The Cuisines of Germany

REGIONAL SPECIALTIES AND TRADITIONAL HOME COOKING

Horst Scharfenberg

POSEIDON PRESS   NEW YORK   LONDON
TORONTO   SYDNEY   TOKYO

POSEIDON PRESS
SIMON & SCHUSTER BUILDING
ROCKEFELLER CENTER
1230 AVENUE OF THE AMERICAS
NEW YORK, NEW YORK 10020

COPYRIGHT © 1980 BY HALLWAG AG BERN
TRANSLATION COPYRIGHT © 1989 BY POSEIDON PRESS,
A DIVISION OF SIMON & SCHUSTER INC.

POSEIDON PRESS IS A REGISTERED TRADEMARK
OF SIMON & SCHUSTER INC.
POSEIDON PRESS COLOPHON IS A TRADEMARK
OF SIMON & SCHUSTER INC.

DESIGNED BY KAROLINA HARRIS
MANUFACTURED IN THE UNITED STATES OF
AMERICA

10 9 8 7 6 5 4 3 2 1

LIBRARY OF CONGRESS CATALOGING IN
PUBLICATION DATA
SCHARFENBERG, HORST.
  [DEUTSCHE KÜCHE. ENGLISH]
  THE CUISINES OF GERMANY: REGIONAL SPECIALTIES AND
  TRADITIONAL HOME COOKING/HORST SCHARFENBERG.
    P. CM.
  TRANSLATION OF: DIE DEUTSCHE KÜCHE.
  INCLUDES INDEX.
  I. COOKERY, GERMAN. I. TITLE.
TX721.S18413 1989   89-8396
641.5943—DC20   CIP

ISBN 0-671-63197-7

Acknowledgments

· · · · · · · · · ·

My heartfelt thanks go out to everyone who has helped me with this book, and there have been hundreds of homemakers, chefs, and cooking enthusiasts whose collective kitchen experiences have been a source of inspiration and support. The contributions of my culinary benefactors with whom I'm personally acquainted (or are at least known to me by name) have been duly recognized in the appropriate places, but there have been many other benefactors—notably the authors of the recipes I have adapted or excerpted in the following pages—whose contributions I would like to acknowledge here.

Also, I would like to thank Walter Putz, of the Brenners Park Hotel, Baden-Baden, and Ernst Birsner and his Burda Kochstudio, Offenburg, for providing me with pictorial material from their astounding collections of cookbooks. In this connection, I would also like to thank all my collaborators at Hallwag Verlag, my original publisher, who put so much love, energy, and skill into the preparation of this book.

My deepest thanks, however, must go to my late parents. My father, a successful engineer and more familiar than most of his countrymen with the culinary delights of the greater world, nevertheless (or perhaps for that very reason) retained a lifelong affection for the cuisine of his native land—an attitude that he was eager to impart to me at every possible opportunity. My mother was one of those brilliant cooks who expected no greater reward for her artistry in the kitchen than the assurance of her family's well-being and satisfaction. Thanks to you both, my beloved parents, for having brought me up in such a delicious environment. . . .

Contents

· · · · · · · · · · · · · · · ·

THE   RECIPES

Map of Germany

. . . .

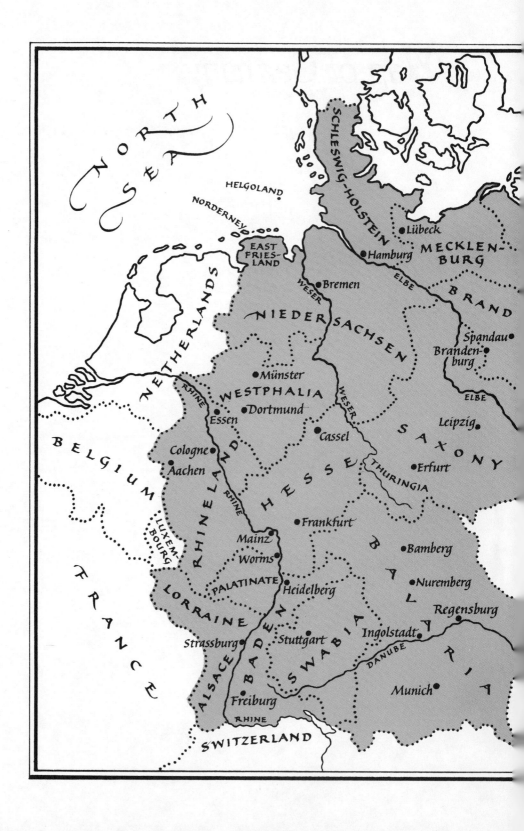

NORTH SEA

HELGOLAND

NORDERNEY

EAST
FRIES-
LAND

SCHLESWIG-HOLSTEIN

Lübeck

MECKLEN-
BURG

Hamburg

BRAND

WESER

Bremen

ELBE

Spandau

NETHERLANDS

NIEDER SACHSEN

Branden-
burg

Münster

WESER

ELBE

RHINE

WESTPHALIA

Dortmund

Leipzig

SAXONY

Essen

Cassel

BELGIUM

Cologne

Aachen

HESSE

Erfurt

THURINGIA

RHINE

FRANCE

LUXEM-
BOURG

RHINELAND

Frankfurt

Bamberg

Mainz

BAVARIA

Worms

Nuremberg

PALATINATE

Heidelberg

LORRAINE

Regensburg

Strassburg

Stuttgart

Ingolstadt

ALSACE

BADEN

SWABIA

DANUBE

Freiburg

Munich

RHINE

SWITZERLAND

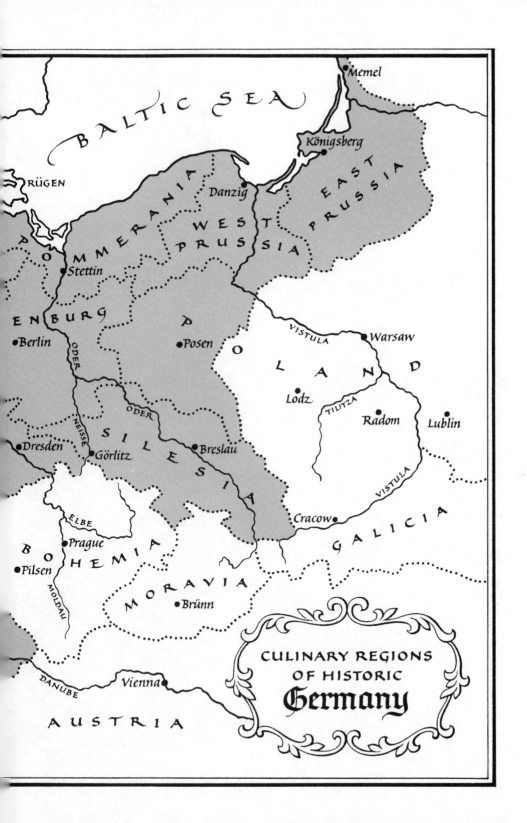

BALTIC SEA

RÜGEN

•Memel

•Königsberg

POMMERANIA

•Danzig

WEST PRUSSIA

EAST PRUSSIA

P O M M E R A N I A

•Stettin

ENBURG

ODER

•Berlin

P O L A N D

VISTULA

•Posen

•Warsaw

ODER

•Lodz

TILITZA

NEISSE

•Radom

•Lublin

S I L E S I A

•Dresden

•Görlitz

•Breslau

ELBE

VISTULA

B O H E M I A

•Prague

•Cracow

G A L I C I A

•Pilsen

MOLDAU

M O R A V I A

•Brünn

DANUBE

•Vienna

CULINARY REGIONS
OF HISTORIC
Germany

AUSTRIA

Introduction

. . . .

Who does not know sauerbraten, hamburger, liverwurst, pumpernickel, or knockwurst? Many of the eating habits and recipes that German immigrants have brought with them over the Atlantic have become classic American dishes, resembling more or less the original. But all of them, however combined and even supplemented by a cook's gastronomical experiences in Bavaria, Heidelberg, or the Rhine valley, are not truly prepared as traditional German cuisine.

Reading about German cuisine will show—so I hope—that the worldwide reputations of certain national recipes are often superficial and misleading about the country's cuisine as a whole: Americans don't eat only hamburgers, doughnuts, and T-bone steaks; Germans don't eat only sauerkraut, potato salad, and pretzels.

Every national cuisine is far more than cooking, it's a way of life determined by the country's national character—the way its people feel and think and behave. Germans tend to be perfectionists. They have boundless appetites. Their fare reflects their love of food, drink, and merrymaking—tasty, hearty, and plentiful. They can be gluttons at noon and gourmets at night. They remember the times when food was scarce. There has hardly been a single generation of Germans within the last five hundred years that hasn't experienced hunger. Marauding foreign soldiers and domestic despots took away their provisions; bad weather ruined their crops. Only when potatoes were brought from America in the eighteenth century did their food supply become more reliable. Potatoes were their salvation. That's why they are such an important part of German cuisine, and why Germans have invented hundreds of ways to prepare them.

Germany is famous for its ancient towns, towering castles, romantic valleys, cozy beer gardens, and genial wine cellars. But each province has developed its own variety of delicious foods, incorporating whatever delicacies could be found in neighboring countries. Climate, soil, and even the inhabitants vary from region to region. The south is beer country; wine prevails in the southwest; and up north, the people are rather fond of hard liquor. Local country food has been created accordingly.

Austria, France, Switzerland, Poland, Czechoslovakia, The Netherlands, Denmark, Belgium, as well as Italy, some Balkan countries, and Hungary have all contributed to the melting pot of German cuisine, which has evolved, over time, to become a most appealing blend of European flavors shaped by German culinary preferences. Here again is a significant parallel between German and American cooking—both have always been open to rich and multifarious outside influences. It's no wonder then that German cuisine has frequently been praised not only domestically, but by travelers from abroad as well. In the sixteenth century, Michel de Montaigne, a famous French philosopher, essayist, and nobleman, wrote about his culinary experiences in southern Germany:

> . . . in good inns, soup, sauces and salads are prepared with such excellent taste that the cuisine of the French nobility can hardly match it . . . new for us were the soups with quinces and dried apples as well as coleslaw. Remarkable is the abundance of excellent fish, game, birds, and young hares that are prepared quite differently from our recipes, but at least as tasty. We have never seen such tender and juicy meat dishes as are served there every day. Together with meat are served stewed plums, pears and apples.

For more than forty years I have collected the typical recipes of my home country from all regions of Germany and have provided in this volume whatever tidbits of information I could find about their history and background. Frequently, one recipe is given in different variations because they have once been or still are in use.

Now, as a part-time resident of the United States, I have had the chance to serve a multitude of German dishes to my American friends and observe their reactions. To my delight, they have been thrilled with the results. One American cooking instructor, Rosa Tusa of West Palm Beach, has even adopted some of my recipes—the specially flavored red cabbage and the authentic potato salad—as part of her program.

These savory meals, which have never been presented in one volume before, are all prepared in the authentic, Old World way. Whether they are known or unknown tastes, I'm sure you'll enjoy the succulent dishes in this book that cooks throughout Germany have been perfecting for generations. I bid you *Guten Appetit.*

HORST SCHARFENBERG

Baden-Baden, Germany
Stuart, Florida

The Cuisines of Germany

. . . .

A Culinary Atlas of Germany's Historic Regions

*B*avaria
Bayern

• • • • • • • •

Germany is divided into cultural superregions by a culinary boundary line that is frequently called the "Weisswurst Equator," in honor of a characteristic Bavarian sausage specialty. In this instance, and perhaps one or two others, the culinary boundaries of the Bavarian state correspond closely to the political ones, which is in no way to suggest that the eating and drinking habits of all Bavarians are the same. The Franconians, for example, in the northern part of the state, continue to enjoy a fair degree of culinary autonomy. Their traditional cuisine is obviously influenced by the relative scarcity or abundance of natural resources—the rocky slopes of the Oberpfalz (Upper Palatinate), for example, versus the lush meadows and fields of Lower Bavaria.

Even Munich, the weisswurst metropolis, has not disdained the sturdy peasant cuisine on which it has fed since infancy, though very Bavarian specialties have made their way into the German culinary mainstream. Bavaria's greatest contribution has undoubtedly been the concept of the *Schmankerl,* which might collectively be described as between-meal treats were it not for the fact that an extra meal, a kind of second breakfast called *Brotzeit,* has had to be fitted into the day to accommodate the Bavarians' fondness for *Schmankerl.* This was not so much a time for bread, as the name seems to imply, as a time for everything that could possibly be eaten *with* bread—which is to say, virtually anything.

In the old days, the foreman sent one of the apprentices

down to the butcher's for a take-out assortment of ready-made *Schmankerln,* possibly including such notable Bavarian specialties as *Lüngerl,* "sour liver," and "pickled tripe." A fondness for liver, kidneys, tripe, and other organ meats is very characteristic of the culinary zone that lies due south of the Weisswurst Equator—comprising Swabia, Baden, and Bavaria—though when it comes to such items as the spleen, heart, and the lungs, the Bavarians are left entirely in possession of the field. The aforementioned weisswurst—the invention of which, like so many of mankind's great discoveries, was the result of a happy accident—is the prince of Bavarian *Würste* and is supposed to be eaten very fresh with plenty of sweet mustard; tradition has it that weisswurst should never be allowed "to hear chimes at noon," i.e., it should be all gone by noon of the day on which it's made.

Tiny *Nürnberger Rostbratwurst* is only slightly less celebrated than weisswurst and tastes remarkably good either when cooked in broth seasoned with vinegar or when fried with sauerkraut; the plump *Regensburger* is the most venerable—the earliest wurst species of which we have historical evidence. Apart from the purely poetic ("cottonwurst," "farmer's sighs"), wurst nomenclature is not always cut-and-dried: *Leberkäs* does not contain a particle of liver (or cheese for that matter), and when the Bavarians borrowed the recipe for *saucisse de Lyons,* they rechristened it *Leoni,* apparently having confused the eating capital of France with a little village of that name on the Starnberger See. Notable Bavarian cheeses include *Allgäuer Emmentaler* (never to be referred to as "Swiss cheese" in the presence of a Bavarian), several varieties of *Bierkäse,* and the piquant *Weisslacker,* so called because its mottled, glazed surface is thought to resemble white lacquer (i.e., shellac). This last is one of Germany's truly unappreciated regional specialties, as it has never really found favor on the other side of the Weisswurst Equator.

The handful of Bavarian specialties that have achieved this sort of national recognition—notably *Schweinshaxen* (Bavarian-style pigs' knuckles) and *Wammerl* (cooked pickled belly meat)—have left us with the not entirely accurate impression that Bavarians feed exclusively on pork. A number of local informants have confirmed my suspicions that Bavarians are so fond of roast pork that they prefer to save it for Sundays, whereas, they explained, "beef was for every day." In former times, this was more likely to have been true of the humble cabbage, the only vegetable apart from the radish (familiarly known as *Radi*) with which the Bavarians have developed a close emotional relationship.

Cabbage is eaten fresh in salads, as well as boiled, braised, and steamed, and salted down in the form of sauerkraut, which Bavarians like to eat with *Reiberdatschi* (potato pancakes); this is considered to be one of their foremost eccentricities by the inhabitants of other regions of Germany. You will find a detailed study of Bavarian dumplings *(Knödel)* in the chapter "Dumplings, Spätzle, and Other Side Dishes," but only a passing mention of the rolls *(Semmel, Weckerl)* and other breadstuffs that go into them; notable among them are the original Kaiser roll *(Kaisersemmel)*, the poppyseed *Mohnweckerl,* the crusty *Rasperl,* and the still crustier *Salzstange,* a short baguette-shape loaf that is heavily salted, studded with

Square in Munich

The kitchen of the Wittelsbach Royal Palace, Munich

Garmisch-Partenkirchen,
Bavaria

caraway seeds, and hard-baked almost to the consistency of a pretzel.

My colleague Erna Horn is convinced that Bavaria's strategic position astride the trade routes that ran north from Italy across the Alps made it the first northern European state (including France) to develop a genuine haute cuisine in imitation of the Italian Renaissance courts. This tradition seems to have lapsed somewhat in more recent times, however, and it's my impression that modern Bavarian specialties have made their reputation more on the basis of quantity than quality.

On the other hand, the Bavarians' corresponding tendencies toward overindulgence in the beer hall and the pub have done little to harm the international reputation, or indeed the quality, of Bavarian beer, which is thought by many to be the best in the world, and which is often used in Bavarian cooking. Other beer-producing countries in the Common Market have been putting pressure on the German government to substitute a less exacting standard of quality control for the celebrated Bavarian "Statute of Purity," which dates back to 1516 and still regulates the purity of the ingredients used by every brewery in West Germany.

The northern fringe of Bavaria—that is, the northern part of the historic region of Franconia—is wine country, and

Franconian wine is traditionally drunk from flasks of the kind that are most conventionally associated with Spanish shepherds and Portuguese fisherfolk. Two of Germany's most remarkable beers are also produced here—Kulmbacher Eisbock is remarkable chiefly for having the highest alcohol content of any beer, and Bamberger Rauchbier, with its distinctive flavor of wood smoke, is surely the strangest-tasting (with the possible exception of Berliner Weisse).

Franconia is in the transition zone between southern *Knödel* and northern potato dumplings, and Franconians, as befits the dwellers in one of Germany's great garden spots, are much fonder of fresh vegetables than their neighbors in Old Bavaria —*Pickelsteiner* (a casserole) is really more of a Franconian than an Old Bavarian specialty—although Franconia market gardeners tend to specialize in the spicier vegetables, such as horseradish, garlic, and of course *Schwarzwurzel* (scorzonera or black salsify). Traces of a native Franconian haute cuisine can perhaps be glimpsed in this extract from a letter written by Margravine Wilhelmine of Bayreuth to her brother, the future Frederick the Great, in 1732: "Each of my ladies-in-waiting is obliged to cook a dish for me in my kitchen that I have dined on with some relish in the past."

The Franconians are also partial to freshwater fish, carp in particular, though in this respect Old Bavarians seem almost

Ingolstadt, Bavaria

fastidious in their fondness for such delicate white-fleshed creatures as *Trüschen* and *Renken* (known in Great Britain as burbot and vendace, respectively), not to mention a Munich specialty fish, rarely encountered these days, called the *Isar-Huchen*. (On the other hand, the gigantic *Wels,* or Danubian catfish, which occasionally exceeds 500 pounds, would seem to be the ideal food fish for those waters.) The inhabitants of both regions have always had a weakness for wild food from the forest, from the lowly *Schwammerl* (mushroom) to the lordly stag, a taste that has been memorialized in countless popular novels dealing with poachers and forest outlaws of the Robin Hood type. Finally, the specialty of the region that has made the greatest name for itself on both sides of the Weisswurst Equator is undoubtedly *Nürnberger Lebkuchen,* "gingerbread," which came into being through the combined efforts of the medieval spice traders of Nuremberg and the beekeepers of Franconia, a good example of the way in which the traditional cuisine of this entire region is basically country cooking with a few international influences.

Regensburg on the Danube
River, Bavaria

Central Germany

In this section, I am going to discuss only the historic regions of Saxony and Thuringia, since Silesia and Berlin and its environs will each have separate sections devoted to them. I should also mention at the outset that I myself have not set foot in either of these regions, which are now in East Germany, since the end of the war, and thus the observations that follow are based on my childhood memories, reports, and letters from visiting friends and relations, and on historical sources of various kinds.

My grandparents lived in Ilmenau, and the edge of the great Thuringian Forest, the Thüringer Wald, was just beyond the little railway station called Ilmenau-Bad. On summer evenings, the family would set off in that direction, and after a brief suburban interlude consisting of flowerbeds, tidy lawns, and gravel paths, we would catch the sound of brass-band music somewhere up ahead and walk toward the sound for a while, past the beer stalls and benches and picnic tables. By now we were on the outskirts of the forest, but no one was much inclined toward wandering very far, since the sausage sellers had already set up their little portable grills, the smoke was billowing out, and the aroma of grilled bratwurst—which for me will always represent the very life's breath of Thuringia—was steadily wafting toward us.

The vendor would pick one of the well-browned bratwursts with a pair of tongs and slap it into a French roll that had been slit lengthwise down the middle, so there still was a fair amount of bratwurst protruding at either end. The skin would have burst in one or two places, so the juices would blend with the mustard on the outside in a truly wonderful

Dresden, former capital of
Saxony (engraving by
Albert H. Payne)

way. There was beer for everyone, of course; even we children were allowed to take a nip or two, for practice. Just a few days ago, I was speaking with an old-time sausage-maker from Thuringia, who was able to assure me that the sausage vendors still wheel their portable grills along the sidewalks and through the parks; he also allowed me to assist him in a session of Thuringian home-style sausage-making—knockwursts, blutwursts, and mettwursts, as well, of course, as bratwursts, all heavily spiced with marjoram, caraway, and coriander, and all of them quite delicious.

Yet despite all this, Thuringia has never been really blessed with abundance. Germany's greatest poet, Johann Wolfgang von Goethe, during his tenure as chief minister to one of the lesser German states, was always begging for food parcels from his mother and friends back home in Frankfurt am Main. The uncertainty of rural life in some of the poorer districts was at least somewhat reduced when the cultivation of the potato was introduced into Thuringia (at about the same time), which not only was useful in staving off hunger but also provided the entire region with a delicious everyday staple in the form of big potato dumplings, *Kartoffelklösse*.

Wild berries, mushrooms, and game abounded in the forests, but since these tend to taste best when prepared in the simplest and most straightforward manner, the Thuringians can hardly be reproached for having failed to accumulate a fund of indigenous recipes. The Thuringians' culinary ingenuity, like that of their neighbors the Saxons, was concentrated mainly on baked goods, particularly rich, buttery fruit tarts and other sorts of pastries that are baked on a metal sheet and accordingly called *Blechkuchen* in German. The Saxons certainly have good reason to be proud of their *Dresdner Christstollen,* the most indispensable of Christmas pastries. A wandering Saxon far from home at Christmastime who manages to provide himself with a genuine Christmas stollen can relive the joys of Goethe feasting on *Frankfurter Brenten* in the midst of a culinary wasteland.

In general, the traditional cuisine is a strange mixture of luxury and austerity, the first of these qualities being exemplified by one of the showiest (and tastiest) of German casseroles, *Leipziger Allerlei,* the second, perhaps more characteristically, by a thin gruel made from millet or flour, formerly the everyday staple of a large part of the Saxon countryside. For the millworkers in the larger towns, a salt herring or an old scrag end of mutton was a delicacy to be savored once or twice a month. At the other end of the social spectrum, the princely capital of Dresden, better known for the production of ingenious, inedible confections in porcelain, marble, and stucco, was easily outshone by the bourgeois hospitality of Leipzig,

Leipzig, Saxony (engraving by Georg M. Kurz)

the seat of a great university and once the center of the German book trade.

The staple beverage of the Leipzig intelligentsia was a sourish-tasting, top-fermented lager known as *Gose,* though the coffeehouse also plays an important part in the social and intellectual history of the city. In the days when coffee was still regarded as a dangerous intoxicant, and consequently illegal in many of the surrounding princely states, the subjects of the luxury-loving kings of Saxony were known as *Kaffeesachsen,* and the oldest of Leipzig's coffeehouses, the Kaffeebaum, was founded in 1694. Such, in fact, were the free-and-easy ways of the Saxons during that period that the practice of dunking coffee cake (*ditschen,* in the local terminology) probably became established at about the same time.

And, finally, some mention ought to be made of Saxony's greatest contribution to the world's great tables—Meissenware and other high-quality porcelain, first produced at the royal workshops at Meissen; Thuringian Henneberger ware, also of very high quality and almost unobtainable today; and a great variety of beautiful glassware. In summary, then, the cuisine of central Germany is basically quite simple, though undoubtedly deserving of praise for several areas of special concentration, and if Thuringia is known on account of its forests as the "green heart of Germany," then Saxony ought to be known on account of its coffee cake as the "*Kuchen* center of the nation."

Silesia

Schlesien

. . . .

The inhabitants of no other German region have developed such a deeply sentimental attachment to the traditional dishes of their native land. This tendency is especially marked in the case of Silesian émigrés who have lived in West Germany for many years, but among those who still dwell in the original "Silesian land" along the banks of the Oder, I have seen a welling of tears at the mention of even such unromantic staples as linseed oil (used in lieu of olive oil, et cetera), or potatoes with herring.

Possibly this passionate attachment to their regional culture and folkways first developed as a result of numerous threats to the Silesian existence that have materialized over the course of the past few centuries. Poles, Bohemians, Austrians, and Prussians have all asserted their claims, often forcibly, to this fertile and defenseless land; the first three of these, along with the Silesians' less acquisitive neighbors in Saxony and Thuringia, have at least contributed to the development of a number of Silesian culinary specialties. The conquering Prussians had little to offer in the way of interesting recipes, and the turn-of-the-century "world capital" of Berlin had to recruit not only a large proportion of its population but also a great many of its favorite *Delikatessen* from the ample surplus of both that was available in Silesia.

The attitude expressed in the statement "My country, right or wrong" also describes the Silesian's indiscriminate attachment to the products of his native soil, including the stunted grapes and sour wines of Bomst and the bizarre concoction known as *Bowle* (see *Maibowle,* page 481). All other attempts to grow wine grapes so far north in Europe have long since been abandoned, but the Silesians are still carefully tending to their scraggly little vines and, in fact, a variety of sparkling white known as Grünberger Sekt has acquired a certain reputation for itself. I haven't yet had the opportunity to taste any since Grünberg is now Zielona Góra, in Poland.

Silesian patriotism has also succeeded in eliminating class distinctions, as far as food is concerned, so that Silesian upper-class cuisine and poor folks' victuals are basically identical. The Silesian poet Friedrich Bischoff was a colleague of mine on the Southwest Radio Network for many years; previous to that he had served as the director of the regional radio station in Breslau (Wroclaw in Polish). He had always struck me as a man of the highest culture, a kind of superaesthete with his immaculate, custom-tailored suits and his fluent, "accentless" radio announcer's German, but as soon as he began to speak of Silesia, of his "home sweet home in the meadows," he instantly became as earthy and colloquial as any mud-caked farmhand in a village pub.

An extract from one of Bischoff's poems celebrating "the good gifts of my homeland" provides a kind of roll call, or really a calendar, of Silesian holiday treats, particularly from a child's point of view. It starts out with two different kinds of sweet biscuits *(Striezel)* and pound cake *(Baben,* similar to the Polish *babka)* plus coffee cake with streusel topping, all of them "delicious in the old Silesian way, moist within and butter-crisp without, whispers all around them of a delicate fragrance," followed by "seven different kinds of *cookies,* on Whitsun and at Easter time—we could take as many as we wanted," then "gingerbread men [*Pfeffermänner*] and anise stars, the Christ Child's loving bounty. . . ." Finally, there were "dumplings big as cannonballs and, from poppyseeds that tasted like earth, our reward from Saint Sylvester." Saint Sylvester's Day is New Year's Day, on which the poppyseed *Mohnstriezel* was traditionally served, and the dumplings are the famous Silesian *Kliessla* (the dialect name, which sounds quite a bit more like an endearment than the High German *Klösse*), of which there are a great many varieties.

Wellwurst is a unique Silesian specialty, but Silesian-style weisswurst was probably introduced by migrants from Franconia. However, Silesian weisswurst and bratwurst are both served in a sweet-sour gherkin sauce, mostly gingerbread spiced. Sweet-and-sour sauce has become a naturalized Silesian specialty that is served with beef and tongue as well as wurst and most notably with the famous Christmas carp, which, in acknowledgment of its Polish origin, is known as Polish carp. Schömberg and Jauer (now named Chelmsko Sklaskie, Jawor) were both renowned for the local wurst, and Oppeln (Opole) surely deserves to be remembered for the little sausages seethed in broth that were sold by hawkers at the railroad station, starting in 1843—the progenitors of many millions of hot sausages (or rather, *"Heisse Wüüürstchen!"*) that have been sold in German railroad stations ever since then. The little town of Tuchmach, now just over the border in Czechoslovakia, was noted for a kind of *Bockwurst* (boiled sausage) called *Tuchmacher Forelle* (Tuchmach trout), just as toasted cheese is Welsh rabbit and canned sardines are Scotch grouse. Perhaps the most distinctively Silesian of these much-beloved specialties are the Christmas pastries, and, to the Silesian ear at least, no other words could even sound half as delicious as *Neisser Pfefferkuchen* or *Liegnitzer Bomben*—the only gratifying bombs I know.

My favorite character in Silesian folklore is Rübezahl (Turnip Tail), the resident goblin of the Riesengebirge (Giant's Mountain), whom I like to imagine with a garland of sausages strung around his neck, a platter with a fresh-baked *Kuchen* balanced in one hand and a *Kliessla* the size of Charlemagne's giant imperial orb in the other; dangling from his belt is a sack full of *Galuschel* (chanterelles) and juicy blueberries, with just the hoofs of a roebuck peeking out of the mouth of the sack. I don't think that Rübezahl, who is capable of making things quite unpleasant for those who have displeased him in some way, would object to such a characterization, since he is, after all, a Silesian himself.

Berlin and Environs

. . . .

Politically at least, the western half of Berlin and its environs have gone their separate ways since the end of the war, but at the beginning of this century, when Berlin first became a real world-class metropolis, the two were quite inseparable, especially from a culinary standpoint. "Metropolis" implies a certain cultural heterogeneity, or even a hodgepodge, and that was certainly true of Berlin. Yet in all those millions of kitchens there were still certain basic tendencies to be discerned, since Berliners have always been known for keeping their *Schnauzen* ("snoots," a favorite Berlin expression) cocked to every passing breeze.

There is also an expression, *"Berliner Luft, Berliner Küchen-duft,"* which is to say that simply taking a breath of air in Berlin also means finding out what's going on in everyone else's kitchen. The kitchen smells may be different in Wedding or in Zehlendorf—for those who have some acquaintance with the city—but Berliners get around quite a bit, and it's not unusual to see a distinguished old gentleman in a fur-collared overcoat relishing a rather less distinguished cold *Bulette* (fried meatball patty) in a street-corner *Kneipe* (saloon).

We have already seen how the Silesians conquered the conquering Berliners, as the Greeks did the conquering Romans, overwhelming them with the sheer superiority of their culinary arts. A note of squirearchical elegance had already been borrowed from the kitchens of the rural nobility in the Mark of Brandenburg, and Swiss confectioners and Huguenot refugees from Louis XIV's France contributed a more practical, everyday refinement to the cuisine of the Prussian capital (which is what Berlin was prior to 1871, when it became the

The Brandenburg
Gate in Berlin

national, or rather "imperial," capital). The most talented chefs from all over the country hoped to make a brilliant career in "Athens-on-the-Spree" (the Spree is one of two sluggish little rivers that flow through the city limits of Berlin), and help convince the *Herren Diplomaten* and other distinguished foreigners that Berlin *"doch keen Dorf is"* (ain't just a village).

Berliners have always been confident enough to acclaim the latest novelties from abroad, and great-hearted enough to adopt them as their own "traditional" specialties. Today's divided Berlin still has a marked cosmopolitan air, both of the old style (*the* gourmet restaurant of the moment is called Maître and the chef is a Frenchman) and the new (the Berlin district of Kreuzberg has the highest per capita consumption of fresh lamb of any German community, since a large number of its inhabitants are recent arrivals from Turkey). But if you asked the average German what sort of food and drink he or she would associate with Berlin, the answer might be something like *Weisse mit Schuss* (sparkling beer specialty with a dash of raspberry syrup, page 475, *Molle und Korn* (same thing as a boilermaker), *Buletten* (Meat Patties), *Hackepeter* (spiced pork tartare), *Berliner Pfannkuchen* (Shrovetide Pancakes), *Harzer mit Gänseschmalz* (Harz Mountain sour-milk cheese with goose schmalz), *Bockwurst* (boiled sausage), *Löffelerbsen mit Speck* (pea soup with pickled pork), or *Pökelkamm mit Sauerkohl* (pickled scrag of pork with sauerkraut)—all simple, "popular" fare, much of it of the free-lunch-counter variety.

Some would probably just answer "Aschinger's," a chain of restaurants—something like the equivalent of Lyon's in London or the Automat in New York—that offered prompt service and an inexpensive menu, the first of its kind in Germany. At Aschinger's you could get virtually any number of *Schrippen* (hard rolls) with even the cheapest dishes, which seems to have been the basis, at least initially, for their considerable success. This is not to say that all Berlin specialties are on the same basic level as scrambled eggs or fried meatballs. Berlin-Style Chicken Fricassee, *Aal Grün* (a delicious eel dish) with cucumber salad, *Schüsselhecht* (Pike Casserole), *Sülzkotelett* (Pork Chops in Aspic), and *Schnitzel Holstein* (Veal Cutlet Holstein) are all very elegant dishes, some of them even rather splendid, and in between we have a great many hearty but quite presentable specialties of medium grade, notably *Schmorgurken* (Braised Cucumbers), *Stolzer Heinrich* (Bratwurst in Beer Sauce), *Falscher Hase* (Mock Hare Meat Loaf), and *Saure Eier mit Specksauce* (Eggs with Sweet-Sour Bacon Sauce).

Very early on, the Berliners got into the habit of making forays into the countryside in quest of fresh meat, fish, fruit, and vegetables; they went out on crayfishing expeditions, or to sample the famous Spreewald pickles, or to pick red currants in Werder, both just outside the city. *Kasseler Rippespeer,* a particularly delicious variety of smoked pork loin, has nothing to do with the city of Kassel, which is in Hesse, but is said to have been named for a master butcher by the name of Cassel, who had his shop at 15 Potsdamer Strasse. Even the world-famous *Wiener Wurst* (here, I must confess, I'm simply repeating what I've been told) are alleged not to be "Vienna sausages" at all, but the invention of a Berlin butcher whose name happened to be Wiener. I have it on somewhat better authority that *Bockwurst* originated at Niquet's, a wholesale butcher shop in the Gendarmen-Markt, but if the Berliners had ever dared to make the claim that the first frankfurters were produced by a Herr Frankfurter from Berlin (or *in* Frankfurt, on the Oder river), I would certainly not be the one to repeat it here.

On the other hand, Berliners have good reason to be proud

of the fact that their city was one of the world capitals of gastronomy during the first three decades of our century, with such fine gourmet restaurants as Hiller's, Dressel's, and Borchardt's; wine bars like Lutter and Wegener's; and coffeehouses like Kranzler's, Café des Westens, and Das Romanische—the latter two of which were genuine artists' cafés. As for the current prospects, I can only say that the famous *Eckkneipen* (corner bars) have grown fewer than they were but otherwise it is like everywhere—you can eat a bad, inexpensive meal, or if you want to reserve a table in advance, you can eat a good, expensive meal, sometimes even an excellent one in and around Berlin.

Kitchens of the old royal castle in Berlin

Mecklenburg and Pomerania

. . . .

Today's West Germans are only dimly aware of Pomerania; perhaps they recall it as a place that used to be divided into two parts, "Hither" and "Further." The inhabitants of Berlin and central Germany have always been much better acquainted with these Baltic Sea provinces (that is, Mecklenburg and Pomerania), which served as both bathing beach and vegetable garden for the more populous regions in the interior. Back-to-the-land enthusiasts should be delighted to hear that both these regions are almost exclusively agrarian and unspoiled, with deep, fertile soil, large tracts of forest and moorlands, miles of sandy beaches along the Baltic, and over six hundred lakes dotted about the plain of Mecklenburg.

Mecklenburg (with the cities of Schwerin and Rostock) and part of Hither Pomerania are part of East Germany today, and much of Further Pomerania, including the capital city of Stettin (Szczecin), was awarded to Poland in 1945. The slow-paced, semifeudal style of life in the countryside encouraged an interest in good food (that, along with hunting and fishing, were the main recreations available to the country squire and his tenant farmer alike). There were gastronomic pearls to be discovered in the sleepy country villages, and the Mecklenburger's table was richly laden with the spoils of his (or rather, the squire's) fields, lakes, and forests. The concoction of fruit relishes and preserves to be eaten with wurst or game was the culinary specialty of the region, but there were no special dishes *"Mecklenburger-Art"* or *à la Mecklenbourgeoise* that were ever brought to the attention of a wider public.

Schwerin castle in
Mecklenburg, East Germany
(after a drawing by Krüsi)

Pomeranian cuisine is quite similar to that of Mecklenburg, though rather more distinctive, due to prevailing Slavic influences. In fact, the "Further" half of Pomerania that lies to the east of the river Oder has been "under Polish administration," as the Germans delicately put it, since the end of the war. Before that, the vast Pomeranian plain was worked by tenant farmers on the great estates, and the social tone of the larger towns was set by the Prussian officers of the garrisons.

German gourmets whose memories extend back to the prewar era still speak of the plump white Pomeranian geese with a reverence that was rarely extended to the human inhabitants of the region—the "thick-skulled Pomeranian" *(Pommerscher dickshädel!)* having been cast for the role of the country bumpkin in the gallery of German regional types. And although Pomeranian farmers were constantly complaining of poor harvests, Pomerania has always impressed visitors from the west as a land of plenty, perhaps beginning with this report sent back by a traveling Catholic priest in the year 1159:

There is an incredible abundance of fishes here, both from the seas and fresh water, and for just a few pence, you could buy yourself a whole wagonload of fresh herring, and if I were to say what I truly believe to be true concerning the size and delectability of the latter, then I would surely be taxed with the vice of gluttony.

Wild game is no less abundant, including stags, bison, wild horses, wild boars, wild pigs, and other creatures, and there is butter from the cows, and milk from the sheep, and the fat of the rams and he-goats, and an abundance of wheat and honey and hemp and poppyseeds as well as every kind of vegetable [except potatoes, of course, which were still to come].

The bison and wild horses, as well as many of the region's human inhabitants, may have been driven farther east by the substantial numbers of German settlers who were soon to arrive in Pomerania, but this inventory was basically still complete several centuries later, and in Mecklenburg as well. It seems odd that this report makes no mention of geese, but perhaps they were not in evidence at that particular moment, due to the old Pomeranian custom, still very much in favor with later generations, of devouring them down to the feathers and toenails (see recipe section for additional details).

Spickgans, one of the great Pomeranian specialties, has at least been able to lead a kind of rootless, detribalized existence —under the name of *geräucherte Gänsebrust,* or "smoked breast of goose"—on gourmet specialty shelves in the West, but the descendants of the splendid haunch of roebuck that I tasted once in Stargard may be lost to us forever. The same holds true of the fish of the eastern Baltic and the inland lakes, and, unfortunately, of crayfish from the river Oder, which were cheap and plentiful and always fresh. A more controversial class of regional specialties is collectively known as *Blutspeisen,* or blood puddings, in which the sharp, sour taste of the blood is balanced by the sweetness of sugar; the Mecklenburgers prefer to make their *Blutspeisen* with pork offal, the Pomeranians of course with miscellaneous goose parts. Non-Pomeranian gourmets may be a little dismayed by the current dearth of genuine blood puddings and will undoubtedly prefer to dream of Pomeranian rivers bristling with crayfish, forests teeming with roebuck, and barnyards loud with the honking of plump, white geese.

East Prussia

Ostpreussen

. . . .

It is a pity that many people tend to remember this eastern-most of Germany's "lost" provinces chiefly for its military-historical associations—Hindenburg and Tannenberg,* Junkerdom, and the religious order of Teutonic Knights. Anyone who has paid more than the briefest of visits to the land between the Weichsel (Vistula) and the Memel (Newman) rivers is more likely to be reminded of beautiful sandy beaches and broad plains stretching out beneath an endless sky, of silent forests and clear lakes that are like the eyes of a prehistoric world. East Prussian hospitality—including a literally staggering assortment of punches, schnapps, and cocktails—was no less memorable.

Certainly the proximity of the Slavic lands to the east and south was the most important influence on East Prussian cookery, as evidenced by the cottage cheese-filled *Keilchen* (dumplings) that are indistinguishable from Polish *pirogi* and the thick beet soup called *Beetenbartsch* that is nothing but borscht with a German accent. The three essential elements of East Prussian cuisine are *Schmant* (crème fraîche), *Glumse* (cottage cheese), and big portions. The basic spices are dill (suggesting a Baltic, even a Finnish, influence) and marjoram, known as *Meiran* in dialect.

The name of the old East Prussian capital may have changed to Kaliningrad, but *Königsberger Klopse* (meatballs), *Königsber-*

* Site of two decisive battles in eastern European history—at the first, in 1410, King Wladislaw II of Poland broke the power of the Teutonic Knights; the second, in 1914, forestalled a Russian invasion of Germany in the opening months of World War I.

Königsberg, East Prussia
(engraving by H. Winkles)

ger Fleck (honeycomb tripe), and *Königsberger Marzipan* have all ensured that the memory of Königsberg will endure for as long as German is spoken. Similarly, Tilsit (now Sovetsk) will long be remembered for its cheese, and Danzig† (Gdansk), among other things, for its remarkable liqueur, Danziger Goldwasser, every bottle of which contains a shower of little flecks of golden tinsel. The *Pillkaller* (the custom of downing a slice of liverwurst with mustard followed immediately by a swig of clear schnapps, named for a little town in the Masurian Lakes district) has its adherents in West Germany as well, and the names of other localities that are associated with specialties of the region—smoked whitefish from Nikolaiken, for example, or smoked flounder from Cranz—can still evoke a nostalgic pang in the breast of many a onetime East Prussian.

Many of the distinctive game dishes and smoked-fish specialties of the region may be gone beyond recall, due to the unavailability of the main ingredient outside its native East Prussian heath (or in the latter case, the broad freshwater lagoons that lie to the north and south of Königsberg); even the field peas ("gray peas" as the Germans call them) that are the

---

† Strictly speaking, Danzig was in West Prussia, but from a culinary standpoint, these two former provinces, along with Baltic fringe areas such as Memel (Klaipéda) and Kurland, can conveniently be regarded as a single entity.

chief constituent of *Grue Afte* are difficult to come by in West Germany today. This is certainly not the case with *Schmant,* which can readily be replaced with sour cream or, less readily but more authentically, with crème fraîche, for those who have in mind to attempt a genuine Masurian-style *Schmant-schinken* (see page 231) with a rich cream sauce. Similarly, *Glumse* has never been in short supply, but for those who are never quite sure what to do with it, the East Prussians have provided recipes for *Glums*-dumplings and *Glums*–potato pancakes *(Glumskeilchen, Glumsflinsen)* as well as *Glums*-noodles, *Glumstorte, Glumskäschen* (soft cheese spread), *Butter-glumse,* even *Schmant mit Glumse.*

It was customary for a real East Prussian meal to begin and end with a battery of before- and after-dinner drinks. Dan-ziger Lachs is produced by the same distillery that makes Dan-ziger Goldwasser. "Lachs" (the name of the firm, so the connection with salmon is purely nominal) is located near the Krantor, the most picturesque landmark of the old Hanseatic City. In spite of the worldwide renown of these two liqueurs, the Danziger's favorite drink was *Machandel* (gin), which was drunk straight but customarily served with a prune swimming in it.

Bärenfang, which means "beartrap," is a kind of instant mead or, in other words, a combination of honey and grain alcohol, and is also produced commercially in West Germany nowadays; for those who would like to make a real East Prussian evening of it, *Bärenfang* (also known as *Meschkinnes,* which is Yiddish for "violent destruction") can easily be made at home by following the recipe in the chapter on "Drinks." The coffee liqueur known as Cossacks' Coffee *(Kasakenkaffee),* a distant cousin of the Black Russian, is also being produced in West Germany these days, and such do-it-yourself concoctions as *Nikolaschka* and *Pillkaller* are readily available to those who intend to carry their East Prussian memorial dinner beyond the point of all subsequent recollection.

The Landgasse and the City Hall spire, Danzig, East Prussia (now Poland)

Schleswig-Holstein

. . . .

Schleswig-Holstein is Germany's northernmost region, a narrow wedge of land between the North Sea and the Baltic that also forms the base of Denmark's Jutland peninsula—thus, a region where land and sea, as well as the German and Danish languages and cultures, are inseparably intertwined; many of the Schleswig-Holstein specialties that are mentioned in this book are also popular in Denmark and are even called by the same names in many cases. The sea may threaten to burst the dikes and flood the little hummocks, called *Hallige,* that have always been the home of Schleswig's fishermen, but it is also the source of numerous delicacies that are very well thought of in other regions of Germany—kippers, bloaters, the famous Kiel sprats *(Kieler Sprotten),* and herrings prepared for the table in a great many different ways. Oyster harvesting, originally established by a Danish king, has almost died out in this century, though encouraging attempts have been made to repopulate the oyster beds since 1974; the beds were plentiful 150 years ago, and in 1835, the pastor on the island of Amrum was offered two fresh oysters out of every *tonne* (2,200 pounds) in return for his prayers for its continued success.

Schleswigers who make their living from the land rather than the sea like to refer to their native region as Germany's "great green larder," and certainly with good reason. Fully a third of all industrial revenues are derived from food processing (which, by German standards, is quite a bit), with meat products, wurst, and not surprisingly, milk and dairy products topping the list. Beef cattle and dairy herds are conspicuous features of the landscape on a drive through the lush countryside, and while pigs maintain less of a public presence, they are abundantly represented by the selection of hams and sausages in the butcher shops. Holstein "cabin-smoked" ham *(Katenrauch-Schinken),* so called because it was once smoked under the roof of farmhouses without chimneys, is the most famous of these regional delicacies, though smoked sausage tastes just about as good, and bacon has always played a commanding role in the cookery of the region.

Summer visitors mainly come to Schleswig-Holstein for the sand and the sun, but even in summer, the climate is fickle enough that they usually have at least a few days to explore the other attractions of the region, including the cuisine. Schleswigers are accustomed to hearty meals; they require a high-calorie intake (including plenty of fats) to face up to the raw winds that come sweeping in off the North Sea. Perhaps because the air itself has a salty flavor, the Schleswigers have acquired an enormous fondness for what they call *broken söt,* "sweet-and-sour flavors." Whatever the reason, whereas cooks in other regions of Germany tend to measure out the sugar in teaspoons, Schleswiger recipes call for many heaping tablespoons. This often comes as a bit of a shock to the first-time visitor, but it's something that you can easily get used to.

Rough winds, rich, heavy meals, and a reverence for the tradition of their forefathers are three reasons—perhaps not even the most important ones—why rum, aquavit, and other high-proof spirits remain the Schleswiger's beverages of choice, though they are not nearly as intolerant of nonalcoholic additives as the Scotch or the Frisians, for example. Thus, *Grog* (rum plus water plus sugar) and *Pharisäer* (rum plus coffee plus whipped cream) are both traditional specialties of the region, though the *Hallig*-dweller's grog is more likely to be a mug of hot rum that may or may not have a little sugar in it. The port of Flensburg is still the principal nexus of the European rum trade.

Admittedly there is a kind of cyclical rationalizing going on as far as the fatty foods and high-proof spirits are concerned; after a typical Schleswig meal, one may very well need a dram or two "to help the food go down"; on the other hand, a rich,

heavy meal is exactly what you're looking for if you're planning on having a dram or two. Modern nutritionists have
made as little headway in the face of the Schleswig-Holstein-
er's culinary conservatism as the temperance parsons of a
hundred years ago. Gigantic flour dumplings *(Mehlklösse)*;
streaky bacon, hams, and wurst with an inimitable smoky
savor; likewise kippers and *Sprotten* with the golden patina of
the smokebox are still very much in favor. Fresh fish, buckwheat pancakes, and prunes are perhaps the only traditional
articles of diet the nutritionists might approve of; though the
fresh vegetables that appear on the Schleswiger's table are
invariably drenched in white milk sauce.

Gruel *(Grütze)* is usually made with fresh berries and eaten
with cream on top of it. The custom of gathering wild greens
in early spring was formerly very common in Germany, and
the marsh-dwellers of Schleswig-Holstein (and their North
Frisian neighbors on the island of Sylt) are said to have gone
out with horse and wagon and the entire family to harvest the
plantain greens that grew along the beaches. There was some
urgency involved, since the moorland sheep were also very
fond of *Suden,* as they were called, and the Schleswigers and
Frisians also had to endure a certain amount of name-calling
and derision ("weed-eaters," et cetera) on their account. The
custom of gathering *Suden* seems to have died out in this
century, though I have met a couple of old-time Schleswigers
who remembered eating them with great relish (and with milk
sauce, naturally) in their younger days.

Finally, prospective visitors to the region should be fore-
warned that Schleswig-Holsteiners are indefatigable hosts and
hostesses, capable of wearing down even the most principled
objections to a second or third helping; the proper etiquette is
to allow oneself to be entreated and cajoled for a considerable
length of time, and then finally to give in and help yourself
generously to "a little bit more of everything."

East Friesland

Ostfriesland

. . . .

In German popular mythology, the Frisians have been made out to be backward peasants, impractical and illogical to the point of imbecility, and thus the butt of countless "Frisian jokes." I lived for a summer in East Friesland—the grim summer of 1945—and since then I've never liked to hear a word said against them. I was a refugee from the city, and in many other rural areas, refugees were being brushed off like blackflies. I never heard a harsh word spoken while I was in Friesland, though, admittedly, I heard very few words spoken, most occurring in very short sentences, but all of them honest and good-hearted.

I remember that tea was in short supply, so we drank a great deal of buttermilk, which has a much older tradition in Friesland than tea or even "the wine of the country," Frisian rye brandy. In the country, the farm wives still know how to make delicious buttermilk soups and porridges, and perhaps the poet Hoffmann von Fallersleben, author of the national anthem, was also thinking gratefully of East Friesland when he composed these lines: "O buttermilk, my favorite dish!/O buttermilk, my life!/What gift more precious could you have given me, my neighbor's wife?" The native-born Frisian's answer to this poetical question would probably have been "a ham," since a gigantic twenty-five- or thirty-pound "wedding ham" was customarily awarded to a newly married couple to give them a start in life; rather than eat the ham themselves, they'd sell it for enough money to buy a set of pots and pans, dishes, and so forth.

After the war was over, I had the pleasure of attending a number of farmhouse banquets, where the food was cooked over an open fire and in accordance with the old Low German motto "a little much and a little fat"★ (the connotations of the phrase "a little much" being entirely favorable in this case). The Frisians were the last to abandon the old-fashioned pewter spoons and the patriarchal custom of having the entire family plus farmhands and servants gather around a single table for their meals. Despite these ancient "peasant" traditions—and there was never a prouder, more independent group of peasants anywhere, every Frisian farmer was like a king in his own farmyard—the Frisians have made very few contributions to mainstream German cuisine. In other regions, they're best known for their strong tea, the beer brewed in Jever, and the juniper-flavored corn liquor known as *Doornkaat*.

Nevertheless, there are some excellent Frisian specialties, including a great many kinds of pancakes. In the old days, it was said that the Emsländer, the Frisians who lived around the mouth of the river Ems, tried to hedge their fields by planting "live pancakes" all around the edges (the prototype of all subsequent Frisian jokes). Corned beef *(Pökelfleisch)*, originally ship's beef that had been salted down so it would keep over a long voyage, remains a staple of the Frisian diet; Frisian bread is baked in huge rectangular eight-pound loaves, and since modern Frisians rarely sit down fifteen or twenty to the dinner table, most people prefer to buy just a few slices at a time. The grandfather, now long dead, of my friends in Jever once told me about the sort of food they ate in the farmhouse where he grew up: Breakfast, at seven o'clock, of black bread and buttermilk soup, perhaps fried eggs and fried potatoes as well; lunch was taken out to the fields and usually consisted of *dörstampt Eeten,* "food that's all mashed up together," or in other words, stew. There were giant pancakes for dinner, with lots of bacon, or just a big wooden platter of boiled potatoes with bacon gravy, bread, salted butter, and *Melkenkoffje,* "coffee with milk," which was actually made

★ "Een beeten veel un een beeten fett!"

with toasted rye (the grain itself, not the whiskey). Extra rations of *Stuten* (homemade white bread) and ham were provided when the next day's work was going to be especially taxing.

The oldest farmers' cooperative association in Germany, the Leegmoor Society (Leegmoor being the name of a place near Norden), has long held title to a piece of farmland, the annual rent of which is divided among the society's eighty-five shareholders, who are referred to as *Löffel,* "spoons," since most of the proceeds are spent on a colossal banquet held every year on *Marta Lichtmess,* or Candlemas Day, February 2.

Each of the "spoons" wears a brown-paper napkin around his neck, like a lobster bib, and the same traditional dishes are served every year: field peas *(graue Erbsen)* with a clear sauce and with onion sauce, roast beef with prunes and beets, followed by currant biscuits with cheese; tea is served afterwards as well as Burgundy and *Doornkaat* with the earlier courses. Quite surprisingly, at a gathering of tight-lipped Frisian farmers, there is a long string of humorous after-dinner speeches —all delivered in broad *Platt,* Low German—and the evening concludes with the members of the honorable company tearing off their butcher-paper bibs, crumpling them up, and hurling them like schoolchildren at one another; this, too, as it turns out, is an ancient Frisian custom.

Norderney, summer resort island in the North Sea

Hamburg, Bremen, and Lübeck

Hanseatic Cities

· · · · · · · · · ·

The pride and wealth and the extensive overseas connections of the Hanseatic traders have given each of these great seaports a very different culinary identity from that of the surrounding regions, which are Lower Saxony, East Friesland, and Schleswig-Holstein, respectively. The three Hanseatic cities have originated or imported an extraordinary number of their own culinary specialties, and what is perhaps more remarkable, quite a few of these have even acquired a modest international celebrity, notably chicken Bremen-style with a tart white wine sauce *(Kükenragout)*, *Lübecker Marzipan*, and *Hamburger Aalsuppe* (Eel Soup).

Bremen, Hanseatic city and port on the Weser estuary (North Sea)

Commemorative
menu from the
National Writers'
and Reporters'
Day Banquet,
Hamburg, 1894

Hamburg-style smoked meats, the fricassee of tender
young chickens known as *Stubenküken, Kluftsteak,* the only
truly indigenous technique of cooking a steak, as well as *Bremer Klaben,* the northern German version of the famous
Christmas stollen, should also be mentioned as culinary high-
lights of Hanseatic cities. The Bremers surely deserve special
credit for having achieved the transformation of *Braunkohl mit
Pinkel,* boiled kale with homemade sausage, into an elegant
banquet dish, and *Labskaus,* originally a simple sailor's hash
made by cooking up pulverized ship's biscuit and bully beef,
is now served as a "traditional specialty" at similarly exalted
functions in Lübeck.

The wine merchants' cellars in Bremen and Lübeck also
served as a kind of finishing school for young Bordeaux,
which were shipped out as fully mature *Rotspon* (dialect for
"claret"), usually bound for Russia, a number of years later.

The rathskeller of Bremen, Germany's largest wine restaurant, was frequented by wine lovers from all over the world and celebrated in verse by Wilhelm Hauff in his *Phantasien im Bremer Ratskeller*. Thomas Mann had certain reservations, to say the least, about the Lübeck patrician class from which he sprang, but certainly the food that appeared on their tables is described in loving detail in his early novel *Buddenbrooks*. Heinrich Heine was treated rather shabbily by his miserly Hamburg uncle, Salomon, but this hardly seems to have dimmed his approval of the Hanseatic City and its cuisine. "Hamburg," he wrote, "is the best of the republics. Its customs are English, and the food is heavenly. The Hamburgers are good people, and they know how to eat well."

The cuisine of all three Hanseatic cities has a certain urbanity that is lacking in other regions of Germany. Unfortunately, during the past few decades, the old mercantile spirit seems to have reasserted itself a little too vigorously, and palatability has often been sacrificed to profitability. In the last few years, however, strenuous efforts have been made to restore the old standards of gastronomic excellence: meat should be the best available, fish should be freshly caught, and spices should still be fragrant, no matter how remote their place of origin.

Certainly this admirable trend has been encouraged by the fact that many of West Germany's most active and talented amateur chefs live in Hamburg or Bremen, and a great many magazines that are concerned with food and wine connoisseurship are currently being published in Hamburg. One of the things that makes it easier for Hamburg restaurateurs to cater to this demanding clientele is the excellent quality of the produce from market gardens in the fertile marshlands of Vierlande, right outside the city, along with the fruit orchards in the district known as the Altes Land.

The fondness for rich, fatty food and sweet-and-sour sauces of devastating sweetness also finds its way into the Hanseatic cities by similar means, though the seasonings are usually toned down quite a bit. The typical sweet wine from almost any region in Germany will stand up tolerably well to a *söt* sauce made with several tablespoons of sugar, but this is certainly not the case with the fine old Bordeaux that the Hamburg gourmet may prefer to drink with dinner. After serving as wholesale grocers to most of northern Europe for several centuries, the Hanseatic burghers have learned the habit of keeping a little of the *very* best for themselves.

Lübeck, Hanseatic city on the Baltic Sea famous for its marzipan

Lower Saxony

Niedersachsen

. . . .

The lower part of Lower Saxony, so to speak, is East Friesland, which we discussed a little earlier, and even when that is subtracted, the portion that remains—including the Lüneburger Heath district and the Harz Mountains—still comprises a very large area.

In fact, Lower Saxony really does not have a very distinctive cuisine of its own, and such culinary distinction as this region may have achieved is based on the reputations of a handful of celebrated local specialties—Braunschweiger wurst (originally from the city or district known as Braunschweig in German and Brunswick in English), bock beer from Einbeck, and *Harzer,* a variety of sour-milk cheese from the Harz region that is very well-known in Germany and, because of its low fat content and very distinctive flavor, may also be destined for an international career. Brunswick sausage-makers tend to specialize in liverwurst and dried smoked sausage (mettwurst), and though the term *Braunschweiger* is often used in a sort of vague generic sense for either of these two products (especially the latter), anyone who has sampled the genuine article will agree that its worldwide reputation is well deserved. Unfortunately the genuine flavor is very seldom found in the American variety. The reputation of Braunschweig asparagus is necessarily confined to a smaller region of the globe, but it is much sought after by local gourmets—one of a comparative handful of German specialties that sounds *("Braunschweiger Spargel!")* as delicious as it tastes.

There is also a kind of pudding called *Welfenspeise* that is associated with the Welf Palace in Brunswick, the headquarters of the old princely family; the Welfs (or Guelphs) were one of Europe's most ancient dynasties, and very prolific, but since they never made up more than a very tiny fraction of the population, this "Welf pudding" is a bit too aristocratic to be regarded as a genuine popular specialty. Einbeck beer, the original bock beer and the chief propellant of the Bavarian *Faschingszeit* (pre-Lenten festivities), is still being brewed today, and has also been blessed with many imitators. The breweries themselves are worth a visit, and it may be worth noting that the word *Bock* is believed to be a medieval corruption of *Einbeck* and has nothing to do with billygoats (despite what you see on the label), which is what *Bock* normally means. Old-fashioned Braunschweig *Mumme,* a strong, dark, top-fermented beer, seems to have become almost extinct, at least as far as the big commercial beer distributors are concerned.

Harzer cheese was originally made in 1787 by a Swiss immigrant called Sommer who had acquired a dairy (or "cheese bakery," as they're inexplicably called in the Harz Mountains dialect) near Dagmarsfeld, in the Bernburg district, and then had the original idea of injecting the local sour-milk cheese with the fungus that causes "noble rot" in certain wine grapes.★

The trout and other fish from the streams in the Harz Mountains have succumbed to the advance of civilization, and wild mushrooms are rarely to be found these days, though wild berries are still plentiful (in a good year), and fresh carp from the Maschsee is likewise recommended. The only creatures in Lower Saxony that gourmets are inclined to make much of a fuss over are the *Heidschnucken,* the half-wild moorland sheep that graze on the Lüneburger Heath and whose flesh is comparable with the finest of game dishes. *Heidschnucken* mutton is sold at venison prices in gourmet specialty shops between the North Sea and the Alps, but it is also served in ordinary country inns in local villages; it is among the very

---

★ For instance, in sauternes and the elite corps of German wines that have the word *Beerenauslese* (grape selection) buried in their names somewhere.

Hameln on the Weser River,
home of the Pied Piper

best of all German traditional meat dishes, and the leg and the saddle are the choicest cuts. "Heath honey" *(Heidhonig)* from the Lüneburger Heath is a lesser delicacy of the region, though it seems to have suffered somewhat in quality over the years due to the widespread use of chemical fertilizers.

In former days, the staple foods of the people of Lower Saxony consisted mainly of hearty stews made with potatoes and "stick turnips" (rutabagas) and as many big chunks of meat as circumstances would permit—good, nourishing fare, hardly calculated to make present-day gourmets start raving and kissing their fingertips. About the only remaining regional specialty worth mentioning is the smoked eels from the broad lake on the flatlands that is grandiosely known as the Steinhuder Meer ("sea"); these, especially when accompanied by a glass of clear schnapps, are a delicacy indeed, and it seems a pity that Wilhelm Busch, a stalwart son of Lower Saxony and certainly the most prolific of Germany's food poets, never wrote a poem in praise of these *Steinhuder Räucheraale.*

Westphalia
Westfalen

· · · · · · · · · ·

Westphalia's political and administrative boundaries have been redrawn many times over the years without greatly affecting the culinary integrity of the region, since good food and drink have not only kept body and soul together but also helped to keep tribes, people, and nations together as well. In the recipe section you will note that a number of Westphalian recipes have been indexed under the name of a particular district or locality (Münsterland, Sauerland, Bergisches Land, et cetera), since this is a region that can afford to have not just a single traditional cuisine but four or five.

Like the French with their gourmets and gourmands, the Germans like to distinguish between the *Feinschmecker,* or gourmet, who is interested primarily in subtlety, novelty, and refinement, and the *Schlemmer,* who is interested in anything that's good as long as the portions are big enough. Westphalia has apparently always been a *Schlemmer*'s paradise. Christoffel von Grimmelshausen, who served as a mercenary during the Thirty Years' War, wrote a novel, *Simplicissimus,* about his experiences (the earliest German novel that is still very much read today), and finally attained respectability as the mayor of a little town in Baden. He provided us with this brief culinary reminiscence of seventeenth-century Westphalia:

> There we found a Paradise, all that we could have wished for, and more—since there were beautiful maidens there and not just angels, and they plied us with so much meat and drink that in a short while my battle-scarred pelt was smooth and glistening once more, since they set down before us the strongest beer, the best

Opladen, Westphalia

Westphalia ham and knockwurst and some very delicious beef that they liked to cook in salt water and then serve cold. It was there that I learnt to spread a finger's breadth of salted butter on a piece of black bread and then spread cheese on top of that to help it go down a little easier. . . .

The following passage from a Latin poem composed by a papal nuncio a couple of years later makes it clear that the *Schlemmer*'s paradise was something more like purgatory for *Feinschmeckers*:

> No Lucullan feast prepared with Apollo's arts
> Adorns the table, since refinement and
> The subtle tricks of cookery
> Are heartily disdained by Westphalia's sturdy sons.
> They heap up all their vegetables on a single platter.

The Westphalians have acquired a reputation for being hardheaded and stubborn, but in certain instances it seems that they are merely being faithful to the traditions of their ancestors.

There is not a great deal that has to be said about some of Westphalia's better-known specialties, including pumpernickel, which always is solid, never soft textured, and Westphalian beer (except to note that it tends to be on the strong side and the old-fashioned top-fermented brewing methods are still being practiced with considerable success). Steinhäger (gin) has been lucky enough to be recognized by the republic as an *appellation contrôlée* (not actually called that, of course), which is to say that only gin that has been distilled in the town of Steinhagen and flavored with actual juniper berries can lawfully be sold under that name.

In the days before such beneficent regulations were in effect, Westphalian ham came to be a great favorite in Paris under the name *jambon de Mayence,* the place of origin not of the ham but of the middlemen who imported it to France. The ham owed its distinctive taste first to the fact that the hogs were free-ranging and fed on acorn mast in the oak forests of Westphalia, which produced a leaner, more muscular ham, and second to the artistry of the smoking process; nowadays, the hogs stay closer to home and no longer feed on acorn mast, but the ham is still in excellent repute—with *Schlemmers* at the delicatessen as well as with the *Feinschmeckers* in the glittering salons of Paris.

In addition to the culinary titans mentioned above, there are a great many lesser-known contenders, many of them indigenous to a particular city or locality, and a fair number of them—namely, *Töttchen, Pfeffer-Potthast, Grünkohl, Blindhuhn, Dicke Bohnen, Pickert,* and *Bergische Kaffeetafel,* and perhaps one or two others—are also to be found in the recipe section of this book. In this conection, it seems appropriate to pay a

Solingen in Westphalia, famous for its quality cutlery

brief tribute to Henriette Davidis-Holle, who lived in a parsonage in Wegeren in the Ruhr valley and came to be the ancestor of all German cookbook authors. In 1844, she published her *Practical Cookbook for Everyday and Fine Cookery,* the first modern (i.e., comprehensive and schematically organized) German cookbook, which has since been translated into many languages and gone into many more editions in its native land and can still be cited as one of the standard works on the subject. She became a model of crisp authority for all subsequent practitioners in the field, and the phrase "*Man nehme . . .*" (Let one take . . .), with which her recipes typically began, was quickly transformed from a culinary to a cultural imperative.

*T*he Rhineland

Rheinland

. . . .

Westphalia, as we have seen, has its own indigenous cuisine and plenty of it, so here the term *Rhineland* can be taken to refer to the middle and lower Rhine regions and a few adjoining river valleys. In general, the traditional cookery of this region is something of a hodgepodge, as if it had evolved out of the collected table scraps of all the robber barons, Crusaders, and foreign merchants who had traveled along the broad highway of the Rhine. The cookery also seems to be characterized by a certain pretentiousness, so that even a dish that is basically quite palatable may be spoiled by fussy and unconvincing flourishes. A further point to consider is that the cuisine of the Rhineland was effectively responsible for bringing all German cuisine into disrepute with our fellow Europeans, particularly the English, during the early nineteenth century.

The trouble started with Lord Byron's poem *Childe Harold's Pilgrimage,* which was enormously popular all over Europe; Childe Harold's (and Byron's) misty-eyed visions of the castles along the Rhine inspired a craze for "doing the Rhine" at the end of the Napoleonic Wars that lasted well into the 1830s. Few of these foreign visitors ever ventured into the other regions of Germany, and as impressed as they might have been by the magnificent beauty of the castles, rocks, and steep vineyards, they were mightily disappointed by the food, which was much too vinegary and much too fatty for their tastes, and which they assumed to be typical of the rest of Germany as well. Thus, it seems ironic that *Rheinischer Sauerbraten,* which is just what all those English tourists were com-

The market square, Aachen, west of Cologne

plaining about, was to become one of Germany's favorite dishes toward the end of the nineteenth century (to be eventually displaced by a mock-Hungarian concoction known as Gypsy schnitzel, *Zigeunerschnitzel*).

The list of Rhineland specialties with less equivocal reputations is a long one and would certainly include *Moselaal* and *Muschlen auf Rheinische Art* (eels and mussels, respectively, in white wine sauce), smoked meats from the Bad Neuenahr-Ahrweiler district (another local specialty whose quality is now strictly regulated by law), the delectable *Aachener Printen* (Aachen Honey Bars), and at least two weeks' worth of variant recipes for the two basic types of Rhenish potato pancake (the smaller ones are called *Rievekooche,* or something similar, the giant-size, loaf-shape ones are *Döppches-Koche*). Other possibilities range from the exquisite (venison and other wild game from the Eifel region, for example) to the extremely basic (*Himmel und Erde,* "heaven and earth," mashed potatoes mixed up with hot applesauce and served with fried blood sausage). Visitors to Cologne (Köln) should not be disappointed if they order a *Halve Hahn* (half chicken) and the waiter brings a rye bread roll spread with cheese; in fact, this makes an excellent accompaniment for a top-fermented local *Alt-Bier,* such as Kölsch or Düssel. Both have been acquiring a national reputation over the past few years.

Rhine wine—more specifically, the wines of the Central Rhine (Mittelrhein) region—may actually persuade one to adopt a more indulgent attitude toward Rhenish cuisine. Sitting on the deck and munching your way through the "Special Tourist Menu" while the excursion boat drifts slowly past the Lorelei rock, you may find yourself lifting your glass—suddenly oblivious to the mediocre quality of an inexpensive meal. Your emotions welling up within you, you will intone Heinrich Heine's famous song that begins: "I don't know why I am so sad. . . ." Well, that's how everybody pays tribute to the ancient sorceress—and to the wine and romanticism of the Rhine.

Cologne on the Rhine (after a drawing by B. Foster)

*H*esse

Hessen

There is a Hessian specialty called *Dorchenannergekochtes,* "all cooked up together," which happens to be the chief distinguishing mark of Hessian cuisine in general, that is, that dishes also enjoyed in other regions are prepared with a distinctive Hessian twist or fillip; they have a "special whistle" to them, as the Germans say. This in turn has a great deal to do with that most highly esteemed of Hessian characteristics, being what they call "vigilant," clever or quick-witted (perhaps embarrassingly, there is no exact equivalent for this term in standard German); it is this quality, at any rate, that has made it a little easier for the Hessians to survive a long succession of foreign occupiers and home-grown despots who, for example, sold their subjects to England to fight in North America.

As in other German regions, there is a certain amount of local variation, partly due to the differences in landscape and climate, so that the traditional dishes that evolved in the mountainous but relatively well-endowed Bergstrasse district, for example, are somewhat different from those of the stony Rhön plateau. As elsewhere, pork products are in the ascendant, and the Hessians have devised not only a special terminology for them ★ but also slightly different ways of preparing them from their neighbors. Hessian *Rippcher* (the singular is *Rippche,* "rib") are a bit thicker and juicier than their counterparts in other regions since the entire rack is cooked at once

---

★ *Wellfleisch* (boiled trimmings), *Solber* (salt pork), *Haspel* (pickled hocks), and *Leiterchen,* literally, "small ladder" (pickled and boiled spareribs).

and then separated afterwards and cut into very thick segments that are still bursting with juice.

Upper Hesse is famous for its wurst, and I suspect that here the Hessian special twist involves nothing more than using a higher proportion of ground meat to organ meat and filler products; the Hessians are rarely stingy, especially when good food is involved. Hessian wurst, called *Aahle* or *Dürre Runde,* is air-dried until all the extra water has evaporated, and ordinary blutwurst is dried out in the same way, cut into very thin slices, and eaten with buttered *Bauernbrot,* which is a delicacy indeed; Upper Hessian *Bauernbrot* is robust, by the way, but not of the ordinary kind that feel like barbed wire when they come in contact with the roof of your mouth.

Cottage cheese is known as *Schmierkäs* (hence "smearcase" in Pennsylvania Dutch) or *Matte,* and the Hessians like it sweet and sharp-flavored and in combination with almost every other edible substance. The custom of making soups and sauces from herbs and wild greens is best exemplified by the famous Frankfurt *Grieh Soos* (green sauce); these herbs were originally gathered as a kind of springtime rite and customarily eaten on Maundy Thursday (called "Green Thursday" in German) or on Ascension Day. Nowadays, green sauce is sold ready mixed and packaged and is available year-round, and has thus been transformed (or reduced?) by hothouse gardening from a regional to a national specialty.

The original frankfurters—*Frankfurter Würstchen,* to give them their rightful name—are manufactured in the suburb of Neu-Isenburg, near the airport; actually this is not strictly correct, since the original *Frankfurt* frankfurters were miniature bratwursts, and in their day kept entire armies on the march. A related species, the Frankfurt beef sausage *(Rindwurst),* has never achieved the international acclaim of its skinnier siblings but still is considered to be very tasty indeed by sausage mavens. Local pastry specialties include *Bethmännchen* and *Frankfurter Brenten,* both of which are included in the recipe section, though the well-known and quite delicious *Frankfurter Kranz,* or "Frankfurt ring," has had to be disqualified, despite the name, since it is not really a feature of the traditional cuisine of the region. *Hartekuchen,* a kind of dry biscuit, is totally indigenous and tastes exactly as if it were invented to go with the local apple wine, a hard cider, tart and refreshing.

Some of Germany's most famous vineyards are also to be found in Hesse, and the Hessians, "vigilant" to the last drop, have even thought of a way of turning the sourest grapes into a delicious delicacy with the help of the Hessian version of zabaglione. The resulting combination is called *Wipp.* In other words—since I feel that at least one recipe in this section should be given verbatim, in the original Hessian—if you take a generous quantity of *Wipp "mit em Schepper aus'm Kumpe, dann werd geachelt"* (. . . with a mug from the jug, then everybody starts feasting). Incidentally, this last expression—*geachelt*—was borrowed from the Yiddish.

Frankfurt am Main

The Palatinate and Rhenish Hesse

Pfalz und Rheinhessen

. . . .

There is considerable rivalry between these two great wine-producing regions, but at the moment it seems as though Rhenish Hesse is ahead by a nose, since they have an additional thousand hectares or so under vine cultivation; the Pfälzers sometimes prefer to beg the question a little by referring to their native region as the Rhineland Palatinate (Rheinpfalz). From a culinary standpoint, these two regions —all the territory between Bingen and Ludwigshafen, if you're looking at a map, and possibly including the Saar—are united rather than divided by a common preoccupation with wine, which, if not included in the sauces or in the marinades, is almost certain to be served with the meal.

A Pfälzer *Trobbe,* which means "drop" (of ordinary table wine), is regarded as a suitable if not obligatory accompaniment for almost any sort of food, as evidenced by the official names of what are essentially wine-tasting festivals held throughout the region: the "wurst market" in Bad Dürkheim, "pretzel festival" in Speyer, "fried fish festival" in Worms, and even the Deidesheim "billygoat auction" *(Geissbocktversteigerung!).* The traditional cuisine of the Palatinate and Rhenish Hesse has two basic virtues, honesty and simplicity (which might even be called naïveté). As far as the names of the dishes themselves are concerned, for example, the Pfälzers tend to be quite uncompromising: *Saumagen,* which, from a technical standpoint, might legitimately be referred to as a ballotine of

Title page of the "Dürckheim Wurst Market Directory," Bad Dürckheim, 1897. The Wurst Market is the world's largest wine festival.

pork, possibly a "stuffed pork maw," is in the land that gave it birth invariably just a *Saumagen,* a name that has the same colloquial force and vigor (though not the same meaning) as "sow belly" in English. For similar reasons, the Pfälzers have never taken to the fancy foreign word *Kartoffel* for potato (actually from the Italian word *tartufo* for truffle) and continue to refer to them as "ground pears," *Grumbeere,* just as the ubiquitous potato dumplings are known to Pfälzers as "hairy buttons," *Hoorische Knepp*. The Pfälzers' relations with the Deity are said to be just as breezy and colloquial, as in the following prayer: "I praise Thee, O Lord, with food and drink, with hairy buttons, sow maw, 'wurscht,' rolls, and wine."★

The difference between a beer- and wine-based cuisine can perhaps be best conveyed by a comparison of the two prepared cheese recipes given on pages 138 and 139, the Bavarian *Obatzter* versus the Pfälzer *Spundekäs,* the former rather bluff and powerful in its impact, the latter sharp, piquant, and restrained. This is not to say, by the way, that either the Palatinate or Rhenish Hesse is a great cheese-making region, since simple hand cheeses of this type and farmer cheese *(Quark)* is about all there is. Everyday cookery is dominated by wurst, especially the home-style *Hauschlachterwürste,* and various ingenious variations on the basic "ground pear" motif, though there is enough sunshine and fertile soil to spare, in the hill country as well as in the flatlands, for a greater variety of garden produce than was available in many other regions. One of the happiest of Palatine inspirations, however, is the combination of a foaming, "impetuous" (as the wine-tasting

★ "Ich lobe dich, o Herr, mit Esse und Trinke, mit Hoorische Knepp, Saumage, Worscht, Weck, und Wein."

Bingen on the Rhine (after a drawing by Abresch)

crowd might say) new wine with roast chestnuts, which is called *Neie un Keschte* in dialect.

There are a great many traditional recipes for rabbit and other small game, which are still quite abundant in these regions because of the ample cover provided by the vineyards, which spread across the hills and meadows of the river valleys. In addition, the forested mountain range called the Pfälzer Wald, actually the western rim of the Upper Rhine basin, comprises one of the largest contiguous woodlands in West Germany today and—apart from the odd NATO base and a variety of top-secret U.S. military installations—still provides hospitality to a fair number of roebuck, perhaps a wild boar or two, and others of its original inhabitants.

Prospective visitors to the Palatinate and Rhenish Hesse can perhaps get a foretaste of the traditional culture (and cookery) by looking at prints of fruitful, smiling landscapes and rural scenes done by some of the region's native painters (somewhat along the lines of Grandma Moses). These works, full of bold primary colors, are evocative of life's simplest and greatest pleasures, notably those—in the words of Rhenish Hesse's most celebrated poet Carl Zuckmayer, who lived as an emigrant until 1948 in Vermont—"of feeding off the fat of the land, and of feeling a powerful fullness from your neck down to your toes."

Geisenheim on the Rhine, known worldwide for its college for wine growing and cellar mastery (engraving by Johann Poppel, after a drawing by L. Rohbock)

*B*aden

. . . .

In the old days, the princely state of Baden was regarded, not always approvingly, as a kind of miniature Switzerland or Black Forest utopia in Germany's southwestern corner—the *Musterländle,* "little model country," as it was called. Whether or not this is true, it seems easy enough to substantiate the claim that Baden has the finest food in Germany. Those who are not in a position to verify this assertion for themselves have only to consult the *Michelin Red Guide,* which reserves a whole galaxy of stars for the hotels and restaurants of Baden; other European restaurant guides say much the same, though perhaps not so succinctly.

I believe there are three basic reasons for this. First, Baden is blessed with sunshine, and the fertile fields, vineyards, and orchards of the Upper Rhine valley have always assured a bountiful supply of vegetables, wines, fruits, and greens of the very best quality. Second, and perhaps more important, the Badeners (the term *Badenser,* though sometimes heard, is considered mildly pejorative) have been heavily, though indirectly, influenced by the two great cuisines of Europe—the Italian and the French—through the good offices of their kinfolk in Switzerland and Alsace. In addition, these Germanic intermediaries seem to have contributed a number of helpful touches of their own, and it should also be noted that Baden was a part of the Hapsburg Empire for many centuries. Thus, they claim, the celebrated Linzer torte is one of *their* regional specialties, likewise the only slightly less celebrated gugelhupf.

One final reason for the culinary preeminence of this region

Baden-Baden, Black Forest,
famous spa and gambling place
(engraving by Johann Poppel,
after a drawing by R. Höfle)

might be that the Badeners are a bit more easygoing than
other Germans and will always take the time to enjoy, to
"visit" for a while with friends or with strangers (*schwätze* is
the local term), a process that often requires the accompaniment of good food and drink. Baden may not be Germany's
most prestigious wine-producing region, but its wines have
always been put to very good use in concocting sauces. Before
the war, the wines of Baden were reserved mainly for local
consumption, but since then they have done extraordinarily
well in the international marketplace; the largest winery in
Europe, for example, is in Breisach, and the winemakers of
Baden tend to show more strength in their dry whites than
some of the other wine-producing regions of Germany.

Baden's culinary specialties are virtually all characterized by
a certain delicacy—snails, frog's legs, freshwater fish in wine-
and-cream sauce, saddle of roebuck Baden-Baden, asparagus,
dandelion salad (the dish itself having a great deal more delicacy about it than the dialect name that it generally goes by,
see pages 114–15), and Black Forest Cake *(Schwarzwälder
Kirschtorte),* a nontraditional café-style pastry of comparatively recent origin, though the traditional pastime of *schwätze*
has always required that a certain number of delicious fine
baked goods be on hand.

Baden's traditional cuisine also enjoys the advantage of being based on cream and butter rather than lard and bacon, but even a dish like pickled pork shoulder with sauerkraut, or *Schäufele* (bladelet), is considerably less robust than other German specialties of this type, and the sauerkraut itself rendered a bit tastier by being cooked in wine. (This might also be the appropriate place to mention the Baden specialty called *Gumbistöpfel,* which simply involves including a certain number of apples in the homemade sauerkraut when the cabbage is salted down; after a suitable interval has elapsed, the apples come out as tender as baked apples and wonderfully tart.)

Smoked hams from the Schwarzwald have a very good reputation, as do such fruit-flavored liqueurs as Schwarzwald *kirschwasser, Zwetschenwasser,* and *Himbeergeist,* the latter two being distilled from the fermented juice of plums and raspberries, respectively. *Topinambur,* a specialty of the Ortenau district, is made from Jerusalem artichokes, which are grown nowhere else in Germany; it is the best digestive schnapps of German manufacture and is also said to contain a certain ingredient that helps diabetics to metabolize sugar. There are a number of well-known distilleries in Baden, though the connoisseurs often prefer homemade schnapps from some farmer's backyard still—the locations of which are less readily divulged by the connoisseurs to their fellow schnapps-fanciers than by moonshiners in other lands to the local tax collectors.

Swabia

Schwaben

•   •   •   •   •   •   •   •   •   •

The Swabians are the Badeners' neighbors, and the inhabitants of both regions have thus been in a position, at least in a manner of speaking, to peer into each other's cooking pots. Part of Bavaria is inhabited by Swabians, so they also find themselves in a state of transition between Badisch elegance and Bavarian heartiness. Gastronomically, all Swabia is divided into two parts—between the "soup-Swabians" and the "spätzle-Swabians," though it is not so easy to trace the physical boundary between their two domains; possibly the soup-Swabians are in the majority to the south of Ulm (and even they like to put spätzle in their soup on occasion).

Flour is the key ingredient in traditional Swabian cookery, just as cream is in Baden, and here, for once, the almighty *Kartoffel* (potato) is obliged to play a secondary role. The baker's art has been developed to a high level of sophistication and refinement in the land between the Neckar and the Danube—the Swabian *Laugenbrezel* (brine pretzel), for example, alternately chewy and crispy, presents a remarkable study in contrasts. Spread with a generous amount of fresh butter, which some Swabians would surely consider an extravagance, a *Laugenbrezel* is truly a morsel for the gods. The list of other notable Swabian baked goods would have to include the crusty white rolls known as *Seelen* (souls) and rolls called *Mutscheln*, then called *Straubeze* and *Wibele*, anise-flavored *Ulmer Brot* as well as *Horaffen*, and *Ulmer Spatzen* (Ulm sparrows), all being something between cookies and rolls.

There is another line of demarcation that has to do with

Heilbronn, Swabia

altitude rather than latitude or location, and that is the culinary contrast between the rich river valleys of the Danube, Lech, and the Iller, for example, and the relatively infertile upland regions of the Alb and the Baar. Sour broth is one of the staples of the latter and is served with spätzle, potatoes, wurst, and vegetables. The dividing line between beer- and wine-based cookery on the Bavarian and Badisch models also runs through Swabia, where more red wine is produced (and consumed) than anywhere else in Germany.

In general, the Swabians are often credited with a kind of fussy, perfectionist spirit combined with a flair for experimentation that has resulted in a booming regional economy, including a number of phenomenally successful large-scale enterprises. I maintain that this same spirit of fruitful tinkering has been no less active in the Swabian kitchen, producing a traditional cuisine that is as rich and various as any of Germany's regions, including a number of adventurous combinations. To choose the obvious example, we have lentils with spätzle, or potatoes with spätzle and sauerkraut, or spätzle with cheese and, in combination with any of the above-mentioned items, served in a vinegary broth. The repertory of possible fillings for *Maultaschen* (the Swabian equivalent of ravioli) is certainly no less impressive.

The Swabians themselves, great efficiency experts by nature, have long since recognized the postulated relationship between gastronomic intake and economic output—*"Wie oiner isst, so schafft er"* is the way they put it, "The way you eat is the way you work." An almost boundless enthusiasm for both of these activities is a truly Swabian characteristic, or as Goethe once observed, "I fully subscribe to the truth of the local adage: Lord, but what a lot of victuals they have there!" *("Hilf Himmel, was gibt's da für Speise!")*

Whoever thinks of Swabians has to think of their many poets and their two most famous products: spätzle and Mercedes cars.

The Recipes

Soups

. . . .

Soup has had an eventful history in traditional German cuisine. It started out as the great staple dish of the farmhouse kitchen, and up until the beginning of this century it was not unusual for it to be served three times a day. The practice of eating soup for breakfast was well nigh universal at one time, and as *Grimm's Fairy Tales* reminds us, it was the usual food not only of poor woodcutters and poor charcoal-burners but of poor people in general. Later literary evidence (the story of Suppenkaspar in Heinrich Hoffmann's *Struwwelpeter,* a book of cautionary tales for children that was enormously popular at around the turn of the century) suggests that the textural monotony of such a diet was keenly represented by the young and that a carefully orchestrated propaganda campaign—comparable to the one involving Popeye and his can of spinach a few decades later—had to be undertaken to make them put up with the stuff at all.

Nowadays, except perhaps at lunchtime, soup has lost its former monopoly. A clear soup, with or without an egg, is sometimes served at business conferences as a late-morning collation, virtually the only modern survival of the fine old custom of serving soup for breakfast. Recently the idea of having soup as a sort of elegant late-night snack is coming into vogue again (perhaps implying a reversal of this historic trend).

Unlike the French, who generally prefer to serve theirs as a prelude to the evening meal, the Germans have not felt the need for an elaborate nomenclature to describe their soups. There is "clear soup," or broth, and there are also such things as *Grützen* (groats, a porridge made from various hulled grains), *Brei* (a thicker porridge or puree, something like the

French *potage*), and *Eintöpfe* (stews, literally "one-pot" meals). Virtually everything that lies in between goes by the name of *Suppe,* which is what (along with a couple of *Grützen*) we're going to be concerned with in the following section—including recipes for such once-popular delights as quince, elderberry, beer-and-wine, and buttermilk soups.

SCHLESWIG/HOLSTEIN

Vegetable Soup with Dumplings   Frische Suppe

The standard vegetable soup of the Rhineland was acquired from the camp kitchens and quartermasters of Napoleon's armies (perhaps even Louis XIV's). The "fresh soup" of northern Germany is a purely local invention, dating back to the previous century and originally flavored with nothing more than a bunch of soup greens. The present version, which calls for additional vegetable reinforcement, is still reasonably authentic. In Schleswig-Holstein today, *Frische Suppe* is an indispensable component of every official banquet or festive dinner party.

. . . .

Wash the meat and soup bones thoroughly. Place them in a heavy 4-quart pot along with the parsley, carrots, celery, and cold water; simmer gently for 1½ hours. Remove from the heat, strain the broth. Return to the stove and reduce until only 1 quart liquid remains, skimming off the fat as necessary. Add the diced vegetables and cook in the broth until tender. Add salt and pepper to taste.

To make the little flour dumplings called *Mehlmusklösschen* in Schleswig-Holstein, place the butter, salt, and water in a heavy 1-quart saucepan and bring to a boil. (The soup should still be simmering gently.) Add the flour and stir until the mixture clings to a wooden spoon in a kind of doughy clump, then remove from heat. Allow to cool for 5 minutes. Add one egg to the dough and beat in thoroughly. Then add the yolk in the same manner. Season with nutmeg to taste. With wet hands form the dough into little dumplings.

Add the dumplings to the hot broth, and cook for 5 more minutes before serving.

MAKES 4–6 SERVINGS

BROTH:
1¾ pounds stew meat
    A couple of marrow
    bones or 1 pound veal
    or beef stock bones
1 bunch of parsley
2 carrots, peeled and
    chopped
2 celery stalks, chopped
1½ quarts cold water
1½ pounds vegetables
    (green beans, peas,
    turnips, carrots,
    asparagus), washed,
    peeled if necessary,
    and diced
    Salt and freshly
    ground black pepper

DUMPLINGS:
1 tablespoon butter
    Pinch of salt
1 cup water
1¼ cups flour
1 egg
1 egg yolk
    Freshly grated nutmeg

SWABIA

Onion Broth with Croutons   Feine Brotsuppe

2 pounds stew meat
6 marrow bones or 2
    pounds veal or beef
    stock bones
2 garlic cloves
1 leek, washed and
    sliced
2 celery stalks, chopped
2 small carrots, peeled
    and chopped
    Salt and pepper
1½ quarts water
4 medium onions
3 tablespoons butter
1 unsliced loaf of
    Bauernbrot *(peasant
    bread)* or light rye
    bread
2 tablespoons finely
    chopped fresh parsley
4–6 tablespoons cream

It was the German philosopher Ludwig Feuerbach who first confirmed what everyone had long suspected: "A human being *is* what he eats." The inhabitants of Swabia in southwestern Germany, like their cuisine, have a reputation for being solid (as well as stolid) and uncompromising, and grandmother's traditional recipes are still held in the highest esteem. Some years ago, an old Swabian recipe for *Brotsuppe* (bread soup) was transformed by Rolf-Dieter Krauth, gentleman chef and co-owner of the Bizerba factory in Balingen, into this remarkable regional delicacy. It was a dish he could be proud to set before the local titans of industry as well as the most exacting foreign visitors . . . and it is one that teaches us that there is more to life than just filet mignon.

•   •   •   •   •   •   •   •   •

Place stew meat, bones, garlic, leek, celery, carrots, and seasonings in a large pot with the water; bring to a boil. Allow to simmer gently for at least 1 hour, skimming off the impurities from the surface.

Halve the onions and cut into semicircular slices. Sauté the onions in butter over medium-high heat, until they turn

Hohenzollern Castle, home of the imperial family, with a view of Hechingen in southwestern Germany (Swabia)

brown (stirring constantly to keep them from turning black). Add half of the onions to the soup; drain the other half on a paper towel and set aside. Cut several slices from a loaf of peasant bread or light rye bread, as thin as you possibly can, and toast these golden brown in the oven. Break into match-box-size pieces.

Strain the bones, stew meat, and vegetables from the broth. Distribute the toast pieces and the remaining crispy onions among the soup plates before pouring the broth over them. Garnish with parsley and float a little dab of cream in the middle of each plate of soup. With the quantities given in the recipe, you'll end up with plenty of *Feine Brotsuppe*.

MAKES 4–6 SERVINGS

SCHLESWIG/HOLSTEIN

Vegetable Soup Schnüsch

*Schnüsch (*also spelled *Schnusch* or *Snusch*) seems to have originated in Angelland, a region along the North Sea coast that also produced the Angles—the ones who, along with the Saxons and Jutes, became the ancestors of the English (Anglo-Saxons). More recently, Angelland has been noted for its fine dairy herds and *Schnüsch,* which, however spelled or pronounced, turns out to be nothing more than vegetable soup with milk in it.

• • • • • • • • •

Wash the vegetables. Parboil the peas and carrots in a little water with salt and sugar. Reserve ⅓ cup of the cooking liquid.

Snap the beans and cook separately in a little salted water until tender. Cut the beans into ½-inch pieces. Boil the potatoes in their jackets, peel, and slice into thin rounds.

Place the parsley, butter, and milk in a large saucepan and bring to a boil. Then add the vegetables with the reserved ⅓ cup cooking liquid. Cook until all ingredients are heated

½ pound carrots, peeled and diced
½ pound fresh peas
½ pound string beans
Salt
Sugar
½ pound potatoes
3 tablespoons finely chopped fresh parsley
¼ cup butter
3 cups milk
½ cup diced ham or bacon, or pickled or matjes herring

through, then season to taste. Garnish with bits of ham or bacon, or pickled or matjes herring.

NOTE: Northern Germany is noted for its sweet-and-sour soups, so don't be too sparing with the sugar if you're striving for an authentic Schleswigian effect. Also note that this is the recipe for "thin *Schnüsch."* To make "thick *Schnüsch,"* melt the butter with a little flour and make a roux before adding it to the milk, as above.

MAKES 4 SERVINGS

SCHLESWIG/HOLSTEIN

Old-Fashioned Hamburger Eel Soup
Alt-Hamburgische Aalsuppe

BROTH:
- 1 medium ham hock
- 1 pound chicken parts (backs and necks)
- 2¾ pounds lean stew beef
- 2 quarts water
- 1 bunch of soup greens (includes: a carrot, a leek, a branch of celery, and a few sprigs of parsley), chopped
- Salt
- 10 peppercorns
- 1 bay leaf
- 2 pounds fresh vegetables in season (peas, carrots, asparagus, plus smaller quantities of cauliflower, kohlrabi, or green beans)
- 1¼ cups pitted prunes

Aalsuppe, the distinctively festive dish of the Hanseatic Free City of Hamburg, sounds like it should mean "eel soup," since *Aal* is the German word for eel. However, the people of Hamburg and neighboring Holstein, like Bostonians in the United States, are renowned for the broadness of their *a*'s, and *aal* (pronounced something like "awl") is the northern German way of saying *alles,* "all" or "everything." And so, *Aalsuppe* is a soup (originally a stew) that has everything. Eventually, perhaps due to the workings of folk etymology, *alles* even came to include an eel or two, since these creatures are quite common in the rivers of Holstein. The early recipes —the oldest one I know of dates back to 1854—all call for substantial quantities of the principal ingredients, since it hardly made sense to go to so much trouble without being handsomely compensated for one's efforts.

.   .   .   .

Rinse the ham hock. In a 6-quart pot put the ham hock, chicken parts, and stewing beef in at least 2 quarts of water. Bring to a boil and allow to simmer gently for around 2 hours, making sure to skim off the fat and impurities from time to time. Add the soup greens, a little salt, peppercorns, and bay leaf. After another half hour, strain out the solid ingredients through a sieve lined with a clean muslin cloth. Reserve the stew meat. Allow the broth to cool and skim off the fat.

Wash, peel, and slice the vegetables (or cut into thin strips where appropriate). Put the broth back onto the heat. Add the vegetables gradually, starting with those that need to be cooked the longest (i.e., carrots, cauliflower, kohlrabi), and cook until barely tender. At the same time, in a stainless steel or non-reactive pot, simmer the fruit in the white wine until tender, making sure that it does not start to disintegrate or get too soft.

To make the fish broth, put all the ingredients except the eel or fish in a non-reactive saucepan with 1 quart water and bring to a boil. Then add the eel or fish and cook for about 10 minutes—until its flesh is tender but still firm. Do not discard the herbs or the liquid once the eel has been cooked, since you're going to be using them later on.

To keep the fish and the fruit from becoming overcooked, it's actually preferable to keep these off the stove in the separate saucepans in which they were prepared until you assemble the soup.

To make dumplings for the soup, boil the milk or water with the butter, add the flour, and stir vigorously with a wooden spoon until a thick clump starts to form and a white residue is visible at the bottom of the saucepan. Take off the heat and allow to cool for 5 minutes, then beat in the eggs, one at a time, mixing thoroughly after each addition. Season to taste with salt and a little fresh nutmeg. Shape the dough into little dumplings using 1 teaspoon of the mixture and wet hands; cook the dumplings separately in water that is just simmering, then remove from the water and allow to drain.

Now the *Aalsuppe* has almost reached the final assembly stage. Reheat the meat broth, adding the herbs and liquid from the eel broth as well; reserve the pieces of eel. Cut the stew meat into thin strips and add to the broth, along with the white wine in which the fruit was cooked. Transfer the eel pieces into a warm tureen, followed by the fruit, then by the broth with the meat, vegetables, and spices.

To season, add the vinegar, salt and pepper, sugar, and

3 cups firmly packed dried or 1½ cups fresh apple slices
3 cups dried or 1½ cups fresh pear slices
1 cup white wine

FISH BROTH:
1 cup white wine
Dash of wine vinegar
1 onion, finely chopped
1 bay leaf
Salt and freshly ground black pepper
Pinch of sugar
4 allspice berries or ⅛ teaspoon ground allspice
1 quart water
1 2-pound eel or monkfish, skinned, cut into bite-size pieces

DUMPLINGS:
1 cup milk or water
1 tablespoon butter
1½ cups flour
2 eggs
Salt
Freshly grated nutmeg

SEASONINGS:
Wine vinegar to taste
Salt and freshly ground black pepper
Sugar to taste
7 teaspoons finely chopped herbs, choosing 7 out of the following: parsley, thyme, marjoram, savory, sage, chervil, basil, tarragon, celery leaves and stalks (chopped up very fine), lemon balm

Finely chopped chives for garnish

Hamburg Harbor, The
Blockhouse

more herbs (parsley, thyme, marjoram . . .), according to
taste, and finally the dumplings. A sprinkling of finely
chopped chives can also be added just before serving.

Bear in mind that *Aalsuppe* should have a rich, heady aroma
and a delicate sweet-sour taste.

MAKES 8–12 SERVINGS

EAST   PRUSSIA

Sorrel Soup   Sauerampfersuppe

Parboil the sorrel in 3 quarts of salted water for 2 minutes.
Let stand for a few minutes more, then strain out the water
and pat the sorrel dry with paper towels. Chop it very fine—
if using a food mill or processor don't mash it too finely.
Chop the parsley and vegetables, but keep these separate from
the sorrel. Cook the vegetables and parsley in the broth for 40
minutes; strain them out. Reserve the broth and puree the
vegetables with a little of the broth.

Melt the butter in a large saucepan. Cook the minced sorrel
in the melted butter for several minutes, stirring constantly.

Add the clear broth and the pureed vegetables, then season

with salt and pepper, lemon juice, and a pinch of sugar. Bring to a boil and cook all the ingredients together for about 10 minutes. Stir the cornstarch into the sour cream, then stir this mixture into the soup with a whisk. Bring to a boil once more. Simmer for 2 minutes. Serve with a poached or hard-boiled egg in each bowl.

VARIATIONS: In East Prussia, the meat from which the stock was prepared was sometimes cut into matchstick strips and added to the soup, which was generally accompanied by boiled potatoes all around (peeled or boiled in their jackets) to make a complete meal.

As a further refinement, the broth can be thickened with 1 or 2 egg yolks and a pat of butter stirred into it just before serving.

Those not overly concerned with regional authenticity or with calorie counting might even prefer to substitute crème fraîche for the sour cream, which makes for a definite improvement.

MAKES 4 SERVINGS

1 pound sorrel, washed, stems removed
1 large bunch of parsley
1 carrot, peeled and chopped
1 stalk celery, chopped
1 leek, washed and chopped
1 tablespoon butter
1 quart clear broth (either chicken or beef)
  Salt and freshly ground black pepper
1 tablespoon lemon juice
  Pinch of sugar
1 heaping tablespoon cornstarch
1 cup sour cream
4 eggs, poached or hard-boiled

BADEN

Chilled Sorrel Soup   Gekühlte Sauerampfersuppe

Cook the sorrel and dill in the water over medium heat for 15 minutes. Stir in the sour cream and remove from heat, then thicken with the egg yolks. Chill for 20 minutes on ice and stir occasionally with a whisk. Salt to taste.

Add the cucumber strips to the soup, then carefully add the hard-boiled eggs. Serve with an ice cube in each soup bowl.

NOTE: Thin strips of leftover roast beef or other cooked meat (or fish fillet) may be added as a garnish.

MAKES 4–6 SERVINGS

3–5 handfuls of sorrel, finely chopped
3 tablespoons finely chopped dill
1½ quarts water
1 cup sour cream
2 egg yolks
  Salt
1 small cucumber, seeded, and sliced into thin strips
2 eggs, hard-boiled, coarsely chopped

HESSE

Potato Soup   Kartoffelsuppe

2 tablespoons butter
  or lard
1 carrot, peeled and
  chopped
1 stalk celery,
  chopped
1 leek, chopped
3 sprigs parsley,
  chopped
1 large onion, diced
1 pound potatoes,
  peeled, washed, and
  sliced
1½–2 quarts beef stock
  Salt and freshly
  ground white pepper
  Splash of vinegar
2 tablespoons chopped
  fresh parsley

Kartoffelsuppe is the sort of dish that people tend to associate with northern European cuisine in general and German cuisine in particular, though in fact the potato was not introduced into northern Europe until fairly late in the eighteenth century. Soon after its arrival, as in Ireland, it became the staple food of the countryfolk in Germany, Poland, and Bohemia and remained so for the next hundred years. Even so, a cookbook from central Germany that was published in 1792 makes no mention of *Kartoffelsuppe,* and it was only a few years earlier that the exotic *Erdepfel* (earth apple) had received its first formal acknowledgment in a German dictionary. The following recipe has been handed down from my grandmother's family.

·   ·   ·   ·   ·   ·   ·   ·   ·

Heat the butter or lard in a 4-quart soup pot. Place the vegetables, parsley, and onion in the soup pot and fry in the hot fat until the onion becomes transparent. Add the potatoes and enough stock to cover all the vegetables. Add salt and white pepper to taste, stir well, and cook until the potatoes are tender all the way through and almost done. Remove about a third of the potatoes from the pot, mash the two thirds (as if for mashed potatoes), and return to the pot as thickening for the soup.

Reheat the soup. Test for seasoning, add just a hint of vinegar, garnish with parsley, and serve.

VARIATIONS: Carnivores might care to add whatever they judge to be a sufficient quantity of little Vienna sausages or about ¾ pound cooked, sliced pork sausage.

The same recipe, with the addition of ¾ pound leftover (cooked) fish or dried codfish (stockfish) that has been "reconstituted" in water, and omitting the vinegar from the seasoning, is called *Kartoffelsuppe mit Fisch,* a dish that originated in Thuringia in Central Germany.

MAKES 4 SERVINGS

BADEN

Potato Soup Baden-Style
Kartoffelsuppe Badische Art

This soup is a particularly fine recipe that has spread to many different regions from its point of origin in Baden.

· · · · · · · · ·

Peel and wash the vegetables and cut into thin slices. Put into the soup pot with the potatoes and add enough water or chicken broth to cover well. Add the pepper and nutmeg. Cook over a low heat until the potatoes and vegetables are tender.

Remove 1 cup of the potatoes from the liquid and set aside. Put the remaining potatoes, vegetables, and liquid through a fine sieve or puree them in a blender. In a small skillet sauté the diced onion in the butter, then add the entire contents of the skillet to the soup. Stir the cream into the soup and add the cup of reserved potatoes. Test for seasoning, cook until the soup is heated through, then garnish with croutons and chives before serving.

MAKES 4–6 SERVINGS

1 carrot
1 small celery root, or
   2–3 stalks of celery
1 leek (white part only)
1 onion
3 medium potatoes,
   peeled, washed, and
   cubed or sliced
1½ quarts water or
   chicken broth
   Salt and freshly
   ground white pepper
   Freshly grated nutmeg
½ cup finely diced onion
1 tablespoon butter
1 cup cream
½ cup white-bread
   croutons
1–2 tablespoons chopped
   fresh chives

Pea Soup   Erbsensuppe

1 pound (2¼ cups) split
peas, preferably green
ones
2 quarts water
½ pound sliced, medium-
lean bacon, cut into thin
strips
1 medium onion, minced
1 bacon rind, if at hand
1 ham bone ("with a
little bit left on it"), or
a smoked ham hock (see
Note)
3 medium potatoes,
peeled, washed, and
diced
Pinch of crushed dried
basil
Pinch of crushed dried
marjoram
Salt and freshly ground
black pepper
¼ cup croutons

Pea soup is one of those simple, incomparable national dishes
that German immigrants and expatriates long for, and even
start dreaming of if they've been away from it for long time.
Pea soup is also one of the few aspects of Germany's long
military tradition, perhaps the only one, that still inspires genuine affection and nostalgia. Pea soup has long been a staple
on the military menu—it was one of King Frederick the
Great's favorite dishes—and there are still a number of sports,
hobby, and hiking clubs in Germany that provide refreshment
for their members by renting an army field kitchen (better
known as a *Gulaschkanone,* or "goulash cannon") and cooking
up an enormous batch of the stuff. While it may be true that
pea soup tastes best when prepared under battlefield conditions, a highly acceptable substitute can be made at home.

·   ·   ·   ·   ·   ·   ·   ·   ·

Soak the dried peas for a few hours in the water. In a large
heavy pot cook the bacon strips briskly until the fat has been
rendered. Add the chopped onion; continue to cook until the
onion starts to turn transparent.

To the pot add the peas along with the water in which they
have been soaking, the bacon rind, and the ham bone. Add
the potatoes, along with some basil and marjoram. Cook for
a good 30 to 40 minutes on medium heat.

Remove the bacon rind and the ham bone; detach any frag-
ments of ham still adhering to the bone and chop these up
very small. If you want a smoother texture, puree ⅓–½ of
the soup. Add the little pieces of ham, season with salt and
pepper to taste, and garnish with croutons.

NOTE: Some recipes advise you to put *all* the soup through the
strainer instead of just half. In my view, this detracts from the
overall sensory experience, since it's important to get the feel
of an occasional pea on one's tongue while eating pea soup.
(To do otherwise would be to fly in the face of centuries of
Gulaschkanone tradition—I've never met a mess sergeant yet
who'd admit to straining his pea soup.)

If a nice meaty ham bone is not available, the bacon rind and/or ham hock will have to do the job. In this case, add the diced meat from the cooked ham hock or heat up some Vienna sausages or other boiled *Würste* in the soup and cut these into slices before serving.

MAKES 4–8 SERVINGS

The town of Blackenburg and the ruined castle of Greifenstein, Thuringia

Lentil Soup   Linsensuppe

½ pound or 1¼ cups
   lentils, cleaned and
   washed
1 large onion, minced
1 tablespoon lard or butter
1 bunch of soup greens
   (leek, celery, carrot,
   parsley), washed and
   finely chopped
1 carrot, peeled and diced
1 large potato, peeled,
   washed, and cubed or
   thinly sliced
½ pound medium-lean
   bacon
   Salt and freshly ground
   black pepper
   Several tablespoons
   wine vinegar

Soak the lentils overnight in a pot with 4–6 cups of water.

In a large saucepan sauté the onion in lard or butter until golden. Add the lentils and the water in which they have been soaking. Add the soup greens, carrot, and potato to the soup along with the bacon. Bring to a boil and cook for 1 hour, or until the lentils are quite tender. Add salt and pepper to taste after the first ½ hour.

When the soup is almost done, remove the bacon and dice or divide into 4 equal servings. (You can also heat up some Vienna sausages or other appropriately sized *Würstchen* in the soup, in which case the bacon that accompanies them should be cut into thin strips.)

If the soup is too thin, press a few tablespoons of lentils through a fine strainer and use this paste to thicken the soup. The soup should be seasoned with a little vinegar just before serving; a cruet of vinegar (a traditional safeguard against flatulence, by the way) is customarily placed on the table so that guests can season their own individual portions.

NOTE: In northern Germany, the land of sweet-and-sour soup, a little sugar might be added as well.

If slab bacon is available, substitute it for sliced bacon. Cook the piece whole in the soup. Then dice it and return it to the soup.

MAKES 4 SERVINGS

BADEN

"German Wheat" Groats   Grünkernsuppe

To paraphrase the famous definition of "oats" in Dr. Johnson's Dictionary, *spelt* (*Triticum spelta,* also called German wheat) is a grain that in North America is mainly fed to cattle, but in Germany and Switzerland it still continues—in a very small way—to support the people. In fact, Baden and Franconia are about the only parts of Germany where this archaic variety of wheat is grown commercially and harvested before full maturity. The special drying kilns in which *Grünkern* is processed—in order to acquire a slightly smoked flavor—are still in operation. *Grünkern* groats can be obtained in health-food stores (perhaps even in unusually well-stocked ones in North America) and taste so good that it is worthwhile to search for them. This recipe for *Grünkernsuppe* has recently made a remarkable comeback from obscurity, not only on its native heath in southwest Germany but at a number of international gastronomic "conferences" that I've attended.

. . . .

In the bottom of a soup pot sauté both the groats and vegetables in butter until the shallots turn yellow. Pour in the stock, then add the stale or dry-baked roll slices to the pot. Add a little salt and cook all together for about 1½ hours, stirring frequently.

Beat the egg yolk(s) into the cream, take the groats off the heat, and use this mixture to thicken the groats.

Add the dumplings *(Markklösschen)* to the groats and put back on the heat until the dumplings are heated through. If using croutons, garnish the groats and serve.

NOTE: In the old days, *Grünkern* groats were always strained in the kitchens of the rich and well-born; some of the early recipes go so far as to recommend that the groats themselves be discarded and only the gruel that passes through the strainer be served. I'm pleased to report that modern *Grünkernsuppe*-fanciers have done away with such finicky notions and have gone back to the old peasant custom of eating their groats unstrained.

The vegetables should be diced *very* fine—to about the same texture as the groats, in fact.

MAKES 4–6 SERVINGS (12–20 DUMPLINGS)

¾ *cup* Grünkern *groats (spelt, German wheat —not flour or meal)*
1 *tablespoon each very finely chopped chard, shallot, and celery root or stalks (see Note)*
2–3 *tablespoons butter*
1½ *quarts rich beef stock*
½ *medium-size stale or dry-baked roll, without crusts, thinly sliced*
Salt
1–2 *egg yolks*
6 *tablespoons heavy cream*
Several Markklösschen *(page 102), or ½ cup croutons*

Fried Semolina Soup   Geröstete Grießsuppe

5 tablespoons lard or
   butter
⅔ cup farina (semolina)
1 quart boiling water
   Salt
3 egg yolks, lightly
   beaten
4 slices white bread,
   browned on both sides
   in a little butter

This dish is very typical of the sort of sturdy, reliable peasant cuisine that is rapidly dying out in Europe after many years of faithful service and, in this case, after tens of millions of servings.

•   •   •   •   •   •   •   •   •   •

Heat up the lard or butter in a large pot and fry the semolina until it turns pale yellow. Pour the boiling water over the semolina, add salt, and cook until the semolina is done, about 10 to 15 minutes. Remove from heat and thicken with the beaten egg yolks. Serve on top of a slice of fried bread.

MAKES 4 SERVINGS

Menu for the banquet celebrating the marriage of Princess Margarethe of Prussia and Prince Karl Friedrich of Hesse, January 23, 1893

City Hall, Breslau, in Silesia (now Polish territory)

Queen's Soup Königinsuppe

This is a dish that was sure to be found on the menus of all prewar restaurants with any sort of gastronomic pretensions. It is a bit too labor-intensive for even the most expensive restaurants to bother with today, but it is still, as the recipe assures us, "a splendid soup" that deserves to be rescued from oblivion. The earliest recipe that I could discover was published in Leipzig in 1773.

•   •   •   •   •   •   •   •   •   •

"Take a loaf of white bread and carefully remove the brown crust, then divide the bread into 4 or 6 pieces, put into a kettle; throw in a few carrots and turnips that have been cut up crosswise [sliced] and a whole parsley as well; then pour in a good strong beef stock and boil until the bread is quite used up [dissolved] and the broth is fairly thick; then take a half-pound crushed almonds, a little roast veal or chicken chopped up very fine, and the yolks of some hard-boiled eggs made into a paste, and add these to the broth one by one, each time stirring them all together. Put back on the fire for a little while, but the almonds and the rest should not be allowed to boil. Next, pass through a fine sieve, so that you are left with a thick white broth. Season with salt and mace. Put back on the fire until ready to serve, so that the soup is scalding hot, but do not allow it to boil or it will become curdled and unsightly. Before you pour the soup into the tureen, put in slices of toast. And then you may also add whatever you please—chicken or marrow bones, or veal bones stuffed with forcemeat or otherwise, or just some forcemeat by itself, either wrapped around a veal bone or molded into the shape desired, smoothed off very fine, lightly scored with the blade of a knife, and baked in a little cake pan, and served up in a bowl—and that will give you a splendid soup."

MY ADVICE: Mix in a blender until smooth. Do not add any bones; replace them with small pieces of precooked meat (veal and/or chicken breast).

MAKES 8 SERVINGS

1 *uncut loaf of white bread*
3 *carrots*
2 *turnips*
1 *small bunch parsley*
2 *quarts rich beef stock*
½ *pound ground almonds*
1 *cup finely diced cooked chicken or roasted veal*
4 *hard-boiled egg yolks, sieved*
Salt
Mace
6 *slices toasted bread*
Chicken or marrow bones, veal bones, or forcemeat (optional)

BADEN

Snail Soup Schneckensüpple

1 cup veal or beef stock
1 cup dry white wine
1 carrot, peeled and cut in
   two pieces
1 onion, coarsely chopped
1 medium celery root,
   peeled, or 3 stalks of
   celery, halved
1 bay leaf
2 dozen canned snails,
   liquid reserved
½ teaspoon finely chopped
   fresh basil
½ teaspoon cornstarch
½ cup crème fraîche
   Garlic salt
   Freshly ground white
   pepper
   Grated nutmeg
2 tablespoons chopped
   fresh parsley

Snails are served quite frequently in old-fashioned farm kitchens and country inns in Baden, but it is a taste that has yet to be acquired by countryfolk in other parts of Germany. There are a great many different ways of preparing snails in Baden, and this particular recipe has recently made something of a reputation for itself in serious gastronomic circles.

. . . .

In a large non-reactive pot cook the stock, white wine, vegetables, and the bay leaf all together for 15 minutes. Add the snails together with the liquid, if any, from the can or container they came in and cook for 15 minutes more. Strain out the solid ingredients. Finely mince half of the snails; cut the rest in half. Cut half the carrot and half the celery root or stalks into julienne strips; put the snails and vegetables back into the broth, add the basil, and heat up once more.

Mix the cornstarch and the crème fraîche, then stir this mixture into the soup with a whisk, and cook until the soup comes to a boil.

Season with garlic salt, white pepper, and nutmeg. Stir half the parsley into the soup; use the rest to garnish the soup in the tureen or the individual bowls.

VARIATIONS: If you're not afraid of a somewhat more insistent garlic aroma, add a few crushed fresh cloves of garlic to the stock, wine, and vegetables instead of garlic salt. Season to taste with salt before serving.

For a richer soup, thicken with 2 egg yolks in place of the cornstarch.

MAKES 4 SERVINGS IN SMALL SOUP BOWLS OR CUPS

Abbey of Benediktbeuren, Bavaria

ALLGÄU

Cheese Soup Käsesuppe

Cheese soup plays an important role in the traditional cuisines of France and Italy, and a few of these recipes seem to have found their way into the kitchens of Renaissance German princes—as evidenced by Marxen Rumpolt's *New Kochbuch,* published in 1581, which refers to such dishes as "Cheese Soup with Poach'd Eggs," "A Cheese Soup Made from a Parmesan Cheese," "Capons in a Soup Strewn with Parmesan Cheese." This recipe from the Allgäu, an Alpine district on the Austrian border, is probably the only indigenous German attempt at a cheese soup, probably invented just before the turn of the century.

⅓ *cup flour*
3 *tablespoons butter*
1 *quart rich beef stock*
½ *pound Swiss cheese,*
grated
1 *egg yolk*
2 *tablespoons heavy cream*
Freshly ground white
pepper
¼ *cup white-bread*
croutons
8 *onion rings, toasted*

·   ·   ·   ·   ·   ·   ·   ·

Place the flour and butter in a heavy-bottomed saucepan. Cook the roux over medium heat, but do not allow it to color. Pour in the stock. Stir well and cook over a low flame for 15 minutes. Gradually stir in the grated cheese and heat thoroughly before removing from the burner.

Beat the egg yolk and the cream with a whisk and thicken the soup with this mixture while the soup is off the heat. Season with white pepper to taste. Garnish with the croutons and toasted onion rings.

MAKES 4 SERVINGS

Crayfish Soup   Krebssuppe

8 crayfish (or 10 or 12, if
  they're especially small;
  2 small lobsters may be
  substituted)
2 quarts fish stock
2 small bunches of dill,
  plus 2–3 tablespoons
  chopped fresh dill
A few sprigs of parsley
Leaves from 3 celery
  stalks
1 tablespoon salt
3 tablespoons butter
2 tablespoons flour
1 cup cauliflower flowerets
  and asparagus tips,
  parboiled (optional)
2 egg yolks

East Prussia (which now belongs to Poland and the Soviet Union) is a flat, well-watered region, one of the few parts of the old German Empire where the local landowners, the Junkers, stoutly resisted industrialization. Hence, at around the turn of the century, the rivers were clean and unpolluted; the crayfish flourished. Nowadays, the crayfish, like the Junkers, are no more—or at any rate, they have to be imported, recently from as far away as Turkey. Homemakers used to wrap crayfish in the leaves of stinging nettles before storing them in the larder—though whether this was to keep them fresh for a little longer or simply a kind of primitive home-security system, I've been unable to determine.

.   .   .   .

Clean the crayfish thoroughly with a brush. Bring the fish stock to a boil, add the dill bunches, parsley, celery leaves, and salt. Push the crayfish under the stock, one by one, and cook for about 10 minutes. Take the crayfish out of the stock, break open their shells, carefully remove the meat, and break the meat into coarse lumps. Set this aside, along with the four heads of the crayfish (the pointed front part of the shell). Reduce the liquid in which the crayfish have been boiled to 1 quart; skim off the impurities.

Crush the shells from the tails and 6 heads very finely and cook for a good 5 minutes in just 1 tablespoon butter. Add the quart of crayfish liquid and simmer for 20 minutes, then pour through a very fine strainer.

Mix 2 tablespoons of butter and the flour in a medium saucepan to make a white roux, add the strained crayfish liquid, and simmer gently for 15 minutes. Heat the crayfish meat in the soup. Then add the cauliflower flowerets and asparagus tips, and heat thoroughly. Remove the soup from the heat and thicken with egg yolks.

Garnish the edge of each plate with a crayfish head filled

with a little crayfish meat—a very striking effect. Sprinkle each soup portion with plenty of chopped dill.

MAKES 4 SERVINGS

SWABIA

Pancake Soup   Flädlesuppe

In southern Germany, *Flädle* are little pancakes; the same recipe is also quite popular in Austria, where it goes by the name of *Fritattensuppe,* "fritter soup." It seems likely that one of these is the authentic original and the other merely an upstart imitation—but that is surely a matter for the Swabians and the Austrians to settle between themselves. *Flädlesuppe* is another of those unpretentious regional delicacies that has recently been taken up in serious gourmet circles.

1 cup flour
2 eggs
1½–2 cups milk
 Pinch of salt
 Bacon drippings or butter to grease pan
1 quart rich, clear broth
2–3 tablespoons chopped fresh chives

• • • • • • • • •

Whisk together the flour, eggs, 1½ cups milk, and salt to make a smooth *Flädle* batter. Allow to sit for at least 30 minutes. Check the consistency; you may need to add up to ½ cup more milk. Take a medium-size skillet and grease the bottom very lightly with bacon fat. Pour 2 to 3 tablespoons of batter onto the hot skillet, using the back of the spoon to spread out the batter if necessary. The pancakes should not be too thick. Roll them up or simply stack them on top of one another when they're done.

Slowly bring the broth to a boil. Cut the *Flädle* into thin strips and allow these to heat up in the broth. Garnish each serving with finely chopped chives.

MAKES 4–6 SERVINGS

Esslingen, Swabia

WÜRTTEMBERG

"Fiddlepeg" Dumplings Geigen-Knöpfle

1 egg
2 tablespoons or more
freshly grated bread
crumbs (a good substitute
for Mutschelmehl)
Small pinch of salt
1 quart clear beef stock
Freshly grated nutmeg
Chopped fresh chives

This is a recipe that transcends narrow regional affiliations. It is also found in Bavaria, where it is known as *Münchner Nockerln,* roughly translatable as "cute little Munich dumplings," and in the region around Ulm, in Württemberg, where it goes by the name of *Mutschelmehlklösse. Mutschelmehl,* a celebrated local specialty, is a savory breading mix that has just the right consistency for making dumplings.

•   •   •   •   •   •   •   •   •

Beat the egg thoroughly, then stir in just enough bread crumbs so that the egg dough comes away from the spoon. Add salt. Wait for 2 or 3 minutes.

Meanwhile, gently simmer the stock. Use the bowls of 2 demitasse spoons to shape the dough into 8 to 10 little dumplings—*Geigen-Knöpfle.* Drop the dumplings into the simmering stock. If your first dumpling starts to disintegrate, then you had better let the rest of them sit for a while longer. If the dumpling sinks straight to the bottom, this means that the dumpling dough is a bit too compact, but it can easily be thinned out by adding a little lukewarm broth or milk.

Once the *Geigen-Knöpfle* are floating nicely, wait for at least 2 minutes before turning them over in the broth. You can expect them to swell up a great deal before they're cooked all the way through.

Serve the *Geigen-Knöpfle* in hot broth. Flavor with a little freshly ground nutmeg and garnish each serving with chopped chives.

MAKES 4 SERVINGS

Cotton Soup   Baumwollsuppe

The name for this recipe, which seems both original and appropriate, was mysteriously altered at around the turn of the century by some officious and literal-minded person to *Einlaufsuppe,* which simply refers to the fact that the egg dough is slowly poured into *(einlaufen)* the broth.

6 eggs
⅓ cup flour
Pinch of salt
Freshly grated nutmeg
1 quart beef stock or salted water
8–12 thin slices white bread
2 tablespoons butter
Chopped fresh chives

In a mixing bowl beat together the eggs, flour, salt, and a little nutmeg.

Bring the beef stock to a boil in a soup pot. Stir 2 tablespoons of hot broth into the egg batter in the mixing bowl, then pour the egg batter into the boiling soup, stirring vigorously and continuously. Reduce the heat. The soup should not be allowed to come to a boil again; keep stirring the egg batter in the broth until it looks as if the soup is covered with little "flecks" of cotton wool or, less prosaically, of coarse hominy grits or semolina.

Fry the slices of bread in the butter, on both sides. Pour the soup into the tureen, float the toast slices on the surface, and garnish with chopped chives.

VARIATION: In the original version, which just called for salted water instead of stock, crispy onions fried in lard were used for a garnish to give a more robust flavor to what was otherwise a rather thin soup.

MAKES 4–6 SERVINGS

Marrow Dumplings   Markklösschen

Beef marrow from 2 pieces of 2" long marrow bones
4 tablespoons butter
1¾ cups fresh dry bread crumbs (see Note)
2 eggs
2 egg yolks
Salt
Pinch of freshly grated nutmeg
1 tablespoon chopped fresh parsley
1 quart clear beef stock

These little soup dumplings made with beef marrow can now be bought ready-made at the butcher shop. *Markklösschen* have yet to achieve a major presence in the overseas market, but this hardly poses a problem, since they seem to taste a lot better if you make them yourself.

. . . .

Knead the marrow in a bowl of cold water until it turns white. Remove from water. Crush the marrow and stir together with the butter, which should be very soft, until you have a nice fluffy mixture.

Put most (but not all) of the bread crumbs in a mixing bowl, add the eggs and the egg yolks, and mix gently. Then let stand for several minutes. If you put in all of the bread crumbs at once, the mixture may be too dry; if it's too soggy, you can always add more bread crumbs.

Combine the bread-crumb mixture with the marrow and butter mixture; knead thoroughly. Season with a little salt and nutmeg. Mix the parsley into the dough, then put it in the refrigerator for a little while. Remove from the refrigerator and roll the dumpling dough into a slender stick or ¾-inch cylinder. Chill once more.

Cut the cylinder of dough into ¾-inch to 1-inch short sections and roll these between the bowls of two wooden ladles or the palms of your hands until you have a bunch of little round dumplings the size of cherries. Cook the dumplings for at least 10 minutes in clear beef stock until done.

NOTE: Prepackaged bread crumbs may have their uses, but they're not really good enough for making *Markklösschen*. It's better to make the bread crumbs by drying out a few slices of white bread in the oven at very low heat (so they don't start to turn brown), then crumbling them up with your fingers or grating them with a grater.

MAKES ABOUT 12 DUMPLINGS (4 SERVINGS)

EAST PRUSSIA

Plum Soup with Dumplings
Pflaumensuppe mit Keilchen

Keilchen (little wedges) are yet another variety of soup dumplings, for which German has almost as rich a nomenclature as Italian does for pasta or Eskimo for snow.

• • • • • • • • • •

First, combine the egg with a pinch of salt and as much flour as it takes to make a fairly firm dough (not too soggy). Use a wet teaspoon to form the dough into small dumplings. Cook in boiling water (these take 15 to 20 minutes to cook) and allow to cool.

Poach the plums in water with the cinnamon stick, cloves, sugar, and lemon peel until soft. Remove the cloves and the cinnamon stick; pour the soup through a very fine sieve, pressing the plums through the sieve in order to mash them. A blender could be used as well.

Reheat. Stir 2 teaspoons cornstarch into a little cold water.

1 egg
Pinch of salt
¾ cup flour
1¼ pounds fresh plums, pitted
1 quart water
1 cinnamon stick
3 whole cloves
1–3 teaspoons sugar, according to sweetness of plums
Grated peel of ½ lemon
2 teaspoons cornstarch

Add it to the broth and bring to a boil. Add the dumplings to the hot soup before serving.

VARIATION: Sometimes *Pflaumensuppe* is cooked with pearl barley instead of thickening it with cornstarch, in which case it's best to tie up the spices in a little muslin bag to make it easier to remove them (and of course the soup shouldn't be strained).

MAKES 4 SERVINGS

SOUTHERN   GERMANY

Lemon Soup   Zitronensuppe

1 *large lemon*
4 *zwiebacks*
3 *cups water*
  Scant ½ cup sugar
2 *cups dry white wine*
3 *eggs, separated*
  A small pinch of salt
2 *or more tablespoons sugar, according to taste*

Starting in the early eighteenth century, lemon soup was served in respectable middle-class households rather than in peasant kitchens. This particular recipe turned up among the papers of a family from the region around Lake Constance.

·   ·   ·   ·   ·   ·   ·   ·   ·

Peel the lemon carefully, removing only the yellow outer peel, and squeeze out the juice; reserve. Place the lemon peel, the zwiebacks, and the water in a stainless steel or non-reactive pot; bring to a boil and simmer gently for about 30 minutes. Pour the liquid through a strainer. Return the liquid to the pot. Add the ½ cup sugar, lemon juice, and white wine; bring to a boil once more, then simmer gently for 5 minutes.

Beat the egg whites with the salt and 2 tablespoons sugar until stiff. Using 2 spoons place dumpling-shaped scoops of the whites on the surface of the simmering soup. Poach for 3 minutes on each side. Remove from the soup with a skimmer or slotted spoon and put on a plate.

Remove the soup from the heat and thicken with beaten egg yolks. Taste for seasoning, garnish with the meringue "dumplings," and serve.

MAKES 4 SERVINGS

THÜRINGER WALD

Cold Bilberry Soup   Blaubeer-Kaltschale

Bilberries and/or blueberries grow almost everywhere in the woods. In summer, families used to go on weekend expeditions out "into the berries," the adults returning with baskets full of booty, we children only with voluptuous purplish smears around our mouths. Bilberries (packed in jars) are sometimes found in gourmet or specialty stores in North America, but for *Blaubeer-Kaltschale* it makes much more sense to use fresh blueberries, or frozen ones if necessary.

1¾–2 pounds blueberries, cleaned and washed
Sugar to taste
1 quart milk

· · · · · · · · ·

Place the berries in a bowl and stir in the sugar. Leave covered for at least 1 hour. Add cold milk and serve in bowls.

VARIATIONS: At my grandparents' house, this dish was always accompanied by thick slices of *Schietchen,* Thuringian–style coffee cake (page 422), which was also served at breakfast and with afternoon coffee.

A somewhat more sophisticated *Kaltschale,* served exclusively to the older crowd on Sundays, substituted a white wine sauce for the milk—1 pint white wine, 1 pint water, juice of a single lemon, to be poured right over the blueberries. Thuringia is far from any wine-producing region, and in the old days, this was one of the ways in which the locally available vintages could be made palatable.

MAKES 4 SERVINGS

NORTHERN GERMANY

Elderberry Soup   Fliederbeersuppe

Elderberries (*Fliederbeeren,* called *Holunderbeeren* in standard German) ripen in the fall, in heavy purplish-black clumps like

DUMPLINGS:
 1 tablespoon butter
  Pinch of salt
½ cup milk
¼ cup flour
 1 egg

BROTH:
 1 quart elderberries,
   stemmed
 1 cup water
2–3 tablespoons sugar
2–3 medium Granny Smith
   apples, peeled, cored,
   and cut into ½" diced
   pieces
½ pound plums or
   greengages, pitted
1–2 teaspoons cornstarch

miniature bunches of grapes. Nowadays, they are only occasionally found in produce markets or fruit stalls in Europe (and only very, very occasionally in North America), so if you don't already live in the country, or at the very least in the suburbs, a little botanizing expedition is in order if you want to try out this recipe, which also introduces you to a new variety of dumpling.

· · · · · · · · · · ·

To make the dumplings (called *Kluntjes* in northern Germany), combine the butter, salt, and milk in a heavy saucepan and bring to a boil. Add the flour and stir vigorously until the flour adheres to a wooden spoon in a doughy clump. Remove from heat, allow to cool down a little, then beat in the egg. Cut up the dough into cherry-size pieces and with wet hands shape into little dumplings ¾" in diameter.

Put the berries and water in a non-reactive saucepan and bring slowly to a boil. If the berries aren't quite as ripe as they should be, you may have to add a few more tablespoons of water. Add sugar and cook for another 10 minutes, then pour the liquid through a very fine strainer, pressing on the solids.

Add the apples to the simmering elderberry broth. Then add the plums to the soup a few minutes after the apples. The soup is done when the apples are cooked through but still firm; they shouldn't be allowed to get too soft. Mix the cornstarch in 2 tablespoons cold water. Add this to the soup and bring to a boil. You may want to add a little sugar at the very end; the soup should taste nice and sweet.

Cook the dumplings in the simmering soup for 5 to 10 minutes, until they're cooked all the way through.

VARIATION: In Saxony, little balls of beaten egg white (see the recipe for *Zitronensuppe*) are substituted for the dumplings.

Also, if you still have a few more elderberries than you know what to do with, see the recipe for *Braunbiersuppe*.

MAKES 4 SERVINGS

SAXONY-ANHALT

Brown Beer Soup   Braunbiersuppe

When the old German customs of serving soup and alcoholic drinks for breakfast (the latter was also quite common in Britain and Colonial America) converged, the result was *Biersuppe,* beer soup. This was sometimes cooked up very thick and served as a hearty mush or porridge, which seems as if it might have had more of a sedative than invigorating effect, especially if eaten every day. The following recipe (not of the thick and hearty variety) dates from around the turn of the nineteenth century. It gives the authentic phrasing.

•   •   •   •   •   •   •   •   •   •

"Cook brown beer with a little coarse-chopped ginger or caraway seeds, thicken with egg yolks and some flour, add butter, sugar, and salt, and pour the soup over black bread that has been cut up in cubes. Or, you may also bring the beer to a boil, thicken with just a little flour, add some elderberry pulp [*Fliedermus*], salt, and pepper, and serve over black bread cut in the same manner."

MAKES 4 SERVINGS

"Brown beer"—about 1 quart dark beer or stout; "Coarse-chopped ginger or caraway seeds"—try ½ teaspoon each of ground caraway seeds and chopped fresh ginger (the latter being by far the more pungent of the two); "Egg yolks and some flour"—3 egg yolks plus 1 tablespoon cornstarch stirred up in a few tablespoons cold water; "Butter"—1 or 2 tablespoons; "Black bread"—2 large or 4 small slices of pumpernickel; "Elderberry pulp"—2–3 tablespoons pureed elderberries (gives the soup a rich, distinctive taste) Sugar and salt to taste

The Berlin suburb of Spandau (engraving by Johann Poppel, after a drawing by L. Rohbock)

EAST   AND   NORTH   FRIESLAND

Barley Soup with Buttermilk
Buttermilchsuppe mit Graupen/Karmelkbree

⅔ cup pearl barley
1 quart crème fraîche, or
1 quart heavy cream
with 4 tablespoons
lemon juice
Salt
Several tablespoons
sugar (to taste)

Friesland is a thin strip of land (as well as numerous offshore islands) that extends along the North Sea coast from Holland to just beyond the Danish border. A keen appreciation of the abundant local dairy products is very characteristic of the Frisians. The buttermilk soup called *Karmelkbree* has a very distinctive, almost sweet-sour sort of taste and was once the basis for an entire industry in East Friesland. There, even after the war, wagons laden with great urns of buttermilk soup used to trundle from door to door at breakfast time. This, unfortunately, is no longer the case, but *Karmelkbree* is still served for breakfast at some of the nicer seaside resort hotels on the North Sea coast and is now sold in several old-fashioned dairies, in heavy-duty plastic bags all ready to be heated up and served at home.

· · · · · · · · · ·

Wash and drain the pearl barley, add to the crème fraîche or heavy cream and lemon mixture along with a pinch of salt, and put on to boil. Simmer gently for 1 hour, adding salt to taste. Make sure that the barley gets cooked until it is nice and tender. Add sugar to taste.

MAKES 4 SERVINGS

Salads and Appetizers

.　　.　　.　　.　　.　　.　　.　　.　　.

Traditional German cuisine does not offer a very large selection in either of these categories, though there are a few old-time customs that have contributed to the store of recipes for *kleine Gerichte,* "little dishes," or appetizers. The first custom is that of hearty snacks between meals, referred to as "Vespers" in Germany—which is well established among city dwellers as well as countryfolk; the second is the prevailingly rural institution of the morning pint of beer or glass of wine *(Frühschoppen),* when the menfolk of the village trot off to the local pub directly after church on Sunday, where they might expect to find an assortment of snacks and little tidbits. Items of this kind were called *Schmankerln* in Bavaria, where the art of concocting them had reached its highest peak.

Finally, in an era of cheap, plentiful eating even in an urban setting, every restaurant has its crowd of regular customers, each with his or her regular table, or *Stammtisch*—a custom that has become synonymous in modern Germany with cronyism and favoritism. Nevertheless, for the sake of providing a little variety for the regulars, German restaurants have produced a number of notable additions to the appetizer menu.

Potato salad undoubtedly ranks first among the salads. Some very popular appetizers are *Zwiebelkuchen* and *Maultauschen,* the Swabian version of ravioli, won tons, or pirogi. Admittedly, the German farmwife or alehouse-keeper would not have been highly motivated to devise new recipes for snacks and tidbits, since an immense amount of these already existed in the convenient, prepackaged form of *Würste,* or sausages, a number of which even found their way into salads.

Coleslaw   Roher Krautsalat

Before greenhouses and refrigeration made fresh lettuce available year-round in northern Europe, coleslaw was much more of a staple than it is today. Now it can be appreciated as an extra-crispy and hearty crudité, rather than merely tolerated as an off-season lettuce replacement. Traditionally, coleslaw, whether made from red or white, raw or parboiled cabbage, was a popular dish in every region of Germany. In his German travel diaries (1580), Michel de Montaigne kept a list of "dishes unfamiliar to me," in which he included, without further comment, the "cabbage salads" that were set before him in the Swabian town of Lindau on Lake Constance. Today, coleslaw is an everyday treat in Bavaria, but somewhat different from the American version because caraway seeds are often used.

. . . .

Remove the torn or damaged outer leaves from the cabbage. Cut into quarters, remove the stem and the tough white part around the base, then finely shred the cabbage leaves. Transfer to a large mixing bowl, add salt, and pound the cabbage with a potato masher until it loses some of its stiffness. Let sit for 15 minutes. Add the onions (or shallots).

Mix the vinegar and sugar until the sugar is completely dissolved. Pour this over the cabbage and toss well. Let sit for another 15 minutes before adding the salad oil and caraway seeds, then mix thoroughly.

NOTE: You may want to add more caraway seeds, which are not only very tasty in their own right but also help to make the cabbage a little easier to digest. You may also want to pour off the liquid that's released from the grated cabbage when you're pounding it with the potato masher.

MAKES 4–6 CUPS

1 2-pound fresh young cabbage head
1 tablespoon salt
2 small onions (or better still, 4 medium shallots), finely chopped
3 tablespoons vinegar
½ teaspoon sugar
3 tablespoons salad oil
½ tablespoon caraway seeds

Red Cabbage Coleslaw   Rotkrautsalat

1 2-pound red cabbage head
1 tablespoon salt
2 small onions, finely
    chopped
3 tablespoons vinegar
1 teaspoon sugar
1 small Granny Smith
    apple, peeled, cored, and
    julienned
3 tablespoons salad oil

This or any other variety of coleslaw makes an excellent accompaniment for roast pork (as well as bratwurst).

•   •   •   •   •   •   •   •

The procedure is as above with the addition of julienned apple. Here the apples replace caraway seeds in the above recipe.

VARIATION: Instead of sugar, try heating up a little red currant jelly to liquefy it, then mix with the coleslaw along with a small pinch of grated nutmeg.

MAKES 4–6 CUPS

Parboiled White Coleslaw
Gerbrühter Weisskrautsalat

1 2-pound cabbage head
3–4 tablespoons mild
    vinegar
7 strips medium-lean
    bacon, cut into small
    squares
Salt and freshly
    ground white pepper
Small pinch of sugar

Another variant on the basic coleslaw recipe is using white cabbage that has been parboiled.

•   •   •   •   •   •   •   •

Cut the cabbage into quarters, remove the stem and tough outer leaves, and grate coarsely. Add the grated cabbage to 4 quarts of boiling salted water and bring to a boil. After 2 or 3 minutes, put it in a colander to drain; shake it dry; and press out the remaining liquid. While the cabbage is still lukewarm, put it into a salad bowl, sprinkle with vinegar, and mix well. Allow this to sit for several minutes.

Shortly before serving, cook the diced bacon until the fat has been rendered and pour the entire contents of the skillet (fat and bacon) over the salad. Season to taste with salt, white pepper, and a little sugar.

MAKES 4 CUPS

Parboiled Red Coleslaw   Gebrühter Rotkrautsalat

This is the red-cabbage version of Parboiled White Coleslaw. Ingredients and procedures are identical except that red cabbage is substituted for white. Also, you should put a tablespoon of vinegar into the water before parboiling the cabbage; this will set the color of the cabbage, so add that much less vinegar afterwards. With red cabbage, many people prefer to substitute ⅓ cup salad oil for the bacon, which should be sprinkled cold over the still lukewarm cabbage.

Celery-Root Salad   Selleriesalat

This is a typical German salad of the old school that usually accompanies a main dish but may also be served as an appetizer.

●   ●   ●   ●   ●   ●   ●   ●   ●

Put the freshly sliced celery root immediately into the stock, which should be flavored with 1 tablespoon each oil and vinegar, ½ teaspoon salt, the sugar, and chopped onion. Cook for about 20 minutes—until the celery root is quite tender and the liquid has almost boiled away. Season the celery root and beef stock with the remaining oil and a dash or two of wine vinegar, as well as with salt if you wish.

NOTE: If the salad is to be served as an appetizer, mix in some coarsely chopped walnuts and garnish with a few walnut halves. This was the way it was always served to us by my grandmother Maximiliane, who was enormously proud of the fact that walnuts grew in the yard of the old family house in Auerbach in the Bergstrasse—which is not a street but a mountainous region in southern Hesse.

Nowadays, in this age of crudités, it may be more usual to substitute grated, uncooked celery root, marinated in oil and vinegar, and possibly mixed with grated raw carrot.

MAKES 2–3 CUPS

1 medium celery root (3" diameter), peeled, washed, and thinly sliced
1 cup beef stock
2–3 tablespoons salad oil
Wine vinegar
Salt
Pinch of sugar
1 small onion, grated or finely chopped

BADEN

Dandelion Salad Löwenzahnsalat/Seicher

2–3 *tablespoons wine*
  vinegar
  Pinch of salt
¼ *teaspoon sugar*
  Freshly ground black
  pepper
6 *handfuls of dandelion*
  greens (at least 1
  pound), washed and
  patted dry
2 *tablespoons salad oil*
1 *medium potato, boiled*
  in its jacket
10 *strips medium-lean*
  bacon, diced

The standard German and English names for the dandelion take note of the fanciful resemblance between its spiky petals and a lion's teeth; its unofficial colloquial names (Badlish *Seicher,* English "pissabed," as well as the official French *pissenlit*) celebrate the potent diuretic properties of the dandelion's stems and greens. An alternate name for this particular dish in Baden is *Rossblumensalat,* "horseflower salad," which would seem to imply that dandelion greens are not the most delicate fare; that is, unless they are treated according to this recipe.

In southwestern Germany and Franconia, prepared dandelion greens are available at markets and greengrocers. Even in North America, with the current revival of interest in various "down-home" and regional cuisines, dandelion greens can probably be found at specialty markets in most large cities. It is recommended to anyone who appreciates a sharp bitter-herb flavor—while bearing in mind, of course, that the pharmaceutical claims that have been made on behalf of the dandelion/*pissenlit*/*Seicher* have by no means been exaggerated.

· · · · · · · · · · ·

Weinsberg, Swabia

In a stainless steel or glass bowl combine the vinegar, salt, and sugar. In another bowl sprinkle a few grindings of pepper over the greens and let stand for a couple of minutes. Meanwhile, whisk the salad oil into the vinegar mixture. Toss the greens with this dressing.

Peel the hot potato that has been boiled in its jacket and mash it thoroughly with a fork. Mix with the dandelion greens. Place the bowl with the greens in a large pot with hot water in it; that way they'll warm up a little and get softer.

Cook the bacon until the fat is rendered; pour the entire contents of the skillet into the salad bowl, toss, and let stand for at least 15 minutes.

NOTE: Dandelion salad is frequently served with a poached egg or simply garnished with hard-boiled egg slices or sprinkled with finely chopped hard-boiled egg.

MAKES 4–6 SERVINGS

HUNSRÜCK

White Radish Salad   Rettichsalat

The Hunsrück is a small mountain range in the southwestern state of the Palatinate, between the Rhine and the French border, and this particular recipe comes from the town of Idar-Oberstein, where white radish salad is served with large steaks *(Spiessbraten)* fresh from the grill.

4–6 medium white radishes
(red radishes are a
definite second choice)
Salt
Small pinch of sugar
Juice of 2 lemons
1 cup sour cream

•   •   •   •   •   •   •   •   •

Peel the radishes and cut into matchstick strips. Add salt to taste and let stand for about 10 minutes, tossing the radish strips 2 or 3 times in the interim. Add the sugar to the lemon juice and pour over the radishes. Mix once more, stir in the sour cream, and serve.

MAKES 4–6 SERVINGS

Potato Salad   Kartoffelsalat

Potato salad, one of the uniquely German contributions to the world banquet (or picnic) table, is not always prepared the right way in German restaurants. The late Alfred Walterspiel, Germany's greatest chef, introduced his own potato salad recipe with the portentous comment, "It should come as no great surprise to anyone that I am including a recipe for potato salad, since it is by no means a simple matter to prepare it properly." Fortunately, the art of making decent potato salad is being carried on by homemakers, amateur chefs, and other nonprofessionals. The food writers and restaurant critics, ostensibly the guardians of public taste, have not, as far as I know, raised any kind of fuss about this scandalous state of affairs—since what is a simple potato salad worth to those who dwell in the rarefied realms of goose-liver mousse and cherimoya parfait?

Somehow, I suspect that in other countries the art of making "German" potato salad could hardly be much better—though on the other hand, it could hardly be worse. At any rate, for those who would rather know how to make a good potato salad than an indifferent cherimoya parfait, remember that we are dealing with one of the great triumphs of traditional German cuisine.

The very first thing to consider, of course, is the raw materials: the potatoes to use are waxy red potatoes. This variety stands up to cooking very well, but they should not be allowed to cook until they get soft and mushy. With the few exceptions noted under the individual entries below, potato salad should be prepared while the potatoes are still warm.

German potato salad is traditionally served as an accompaniment to a great many things, among them: bratwurst, *Buletten* (see page 250) or *Frikadellen* (Meat Patties or rissoles, served hot or cold), Wiener Schnitzel, sweetbreads (or brains) cooked in a pastry shell, broiled fish, roast shank of veal, and finally, in Swabia, roast meat with a thick, hearty gravy—hardly the sort of light, outdoorsy fare that we normally associate with potato salad, but a combination that I highly recommend.

It must be admitted that in the northern half of Germany, potato salad is prepared with mayonnaise. But, being a "southerner" myself, I find that offensive.

Alfred Walterspiel's Potato Salad

This is the definitive German potato salad as presented by the great chef in his book, *My Art in Kitchen and Restaurant.* Though he achieved some of his greatest professional triumphs in Berlin, Walterspiel is a native of Baden, where they prefer the sort of potato salad that's best described as *glitschig* ("slippery," "slithery"—linguistically akin to "glitch," a word that was first introduced into the American vernacular by German rocket scientists at Cape Canaveral). Typically, the neighboring Swabians have grabbed the credit for a recipe that's popular all over southwestern Germany and so it is frequently referred to as *Schwäbischer Kartoffelsalat.* You'll note that Walterspiel's recipe calls for special salad potatoes, a thinnish, elongated variety known as *Mäuschen,* "little mice," in Germany; red potatoes make an adequate substitute.

2½ pounds red potatoes
½ cup beef stock
½ cup olive oil
3 tablespoons wine vinegar
1 tablespoon fine herbs (parsley, tarragon, and chervil)
1 tablespoon onion juice
1 tablespoon Dijon mustard
1 tablespoon sugar
Salt and freshly ground black pepper

• • • • • • • • •

"Potato salad should not be served ice-cold; it tastes best when it is almost lukewarm. The *Mäuschen* (a kind of potato from the region around Mainz and Mannheim) should be cooked in a steamer and, after they have cooled down about halfway, peeled and uniformly cut into very thin slices; then put into the dressing one by one, so they won't stick together. The dressing is prepared in the following manner: To serve eight people, combine ½ cup beef stock with ½ cup olive oil, 3 tablespoons wine vinegar, 1 tablespoon fine herbs (parsley, tarragon, and chervil), 1 tablespoon raw onion juice, 1 tablespoon Dijon mustard, 1 tablespoon sugar, salt to taste, and a few grindings of pepper from the mill. The resulting mixture should be stirred well and the potato slices added very carefully and gradually. Actually, since it takes half an hour for the potatoes to absorb just half of the dressing, I prefer to wait until then before mixing the salad, being very careful not to break the delicate potato slices."

MAKES 8 SERVINGS

SWABIA

Grated Potato Salad   Geriebener Kartoffelsalat

2 pounds red potatoes,
  boiled in their jackets
1 cup beef stock
3–4 tablespoons vinegar
1 large onion, finely
  chopped or grated
¼ cup salad oil
Salt and freshly
  ground black pepper

Peel the potatoes while still warm, and allow to cool. Grate them with a hand grater or in a food mill. Heat the stock and pour over the grated potatoes. Toss briefly and then immediately add the vinegar and onion. Finally, mix in the salad oil, add salt and pepper to taste, and let stand for 1 or 2 hours.

When served, the potato salad should be thick enough so that a spoon will stand up in it without toppling over. Customarily, the salad is molded into a smooth dome shape by pressing a round bowl over it and then smoothing it out; decorative patterns may be applied with a knife or the handle of a spoon.

NOTE: On special occasions (birthdays, christenings, et cetera) an extra decorative effect is achieved by reserving about a quarter of the potato salad, mixing with grated beets, and then using this mixture as a garnish. Alternately (or additionally), garnish with hard-boiled eggs, quartered or thinly sliced.

MAKES 4–6 SERVINGS

RHENISH HESSE, LOWER SAXONY

Potato Salad with Bacon
Kartoffelsalat mit Speck

Peel the potatoes while still warm, and cut them into slices. In a skillet fry the bacon with the onion until both are translucent. Add the vinegar to the skillet, stir, and then pour the entire contents of the skillet over the potato slices and toss briefly. Pour the warm stock over the potatoes a little at a time and mix well each time. Add salt and pepper to taste.

Let the salad stand for a while to allow the ingredients to blend nicely and, if possible, serve while still lukewarm (in the old days, they would have left the salad bowl on the edge of the hearth to keep the potato salad from getting cold). Sprinkle with chopped fresh chives shortly before serving.

MAKES 4–6 SERVINGS

2 pounds red potatoes, boiled in their jackets
7 strips medium-lean bacon, cut into matchstick strips
1 small onion, finely chopped
3 tablespoons vinegar
1 cup warm beef stock
Salt and freshly ground black pepper
2–3 tablespoons chopped fresh chives

Würzburg, Franconia

BADEN

"Gentleman's Relish" with Blackberries
Herrensalat mit Brombeeren

3 medium apples
2 small onions
Salt
1 tablespoon lemon
juice
½–¾ pint blackberries
1 tablespoon freshly
grated horseradish
⅓ cup mayonnaise
Few drops of
Worcestershire sauce
(optional)

This is really more of a condiment than a salad, and so it is only technically eligible for inclusion in this section. Still, it provides us with a tasty bit of evidence for the culinary daring and ingenuity of our nineteenth-century forebears, who are so often underrated in that department. This version is taken verbatim, with abbreviations, from a handwritten book of recipes.

•   •   •   •   •   •   •   •

"Grate 3 peeled ripe apples, likewise 2 sm. onions. Mix with salt and 1 tbsp. lemon juice to keep the apples from turning brown. Add 300 grams [½–¾ pint] ripe blackberries. Stir up 1 tbsp. grated horseradish into a l[ight] mayonnaise. You may add a few drops of Engl. relish [Worcestershire sauce]. Mix all these together well. Very good w. [with] a cold joint [of meat]."

MAKES 4 SERVINGS

SWABIA

Cold Beef Salad   Rindfleischsalat

In current parlance, "cold beef salad" *fleischsalat* is a euphemism appropriated from traditional peasant cuisine and used to denote an otherwise indescribable mishmash of delicatessen leftovers. In former days, the basic ingredients of such a dish could be identified at a glance, since it was only made when there was leftover roast beef or when the meat had already been boiled for stock.

.   .   .   .

Cut the quartered onions into thin slices. Combine the vinegar, sugar, and salt, then add the salad oil and sour cream, and mix together into a smooth dressing. Place the beef and the onion rings in the dressing, season with a little pepper, and let stand for at least 1 hour.

Serve garnished with chopped parsley; at the very last moment, add the hard-boiled quartered eggs. As an untraditional but decorative touch, you can also add a sweet pepper (preferably half of a green and half of a red or yellow one) cut up into very thin strips.

MAKES 4–6 SERVINGS

2 medium onions, quartered
2–3 tablespoons wine vinegar
Small pinch of sugar
½ teaspoon salt
3 tablespoons salad oil
2–3 tablespoons sour cream
1¼ pounds cooked lean beef, cut into thin strips
Freshly ground black pepper to taste
2–3 tablespoons chopped fresh parsley
1–2 eggs, hard-boiled and quartered
Sweet pepper strips (optional)

FRANCONIA

Beef Muzzle Salad   Ochsenmaulsalat

This salad is customarily served with a loaf of hearty brown or black bread, with or without butter.

.   .   .   .

Combine the vinegar, salt, and sugar; then pour in the oil and white wine and mix into a smooth dressing. Toss the beef slices in the dressing and allow to soak for at least 1 hour; season generously with pepper.

Slice the halved onions thinly. Mix these in with the salad and let stand for another hour.

NOTE: Muzzle is sold precooked and boneless.

MAKES 4 SERVINGS

2 tablespoons vinegar
½ teaspoon salt
Small pinch of sugar
¼ cup salad oil
2 tablespoons dry white wine
1¼ pounds beef muzzle (beef palate or boneless beef head), cut into thin strips or slices (see Note)
Freshly ground black pepper
2 medium onions, halved

BADEN

"Strasbourg" Wurst Salad
Strassburger Wurstsalat

Pinch of salt
Pinch of sugar
2–3 tablespoons wine
vinegar
3–4 tablespoons salad oil
¾ pound bologna, cut
into thin strips
½ pound Swiss cheese
(or mild cheddar), cut
into thin strips
1 medium onion,
quartered, thinly
sliced
Coarsely ground black
pepper

In spite of the name indicating that it originated on the left bank of the Rhine, this dish seems to have originated in Baden, on the other side of the river. Nowadays, it's served in virtually every restaurant in the German Upper Rhine region, usually with peasant bread.

•   •   •   •   •   •   •   •   •

Combine the salt, sugar, and vinegar, pour in the oil, and whisk vigorously to make a smooth dressing. Add the bologna and cheese, plus the onion, and let stand for at least 30 minutes. Sprinkle with the ground pepper.

MAKES 4 SERVINGS

"Spyglasses"   Feldkieker

10 pounds fresh ham or
pork shoulder (⅔ lean
and ⅓ fat, finely
ground; grains about
⅛" in diameter), at
room temperature
1–2 garlic cloves, mashed
or very finely chopped
4–6 tablespoons salt
1 teaspoon ground white
pepper
½ teaspoon grated
nutmeg
1 teaspoon saltpeter
(potassium nitrate,
available at the
drugstore)
Sausage casings

Even if Germany is no longer quite the "Land of Poets and Thinkers" *(Land der Dichter und Denker)* that she might have once been, her reputation as the preeminent *Land der Würste* is still triumphantly intact. Germany still holds all the records for per capita consumption, total production, and greatest available selection. As far as this last point is concerned, however, instead of providing a brief description of the many regional varieties of wurst (with recipes), I would like to appoint a single representative from this vast but worthy throng to stand in for all the rest. It is a Thuringian specialty and, in my opinion, the very best tasting of all German *Würste*. Its name is *Feldkieker,* which means "spyglasses." They are made in Eichsfeld, the northwestern tip of Thuringia (now part of East Germany) that pokes out into the territory of the Federal Republic between Göttingen and Eschwege.

My old friend Bernhard Richardt, known as "Kratschel," comes from Birkungen and, after consulting with his favorite butcher, has obliged me with the following recipe for genuine *Feldkieker*. For very dedicated amateur sausage-makers, it is worthwhile trying.

. . . .

The sausage meat should be still warm (the temperature of the freshly slaughtered pig) when it is kneaded together with the garlic and other spices. Pack the well-blended sausage mixture tightly into the sausage casings (the original recipe calls for medium-size calves' bladders). Before the sausages are tied off at the ends, they should be tightly compressed inside the casings (you can do this by twisting the long sausages at intervals) and then punctured with the tines of a fork.

The sausages have to be hung up to dry for quite some time —in the case of the *Feldkieker,* at least 3 or 4 months before they're really ready to eat. Traditionally, sausages were made in the early winter and ready by early spring ("When the cuckoo calls/Then the *Feldkieker* are ripe"—Eichsfelder folk wisdom, as relayed by Kratschel Richardt). They should not be hung in a draft or near a radiator or other source of heat. In short, the air should be dry, but not too dry; a place with low humidity is best. Smoking is not recommended for *Feldkieker,* though they can be smoked "cold," using beechwood sawdust. In any case, depending on conditions in the pantry, the *Feldkieker* should keep for 1 to 2 years.

MAKES 12–15 LARGE SAUSAGES

Marbach, Swabia

BADEN

Mock Goose Liver   Falsche Gänseleber

½ pound lightly smoked
  fatty bacon, diced
1¼ pounds calves' liver,
  cubed
3–4 hard-boiled egg yolks
  Salt and freshly
  ground white pepper
  to taste
  Pinch of ground
  coriander
  Jigger (1 ounce) of
  Madeira
  A few truffle slices
  that have been soaked
  in Madeira and diced
  (optional)

Once again inspired by the culinary fame of their left-bank neighbors in Strasbourg (the left bank of the Rhine), the chefs and innkeepers of Baden concocted this counterfeit foie gras recipe. This particular version was written down about one hundred years ago by an anonymous guesthouse chef in Offenburg.

·   ·   ·   ·   ·   ·   ·   ·   ·

In a skillet start frying the bacon, then add the liver. Continue cooking, stirring constantly, for 5 minutes, until the bacon is translucent and the liver is just cooked all the way through. Allow to cool and then puree—either in the food processor or food mill (and then put through a fine strainer in the second case). Mash the yolks of the hard-boiled eggs and add to the puree. Season with salt and white pepper, ground coriander, Madeira, and (if circumstances permit) truffles. Cool the mixture in a bowl placed in an ice bath, then chill in the refrigerator.

NOTE: A more elaborate presentation can be achieved by coating the inside of a mold with Madeira aspic; allow it to gel, then fill up the mold with the mock goose liver while it is still soft and malleable, and smooth off the top. (A layer of aspic can also be poured over the top of the mock goose liver after it has been chilled in the refrigerator and then allow this to set.) Just before serving, turn over the mold and cut the "pâté" into slices. Serve with buttered toast.

MAKES 4–6 SERVINGS

Cracklings Grieben
(also called *Grammeln, Schreiwen, Spirkeln, Krappen*)

The solids that remain when pork fat has been rendered have a hearty, crunchy taste and are naturally not held in particularly high esteem by health-conscious moderns. Actually, since they've already had the fat cooked out of them (or most of it, anyway), cracklings have a lot fewer calories than a number of other crunchy tidbits one might be tempted to eat instead—dry-roasted peanuts, for instance. *Grieben* were frequently to be had for the asking in my grandmother's kitchen, and they can also be put to less frivolous uses, substituting for chemical-laced and ridiculously overpriced "bacon bits" and other store-bought garnishes for potato and vegetable salad, pea soup, baked or mashed potatoes, or in stuffing for turkey or goose and in *Buletten* (Meat Patties).

·   ·   ·   ·   ·   ·   ·   ·   ·

Take pork suet (the fat around the kidneys, also called "fresh leaf fat"), cut into little cubes, and fry over low to moderate heat until the cubes are golden brown and crispy and the fat has been rendered. Pour off the fat, drain the cracklings on paper towels, and store in a glass jar.

VARIATION: To make a truly delicious spread to put on bread, redolent of the old-time farmhouse kitchen, you can refry the cracklings in the fat along with a diced apple and onion, seasoned with marjoram and sprinkled with salt.

EAST PRUSSIA

Shoemaker's Pie   Schusterpastete

8–10 *small to medium-size*
all-purpose potatoes,
boiled in their jackets
4–5 *tablespoons plus 1*
teaspoon butter
Freshly ground black
pepper
2½ *cups leftover roast*
(or an equivalent
amount of cooked
stew meat), cut into
cubes
1 *large onion, diced*
2–3 *cooked herring fillets,*
diced
1 *cup sour cream*
2–3 *heaping tablespoons*
fresh bread crumbs

In the titles of old-time German recipes, the shoemaker some-times figures as a poor but enterprising fellow who has to make the best of a slightly unpromising combination of low-cost ingredients. This one, from East Prussia, represents one of his most notable triumphs over adversity, though nowa-days, of course, the main ingredients aren't necessarily all that cheap.

Serve with a green salad or a salad of winter vegetables.

•   •   •   •   •   •   •   •   •   •

Preheat the oven to 425°F. Peel the cooked potatoes and cut into thick slices. Coat the inside of an ovenproof casserole with 2 tablespoons butter and put in a third of the potato slices; sprinkle with a little pepper. Next, put in the cubes of roast, then add another third of the potato slices.

Fry the onion in 1 teaspoon butter until it just starts to become transparent, and mix with the herring. Put this in on top of the second layer of potatoes. Cover with the remaining potato slices; sprinkle lightly with pepper; spread the sour cream over the top; sprinkle the bread crumbs over this; and dot with the remaining 2–3 tablespoons butter. Bake for about 30 minutes, by which time the *Schusterpastete* should have acquired a nice crispy crust.

MAKES 4 SERVINGS

HAMBURG, LOWER SAXONY

Herring Spread   Heringsbutter

Herring mavens will instantly recognize this dish as a stripped-down version of *Heringshäckerle,* though it may seem strange that the dirt-poor miners and millhands of Silesia put together a much more sumptuous salad than the well-fed burghers of Hamburg and environs. Perhaps the reason for this is that the burghers liked to keep in reserve a salty, savory antidote to all those sugary Yuletide treats they were expected to get through between Christmas and New Year's. Spread on slices of peasant bread *(Bauernbrot)* or hearty rye.

*   *   *   *   *   *   *   *   *

Soak the herring fillets in water for 10 minutes (if necessary), pat dry, and chop up very fine. Add the minced onion and butter and mix together thoroughly. Let sit refrigerated overnight, or at least a couple of hours. Remove from the refrigerator 30 minutes before serving.

MAKES 1 CUP

4 matjes herring fillets
2 tablespoons minced onions
9 tablespoons butter, softened

Herring Salad   Heringssalat

Also known as Polish salad, red salad, and as confetti salad in the city of Mainz, this dish was traditionally made up in washtub size batches for guests who came to watch the annual pre-Lenten parade. In my hometown, Frankfurt, it was called "Christmas salad" and served with the original *Frankfurter Würstchen* as an appetizer on Christmas Eve. You can serve it with hot wurst and crusty rolls *(Wasserbrötchen)*.

*   *   *   *   *   *   *   *   *

The boiled potatoes, beets, beef, sausage, and pickles should either be diced or sliced into thin strips (either is permissible, as long as all ingredients receive the same treatment). In a large bowl mix these with the apple, the liquid from the beets, the capers, and the brine from the caper jar as well.

The herring fillets should be soaked in water for 10 minutes, then cut up and mixed in with everything else. Season the salad, with pepper, oil, and vinegar; salt probably won't be necessary. The salad should be allowed to stand for at least 10 hours. Garnish with mayonnaise and hard-boiled eggs.

MAKES 4-6 SERVINGS

4–5 medium-size red potatoes, cooked in their jackets the day before and peeled
2 cups pickled beets; reserve ¼ cup liquid
¾–1 pound cooked lean beef
½ pound cooked pork sausage or knockwurst
4 big kosher dill pickles
1 Granny Smith apple, peeled, cored, and diced or sliced thinly
1 small jar of capers
4–5 matjes herring fillets
Freshly ground black pepper
2 tablespoons salad oil
2 tablespoons wine vinegar
1 cup mayonnaise
2 eggs, hard-boiled and quartered

City Hall, Brieg (engraving by
J. Richter, after a drawing by
L. Rohbock), Silesia

SILESIA

Chopped Herring Salad   (Heringshäckerle)

8 matjes herring fillets
1 large Granny Smith
  apple, peeled, cored,
  and diced
1 tablespoon lemon juice
8 strips medium-lean
  bacon, diced and
  cooked
1 large onion, finely
  chopped
2 eggs, hard-boiled, 1
  finely chopped
2 tablespoons sour cream
½ teaspoon hot mustard
1–2 tablespoons chopped
  fresh parsley

My Silesian friend Heinz Schwarz made up a batch of this salad on my TV cooking program a number of years ago and, for the next couple of months thereafter, was deluged with requests to repeat this memorable performance on every possible occasion. Heinz, who soon came to be burdened with the nickname "Mr. Häckerle," has been a very good sport about it all and has certainly never wavered in his affections for *Heringshäckerle,* which incidentally is known in other parts of Germany as *Heringsstippe* or just *Stippe.*

Serve with hot potatoes boiled in their jackets; it also tastes delicious when spread over a slice of pumpernickel or hearty rye bread—and if the price of matjes herring keeps going up, this former poor man's delicacy from Silesia may eventually replace caviar as the higher-priced spread *par excellence.*

•   •   •   •   •   •   •   •   •

Soak the herring fillets for ten minutes, then pat dry with a paper towel and cut into little cubes. Toss the freshly cut apple with the lemon juice. Combine the herring, apple, bacon, onion, and the finely chopped egg with the sour cream and mustard.

To garnish, cut the other hard-boiled egg into slices or eighths and sprinkle the parsley in the center of the salad.

MAKES 6 SERVINGS

EAST PRUSSIA

Courland Bacon Rolls Kurländer Speckkuchen

Courland is a stretch of Baltic coastline that has occasionally fallen under Prussian rule (not to mention Polish, Lithuanian, Swedish, and Russian), and it was probably during one of these comparatively brief periods that this hearty onion-roll recipe became firmly established in all of East Prussia and so is happily eligible for inclusion in this book.

. . . .

Sift the flour into a large mixing bowl. Make a crater in the center. Pour the milk into the crater. Sprinkle the yeast and sugar over the milk; let sit 10–15 minutes, until the yeast begins to foam. Add the butter, egg, and salt and mix into a dough. Knead the dough until smooth and elastic. Allow the dough to rise for 1–2 hours.

In a skillet fry the bacon and remove from the pan. In the fat that remains in the skillet, sauté the onions until they begin to turn transparent. Allow to cool, then mix them with the bacon and hard-boiled egg. Season with salt and plenty of pepper.

Preheat the oven to 350°F. Grease a baking sheet with the lard. Roll out the dough into thin sheets. Use a cup or 3″ cookie cutter to cut out circular pieces of dough. Put a little of the filling (about 1 teaspoon) on each piece, then coat the edges of the circles of dough with beaten egg white so they'll adhere properly, fold in half, and press the edges together. Glaze the tops with beaten egg yolk and sprinkle with caraway seeds.

Place the onion rolls on the baking sheet, and let sit for 10–15 minutes. Bake for 20 minutes, until golden brown. To get the full effect, taste some of the rolls while they're still hot, some while they're warm, some while they're cold.

MAKES ABOUT 35 ROLLS

DOUGH:
3¼ *cups flour*
  1 *cup lukewarm milk*
  3 *teaspoons yeast*
    Small pinch of sugar ("enough to fit on the point of a knife")
  7 *tablespoons butter, softened*
  1 *egg*
 ½ *teaspoon salt*

FILLING:
½ *pound Canadian bacon, finely diced*
  2 *onions, finely diced*
  1 *large egg, hard-boiled, finely chopped*
    Salt and freshly ground black pepper

  1 *tablespoon lard or butter*
  2 *eggs, separated*
    Caraway seeds

Swabian Pockets   Maultaschen

DOUGH:
2¾ cups flour
4 eggs
Salt

FILLING:
1 tablespoon butter
6 strips medium-lean
bacon, cut into cubes
3 medium onions, diced
¼ pound fresh sausage
meat (from sweet
Italian sausage
preferably)
1 hard roll, without
crust, and best when
stale
½ pound cooked spinach
½ pound ground meat or
lightly smoked farm
sausage
1 cup (bauernbratwurst)
or leftover roast, stew
meat, etc., diced
3 eggs
3–4 tablespoons chopped
fresh parsley
Salt and freshly
ground black pepper
Grated nutmeg

1 egg
3 tablespoons canned
milk
Enough beef stock or
salted water to cook
the Maultaschen

Certainly if anyone were to insist that *Maultaschen* were the most delicious of all Swabian specialties, I would hardly be prepared to deny it. In fact, as indicated earlier, I suspect that *Maultaschen* would have very good chances in a four-way international competition with ravioli, won tons, and pirogi for the championship of the Roughly Rectangular Pasta with Meat (plus Miscellaneous) Filling division.

It has been said that *Maultaschen* were originally invented in order to allow the Swabians to keep eating meat during Lent by concealing it beneath the pasta shell and amidst the spinach filling from the eye of the parish priest (if not the omniscient Deity Himself). The following recipe is typical but far from definitive, especially where the ingredients for the filling are concerned. Feel free to use whatever you have on hand or whatever your fancy (or your conscience) dictates.

·   ·   ·   ·   ·   ·   ·   ·

Combine the flour, eggs, and salt in a bowl and mix to make a pasta dough *(Nudelteig)*. Then add a little water and knead until it has a firm, but elastic consistency.

To make the filling, melt the butter in a skillet and fry the bacon with the onions until both are quite translucent. Combine the bacon mixture with the sausage meat.

Moisten the hard roll in water, press dry, and put through the meat grinder (better than the food mill or food processor), along with the bacon mixture, cooked spinach, ground meat or smoked farm sausage, leftover roast, etc. Then fold in the eggs, parsley, and seasonings; mix together. The filling should be very spicy indeed.

On a board that has been sprinkled with flour, roll out the dough into rectangular sheets (about twice as wide as you want your *Maultaschen* to be). Take a tablespoon measure and put little dabs of filling at equally spaced 3-inch intervals all down the middle of one side of the sheet of dough. Mix together the egg and canned milk and apply it to the spaces in between, the outer edge and the fold line. Fold the plain half of the sheet of dough over to cover the filling, press down firmly on the spaces around the little packets of filling, and use a pastry wheel or knife to separate the packets into 3-inch square- or diamond-shape *Maultaschen*. The process is similar to making ravioli.

Cook thoroughly in beef stock or boiling salted water for about 10 to 15 minutes, depending on the size of the *Maultaschen*. They'll bob up to the surface when they're done; remove them with a slotted spoon and allow to drain.

SERVING SUGGESTIONS: Cut an onion or two into half-rings, fry in butter until golden brown, and empty the contents of the skillet over the *Maultaschen* on the serving dish. Serve with *glitschige* (slippery) potato salad or a mixed green salad.

Swabian Wonton Soup: Serve a couple of *Maultaschen* in a bowl of hearty beef broth; garnish liberally with finely chopped onion.

Swabian Fried Won Tons: Allow the boiled *Maultaschen* to cool and then cut into strips. Sauté in a skillet until crisp on the outside. Serve with potato salad.

Maultaschen Croque Monsieur: Arrange several portions in an ovenproof casserole, cover with boiled ham and a couple of slices of cheese, and heat in the oven until the cheese reaches the desired consistency. Serve with green salad.

MAKES 4–6 SERVINGS

Abbey cloister, Berchtesgaden, Bavaria

Onion Tart   Zwiebelkuchen

DOUGH:
- *2 cups flour*
- *⅔ cup lukewarm milk*
- *2 teaspoons yeast*
- *2½ tablespoons butter*
- *Pinch of salt*
- *½ tablespoon butter for springform pan*

TOPPING:
- *2–3 tablespoons butter or lard*
- *½ pound medium-lean bacon, diced (if available use thickly sliced bacon)*
- *2 pounds or 3 extra-large onions, finely chopped*
- *Salt and freshly ground black pepper*
- *Large pinch of caraway seeds*
- *2 eggs*
- *2 egg yolks*
- *1 cup sour cream*

Throughout the wine-growing valleys of the Rhine, the Main, and the Neckar, the *Zwiebelkuchen* is an autumnal delicacy that is closely linked with the appearance of the new wine, when every self-respecting drinking establishment puts out a placard advertising *"Neuer [Wein] und Zwiebelkuchen"* and every true Rhinelander who has wandered far from home becomes almost unbearably nostalgic. *Zwiebelkuchen* is also referred to in certain areas as *"Posaunertorte"* (trombone tart). It should be eaten while still warm, preferably of course with a new wine (and ideally, with one that still has a little bite to it); a sturdy dry white wine also goes down quite well with *Zwiebelkuchen.*

•   •   •   •   •   •   •   •   •   •

Make the dough following the technique in the Courland Bacon roll recipe (page 129), but using the ingredients listed here. This dough should rise for only 1 hour. Grease a 10″ springform pan with ½ tablespoon butter. Pressing it with fingertips, use the dough to cover the bottom and sides of the pan, coming up about 1 inch from the top edge.

To make the topping, melt the butter or lard, then fry the bacon until it turns translucent. Add the chopped onions at that point and sauté, stirring frequently, until they turn clear yellow in color. Add salt, pepper, and caraway seeds to taste; allow to cool.

Preheat the oven to 400°F. Thoroughly beat the eggs and yolks into the sour cream. Spread the onions and bacon on the dough, then pour in the sour cream mixture, slowly enough so that it's able to penetrate past the onions. Bake for 35 to 40 minutes, until golden brown. After 15 minutes of cooking reduce heat to 350°F.

VARIATIONS: Badische Zwiebelkuchen (Baden-style onion tarts) can be made with ordinary bread dough, and in the old days they used to be put in last of all with every batch of bread that went into the baker's big oven—year-round, not just during

the new-wine season. Nowadays, *Zwiebelkuchen* is still occasionally made in the old way, on large baking sheets, starting out with just a thin layer of dough and a thin onion/sour cream topping.

In Swabia, *Zwiwlwähe* are baked in flat baking pans, like Sicilian-style pizza, and finely chopped scallions are used for the topping. Shortcrust dough (used for pies) can also be used for these Swabian-style *Zwiebelkuchen,* or frozen puff-pastry dough as well.

MAKES 6 SERVINGS

The poet Eduard Mörike (1804–75) was also a clergyman, a Swabian, and a connoisseur of *Zwiwlwähe.* On one occasion, he spent the night in the rectory of a colleague in a spare room where onions were being stored —an experience commemorated in the following poem (not, regrettably, one of the ones that was set to music):

So oft I've heard it said,	*Ganz richtig hört' ich sagen,*
And truthfully, it seems,	*Daß, wer in Zwiebeln*
That onions round the bed	*schlief,*
Bring harsh and heavy	*Hinunter werd' getragen*
dreams.	*In Traüme schwer und tief.*
It's Hahnemann's ★	*Und gegen dieses Übel,*
position,	*Das gar nicht angenehm,*
And rightly so, I'm sure,	*Hilft selber nur die Zwiebel*
That the cause of the	*Nach Hahnemanns System.*
condition	
Must also be the cure.	
The cure for my	*Das laßt uns gleich*
condition?	*versuchen!*
Pray God it comes in	*Gott gebe, daß es glückt!*
time—	*Und schafft mir*
A plate of *Zwiebelkuchen,*	*Zwiebelkuchen!*
Or else I've lost my mind!	*Sonst werd' ich noch*
	verrückt.

★ Famous physician of the time.

WESTPHALIA

Sausage Rolls Wurstbrötchen

¾ *pound large fresh
    bratwursts or sweet
    Italian sausage*
1 *stale or dry-baked hard
    roll or kaiser roll
    Salt and freshly ground
    black pepper*
1 *pound frozen puff-
    pastry dough*
1 *egg beaten with a little
    water*

Formerly made with bread or biscuit dough, these are now made with frozen puff-pastry dough, which not only tastes better but saves a lot of work. Serve fresh from the oven, with mustard and, of course, beer.

•   •   •   •   •   •   •   •   •

Remove the sausage meat from the casing. Remove the crust from the roll, cut the roll into thin slices, and soak in water. Press firmly to squeeze out the water; knead together with the sausage meat; season the mixture with salt and pepper. Preheat the oven to 425°F.

On a board that has been sprinkled with a little flour, roll out the puff-pastry dough, but not too thin, cut into squares, 2½″ on a side; mold the sausage meat mixture back into little sausage shapes and roll these up in the squares of dough. Brush the edges of the dough with a little egg wash and press together so they are completely sealed cylinders.

Sprinkle a baking sheet with cold water, arrange the sausage rolls on it with the seams facing down, glaze with the remaining egg wash, and bake until golden brown, about 20 to 25 minutes.

MAKES ABOUT 15 ROLLS

Cheese, Eggs, and Breakfast Cakes

· · · · · · · · · ·

Cottage Cheese Quark

Cottage cheese is a dish of great antiquity, a dish not actually invented by Germans but one that has been eagerly consumed by them in more different forms and under more different names than by anyone else. Apart from *Quark,* the more or less official name, we also have *Smierkäse* (a name that is also widely used, though generally spelled *smeercase,* in the eastern and midwestern United States), *Siebkäse* (sieve cheese), *Topfen* (pot [cheese], another name that is sometimes used in English-speaking countries), *Zieger* (not to be confused with *Ziegenkäse,* which is goat cheese), *Glumse,* as well as a couple of others. In Germany, *Quark* is always low-fat and has the smooth consistency of cream cheese.

In North America, low-fat cottage cheese is associated with dieting, abstinence, even penitence, but the Germans have discovered a number of different ways of getting around such restrictions where necessary. *Quark* can be salted, sweetened, hot and spicy, eaten with fish or fruit, used as a dip (also, admittedly, not a German invention), as a filling for dumplings, a freshening agent in pastries and cake mixes, or even mixed together with wurst and vegetables to make splendid *Herrentorten.* A recent competition for "the very best *Quark* recipe" in a West German newspaper elicited more than six thousand entries, enough to suit every occasion, time of day, and just about every conceivable taste. Over the last few decades, *Quark* has enlarged its culinary domain to include a great many novel methods of preparation and subtle taste sensations that would certainly have astounded the inventors of the sturdy, pioneering recipes that appear on the next few pages.

When using American cottage cheese, it is most strongly recommended that a low-fat variety be used and put through a fine sieve first in order to smooth it, unless the recipe indicates otherwise. Lump-free cottage cheese should be used in all German *Quark* recipes. *Fromage blanc,* available in some specialty-food stores, is a good substitute.

Gumbinnen (engraving by Navellier, after a drawing by Clerget), East Prussia

EAST PRUSSIA
Cottage Cheese with Sour Cream and Onions
Schmant mit Glumse

This is a simple summertime *Quark* recipe that in Frankfurt we simply called *Kräuterquark,* because of the chives and onions. It also appears to have been a very big favorite in East Prussia, where *Quark* was referred to, almost cooingly, as *Glumse.* This variety of *Quark* was usually accompanied by potatoes boiled in their jackets or the cheese was spread on bread, with or without butter, though it might be more in accordance with contemporary tastes to serve it with a green salad.

• • • • • • • • •

Stir together the cottage cheese, sour cream, and grated onion very vigorously. Stir the chives into the cottage cheese along with the salt and white pepper. The mixture should be smooth and creamy; you may want to add a tiny pinch of sugar, as well as hard-boiled eggs, chopped up very finely.

MAKES 4 SERVINGS

2 cups cottage cheese
  pressed through a fine
  sieve
1 cup sour cream
1 small onion, grated
½ cup minced chives
  Salt and freshly ground
  white pepper

OPTIONAL:
  Pinch of sugar
2 eggs, hard-boiled and
  finely chopped

HESSE, CENTRAL GERMANY

Cooked Cheese Kochkäse

This was a great favorite in farmhouse kitchens during prewar days. *Kochkäse* is easy to make (especially when you're allowed to start out with store-bought cottage cheese instead of the more traditional skim milk), light, low in calories, and very good-tasting, so it seems about due for revival.

Cooked cheese was customarily spread on a light rye bread (*Bauernbrot*) or, in rural households, eaten with potatoes as an evening meal.

• • • • • • • • •

Sieve the cottage cheese and mix with the baking soda. Set out in a flat, shallow baking dish, covered with a cloth, and allow to "ripen" for a couple of days in a cool room. Then, in a saucepan, combine it with the butter, caraway seeds, salt, and milk, bring to a boil, and allow to cool a little before thickening with the egg yolk.

Transfer to a larger flat-bottomed vessel (or to several smaller ones, resulting in what was called "cup cheese" in the old days) and allow the cheese to set. It should be yellow in color, with a smooth, shiny surface (which you can sprinkle with caraway seeds if you wish). To store the cheese, refrigerate it.

2 pounds cottage cheese
1 teaspoon baking soda
2 tablespoons butter
1 teaspoon caraway seeds
1 teaspoon salt
½ cup milk
1 egg yolk

VARIATIONS: The baking soda and egg yolk can be omitted, in which case it will take the cheese somewhat longer to solidify.

The milk can also be replaced with cream (and the butter reduced accordingly or omitted altogether); unfortunately, as with regular cheese, the higher the butterfat content, the better it tastes.

MAKES 8 SERVINGS

B A V A R I A

Liptauer

PER PERSON:

⅔ cup creamed cottage
  cheese
½ cup finely grated
  Swiss cheese
2–3 tablespoons sour cream
1–2 teaspoons finely
  chopped onion
  Salt and freshly
  ground black pepper
  Mild paprika

Liptau, now called Liptovský Mikuláš, is a town in Slovakia where this popular cheese spread seems to have originated. Actually, Bavarians who lived south of the Danube puristically insisted that genuine Liptauer could only be made with smooth cottage cheese; a preparation (like this one) in which other kinds of cheese were involved was called an *Obatzter* (see following entry). The more permissive folk to the north of the Danube tended to use these terms interchangeably, as does pretty much everyone today. The recipe for *Liptauer/ Obatzter,* at any rate, is simplicity itself. Serve with white bread or *Mischbrot* (made with a mixture of rye and whole-wheat flour).

•   •   •   •   •   •   •   •   •

Mix all ingredients thoroughly.

VARIATIONS: Sharp cheddar, Camembert, or Romadur can be substituted for Swiss cheese (Emmentaler), though a mixture of cottage cheese and Weisslacker—a sharp, semisoft cheese with a runny, shellac-like surface (*Weisslacker*-white lacquer) —gives a closer approximation of the authentic Liptauer taste.

For a little extra body, you can add butter to the cheese mixture, and for a little extra piquancy, one or more of the following: ground caraway seeds, finely chopped anchovies, hot mustard.

MAKES ½ POUND CHEESE

BAVARIA

Obatzter

Mash all the ingredients with a fork and mix thoroughly.

VARIATIONS: Those in search of a heartier taste can replace about a third of the Camembert with Limburger or Romadur, and those in search of a milder one can substitute cream cheese or cottage cheese for some of the Camembert—which brings us perilously close to Liptauer—or thicken with 1 egg yolk for a smoother blend, or coarsely chop the onions for a little more textural variety.

Optional condiments might also include caraway seeds, finely chopped gherkins, finely chopped (sweet) red peppers, and paprika (which should be mixed separately with the butter and then combined with the rest of the ingredients to ensure a homogeneous mix).

Finally, those who prefer to delegate their responsibilities in these matters can follow the basic *Obatzter* recipe, as given above, then set the cheese in the middle of a big platter surrounded by all spices and savories, plus an additional supply of finely chopped onions, and encourage their guests to fend for themselves.

MAKES ABOUT ¼ POUND CHEESE

PER PERSON:
¼ pound Camembert
1–2 teaspoons butter
1–2 teaspoons finely chopped onion (Optional: caraway seeds, chopped gherkins, chopped red pepper, paprika)

ALLGÄU

Cheese Salad with Oil and Vinegar
Saurer Käse

This seems to be a rare ancestral form of the cheese salads (or cheese and wurst salads) that abound in modern German cuisine. Serve with rings of raw onion and *Bauernbrot* or potatoes boiled in their jackets.

.   .   .   .

½ teaspoon salt
  Small pinch of sugar
1–2 tablespoons wine
  vinegar
¼ cup salad oil
1 cup lukewarm water
1 pound Limburger

Mix the salt and sugar with the vinegar until both are dissolved. Stir in the oil and the water; cut the cheese into slices and add to this mixture. Let sit for 1 hour, turning the cheese slices in the dressing frequently. Transfer the cheese to a porcelain bowl, pour the dressing over it, and allow to sit overnight.

MAKES 4–6 SERVINGS

ALLGÄU

Cheese Spätzle   Käsespätzle

Served with a green salad, this makes an excellent light lunch or dinner in summertime (or wintertime, for that matter).

•   •   •   •   •   •   •   •   •   •

1 tablespoon oil
1 recipe spätzle (page
  318)
½ cup butter
½ pound Emmentaler
  (Swiss cheese), grated
4 small onions, sliced into
  rings

Boil salted water in a saucepan along with 1 tablespoon oil. Cook the fresh spätzle. As the cooked spätzle bob up to the surface of the boiling water, remove them carefully with a skimmer or slotted spoon and allow to drain thoroughly.

Coat the bottom of a warm bowl with about 1 tablespoon butter. Start filling up with alternate layers of spätzle and grated cheese, then sprinkle a few little dabs of butter on top and toss gently but thoroughly. Save a little butter and fry the onion rings until golden brown, then pour the entire contents of the skillet over the spätzle.

MAKES 6–8 SERVINGS

BERLIN

Fried Potatoes with Eggs Hoppel-Poppel

This traditional dish can be found in a great many different versions, all of them involving fried potatoes with a fluffy coverlet of scrambled eggs. Christened *Hoppel-Poppel* by the Berliners for purely phonetic reasons, it is known in many other parts of Germany as *Bauernfrühstück* (farmer's breakfast), on the supposition that the leftovers from a thrifty farm family's dinner table (which were likely to be potatoes) were certain to turn up again at breakfast the next morning. Nowadays, our working and eating habits having changed considerably, *Hoppel-Poppel* is usually served for lunch.

· · · · · · · · ·

Dice the cooked potatoes. Melt the butter in a skillet and fry the bacon with the onions. Add the potatoes and fry, turning occasionally, until well browned. Add salt and pepper to taste.

Crack the eggs in a bowl and beat them well, then pour them over the fried potatoes. Mix together, and continue to cook until the eggs are nice and fluffy. Serve at once with bread or salad (or both).

MAKES 3 SERVINGS

1½ pounds or 4 medium all-purpose potatoes, boiled in their jackets, cooled, peeled
2–3 tablespoons butter or lard
½ pound medium-lean or fatty bacon (or a larger quantity of leftover roast or other cooked meat may be substituted), cubed
1 medium onion, finely chopped
Salt and freshly ground black pepper
6 eggs

Heidelberg, Baden

BERGSTRASSE

Stuffed Eggs with Sorrel Eier mit Sauerampfer

8 eggs
3 tablespoons sour cream
2–3 cups coarsely chopped
   sorrel (or substitute
   3–4 cups chopped
   watercress and 1
   tablespoon vinegar)
2 tablespoons butter
Salt to taste
Grated nutmeg
1 tablespoon butter for
   greasing baking dish
2–3 tablespoons heavy
   sweet cream

Here is a delicious dish that I first tasted some years ago at the house of some of my grandmother's relatives in Bensheim in the mountainous Bergstrasse region (Hesse). This is not, strictly speaking, a regional specialty, and I was given to understand at the time that the recipe had been handed down in the family for many generations. Since I was not exactly in the direct line of descent, I was never initiated into the family secret, and I had to wait until many years later to reconstruct the recipe from memory.

Serve hot with freshly baked white bread. Makes a very nice appetizer—also perfect for brunch if prepared in advance.

•   •   •   •   •   •   •   •   •

Hard-boil 6 of the eggs, plunge into cold water, remove the shells, and halve lengthwise. To keep the yolks from discoloring cook the eggs only 10 minutes after they have come to a boil. The other 2 fresh eggs should be cracked and beaten together. Remove yolks from the hard-boiled eggs, mash, and transfer to a mixing bowl. Combine with the beaten eggs and the sour cream. Reserve the egg white halves.

Wash the sorrel (or watercress), press out as much of the water as you can, and then cook for just a little while in the butter along with some salt and a little ground nutmeg. Allow it to cool, then finely chop the sorrel on a cutting board. Put the sorrel and the butter from the skillet into the mixing bowl with the eggs and sour cream; mix everything together thoroughly. Fill the hard-boiled egg white halves with this mixture. (When using watercress, add 1 tablespoon vinegar.)

Preheat the oven to 300°F. Butter a shallow baking dish large enough to accommodate the hard-boiled egg halves comfortably, but not a great deal larger, with the remaining tablespoon of butter; put in the egg halves with the filled side down. Add a little extra salt and nutmeg to the remaining filling mixture, stir in the sweet cream, and fill up the spaces in the dish between the stuffed egg halves with this mixture.

Bake in the oven until the filling has thickened and stiffened, about 10 to 15 minutes.

MAKES 3 SERVINGS

BERLIN

Eggs with Sweet-Sour Bacon Sauce
Saure Eier mit Specksauce

The Berliners usually serve this dish with mashed potatoes, which they call *Quetschkartoffeln,* or, roughly, "smashed potatoes."

• • • • • • • • • •

Keep the eggs warm in hot water while preparing the sauce.

In a skillet fry the bacon and onions until both start to turn translucent. Then add the lard or butter; when the onions have turned clear yellow, add the flour and continue to heat until you have a light brown roux. Pour in the stock and stir into a smooth sauce, then season with salt and pepper, bay leaves, vinegar, and a little sugar. Simmer for about 15 minutes longer; remove the bay leaves. Serve the whole eggs with the sauce poured over them.

MAKES 4 SERVINGS

8 eggs, hard-boiled (shells removed) or poached
10 strips medium-lean bacon, cut into little strips or diced
2 medium onions, diced
1 tablespoon lard or butter
2 tablespoons flour
2 cups beef stock
Salt and freshly ground black pepper
2 bay leaves
Vinegar
Sugar

Eggs Pickled in Brine   Soleier

12 eggs
5–6 tablespoons salt
  1 quart lukewarm water
    Salt and freshly
    ground black pepper
    Mustard
    Vinegar
    Oil

This is a delicacy that is said to have originated in the salt-works in the city of Halle in Saxony, where the workers used to make pickled eggs by lowering them in string bags into the natural brine wells. From there, it was but a short step to the glass-fronted "cake safe" (see illustration) that was perched on the bar of every street-corner saloon in Berlin. Surprisingly, this staple item of the old-time free-lunch counter was revived as a fashionable *amuse-gueule* in the seventies and has even enjoyed a certain vogue in Paris over the last couple of years.

Hard-boil the eggs for 10 minutes, then plunge into cold water. Dissolve the salt in the lukewarm water.

Roll the eggs around on a hard, flat surface until cracks begin to appear in their shells, but do not remove the shells. Put the eggs into mason jars (or any other kind of jar that has a lid), cover with salted water, and let sit (covered) for 3 to 6 days, depending on how salty you'd like to make them.

To eat them remove the shells and slice the eggs in half—there is some controversy among the experts as to whether the eggs should be sliced lengthwise or crosswise, which, like most learned controversies of this kind, can be safely ignored. The complicated part actually comes next: Carefully remove the half-yolks and apply salt, pepper, mustard, vinegar, and oil to taste in the space where the yolks used to be, then carefully put the half-yolks back upside down, with the rounded part rather than the flat side facing up.

Now, at long last, the *Soleier* are ready to eat. In order to experience their fully briny charm, they should definitely be eaten with one's fingers—old-time saloon habitués, for example, developed a two-handed technique whereby the yolk was extracted from the white with one hand and the condiments applied with the other.

YIELDS ONE DOZEN EGGS

WESTPHALIA

Pickled Eggs Marinierte Eier

Unlike the brine-cured eggs in the previous entry, this recipe from the nineteenth century for pickled eggs is still awaiting a major revival. Perhaps it might help to point out that the ingredients are inexpensive, the preparation is not the least bit difficult, and the results are entirely worth the effort.

. . . .

Hard-boil the eggs in generously salted water for 10 minutes. Plunge into cold water and remove shells.

Crack the peppercorns and allspice (but do not pulverize completely). Simmer all the spices gently with the vinegar in a non-reactive saucepan for a good 10 minutes.

Put the peeled eggs in a tall glass jar or a stoneware crock; allow the pickling liquid to cool, then pour it over the eggs through a fine strainer in order to remove the spices. Seal the mouth of the jar or crock with wax paper, then put the jar in a cool place (not the refrigerator). In the old days—when such things were done right or not at all—the eggs would be left in the pickling brine for a month or so, but they should be quite ready to eat after about a week. When the time has come, take the eggs out of the jar, allow to drain, pat dry with a paper towel, and serve with bread and butter.

YIELDS ONE DOZEN EGGS

12 eggs
Salt
1 heaping tablespoon
* peppercorns*
2 tablespoons allspice
* berries*
1 1-inch piece thinly
* sliced fresh ginger, or 1*
* tablespoon and 2*
* teaspoons powdered*
1 quart diluted (mild)
* vinegar*

BALTIC COAST

Scrambled Eggs with Kippers
Rührei mit Bückling

PER PERSON:
  ½ *small onion, sliced
    paper-thin*
  1 *tablespoon clarified
    butter*
  ½ *filleted kipper (or
    1 Kiel sprat—see
    Notes)*
  1 *teaspoon (or more)
    finely chopped dill*
2–3 *eggs
    Salt and freshly
    ground black pepper*

Here is another regional specialty that has gradually been accepted into the ranks of *haute gastronomie* over the past couple of decades. *Rührei mit Bückling* is customarily served on top of a slice of toasted *Mischbrot* (a mixture of rye and whole-wheat bread); the best substitute is rye bread.

•   •   •   •   •   •   •   •   •

In a large skillet sauté the onion in the clarified butter over moderate heat. When the onion starts to turn translucent, place the kipper fillet on top of the onion and allow to cook for 2 to 3 minutes, turning the kipper once, very carefully. Sprinkle with dill.

Beat the eggs together briefly with a little salt. Add to the skillet and, using a fork as a pusher, scramble the eggs by "sweeping" around the outer part of the skillet without disturbing the kipper fillet. Then season with a little pepper; you may want to add some more dill as a garnish.

NOTES: This dish can easily be transformed from a breakfast special or a snack into a main dish for lunch or dinner by using a whole kipper fillet (not too big a one, preferably) plus 3 or 4 eggs per person. Serve with fried potatoes and a lettuce or cucumber salad.

In Germany, a smaller relative of the herring called the sprat (*Kieler Sprotte,* "Kiel sprat," a specialty of the Baltic seaport of that name) would be substituted, but these may be even more difficult to come by outside the Baltic and vicinity.

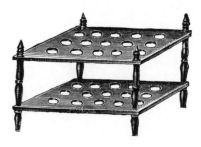

Basic Pancake Recipe   Eierpfannkuchen

Actually, the German *Eierpfannkuchen* is like a sort of tomboy cousin of the French crêpe—ideally making up in vigor and flexibility for whatever it might lack in sophistication or refinement. *Eierpfannkuchen* are often served as an accompaniment to fresh seasonal vegetables—savoy cabbage in the fall, asparagus in the spring, and so forth.

1½ cups flour
1¼ cups milk
4 eggs, separated
   Small pinch of salt
2 tablespoons butter
1 tablespoon oil

.   .   .   .

Mix together the flour, milk, egg yolks, and salt into a batter and let sit for 15 minutes. Beat the egg whites into stiff peaks and fold into the batter.

Heat some of the butter and oil in an omelette pan (or an 8″ to 10″ skillet), then use a ladle to pour the batter into the skillet and allow to cook on one side. When the upper edge of the batter is no longer liquid or runny, flip over onto the other side (with as much elegance and panache as you can manage). For an extra buttery taste slip an additional pat of butter under the pancake, and cook until the other side is also golden brown.

MAKES 2 SERVINGS

Fluffy "Omelette"   Aufgezogener Eierpfannkuchen

Combine the milk, flour, egg yolks, and pinch of salt. Stir into a smooth batter, then let sit for 30 minutes. Beat the egg whites until stiff, then fold them into the batter.

2 tablespoons milk
1 tablespoon flour
2 eggs, separated
   Small pinch of salt
   Butter to grease the pan

Preheat the oven to 400°F. Heat the butter in the omelette pan (or 8″ to 10″ ovenproof skillet), pour in the batter, and cook for a very short time on one side over medium-high heat. Bake the omelette in the oven for just about 5 minutes, which is supposed to make it especially light and fluffy—"pulls it up," as the Germans say. You can also put the omelette under the broiler for a couple of minutes, but watch it closely.

VARIATIONS: Adding 4 to 6 heaping tablespoons of finely chopped chives will transform the basic *Eierpfannkuchen* into a *Kräuterpfannkuchen,* an "herb omelette," to which basil, parsley, or other herbs (in limited quantities) can also be added.

Speckpfannkuchen: Fry up a few slices of fatty smoked bacon in the omelette pan until the fat has been rendered before adding the *Eierpfannkuchen* batter. Serve with a green salad. Similarly, adding a few pieces of kipper fillet makes a *Bücklingpfannkuchen;* a few little slices of Edam or Swiss cheese makes a *Käsepfannkuchen,* both of which are also quite good with a green salad. If you ever come to Cologne and intend to order *Eierpfannkuchen,* better remember a little poem by Heinrich Heine, who wrote: " . . . there I ate *Eierpfannkuchen* with ham and it was so salty, I had to drink lots of Rhine wine."

Gefüllte (stuffed) *Pfannkuchen,* spicy filling: Follow the basic recipe and use one of these fillings, which can be stirred or folded into the batter: fried chicken livers, chopped; ground meat with diced tomato; dried forest mushrooms (chanterelles, *Steinpilze,* et cetera), soaked and coarsely chopped; creamed spinach.

Gefüllte Pfannkuchen, sweet filling: Follow the fluffy omelette recipe. Add 1 teaspoon sugar (or vanilla sugar) to the batter; use marmalade or fruit preserves for the filling.

MAKES 1 OMELETTE

Basic Buckwheat Cake Recipe
Buchweizenpfannkuchen

2¼ cups buckwheat flour
2½ cups milk
4 eggs
Salt
Small pinch of sugar
Butter (lard, vegetable oil) to grease the pan

Cosmopolites and socialites will note that these buckwheat pancakes are essentially the same as the famous Russian blinis, and though they're just as good with caviar, they were never embraced by the German upper crust with the same desperate passion as they were by their Russian counterparts, the czarist aristocracy. Consequently, these pancakes are still more at home in the old-time country kitchen than at embassy receptions, boutique openings, and so on.

•   •   •   •   •   •   •   •   •

Mix the buckwheat flour with the milk, eggs, salt, and a very little sugar to make a smooth dough. After that, it's best to allow the dough to sit for several hours, if possible. Then heat a little butter in a skillet; use about ¼ cup of batter per pancake, customarily about the size of the palm of your hand, and cook until crispy on both sides. For a lighter pancake use ½ cup more milk.

VARIATIONS: In the Lower Rhine region (where they're euphoniously called *Bookweetpannekoke* in Plattdeutsch), buckwheat cakes are traditionally eaten with dark syrup or plum jam.

Similarly, the *Heensch-Kuchen* that they make a bit further south in the Eifel region (southwest of Bonn) have yeast added to the batter, plus mace, pepper, and salt, and are served with the usual sweet-sour alternative, in this case either molasses or corn syrup.

MAKES 4–6 SERVINGS

EAST   FRIESLAND,   WESTPHALIA

Buckwheat Cakes
Bookweetenschubber/Janhinnerks

In former days, the Frisians practiced a fairly wasteful form of agriculture, burning off the grasses on the moorlands and sowing *Bookweet* in the ashes, which would get them a couple of good harvests (and numerous buckwheat cakes) before the soil was exhausted.

•   •   •   •   •   •   •   •   •

The basic recipe above is followed, except that tea is substituted for the milk and lots of little pieces of bacon (¾ cup, diced) are added to the pan while cooking the buckwheat cakes. Serve with blueberry jam or preserves.

To make *Janhinnerks,* the Westphalians used coffee instead of tea or milk; in addition to the bacon in the pan, currants or even cranberries may be added to the batter. Serve with dark syrup or honey.

EAST FRIESLAND

Frisian-Style Waffles   Speckendicken

2¼ cups rye flour
1¾ cups whole-wheat flour
    Scant tablespoon
    baking powder
3–4 eggs
  2 cups milk
⅓ cup cane or corn syrup
¼ pound lard
    Scant ½ cup sugar
½ teaspoon powdered
    cinnamon
½ teaspoon ground
    cardamom
¼ teaspoon ground anise
    Bacon fat to grease the
    waffle iron
    Smoked hard sausage
    (mettwurst)

Speckendicken were traditionally served on New Year's Day, and the preparation, especially in its final stages, was a group effort in which the entire family could take part. Those concerned with total authenticity should serve the waffles with tea or *Doornkaat* (juniper-flavored rye liquor) rather than coffee. They also taste pretty good cold, so they need not necessarily be consumed on the spot.

•   •   •   •   •   •   •   •

In a large mixing bowl combine the flours and baking powder. Beat the eggs and add to the flour.

In a small saucepan combine the milk, syrup, lard, and sugar, then heat until the lard is melted. This should be lukewarm before adding to the mixing bowl with flours and eggs.

Add in the spices and mix all these ingredients into a thick batter. In the old days, the dough would have been taken down to the cellar to sit for a day or so, but just letting it sit overnight in a cool place should be sufficient.

Grease the waffle iron with bacon fat (or other fat). If you have an old-fashioned wrought-iron waffle iron with three little heart-shape compartments, you can press a little circle of smoked hard sausage into the center of each of the waffle compartments as a garnish, pour in the waffle batter, and bake about 2 minutes—until the outsides are golden brown and crispy.

MAKES 6 SERVINGS

*F*ish

. . . .

It has been pointed out that the Germans are not great fish
eaters, and this is to some extent true, though in former times,
this could be explained as more a matter of opportunity (or
the lack of it) than taste. The inhabitants of the Baltic and
North Sea coasts may have had more than their share of fish,
but for some reason they failed to provide us with a great
many classic seafood recipes. In the Catholic areas of the country, primarily in the south, fish was supposed to be eaten on
fast days, which were surprisingly numerous (not just Fri-
days, in other words) and quite strictly observed. Some excellent fish recipes were devised in monastery kitchens and the
households of the gentry, but ordinary people could hardly
afford to "fast" on such a luxury. Salted herring and salt cod
(Stockfisch) were the only kinds of coastal fish that could be
transported inland in substantial quantities. The carp, which
was raised in monastery pools, was a native freshwater fish
that played an important role in traditional German cuisine.
Other favorites were eel, pike, and small whitings.

Nowadays, everywhere in Germany you'll find rainbow
trout. It was introduced from North America only in the
1880s. The *Bachforelle,* the native European brook trout, has
always been fairly rare—though less so than it is today—and
was available to only a handful of intrepid anglers. Unlike the
rainbow, it can survive only in the cold, clear, oxygen-rich
water of a mountain stream and cannot be raised successfully
in commercial hatcheries. This is in no way to impugn the
deliciousness of the famous German specialty, smoked rainbow fillets *(geräucherte Forellenfilets),* but merely to point out
that as a creation of the modern age, they are not strictly
eligible for inclusion in this book.

Admirers of the famous Kiel sprats *(Kieler Sprotten)* might object that a number of excellent smoked-fish preparations have been given short shrift in the following pages. The same holds true of the many old-time recipes for marinated fish, which may have been commercially processed or served in restaurants, but were rarely made from scratch in the family kitchen.

EAST FRIESLAND, HAMBURG,
BREMEN, SCHLESWIG-HOLSTEIN

Pfannfisch

"Panfish" is a popular means of recycling leftovers in these parts of Germany.

•   •   •   •   •   •   •   •   •

Wait till the potatoes have cooled off before peeling and dicing (or slicing) them. Melt 1 tablespoon butter in a skillet and fry the bacon. When the bacon turns translucent, add the potatoes, then a little salt and pepper, and fry over high heat. Separate the fish into pieces (not too small), sprinkle with pepper, and set aside.

In another large skillet melt 2 tablespoons butter and lightly brown the onions. Add these to the potatoes.

To the potato mixture add the remaining 2 tablespoons butter together with the pieces of fish. Mix carefully so that the fish pieces remain essentially intact. When thoroughly heated transfer it to a serving platter, pour the liquid remaining in the skillet over the fish, and garnish with chopped parsley.

For a richer *Pfannfisch* mix, stir the dry mustard with water or fish stock and mix with the beaten eggs (perhaps stirring in a little chopped parsley as well). Season (cautiously!) with salt and pepper. Shortly after the fish pieces are added to the skillet with the onion rings, pour this mixture over both and cook until the eggs are scrambled.

NOTE: Smoked fish is often substituted for a portion of the cooked fillet (it would have generally been called salt cod or stockfish in the old days) to provide the *Pfannfisch* with a little extra zest; in either case, serve with a pickled vegetable— mixed pickles, pickled beets, et cetera.

MAKES 4 SERVINGS

2 pounds potatoes, boiled in their jackets
5 tablespoons butter
¼ pound medium-lean bacon
Salt and freshly ground black pepper
1 pound cooked fillet of fish, or only ¾ pound and additional ¼ pound smoked fish (see Note)
3 medium onions, thinly sliced
2 tablespoons chopped fresh parsley

OPTIONAL:
1 teaspoon dry mustard
4 tablespoons water or fish stock
3–4 eggs, beaten
Chopped parsley
Salt and freshly ground black pepper

Fish and Potato Casserole   Fischkartoffeln

*2 pounds potatoes,
   boiled in their
   jackets
3 tablespoons butter
3 tablespoons flour
1 medium onion,
   grated
1 cup fish stock, light
   beef stock, or water
½ cup heavy cream or
   crème fraîche
   Salt and freshly
   ground white pepper
1–2 egg yolks
1–1¼ pounds leftover
   cooked fish,
   deboned, separated
   into pieces
2 tablespoons grated
   Swiss cheese
   Chopped fresh
   parsley or anchovies
   (optional)*

This dish contains basically the same ingredients as *Pfannfisch* with much the same intent. The basic recipe is common to several different regions, not just along the Baltic or North Sea coasts, and was particularly popular in central Germany at one time. Serve with a green salad or (as is customary in central Germany) with peas and carrots, boiled together.

•   •   •   •   •   •   •   •

Peel the boiled potatoes and slice into thin rounds. In a saucepan combine the butter, 1½ tablespoons flour, and the onion and cook to make a light roux. Add the stock or water, and the cream, mix thoroughly, and season with salt and pepper. Bring this to a boil and cook for several minutes. Remove from heat and thicken with the egg yolks.

Preheat the oven to 350°F. Coat the inside of a soufflé dish with 1 tablespoon butter. Arrange the fish and potato slices in alternate layers, pouring some of the sauce over each layer, then cover the top layer with the remaining sauce, dot the top layer with the remaining butter, and sprinkle with grated cheese. Bake for about 20 minutes; you may want to increase the heat a little toward the end to make sure that a golden-brown crust forms on top.

You can also sprinkle a generous amount of chopped parsley or a couple of chopped anchovies in between the layers of fish and potatoes.

MAKES 4 SERVINGS

Haddock or Cod in Mustard Sauce
Schellfisch oder Kabeljau in Senfsauce

When this dish is prepared in a slapdash or, as the Germans say, "stepmotherly" fashion, it does less than justice to that excellent fish, the haddock. The obvious pitfall is that the sharpness of the mustard sauce can easily overpower the delicate taste of the haddock—though in the old days, especially in inland regions where the fish might not have been at its freshest, this was probably regarded as the lesser of two evils.

. . . .

To make the stock, combine all the stock ingredients in a large non-reactive pot and bring to a boil. Simmer for 30 minutes.

Remove the scales from the fish (or have them do this for you at the fish store), remove the fins, wash thoroughly, and rub with lemon juice. Sprinkle with a pinch of salt and let stand for 20 minutes, then add the fish to the hot stock and bring to a boil. Reduce heat and simmer for 15 to 20 minutes.

In the meantime, you can start to prepare the mustard sauce. In a saucepan melt the butter and sauté the onion, then add the flour. Cook the roux till golden, then add enough of the stock to make a smooth sauce. Season it with lemon juice and cook for another 10 minutes. Stir in the mustard and add salt and pepper if necessary.

Remove the fish from the broth and allow to drain. Serve the fish with the mustard sauce, and the hard-boiled egg on the side.

NOTE: This dish is usually accompanied by plain potatoes boiled in salted water. As an optional garnish for the potatoes, fry onion rings in butter till well browned, then pour the entire contents of the skillet over the potatoes.

MAKES 4 SERVINGS

STOCK:
- 1 cup dry white wine
- ½ cup vinegar
- 2 quarts water
- 1 large onion, sliced
- 1 leek, white part only, thoroughly washed
- 1 carrot, peeled
- 1 celery root
- 10 peppercorns
- 6 allspice berries, or 1 whole clove
- 1 bay leaf
- 1 teaspoon salt

- 2 pounds haddock or cod (a single large tailpiece, if possible)
- 1–2 tablespoons lemon juice
- Salt

MUSTARD SAUCE:
- 2 tablespoons butter
- 1 tablespoon minced or grated onion
- 2 tablespoons flour
- 2 tablespoons lemon juice
- 2 tablespoons Dijon-style mustard
- Salt and freshly ground white pepper

- 1 egg, hard-boiled and chopped

COASTAL REGIONS

Fried Fishcakes   Gebratene Fischklopse

2 *large stale or dry-baked
 rolls*
1 *pound fresh or cooked
 fish*
2 *tablespoons butter*
1 *medium onion, diced*
2 *eggs, beaten*
 *Finely chopped parsley
 or grated lemon peel
 (optional)*
 *Salt and freshly ground
 black pepper*
2 *tablespoons flour*
 *Butter or drippings for
 frying*

Here is another means of recycling leftover fish, which has been elevated to the status of a first-run recipe made from fresh fillets (freshwater fish fillets in inland regions). Serve with potato salad prepared the north German way with mayonnaise.

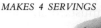

Remove the crust from the rolls, cut the rolls into slices, and soak in water or milk to soften. Press the moisture out of the rolls, combine with the fish, and put through the meat grinder, food mill, or processor—but it should not become too fine. Knead 1 tablespoon soft butter into the mixture to make a sort of dough.

Melt 1 tablespoon butter and sauté the onion until it starts to turn translucent. Add this to the fishcake dough along with the beaten eggs. If you wish, you can add a little parsley or a very little bit of grated lemon peel to the fishcake dough as well. Add salt and pepper to taste.

Shape the dough into small flat cakes, dust lightly with flour, and fry until they are golden brown on both sides.

MAKES 4 SERVINGS

Danzig harbor, East Prussia (now called Gdańsk and
belonging to Poland)

Steamed Fish Pudding Fischpudding Bürgerlich

Savory "steamed puddings" that were cooked in a special mold immersed in boiling water were popular specialties of the Wilhelminian (or Victorian) era that seem to have fallen from favor during the early years of this century. This is a good example of the *Bürgerliche* cuisine, roughly equivalent to the French *cuisine bourgeoise* that was developed in the households of the prosperous urban burghers and the gentry.

· · · · · · · · · ·

Combine the fish with the fatty pork, onion, and potato. Adjust the meat grinder or food mill to its finest setting, and run this mixture through it *twice* (or puree, just once, in the blender or food processor).

Remove the crust from the roll, slice the roll, and soften by soaking in the milk. Whip 3 tablespoons butter until creamy, squeeze the moisture out of the roll slices, and knead this together with the butter.

Mix the yolks together with the pureed fish dough and add the roll slices and butter. Season with salt, pepper, and parsley. Beat egg whites until stiff and fold them into the fish mixture, being careful not to overmix. Butter the mold (see Note). Fill pudding mold with this mixture. Lock the mold (or securely cover with wax paper and foil over that), immerse in hot water bath, and cook for about 80 minutes.

To serve, turn the mold out onto a serving platter, garnish with tomato or anchovy sauce,* and serve with bread or potatoes boiled in salted water.

NOTE: You can use a ring mold or a fluted mold. Any mold will do as long as it can be submerged in a water bath.

MAKES 6 SERVINGS

2 pounds saltwater or freshwater fish fillet, skinned
¼ cup cubed fresh fatty pork (originally, fatback)
1 medium onion, diced
1 small potato, boiled in its jacket, peeled
1 4" piece stale or dry-baked French bread
A few tablespoons milk
4 tablespoons butter
5 eggs, separated
Salt and freshly ground black pepper
2 tablespoons finely chopped fresh parsley
Tomato or anchovy sauce

★ Anchovy sauce: white sauce (Béchamel sauce) seasoned with anchovy paste or anchovy fillets pounded to a paste.

THURINGIA, SAXONY

Fish Casserole   Fisch Pickelsteiner

2 pounds cod, haddock,
or other saltwater fish,
filleted
2–3 tablespoons butter,
lard, or (preferably)
clarified butter
½ pound carrots, peeled
and cut into fat sticks
2" long
½ pound celery stalks,
cut into fat sticks
2" long
1 large onion, cut into
rounds
½ pound potatoes, peeled
and sliced
Salt and freshly
ground black pepper
2 cups beef stock

This family recipe for fish casserole originated in the Vogtland district of central Germany. The original *Pickelsteiner* is a hearty Franconian beef stew with lots of vegetables, the recipe for which can be found in the chapter "Vegetables, Potatoes, and Stews."

• • • • • • • • •

Cut the fish into bite-size pieces. Thoroughly butter a pot or casserole with a tight-fitting lid. Arrange the fish, carrots, celery, onion, and potatoes in layers inside the pot, ending with the potatoes as the top layer. Season each layer with salt and pepper as you go along. Pour the beef stock into the pot, dot the top of the potatoes with the remaining fat. Cover and cook over very low heat for 3 hours.

MAKES 6 SERVINGS

EAST PRUSSIA

Cabbage Rolls with Codfish
Kohlrouladen mit Dorsch

The *Dorsch,* or *Pomuchel,* the kind of codfish that's found in the Baltic, is a little smaller than its North Sea cousin and has a disproportionately thick head; it was in reference to this latter trait that the German inhabitants of Danzig (Gdańsk) were known as *Pommuchelsköpp,* "codfish-heads."

• • • • • • • • •

Peel off 8 to 16 of the freshest, crispiest leaves from a large cabbage and parboil them for a couple of minutes in salted water. Remove from the water, press flat, and spread out to dry.

Mince the fillet in the meat grinder or the food mill, knead this together thoroughly with salt and pepper, lemon juice, and the grated lemon peel. Roll up a small portion of codfish filling in each cabbage leaf; tie with cooking twine if necessary.

Melt the butter and brown the cabbage rolls on all sides. Add a few tablespoons of water and simmer for about 1 hour, covered, until done, turning the rolls in the liquid several times. Remove the cabbage rolls, keep them warm in an oven; retain the liquid in the pan.

Mix the cream and cornstarch, combine with the liquid in the pan, bring to a boil to make a sauce, and pour this over the cabbage rolls.

MAKES 4–6 SERVINGS

1 medium head of
   cabbage (2½–2¾
   pounds)
1¼ pounds codfish fillet
   Salt and freshly
   ground black pepper
   Juice of 1 lemon
   Grated peel of ½
   lemon
3–4 tablespoons butter
1 cup heavy cream
1 teaspoon cornstarch

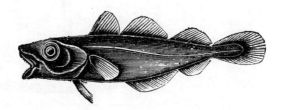

Herring

It would be difficult for us to overestimate the importance of herring both as a staple foodstuff and as an article of trade in the early days. The trick of salting down the day's catch to make it last practically indefinitely was learned by North Sea fishermen about a thousand years ago, and it was the basis for the considerable fortunes amassed by the trading cities of the Hanseatic League (notably Hamburg, Bremen, and Lübeck).

At the beginning of the twentieth century, herring was still enough of a staple that a grocer, for example, was still jocularly referred to as a "herring-tamer" *(Heringsbändiger)*. Primarily thought of as poor people's food, especially in the milltowns of Saxony and Silesia, "millworker's trout" was allegedly a salted herring suspended over the communal bowl of potatoes. Everyone at the table was allowed to lick the fish once during every meal and so it was supposed to last the entire family for a week.

One may wonder then why marinated "Bismarck Herring"

came to be so called—why this humble poor man's fish should be named for such a lofty and powerful dignitary. It is undoubtedly true that Otto von Bismarck was a keen appreciator of herring. He is reported to have said, for example, that if we only had to pay a lot of money for herring, then we would surely learn to revere it as one of our greatest delicacies. Nowadays, of course, we do, and consequently, we have. Small barrels of salted herring are available at American gourmet stores that import German/Scandinavian specialties.

"Fold the napkin in thirds to produce Fig. I, then fold in half again and you have Fig. II. Fold over the corners marked 1 and bring them up to the midline so as to produce Fig. III. Fold over the upper part of Fig. III to produce Fig. IV. Now place one of the peaks marked 2 on top of the other while you bring together the inner edges of the napkin so as to produce Fig. V. Then place the corner marked 3 on top of corner 4, and turn around and do likewise with the other two corners, so that you will have Fig. VI. Now you place one of the peaks marked 5 over the other, in the same way as you did the peaks marked 2 earlier, then pull out the opposing corner toward the left and the right."

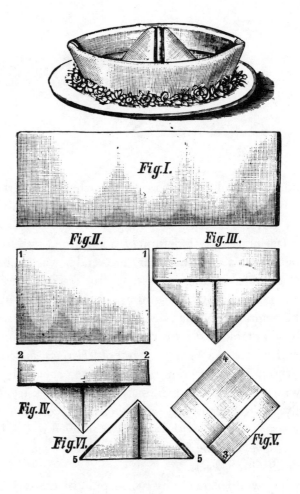

Fried and Marinated Herring
Gebratene Hering zum Marinieren

Ready-made versions of this dish, nowadays called *Bratheringe* in Germany, are abundantly available, but herring mavens willing to defer gratification for a couple of days may find it worthwhile to try out this nineteenth-century recipe.

These marinated herrings will taste equally good with bread and butter or potatoes boiled in their jackets. In the Rhineland, they would have served the herring with mashed potatoes garnished with bits of bacon; in central Germany, with fried instead of boiled potatoes. In the eighteenth century, the herrings were grilled (without the flour, of course) and salted away in casks as provisions.

·   ·   ·   ·   ·   ·   ·   ·   ·

Scale, eviscerate, and wash the herrings. Wipe dry, rub inside and out with lemon juice and sprinkle with a little salt and pepper. Let them sit for about 1 hour. Wipe the outside dry again, dredge them in flour, and tap lightly to remove the excess flour. Heat the oil and sauté the fish till crisp on both sides. Allow to cool.

In a non-reactive pot combine the vinegar, water, 1 onion (chopped or sliced), and spices (except the bay leaves). Bring this to a boil and cook for 15 minutes to make the marinade. Strain out the solid ingredients and allow it to cool.

Put the fried herrings in a ceramic crock with a lid; layer with the raw onion rings from 2 onions and the bay leaves. Pour in the marinade. Cover and allow to marinate for at least 2 days.

MAKES 1 DOZEN HERRINGS

12 fresh herrings
  Lemon juice
  Salt and freshly ground white pepper
  Flour to dredge the fish
  Cooking oil
2 cups vinegar
1 cup water
3 onions, thinly sliced
6 allspice berries, or 2 whole cloves
10 peppercorns
  Small pinch of dried thyme
  Large pinch of dried basil
  Thumbnail-size piece of fresh ginger, very thinly sliced
3 bay leaves

Herring Fishcakes   Heringskoteletts

The landlubber's version of fishcakes *(Fischklopse)* from a few pages earlier was set down by an aunt of mine who lived to a

2 large salted herrings
  Milk or mineral water
1 small bunch of parsley
1 small onion, grated
1 tablespoon butter, plus
  butter (or lard) for
  frying
1 egg
1 kaiser roll
2 tablespoons sour cream
  Freshly ground black
  pepper
2 tablespoons bread crumbs

ripe old age without ever setting eyes on the ocean. Serve the fishcakes with potato salad and a green salad as well.

•   •   •   •   •   •   •   •   •   •

Soak the salted herrings overnight in milk or mineral water. The next day, remove the skin and bones (also the head and fins if necessary). Finely chop the herring fillets and the parsley, mix these together with the grated onion, then knead in the butter and egg.

Remove the crusts from the roll, slice the roll, soak in milk or water to soften, and press out the moisture. Mix this together with the fishcake dough, then add in the sour cream, and add a little pepper (to taste). Form the dough into 4 cakes or patties and coat each with bread crumbs. Melt the butter or lard in a skillet and fry the cakes until brown on both sides.

MAKES 2 SERVINGS

Homemaker's Herring   Hering Hausfrauenart

4 salted herrings (see
  Note)
2 cups sour cream
  Lemon juice
  Pinch of sugar
  Freshly ground white
  pepper
2 medium onions, cut into
  thin rounds
1 large Granny Smith
  apple, peeled, cored, and
  sliced
1 large half-sour (dill)
  pickle, sliced
1 teaspoon mustard seed
2 bay leaves

The name means "the way the homemaker makes it" or "herring *bonne femme*" or something of the sort; the dish itself seems to have originated in East Prussia, where it was simply called "creamed herring" *(Schmantheringe)*. Nowadays, it often turns up on restaurant menus (sometimes under the alias *Matjesfilets Hausfrauenart)*, though the original recipe has slowly but surely succumbed to modern mass-production techniques and dubious methods of "presentation."

The herrings rarely have time for a long, leisurely soak in marinade these days, so they're served with pickled gherkins rather than half-sour (dill) pickles, which in my view tends to spoil the effect. Also, using salt herring rather than matjes fillets involves a little extra effort in preparing the fish for the marinade, the sort of extra effort that was rarely withheld in those days when good food was prepared. This recipe is one that my mother learned from her mother.

Island of Rügen, Baltic Sea

Tradition absolutely requires that the herring be served with potatoes boiled in their jackets, and even the most inveterate wine drinkers are advised to switch over to beer for the occasion.

· · · · · · · · ·

Wash the salt herrings and reserve the "soft roe" (milt) packets. Soak the herrings thoroughly, changing the water frequently, until only a mild salty taste remains. Remove the skin and bones from the herrings. Press the "soft roe" (milt) through a sieve. Then combine the sour cream, lemon juice, mashed "soft roe," sugar, and pepper to make a marinade. Blend this together thoroughly with a whisk.

Arrange the herring fillets in layers in an earthenware crock, interspersed with the onion, apple, and pickle slices, plus a sprinkling of mustard seed; insert the bay leaves into the center. Pour a little marinade over each layer and then the remaining marinade over the top; there should be enough marinade to cover the herring and other ingredients to a depth of a quarter inch or so.

Let it stand overnight so that all the various flavors will be able to blend and work their pungent magic on one another.

NOTE: When you're buying the herrings at the fish store, try to make sure that at least 1 male herring, or "milter," is included (and preferably 2); I'm not suggesting this in the interests of sexual equality, but because you really won't get the full taste sensation if you don't start out with a mixed batch.

If milters are not available, simply omit the milt from the marinade and prepare as otherwise directed.

VARIATION: In the Rhineland, they make a dish called *Rheinischer Heringstipp,* which is identical to the above except that the herring fillets are cut up into bite-size pieces before marinating. Nowadays, the rectangular terrines, called *Heringtöpfe,* that were made especially for the purpose of marinating herrings (large enough that the fillets could be stretched out comfortably at full length) are difficult to come by and accordingly sought after by herring fanciers. You may want to consider this alternative method if you have trouble improvising a suitable substitute *Heringtopf.*

A rather good substitute for this dish can be prepared with "creamed herring" from the supermarket shelf. Simply add more sour cream, sliced dill pickles, mustard seed, and tart apples. A little bit of anchovy paste mixed with the sour cream will enhance the flavor.

MAKES 2 SERVINGS

NORTHERN GERMANY

Herring Fillets with Green Bean Salad
Matjesfilets mit Grünen Bohnen

8 matjes fillets
  Mineral water
2 pounds green beans,
  cleaned and washed
1 tablespoon butter
4 onions, 2 diced, 2 cut
  into thin rings
¼ pound medium-lean
  bacon, diced
  Salt and freshly ground
  black pepper
  Pinch of savory
¼ cup chopped fresh
  parsley

Serve with new potatoes boiled in their jackets and (for those more concerned with paying homage to age-old culinary tradition than counting calories) well buttered. Beer and a clear schnapps (aquavit, Steinhäger, or vodka) is the beverage combination of choice here.

•   •   •   •   •   •   •   •

First, the fillets should be soaked in mineral water for about 5 minutes—the sharper and more pungent their original taste, the longer they should soak. Then put them on crushed ice or in the refrigerator to keep cool.

Snap the beans and cook them in water until they're well cooked but still crispy.

In a skillet melt the butter and sauté the diced onions and bacon until they turn translucent. Season the cooked beans with the salt, pepper, and savory. Combine the beans with the onions, bacon, and melted butter and toss together. Let sit for several minutes. Sprinkle with chopped parsley as a garnish.

Garnish the matjes fillets with the onion rings and serve, as they are, on a bed of crushed ice. Serve the bean salad on the side.

MAKES 4 SERVINGS

Salt Cod   Stockfisch

A "stockfish" is a codfish that has been filleted, salted, and dried—a universal staple of former days that has not fared very well in the "Age of Refrigeration." Nowadays, salt cod is something of a rarity in Germany (and rather expensive). It is usually sold at fish stores in presoaked, "reconstituted" form rather than in the old flat triangular sheets, which have to be soaked for 24 hours (after being pounded to tenderize them and treated with baking soda). In the United States you can buy it under the names "salt cod" or "bacalao."

In southwest Germany, the tradition of eating stockfish for

Helgoland, North Sea

dinner on Ash Wednesday, the first day of Lent, has survived since medieval days; restaurants in the south of Baden, for example, still advertise a "complete stockfish dinner"—a reliable indication that the pre-Lenten carnival revelry is about to come to an end. The recipe that follows was set down in 1796 by the proprietress of the Grüner Baum country inn at Wolfach, in the Schwarzwald (Black Forest), and is reprinted here courtesy of the present proprietor, Günter Endres.

To Cook Stockfish   Stockfisch zu Kochen

2 pounds salt cod
  (stockfish)
3 tablespoons butter
4 shallots, finely
  chopped
  Parsley
1½ tablespoons flour
2 cups beef broth
½ cup heavy cream
  Salt and freshly
  ground black pepper
½ teaspoon ground ginger
  Pinch of nutmeg
  Pinch of mace

Use at least 2 pounds salt cod that has been soaked overnight. Heat up 4 finely chopped shallots and 3 tablespoons butter in a skillet; add 1½ tablespoons flour and cook to make a light roux, and carry on from there as described below. Serve the stockfish with potatoes that have been boiled in salt water.

•   •   •   •   •   •   •   •   •

"Set the stockfish for 3 hours [in a large quantity of water] by the fire, but it must not come to boil. If it starts to boil, move it a little away from the fire. If you wish its flesh to remain white, then wrap your fish in a napkin before you put it in the water. When it is ready to come out of the water, then you can bone your fish. Put a good-size piece of butter in a cahserol [sic] immediately and start to heat it up. Then add some shallots, a little parsley chopped up fine, and a little flour as well, and allow these to toast over the fire. Then add beef broth, a good bit of cream, pepper, [powdered] ginger, n[utmeg], mace, salt. Let this all come to a boil and cook until it turns to a thickish broth. Then put your fish into the broth and allow to cook for a little while and bring it to the table straightaway."

Badenweiler, Baden

S C H W A R Z W A L D

"Ash Wednesday" Salt Cod with Potatoes
Aschermittwoch-Stockfisch

This is a more contemporary recipe, also from Wolfach in Schwarzwald, a picturesque medieval community where on Ash Wednesday—called *Fasnet*'s [*Fastnacht*'s] end—carnival buffoons in mourning attire still enact a springtime fertility rite of sorts—soaking their "moneybags" in the fountain in the town square and then "planting" them, with great solemnity, on long bean poles in front of the tax collector's office. After that, of course, everybody goes to the nearest restaurant to eat stockfish and potatoes, drink lots of beer, and look forward to next year's *Fasnet*.

*¾ pound salt cod
   (stockfish)
2 pounds potatoes
5 tablespoons butter
2 medium onions, thinly
   sliced*

· · · · · · · · ·

Wash the stockfish very thoroughly in cold running water. Then heat it in a generous amount of water until just before it starts to boil. Remove the pot from the heat and just let it sit in the water for another 20 or 30 minutes. Peel the potatoes, cut into slices, cook in salted water, and drain.

Remove the stockfish from the water, skin, fillet, and divide into pieces. In a warm terrine, place alternate layers of boiled potato slices and pieces of stockfish. Melt 4 tablespoons butter (but do not allow to brown) and pour this over the contents of the terrine. Lightly brown the onions in the remaining 1 tablespoon butter and use these to garnish the top of the stockfish and potatoes.

MAKES 4 SERVINGS

Smoked Fish   Räucherfische

What follows are a couple of dishes more likely to bring tears to the eyes than tingles of anticipation to the palate—since none of these traditional East Prussian specialties is currently available, even in Germany, except to those dedicated fish fanciers who have their own smokeboxes or smokehouses.

A specialty of the Danzig waterfront used to be *Spaltaal,* or "split eel." A large eel, weighing at least 2 pounds and about 3 inches in diameter, was smoked over a fire of blazing pinecones; the eel was split lengthwise down the middle to ensure maximum retention of the tangy, resinous taste of the smokehouse.

Long after herring was no longer plentiful, the Baltic coast continued to abound in gigantic salmon, which immediately suggests the possibility of lox—a word that derives, via Yiddish, from the Old German *lahs,* "salmon"; the modern German word is spelled *Lachs* but pronounced the same way.

Smoked flounder used to be the specialty of the coastal towns of Cranz and Sarkau; the fish were smoked between bricks in the first of these localities, and in an underground pit in the second. The fire was fed with pinecones.

Smoked sturgeon, the regal companion of the smoked salmon in North American delicatessens, was another East Prussian specialty. Its meat is still held in great esteem by connoisseurs because it is said to have seven distinct and dif-

ferent tastes; the various "cuts" of the sturgeon were likened in an old book on gastronomy to "the flesh of a calf, a turtle, a fowl," not even counting the caviar. (All genuine caviar stems from sturgeons.)

The mysterious, prehistoric-looking freshwater fish called the *Maräne,* a kind of whitefish *(Coregonus),* was one of the great culinary attractions of the beautiful Masurian Lakes in East Prussia. On occasion, a good half of the passengers on the excursion steamers from Lötzen (now Giżycko, in Poland) used to get off at the little town of Nikolaiken (Mikolajki), not because of anything special about the landscape, but because this was where the freshest smoked *Maränen* was to be found. Smoked-fish fanciers insist that the fish is only at its absolute peak as long as the warmth of the smokehouse still lingers, and a fish that was smoked as long ago as the day before yesterday is no longer worthy of serious consideration. (A smaller version of the *Maräne* still exists in the lakes of Schleswig-Holstein, but not in sufficient numbers to provide the basis for an extensive excursion industry.)

The lamprey, another primeval- and even rather sinister-looking creature, is called *Neunaugen* (nine eyes) in German because of the long row of circular gill pouches behind its real eye. The lamprey is still considered a great gourmet delicacy in the region around Bordeaux, where it naturally takes the form of *lamproie au vin.* In East Prussia, the lamprey was not smoked, but grilled in an oven that was made expressly for that purpose, then put up in vinegar in a little wooden keg. It was a specialty of the port city of Memel (now Klaipėda, in Lithuania) and the Gulf of Courland.

To conclude our discussion of the smoked-fish specialties of yesteryear, here is a bit of inspirational verse that was formerly emblazoned on the wall of a little waterfront tavern in Danzig:

The kipper is golden,
The eel full of fat,
The flounder looks
cross-eyed—
Let's all drink to that!

Goldig ist der Bückling,
Fettig ist der All,
Schielen tut die Flunder
Und wir trinken noch einmal!

BERLIN

Fresh Eel Aal Grün

2 pounds fresh eel
(skinned or not,
depending on
preference)
1 cup dry white wine
2 cups water
2 tablespoons lemon
juice
1 small bunch of dill,
well mashed
1 small bunch of
parsley, well mashed
A few sprigs of chervil
1–2 sage leaves
2 bay leaves
½ teaspoon salt
8 peppercorns
½ onion
1 tablespoon butter
1 tablespoon flour
2 egg yolks
4 tablespoons sour cream
Small pinch of sugar
2 tablespoons finely
chopped fresh parsley
2 tablespoons finely
chopped fresh dill
1 tablespoon finely
chopped fresh chervil

Since medieval times, eels have been a favorite of German urbanites. Just as London Cockneys have their jellied eels, Berliners have always doted on *Aal Jrün* (roughly, "yuh-RINN," the substitution of *j*—which is pronounced like *y*—for *g* being one chief peculiarity of the Berliner dialect) and, in former days, everyone had his or her favorite eel restaurant somewhere out in the suburbs.

Currently, in spite of the fact that smoked eel now costs even more than lox, West Germans still consume some 5,000 or 6,000 metric tons of eel every year (mostly in the form of smoked eel), of which only about 600 tons is actually caught in German waters; the rest has to be imported. The catastrophic toxic spill that decimated the eel population of the Upper Rhine in 1986–87, and briefly made world headlines, should give some indication of why this might be the case.

Tradition dictates (if not positively demands) that *Aal Grün* be accompanied by new potatoes boiled in their jackets and by cucumber salad with creamy dressing.

·   ·   ·   ·   ·   ·   ·   ·   ·

Wash the eel thoroughly and cut into about 12 pieces, none of which should be too thick. Combine the white wine, water, lemon juice, spices, seasonings, and onion in a large non-reactive saucepan; bring to a boil, and allow to cook for about 15 minutes. Then add the eel pieces, reduce heat, and simmer for another 15 minutes. Remove the eel from the broth, and keep warm in a serving dish.

Combine the butter and flour in a saucepan and cook briefly over medium heat to make a white roux. Strain out the solid ingredients from the broth, and add enough broth to the roux to make a smooth sauce. Beat the egg yolks with the sour cream and stir into the sauce with a whisk. Continue to heat slowly, but do not allow to come to a boil. Taste for seasoning —you may especially want to add a small pinch of sugar—

and add the finely chopped herbs. Pour the sauce over the warm eel pieces and serve.

MAKES 4 SERVINGS

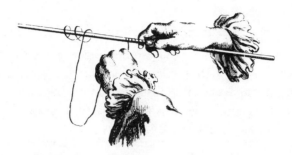

M O S E L   V A L L E Y

Eel in Wine Sauce   Moselaal in Weinsauce

No tourist in Europe should miss the Mosel region—for its scenery, its wines and . . . this special eel dish. Serve it with mashed potatoes and a salad. A Mosel-Riesling wine is best, but not a sweet one.

Clean the eels and cut into 2-inch lengths. Melt the butter in a heavy-bottomed non-reactive saucepan and sauté the onion. Stir in the flour and cook the roux but do not let it color; stir in the veal stock. Add the wine and season with salt and pepper. Cook for 5 minutes until heated through, stirring continuously.

Put in the eel pieces, reduce heat, and cover. Allow the eels to cook for a good 20 minutes, turning them occasionally in the sauce. Remove the eels from the sauce and keep them warm in a serving dish.

Stir the sour cream, lemon juice, and dill into the sauce, test for seasoning, and pour the sauce over the eel pieces.

VARIATION: In recent years, the sauce is frequently enriched by the addition of mushrooms and capers. Some might object that the combination of mushrooms, capers, and dill is a little

1½ pounds eel, skinned
3 tablespoons butter
4 tablespoons minced onion
2 tablespoons flour
1 cup veal stock (chicken broth could be substituted)
1 cup dry Riesling Salt and freshly ground white pepper
3 tablespoons sour cream
2 tablespoons lemon juice
2 tablespoons finely chopped fresh dill

overpowering; purists and antiquarians would insist that this is not the authentic *Moselaal* recipe. (All would certainly agree that the mushrooms should not come out of a can.)

MAKES 4 SERVINGS

"In America eels are only something of a gastronomic curiosity . . ." writes Craig Claiborne. "The eel is among the fishes what Helena was among women . . ." wrote the German gastrosopher (gastronomical writer) Eugen Baron Vaerst in 1854.

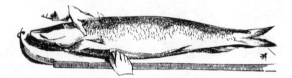

Pike   Hecht

This fish is very popular in southern Germany. It is used in casseroles as *Schüssehelhecht* or baked (larded or basted with sour cream). Whenever traveling in Germany, don't miss a delicious pike *(Hecht)* dish.

BERLIN

Old-Fashioned Fish Casserole
Altberliner Fischgericht

The name literally means "old-time Berlin fish dish," though like many Berliners, the recipe itself (provided in its present version by my aunt Erna Frickert) is said to have come from Silesia.

•   •   •   •   •   •   •   •   •   •

"Cook the carp, tench, eel, pike, crucian [another kind of carp] in water that has been well seasoned [see Note, below]. Drain. Arrange the different kinds of fish on a platter and pour the Polish fish sauce over them; serve the remaining fish sauce on the side.

"Polish fish sauce: Put the fish heads in dark beer along with an onion, bay leaf, parsley stems and sprigs, and allspice berries. Bring to a boil and simmer for ½ hour. Bind the sauce with crumbled gingerbread [for which a gingersnap or other gingerbread cookie may be substituted] or flour, strain through a sieve, add 2 tablespoons soaked raisins, and season to taste with lemon juice, a pinch of sugar, salt, a generous quantity of butter, and red wine." Serve with potatoes boiled in salted water.

NOTE: The essential idea is to provide an interesting variety of flavors and textures from among the different kinds of fish that are locally available, not to reproduce the exact selection called for in Aunt Erna's recipe. (North Americans will find catfish, whitefish, or lake trout a lot easier to come by, for example, than tench or crucian carp.) Also, remember that the eyes and gills should be removed from the fish heads before they go into the pot.

The water in which the fish themselves are cooked should be seasoned with 1 bay leaf, 1 onion, 1 carrot, a couple of lemon slices (including the peel), salt, and a couple of peppercorns. Bring water to a boil and cook for several minutes after adding all these ingredients, then reduce heat and start to cook the larger fish first so they'll all be done at approximately the same time.

Carp Karpfen

The carp has had a great deal more importance as a food fish in Germany than in most other European countries. Perhaps this is because the German monks were particularly fond of tending them in their carp pond. They needed a constant supply of fish because, as mentioned earlier, the meatless "fast" days made up a very large proportion of the medieval church calendar. In later years, carp was primarily a festive dish reserved for Christmas or New Year's. In Bavaria, it is eaten all year round, and the carp from the Aischgründen in central Franconia are held in particular esteem. South German carp fanciers tend to prefer the smaller specimens, weighing not much more than a kilo (2.2 pounds), and North Germans, the larger ones. Carp is frequently eaten halved, breaded, and deep-fried, or served with the following sauce.

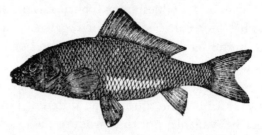

EASTERN AND CENTRAL GERMANY

Carp in Beer Sauce   Karpfen in Biersauce

1 carp, 3½–4 pounds
Salt
Vinegar
2 medium onions, thinly
  sliced
1 carrot, peeled and sliced
Peel of ¼ lemon (pith
  removed), coarsely
  chopped
1 bay leaf
1 whole clove
3 cups dark beer
¾ cup ginger cookie
  crumbs (gingersnaps,
  etc.)
1 tablespoon butter
1 tablespoon flour
1 tablespoon sugar or corn
  syrup
Lemon juice

Other variations on this recipe are known as Carp in Polish Sauce and Bohemian Carp. I have chosen the present recipe in favor of the others on strictly nationalistic grounds; all three were traditionally served on New Year's Day in the eastern parts of Germany. Potatoes boiled in salted water furnish the traditional accompaniment to this dish.

•   •   •   •   •   •   •   •   •

Clean, scale, and wash the carp; cut into slices, in the manner of fish steaks, and sprinkle with salt. Set aside. (The original recipe also suggests that you catch the fish's blood in a bowl and mix with a little vinegar.)

Place the onions, carrot, and lemon peel on the bottom of a large pot and put the fish slices on top of them. Add the bay leaf and clove. Pour in 1½ cups of the beer. Add the ginger cookie crumbs to the pot. Cover and bring to a boil, then allow to simmer very gently for about 15 minutes.

In the meantime, cook the butter and flour until the roux is brown, pour in the rest of the beer (1½ cups), and stir. Stir in the vinegar (and fish blood, if any), add this to the fish slices, and allow it to finish cooking. When the fish slices are ready, take them out of the pot and keep them warm in a serving dish.

Pass the sauce through a strainer. Sweeten with a little sugar (or corn syrup) and lemon juice. Bring the sauce once more to a boil and pour some of it over the carp slices, and serve some of it separately.

MAKES 4–6 SERVINGS

BADEN

Mock Oysters   Falsche Austern

This recipe was handed down for many years in the Seidel family (and dictated to me by Aunt Marthel). Readers who live in places where carp milt is a great deal harder to come by than oysters but who are still interested in practicing the same sort of clever deception may feel free to substitute shad or herring miltner, or whatever is locally available. If you don't know how to obtain oyster shells, simply use other shells or small au gratin cups.

•   •   •   •   •   •   •   •   •

Wash the milt thoroughly in cold water to which a little milk has been added, then change the water, add a little more milk, and soak the milt for several hours. Clean out the oyster shells, divide the milt into 8 equal portions, and place one of these in each of the empty shells. Sprinkle with lemon juice and turn over the milt once in it.

Preheat the oven to 400°F. Cook the mushrooms in the fish broth with the anchovies or anchovy paste until the mushrooms are quite tender. Press through a fine strainer, or food mill or processor, reheat (if necessary), then remove from heat

1 carp milt, or 2 or 3 if the "packets" are fairly small
2 cups milk
8 empty oyster shells
Juice of 1 lemon
1½ cups thinly sliced fresh mushrooms
1 cup strong or concentrated fish broth
4 anchovies, chopped, or 1 tablespoon anchovy paste
2 egg yolks
1 tablespoon butter
Coarse salt
2 lemons, cut into wedges

and stir in the egg yolks with a whisk until you have a smooth, creamy sauce. Pour this over the carp milt in the oyster shells; sprinkle on some more lemon juice and a few little dabs of butter. Arrange the oyster shells on a baking sheet (balance them on little mounds of coarse salt, if necessary, to keep them from tipping over) and bake in the hot oven until they have acquired a nice golden brown crust. Garnish with lemon wedges and serve with butter and squares of toast.

MAKES 4 SERVINGS

LAKE CONSTANCE

Perch à la Mode de Reichenau
Kretzer Reichenauerart

Kretzer or *Aegli* is the local name for the perch (*Barsch* in standard German), and Reichenau is an island in the Untersee (western branch of Lake Constance) best known for its medi-

Frauenchiemsee, island with monastery in Lake Chiem, Bavaria

eval monastery and vegetables, first cultivated by the monks about a thousand years ago. This is a recipe devised by the local fishermen; I have yet to come across it on any restaurant menu. It is best served with boiled potatoes and a salad.

•   •   •   •   •   •   •   •   •   •

Clean, scale, and wash the perch. Rub it with salt, and let it stand for about 2 hours.

Melt half of the butter in a large skillet, and sauté the onions until quite translucent. Dredge the fish in the flour, push the onion rings to one side of the skillet, add the rest of the butter to the skillet, and fry the fish over high heat.

Mix the sour cream with the wine and sage. As soon as the fish is well browned on both sides, reduce heat, and pour in the sour cream and wine mixture. Cover and cook everything together for another couple of minutes or until the fish is done.

MAKES 4 SERVINGS

4 small (½ pound)
   yellow perch
   Salt
3–4 tablespoons butter
   2 medium onions, sliced
   Flour to dredge the
   fish
½ cup sour cream
½ cup white wine
½ teaspoon crushed sage

FRANCONIA, WÜRZBURG

Fried Fish   Meefischle

The German word for this dish is pronounced "May-fish-leh," which simply means that this dish is originally made with little fish from the river Main, on which the city of Würzburg is situated. In Trier, they serve deep-fried fingerlings from the Moselle with local apple wine (hard cider) called *Viez,* coming to the table in white mugs, but the advantage of the Würzburger recipe (which is otherwise identical) is that the *Meefischle* are supposed to be accompanied by a dry Silvaner, which tastes infinitely better than apple wine. Another important point is that the fish should be very small indeed, literally not much bigger than your finger.

Serve with a dry white wine (preferably from Franconia if not actually a genuine Silvaner) as well as white bread, potato salad, and a tossed salad.

1¾ pounds very small
   freshwater fish, about
   the size of minnows or
   whitebait
   Salt
   Lemon juice
1 cup flour
⅓ teaspoon ground
   cinnamon
   Fat for deep-frying
   Lemon halves

•   •   •   •   •   •   •   •   •

The fish should be scaled, if necessary, and washed (but not eviscerated). Allow to drain and then sprinkle them with salt and lemon juice. Let them sit for at least 30 minutes.

Mix the flour with the cinnamon; dredge the fish in the flour, one by one, and fry in boiling fat (not too many at a time) until crispy and golden brown.

Connoisseurs usually eat their *Meefischle* head first; some prefer to throw away the tail, like a shrimp's, even though the tail of a *Mainfische,* when cooked to the proper crispy consistency, has a delicious roasted-almond sort of taste. Garnish with lemon halves.

MAKES 4 SERVINGS

LAKE   CONSTANCE

Perch Fillets in Cream Sauce   Eglifilets in Sahne

This recipe demonstrates a time-honored method of preparing small perch fillets that has long been a favorite at the Krone ("Crown") Restaurant in Schnetzenhausen, near Friedrichshafen, and has been somewhat modernized and refined over the years.

•   •   •   •   •   •   •   •   •

Wash the fillets and pat dry. Add a little salt and pepper to the flour; dredge the fillets in the flour and tap lightly to remove the excess flour.

In a skillet brown the fish on both sides in the clarified butter. When they're almost done, melt a few little dabs of butter on top of the fillets. Remove from the skillet and keep warm.

Stir the cream together with the contents of the skillet, heat through, add lemon slices, and the Worcestershire sauce. Test for seasoning. Pour the cream sauce over the fillets and garnish with separately cooked fresh green peas tossed in softened butter.

MAKES 4 SERVINGS

2 pounds small perch fillets (fillets of small freshwater fish that are not fatty can be used as well; rainbow trout would be good)
Salt and freshly ground white pepper
1 cup flour
2–3 tablespoons clarified butter
1 tablespoon butter
1 cup cream
1 lemon, sliced
Dash or two of Worcestershire sauce
Fresh green peas tossed in butter

EAST PRUSSIA

Baked Pike Perch   Gebackener Zander

Here is a recipe from the region around the Gulf of Courland, which is a sort of freshwater lagoon separated from the Baltic by a very narrow neck of land, formerly (and perhaps still) an earthly paradise for swimmers, sailors, and fishermen. Formerly attached to East Prussia, Courland is now part of the Soviet Union and, accordingly, this recipe, submitted by Frau Sophie Frühling, was awarded first prize by the German Academy of Gastronomy in the category "Recipes from Former German Territories" for 1978.

The European pike perch is actually a kind of perch—large, aggressive, and otherwise reminiscent of pike in its habits and appearance; the same name is sometimes given to the North American walleye and some of its relatives. Accompany this

1 2–3-pound pike perch
Salt
¼ pound fresh fatty bacon (or blanched smoked bacon, thinly sliced)
1 cup fish stock
6 tablespoons butter
2 tablespoons flour
½ cup cream
2–3 tablespoons chopped fresh dill

dish with potatoes boiled in salted water, and peas and carrots
—mixed together in the German style, if you wish—or cauliflower.

.   .   .   .

Scale, wash, and salt the fish. Line the bottom of a large
baking pan with the bacon. Place the fish on top and pour the
stock over the fish. Bake for about 35 minutes. Cut up 4
tablespoons of the butter into little pats and place on top of
the fish, then bake for an additional 5 minutes. Remove the
fish and keep warm on a serving dish.

In a saucepan, cook the remaining 2 tablespoons of butter
with the flour to make a light roux. Add the juices from the
baking pan to the roux along with the cream, stir with a
whisk, cook for a few minutes, and sprinkle in the chopped
dill. Pour this sauce over the perch and serve.

MAKES 4 SERVINGS

Poultry

.   .   .   .

Chickens and geese, unlike fish, could generally be found in the backyard of even the humblest householder (though ducks, like carp, would at least require a pond). Over the last several centuries, the way we have defined the term *poultry* has been broadened in some respects, and narrowed down in a number of others. We tend to believe that such birds as the swan and peacock should give pleasure to the eye exclusively, whereas in former days they often found their way into the stewpot or the roasting pan. Turkey, on the other hand, was commonly known as the "outlandish chicken" *(Welschhahn)* and as such was reserved for the tables of the wealthy until relatively recently. Even though it had been introduced into Europe as early as 1530, there are no truly popular or traditional turkey recipes of German origin. The turkey was also known as "Indian cock," "Calicut cock" (named for a seaport in southern India), or "Turkish cock."

Roast Chicken, Grandma's Way

Grandma's wood- or coal-burning stove did not get as hot as a modern electric range, which was perfectly all right as far as poultry was concerned; all poultry turns out juicier when cooked at a temperature between 350° and 400°F. Since the breast is the tenderest part of the bird, *Grossmutter*'s recipes always called for poultry to be roasted with the breast turned downward; even after the bird had been taken out of the oven

and before it was brought to the table, it was supposed to remain in this position so all the juices would flow down into the breast. The breasts of game birds might be covered with slices of bacon, a practice that is still recommended today.

A roast chicken looks and tastes best when the skin is good and crispy, but not of course when it gets dried out; Grandma avoided that by flicking drops of water onto the bird with the fingertips and then spreading these around with a feather to keep the skin from drying out during the second half of the cooking period. As soon as the skin had reached the desired crispness, the bird was removed from the oven and covered with a large upturned bowl to keep it from cooling off too much while awaiting the carving knife (the bowl was warmed first by immersing it in boiling water). The bird was invariably allowed to "rest" for at least 10 minutes to give the juices a chance to be absorbed back into the meat so they wouldn't come streaming out as soon as the carving knife was inserted.

Nineteenth-century cookbooks invariably recommend that a chicken, no matter how it's going to be prepared, should be soaked first in lukewarm water, then in cold water to make it as juicy and tender as possible.

LOWER RHINE REGION

Stuffed Pullet   Gefüllte Hühnchen

The birds originally called for in this recipe were small pullets, or in other words, extremely small chickens. This was before the days of modern assembly-line poultry farming, when the homemaker might have to choose between the tough old rooster, best fitted for the stewpot, and an undersized pullet whose flesh was tender enough for roasting but far less abundant. This recipe was first published in 1900 in a collection called *The Lower Rhine Cookbook* (containing "the best recipes for the luncheon tables of gentlefolk").

.   .   .   .

"For this recipe, you should only use chickens that would be too small to make a decent meal when roasted by themselves. Make a small cut in the skin of the breast, starting up at the neck and moving downward, then insert the blade of a little knife and very carefully detach the skin from the breast on either side of the cut. Then, by blowing through the quill of a feather, lift up this loose skin from the flesh of the breast, thus creating an empty space which you can fill up with the dressing of your choice. If the skin is still too tight, you can work it loose with the blade of a very thin knife, taking great care not to break the skin in any other place.

"Be sure to use enough dressing so that the skin is stretched taut, yet not so much so that it is likely to burst; the flap of loose skin at the neck can be readily sewn up with a few stitches, and then the pullet is ready for roasting."

NOTES: Readers interested in experimenting with this method should seek out an especially scrawny supermarket chicken and they may find it more convenient to use a plastic drinking straw to inflate the skin, rather than the "quill of a feather."

For the forcemeat, I like to use ground veal mixed up with some ground bacon, a little grated lemon peel, salt, and pepper.

CENTRAL RHINE REGION

Stuffed Roasting Chicken Gefülltes Brathuhn

Here is a dish I remember being served many times as a child while on Rhineland excursions with my parents. The stuffing was not only delicious but (as I came to realize later) also served as a kind of low-cost "extender" for the restaurateur, since a roasting chicken was still pretty expensive in those days.

. . . .

To prepare the chicken for roasting, dry it off thoroughly after washing, then rub it with salt and pepper inside and out.

Remove the crusts from the rolls, cut the rolls into slices, and soak these in water to soften. Press down firmly to remove the excess moisture and mix this with the eggs, seasonings, and grated lemon peel to make a smooth stuffing. Whip 2 heaping tablespoons of butter until creamy and then mix thoroughly with the stuffing.

Preheat the oven to 350°F. Stuff the bird and sew up the cavity. Roast, for about 1½ hours (20 minutes per pound), basting frequently with the remaining butter and accumulated juices. The bird is customarily cut in half, lengthwise, with poultry shears and then opened up like an oyster; the stuffing is cut into thick slices and served as a garnish for the chicken slices.

MAKES 4 SERVINGS

1 large (4½ pounds) roaster
Salt and freshly ground white pepper
3 kaiser rolls
2 eggs
1 tablespoon chopped fresh parsley
Pinch of dried basil
Grated nutmeg
Grated peel of ½ lemon
3 tablespoons butter

Chicken with Rice Huhn mit Reis

This popular recipe from the old days seems to have evolved in two different directions in recent years—either downgraded into a slushy chicken-and-rice soup or "upgraded," thanks to the lavish use of turmeric and other exotic spices, into an *ersatz* chicken curry. The following recipe dates from the nineteenth century and is not only authentic but also has a

1 good-size chicken, not too elderly (4 or more pounds)
1 medium onion
1 carrot, peeled
1 celery stalk
Salt
10 peppercorns
1 bay leaf
1 quart stock (preferably made from veal bones or rich chicken stock)
2¼ cups uncooked long-grain rice
1 small onion stuck with 2 cloves
3½ tablespoons butter
2 tablespoons flour
4 egg yolks
Freshly ground white pepper to taste

very distinguished pedigree, since it was devised by the master chef to one of the noble houses of Germany.

It was customary to garnish this dish with little crescents of puff pastry called *Fleurons,* shaped something like miniature croissants, which look very elegant and taste good as well. Serve with a green salad.

•   •   •   •   •   •   •   •   •

Wash and prepare the chicken. Wash and chop the onion, carrot, and celery. Place them in a large pot with the chicken; add the salt, peppercorns, and bay leaf. Pour in the stock until the chicken is well covered. Slowly bring to a boil, skim the surface, and simmer about 1½ hours. Remove the chicken from the pot and cut into at least 8 serving pieces; keep warm. Strain the broth and reserve it.

Wash and drain the rice; transfer to a medium-size saucepan. Add the clove-studded onion to the saucepan, along with a little salt and ½ tablespoon butter. Add enough broth to cover the rice by about 2 or 3 finger's breadths. Bring to a boil, stir, cover, and allow to absorb the broth over very low heat for about 20 minutes.

In the meantime, heat 2 tablespoons butter in a saucepan, then stir in the flour and cook to make a light roux. Add enough chicken broth to make a light, smooth sauce and allow it to cook for about 20 minutes. Originally, the chicken pieces would have been kept warm in the steam from the sauce, though you may prefer to wrap them in well-buttered aluminum foil and keep them warm in the oven. To keep the sauce from having a floury taste, cook for the full 20 minutes, then remove from heat, season with white pepper, and beat the egg yolks and remaining tablespoon of butter into the sauce so it is smooth and glistening.

Remove the onion from the rice and place it in a mound on a serving dish; arrange the chicken pieces around it and pour the sauce over both the chicken and rice.

MAKES 4 SERVINGS

Bremen-Style Chicken Stew/Berlin-Style Chicken Fricassee
Bremer Kükenragout/Berliner Hühnerfrikassee

These are two local variations on the same basic recipe. Both originated in the kitchens of the prosperous urban middle classes and in recent years have largely disappeared from the repertory, mostly because the prosperous middle classes are currently more interested in *nouvelle* French than old-time German cuisine. Be that as it may, these two recipes are heartily recommended to lovers of good food whatever their party affiliations; Cordon Bleu chefs among my readers are also advised that both these dishes can even be made with high-cost, high-quality *poulet de Bresse* (shorter cooking time!).

. . . .

Wash the hen thoroughly and scrub the veal tongue with a brush; chop the carrot, leek, and celery, then place all the above plus the bay leaf and peppercorns in a generous amount of salted water and cook for about 1½ hours, or until the chicken is just tender but not about to fall off the bones.

While the chicken and tongue are still cooking, you can be preparing all vegetables, as well as the sweetbread. The sweetbread should be soaked in water for about 15 minutes, then parboiled in a little barely simmering vinegar water for 5 minutes. Remove it from the water, remove the tough membranes and blood vessels from the surface of the sweetbread, then cook it in salted water for about 12 minutes; the water should not be allowed to come to a boil. Remove it from the water and drain, then press it between 2 small cutting boards with a weight of some kind on top; this should make it a little easier to cut the sweetbread into slices when it has cooled off. Set this aside for the moment.

In a skillet heat 2 tablespoons butter and sauté the mushrooms. Salt lightly and set aside.

1 4½-pound stewing hen (fowl)
1 fresh, precooked, or pickled veal tongue
1 carrot, peeled
1 leek
1 stalk celery
1 bay leaf
10 peppercorns
2 large or 4 small veal bratwursts
1 sweetbread
1 tablespoon vinegar
5 tablespoons butter
2 cups fresh mushrooms, washed and halved or quartered
Salt
½ pound asparagus (preferably white; tinned asparagus may be used), trimmed
Pinch of sugar
½ cup dried morels
2 tablespoons flour
2–3 tablespoons lemon juice
1 cup white wine
2 egg yolks
½ cup heavy cream
8 Fleurons (or miniature puff pastry crescents)

Cook the asparagus in salted water to which a pinch of sugar has been added. Cut it into pieces 2 inches long.

Soak the morels and wash thoroughly. Cook them in just a little bit of stock.

Remove the chicken and the veal tongue from the broth, then cook the bratwursts in the broth for about 10 minutes. Skin the tongue and cut it into bite-size cubes. Take the chicken meat off the bones and cut it into bite-size pieces; place both in a little of the strained broth and keep warm. When the bratwursts are ready, remove the casings and cut into ¾-inch thick slices, which should be kept warm in the broth along with the chicken pieces and veal tongue.

Heat 3 tablespoons butter in a large heavy-bottomed, non-reactive saucepan, add the flour, cook to make a light roux, then add in 2 cups chicken broth. Add the lemon juice and white wine and cook for a good 15 minutes. Stir the egg yolks into the cream with a whisk and add this mixture to thicken the sauce. Do not allow the sauce to boil.

Cut the sweetbread into bite-size pieces.

Add all the other prepared ingredients to the sauce, which should not be allowed to come to a boil again, and cook until everything is heated through. Garnish with *Fleurons,* if available.

VARIATIONS: The recipes for the Bremen version of this dish always call for a young pullet, but an older "fowl," or stewing hen, can really be just as good.

Customarily a number of other ingredients can also be added to the ragout/fricassee (some of them not unreminiscent of *la nouvelle cuisine*), including artichoke bottoms, pistachio nuts (shelled), and chopped anchovies (in the Bremen version), crayfish tails, and stuffed crayfish "snouts" (see recipe for Crayfish Soup, page 98) and Semolina Dumplings (Griessklösse, pages 309–10) as a garnish (in the Berlin version). Both versions can easily benefit from the addition of a little crayfish butter.

MAKES 8–10 SERVINGS

HAMBURG

Baby Chicken Hamburger Stubenküken

Here we have another German specialty of truly world–class caliber. This dish is thought to have originated not in Hamburg itself but in the little fishing villages along the banks of the Elbe, where, as the story has it, the fishermen used to bring the baby chicks (Küken) indoors to keep them safe from winter weather. A *Stube* is a room, with an extra connotation of closeness, stuffiness, enforced intimacy, as might be experienced in a tavern or, in this case, a one-room fisherman's cottage with a flock of half-grown *Stubenküken* scurrying underfoot. Nowadays, however, *Stubenküken* have come up in the world and are only to be found in the most exclusive restaurants in Hamburg and the surrounding countryside. *Stubenküken* are customarily served on fried bread, though baby peas or other "fancy" vegetables are also a possibility.

4 baby chickens or
  Cornish hens (1¼
  pounds each)
  Salt and freshly
  ground white pepper
4 tablespoons butter
2 medium onions,
  diced
2 cups fresh
  mushrooms, washed
  and thinly sliced
¼–½ pound chicken livers
2 tablespoons fresh
  bread crumbs
2 eggs
  Large pinch of fresh
  or dried crushed
  basil
2 tablespoons cream
1 cup chicken stock

Wash the chickens and dry thoroughly. Rub them with salt and pepper inside and out and let sit for 1 hour.

In the meantime, prepare the stuffing. In a skillet melt 2 tablespoons butter and sauté the onions and mushrooms until the onions are just barely translucent. Add the chicken livers to the skillet, stirring constantly, and cook until they are firm.

Allow the contents of the skillet to cool for a little while, then finely chop the cooked onions, mushrooms, and chicken livers and knead together, with the liquids and remaining fat from the skillet, the fresh bread crumbs, eggs, basil, and cream. If this mixture is too soft to be readily kneaded, add more bread crumbs. Season to taste with pepper and a healthy pinch of salt.

Preheat the oven to 475°F. Stuff the chickens and close up the cavity with long wooden toothpicks. Baste with 2 tablespoons melted butter and roast; after 10 minutes, reduce heat to about 400°. Baste the chickens again with butter and pour the stock over the chicken. Total cooking time is 30 to 40 minutes; you may want to cover the chickens with greased parchment paper. Baste the chickens often.

MAKES 4 SERVINGS

Chicken Stew Made with Roast Chicken
Braunes Geflügelragout

3 tablespoons butter
2 tablespoons chopped onions
2 tablespoons flour
2 cups beef stock
¼ cup dry Port
2 thick lemon slices (including the peel)
2 bay leaves
Salt and freshly ground black pepper
Dash or two of wine vinegar
1¼ pounds roast chicken (just the meat), cut into bite-size pieces

This dish would have been made with leftovers in the old days; today one of its great advantages is that a ready-made roast chicken can be picked up at the market or butcher shop, and the sauce can be made in advance and reheated, so that last-minute preparation time is reduced to a minimum. Just serve with bread as an appetizer or late-night snack, or with noodles or mashed potatoes as a main dish.

•   •   •   •   •   •   •   •   •

Melt the butter in a non-reactive heavy-bottomed saucepan; add the chopped onions and cook until translucent. Add the flour and cook the roux until golden brown. Pour in the beef stock and red wine. Add lemon slices, bay leaves, salt and pepper. Allow the sauce to cook for about 20 minutes, stirring occasionally, then pour through a fine strainer, test for seasoning, add vinegar and salt or pepper. Add the chicken pieces and heat over a low flame.

MAKES 4 SERVINGS

Roast Goose   Gänsebraten

Goose has always been regarded as a particularly German specialty, especially in Mecklenburg and Pomerania in the northeast. Nowadays, all over Germany the Christmas dinner consists of *Gänsebraten* (roast goose). A certain Herr von Seld, a "moral philosopher" who had embarked on a lecture tour of these two provinces around the middle of the previous century, philosophically recounted that

> . . . on one occasion I was served a fat roast goose every day, twice a day, for three entire weeks, since the good countrymen who were my hosts could none of them conceive of anything finer that they could possibly have served me. Moreover, as I continued on my travels, it does not seem to have occurred to anyone that I could have fed on anything else—or indeed that everyone else might not have had the same conception.

Southerners like Goethe, who was from Frankfurt, were generally more temperate in their enthusiasm. Goethe never wrote a poem on the subject of roast goose, though his biographers record that he always helped himself to an extra-large portion, and the Austrian novelist Adalbert Stifter, one of the first to celebrate the joys and pleasures of rural life, confided to his diary that after he and his wife had consumed "a splendid goose" between them, they turned their attention to "a mighty ham" at their next meal. On the other hand, the minor poet Joseph von Lauff did devote one whole canto of his pastoral epic of life in the Moselle valley to a discussion of the

Martingans, or "St. Martin's goose," which includes such lines as these:

The year was good, the wine is in the butt,	*Das Jahr war gut, der Wein geraten,*
The misty Moselle valley shimmers in the dusk,	*Das Moseltal voll Nebelglanz,*
From all directions comes the delicate	*Und allwärts duftete der Braten*
Aroma of roast goose on Martinmas.	*Der delikaten Martingans.*

This sounds a little less silly in German than it does in English; the basic idea is that most of the geese were raised by tenant farmers who paid their yearly rent (including one goose out of every ten) to the local squire on November 11, which is Martinmas, or St. Martin's Day. This was also a time when geese were very plentiful on the open market, hence a very good time to invest in one. For the thrifty consumer who was eager to recoup as much of his investment as possible, a farmer's almanac published in 1900 suggests a couple of homemade "toys that the goose can provide the children." For example:

. . . if you put a couple of peas inside the gullet while it is still moist and supple, then fasten the ends together, and hang it up to dry, you will have made yourself a very fine baby's rattle. Also, when the wishbone is dried out, if you fasten the two ends together tightly with a double loop of twine and insert a short stick through the twine, then you have a wind-up "jumper toy" that will leap about on the table as merrily as a grasshopper in the meadow in the summertime.

Below you will find some favorite stuffings for roast goose, which are equally as good for American domestic duck or even turkey. Don't forget to reduce or increase the quantities accordingly.

"Please, that's what it says in the cookbook!" (original engraving by H. Merté)

Apple Stuffing Apfelfüllung

The apples should be tart and firm-fleshed (i.e., Granny Smith), and can be used whole or coarsely chopped; they taste especially good if the stem and cores are removed, but the skins are left on. Precooked, peeled chestnuts or raisins that have been soaked in brandy can also be mixed in with the apples, as well as finely chopped onions that have been sautéed in butter or goose fat until translucent. In either case, the inside of the goose should be rubbed with a mixture of salt, pepper, and a little sage beforehand. Good proportions would be: 1 part onion, 1 part chestnut or raisins, and 3 parts apples.

Potato Stuffing   Kartoffelfüllung

Peel and wash 3–4 medium potatoes, then cut them into ½-inch cubes. Cook them for about 5 minutes in salted water, then drain. Sauté the heart and liver of the goose or duck in butter, along with 1 or 2 tablespoons of minced onion until the onion becomes translucent. Combine the contents of the skillet with the potatoes and 3 tablespoons chopped parsley, season with salt and crushed, dried marjoram, and fill the cavity of the bird with this mixture.

BERLIN

"Testament" Stuffing   Füllung "Testament"

The name of this traditional stuffing recipe is equally cryptic in German or English; this particular version, perhaps the original, dates from 1904.

"Take enough grated black bread to cover a whole plate, as much again of chopped apple, a little sugar, and as many sultana raisins, thoroughly washed, as you would care to add, then mix together and stuff the goose with all these in the usual way."

BADEN

Steinbach Stuffing   Steinbacher Füllung

The master chef Alfred Walterspiel, who grew up in the little town of Steinbach (now part of the city of Baden–Baden), learned this recipe from his mother. He recommends this stuffing for turkey, but this has also been our favorite goose stuffing in the Scharfenberg family for a number of years now.

· · · · · · · · ·

   "My mother used 2 tablespoons of finely chopped goose cracklings, 1½ to 2 pounds of chestnuts (softened by parboiling in milk), 3 or 4 peeled ripe apples, cored, cut into thin strips, and then cooked like fried potatoes, ½ teaspoon chopped rosemary, the finely chopped liver of the bird, a few shallots, the forcemeat from 2 pork sausages [bratwurst], and a whole beaten egg, salted and seasoned very carefully."

MAKES STUFFING FOR 1 LARGE GOOSE OR TURKEY

2 tablespoons goose cracklings
1½–2 pounds chestnuts
3–4 Granny Smith apples
½ teaspoon finely chopped dried rosemary
2 finely chopped shallots
1 goose liver
2 bratwurst
1 egg

RHINELAND

Goose with Pearl Barley   Gans mit Graupen

This was a very popular recipe before the First World War, especially suitable for the old patriarchs of the flock that no amount of roasting could tenderize. This particular version comes from a handwritten collection dating from 1905; "a very tasty dish," notes the author, "also quite economical"— since a tough old gander could generally be had at bargain prices—"and can also be made with the giblets." At the other end from the tough old ganders were the very tenderest goslings, called *Stoppelgänschen,* "pinfeather goslings," a category that no longer exists today. These, as *The Lower Rhine Cookbook* explains, were "very young goslings, no more than ten

1 6-pound goose
1 onion, sliced
1 bay leaf
1 cup pearl barley
Salt and pepper
1–2 tablespoons rendered goose fat (schmalz)

to fourteen weeks old, which should be roasted with butter, like ducks, since they have so little fat of their own."

•   •   •   •   •   •   •   •   •   •   •

Wash the goose and cut into 8 or 10 serving pieces. Simmer for 2 hours in salted water with the onion and bay leaf until the goose is quite tender (i.e., the point of a knife goes in without resistance).

At the same time, cook the pearl barley in a small amount of water until it cooks down to thick paste. Salt it lightly. Remove the goose pieces from the water. Stir the liquefied goose fat into the pearl barley, add the goose pieces, and cook over very low heat for another 30 minutes. Add salt and pepper if necessary.

MAKES 8 SERVINGS

POMERANIA,   MECKLENBURG,
BERLIN

Geese in Aspic, or "Vinegar Geese"
Gänsesülze oder Gänseweissauer

Dark meat from 2 geese (all meat but the breasts)
Giblets plus 3 or 4 additional goose drumsticks
3 split calves' feet (optional, see Note)
4 cloves
2 bay leaves
1 large onion
2 carrots, peeled and halved
12 peppercorns
Salt
1 quart water
½–1 cup vinegar
Large pinch of sugar

This dish is called "geese" rather than "goose" in aspic because it really should be made in substantial quantities to repay the substantial effort involved. The quantities suggested below should yield about 10 or 12 portions, and this dish keeps very well and makes for delicious leftovers later on. Accompany the geese with fried potatoes and a green salad as well as mixed pickles (chow-chow) as a garnish or condiment.

•   •   •   •   •   •   •   •   •   •

Wash the goose pieces and the calves' feet very thoroughly. Using the cloves pin the bay leaves into the onion. Put these along with the goose, calves' feet, carrots, peppercorns, and salt in the water and simmer for at least 2 hours. Remove the goose meat from the broth after about an hour, or as soon as it's thoroughly cooked; remove the carrots and set aside; after 2 hours discard the onion and the calves' feet.

Separate the meat from the goose pieces and cut into large pieces. Dice the carrots. Place the meat and carrots in a rectangular terrine or casserole dish. Season the broth with vinegar and sugar so it has a sweet-sour taste, and pour it over the contents of the terrine. Chill in the refrigerator until set. *Gänsesülze* should be cut up into serving slices.

NOTE: The calves' feet can actually be dispensed with if you prefer. Substitute 2 heaping tablespoons powdered gelatin mixed with cold water and stir this in the simmering broth at the very end. (The traditional means of safeguarding the leftovers, by the way, was to pour beef suet over the aspic, which would harden into a thick protective layer that could easily be removed later on.)

MAKES 10–12 SERVINGS

MECKLENBURG

Goose Liverwurst Gänseleberwurst

Here's a recipe that originated on a great estate in Mecklenburg. It is a dish that is far too good to be allowed to fade from memory. Though goose livers may have been far more plentiful in Mecklenburg, chicken livers may be substituted if you prefer. The original recipe calls for goose necks, but more conventional sausage casings (pork intestines) may be a bit more practical. You can also dispense with the packaging entirely and store this delicious homemade *Leberwurst* in sterilized mason jars.

.   .   .   .

Cook the pork in salted water until tender. Soak the livers in cold water for several hours, dry them, chop them finely, combine them with the liquefied goose fat (schmalz), and press this through a fine strainer. Cut the pork into small pieces; adjust the meat grinder or food mill to its finest setting, and put the pork through twice, along with the onion and goose fat (in case you're using raw goose fat instead of

2 pounds fresh pork belly or other fatty pork
3½ pounds goose, duck, or chicken livers
¼ pound goose fat (or schmalz, liquid goose fat)
1 medium onion, quartered
Freshly ground black pepper
½ teaspoon crushed allspice berries
1 teaspoon crushed marjoram
½ teaspoon sugar
1 tablespoon salt
Goose necks or sausage casings, cleaned

schmalz). Combine all the ingredients in a mixing bowl, add the spices, and knead this together into a stuffing mixture of uniform consistency.

Fill the goose necks—or sausage casings—though not too tightly and tie off the ends. (The sausage casings in particular should be very thoroughly washed beforehand.) Place the *Leberwurst* in a generous amount of water, bring gradually to a boil, and simmer gently for about 30 minutes. Cool in cold water.

MAKES 6 POUNDS WURST

BRANDENBURG

Duck with Turnips   Ente mit Rüben

1 duckling, 2–3 pounds
1–2 tablespoons butter
2 tablespoons flour
1 teaspoon sugar
    Salt
1 large onion, sliced
3 cups water
2 drops gravy browning
1 pound white turnips,
    washed, peeled, and
    sliced
    Pinch of baking soda
    Freshly ground white
    pepper

This is from a handwritten recipe in the possession of a Berlin family that originally came from the Mark Brandenburg region (the historic part of the Kingdom of Prussia, of which Berlin was the capital).

•   •   •   •   •   •   •   •

Cut the duck into 8 serving pieces. Fry them in butter and brown on all sides; into the pan sprinkle flour, sugar, and ½ teaspoon salt. Add the onion slices to the pan and sauté them. When the flour is lightly browned, add the water, mixing well with the pan juices, and color with a little gravy browning.

Parboil the turnips very briefly 3 to 5 minutes, in water to which a pinch of baking soda has been added. Drain, run water over the turnip slices to cool them, and place them in the skillet with the duck pieces. The duck and turnip slices should simmer, covered, over moderate heat for about 1 hour, or until both are tender. Season to taste with salt and pepper; you may want to take off the cover for the last 15 minutes or so to reduce the liquid to the consistency of a sauce.

MAKES 4 SERVINGS

LOWER SAXONY

Duck with Savoy Cabbage   Ente in Wirsing

Serve with potatoes boiled in salted water or small new potatoes boiled in their jackets, peeled and fried afterwards.

.   .   .   .

Clean, wash, and dry off the duck, inside and out. Melt the
butter in a large skillet and rapidly sear the duck on all sides,
then remove it from the pan.

Lay out the strips of bacon on the bottom of the skillet (do
not pour out the remaining pan juices, however). Rub the
duck inside and out with salt and pepper and place on top of
the bacon strips, with the breast side upward.

Wash the savoy cabbage and press dry. Cut the 2 cabbage
heads in half and cut away the thick ribs, though the leaves
should still be attached to one another. Cut it into quarters if
these fit better in the skillet. Sprinkle a little salt between the
leaves and place the cabbage with the duck in the skillet. Carefully pour in the water, cover, and cook for at least 1½ hours
over moderate heat.

MAKES 6 SERVINGS

*1 meaty duck, about 4
   pounds*
*2 tablespoons butter
   Several slices fresh bacon
   (or smoked bacon that
   has been blanched in
   boiling water)
   Salt and freshly ground
   black pepper*
2 savoy cabbages
1 cup water

CENTRAL GERMANY

Duck with Pomegranate Juice
Ente mit Pomeranzensaft

Nowadays, roast duck that's still a bit pink inside is considered the last word *(der letzte Schrei,* in fact) in German
culinary circles. Admirers of *nouvelle* cuisine might be interested in the following recipe from a trendy little compendium

1 duck, 3½–4 pounds
  Salt
  Freshly ground pepper
  Juice of 2 pomegranates

entitled *The Magdeburg Cookbook for Beginning Housewives, Housekeepers, and Cooks,* first published in 1795:

• • • • • • • • •

"Leave the duck to turn on the spit until it is halfway done, then put it in a bowl, cut the meat into long strips, though without detaching it from the duck. Put salt, ground pepper, and the juice of two pomegranates in the bowl, turn the duck around in this, then press down on it with a plate, turn it around again [in the juice], and serve in its still-warm juices."

NOTES: If straight pomegranate juice is not readily available, substitute grenadine or some other liqueur that has pomegranate flavoring in it, mixed with a little orange peel; rub this mixture into the skin of the duck. Freshly ground green peppercorns are also very good in this recipe.

Instead of a bowl, transfer the duck from the roasting pan into a large skillet that has been well greased with butter and sprinkle with the pomegranate juice (or grenadine), so that none of the juice goes to waste. Also, the thigh and drumsticks should be cooked for an extra 5 minutes in the skillet. Mix the rest of the pomegranate juice or liqueur with a little of the clear cooking juices from the roasting pan to make a little bit of sauce for the duck. It will yield only about 2 or 3 tablespoons of sauce per person.

MAKES 4 SERVINGS

Beef, Veal, and Pork

. . . .

The early Germans believed, as do many modern ones, that beef makes you strong—and it is certainly true that a bull, or even a cow, makes much more of an impression than a chicken or a sheep. Lately, we have learned that in fact it is possible to eat too much red meat, though this was rarely a problem for our medieval forebears. Next to scarcity and the threat of starvation, the biggest problem was spoilage.

In the Middle Ages, large amounts of spices were used and people put up salt pork in casks (later a great convenience for long-distance mariners as well), cured beef in brine (a process that came to be called "corning"), smoked bacon, and preserved all sorts of things in the form of sausages. For the gentry and the peasantry alike, wild game provided a welcome relief from grain and gruel during the long, hungry intervals between hog-butchering days.

Pork has always had a special place of honor in the German larder. As far as per capita consumption figures for the Federal Republic are concerned—an astounding 190 pounds of meat are consumed annually, of which 110 pounds are pork. No less an authority than Wilhelm Busch assures us that the pig may not cut quite as attractive a figure as the bull (or even the sheep or the chicken) but it is still to be esteemed for its inner qualities:

The clever man reveres the hog,	*Ein kluger Mann verehrt das Schwein,*
In this he's not mistaken;	*Er denkt an dessen Zweck,*
His outer husk *is* rather odd,	*Von Außen ist es ja nicht fein,*
But therein lies the bacon.	*Doch drinnen sitzt der Speck.*

Bifflamot

This is, or was, a generic term for a kind of pot roast or stewed beef that was (usually) cooked in red wine, a very popular dish in the southwest especially. The name itself, as you may have guessed, is a corruption of *boeuf à la mode,* though the dish itself seems to have been prepared pretty much *à la mode,* anyway, and a great many variants on the basic recipe have come down to us.

South of the river Main,* the roast was often steeped in vinegar—thus making it a variety of sauerbraten as well—and served with wheat-flour dumplings. In Bavaria, the name was often spelled *Böfflamot,* and the roast was always larded with bacon, usually marinated in a little vinegar beforehand and served with a dark, rich red wine sauce.

The basic idea of *Bifflamot* seems to have been borrowed from the French in the decades after the Thirty Years' War (1618–48), in the course of which more than a third of the population of Germany is thought to have succumbed to famine, pestilence, and other horrors of war, and *Bifflamot* was eagerly embraced by the German burgher as a comforting symbol of postwar prosperity and contentment. It was still the favorite *bürgerlich* Sunday dinner two centuries later, though more frequently under the German name of *Schmorbraten* (pot roast) than *Bifflamot.*

Boeuf à la Mode

This recipe was included in a collection called *New Comprehensible Cookbook,* published in Quedlinburg in 1819; apart from the title of the recipe itself, it uses a couple of French cooking

* The so-called Main (pronounced "Mīne," as in "yours and mine") Line serves much the same function in Germany as the Mason-Dixon Line in the United States.

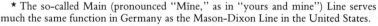

terms that would probably be less comprehensible to most German cooks today.

• • • • • • • • • • •

"Take a nice rump steak [round steak] or a cut off the joint, pound until tender, and lard [wrap] with strips of bacon about 5 inches long and ½ inch wide, which have already been dredged in a mixture of salt, pepper, cloves, finely chopped shallots, and thyme. Then place slices of ham, bacon, and onion with [2 tablespoons] butter in a casserole or stewing pot and cook until golden brown, set the meat on top of these and likewise cook over a gentle flame until golden brown. Pour over the good *jus* [i.e., rich beef stock], add some salt, and cook over a gentle flame for 3 or 4 hours, or until the liquid clings to the meat like a heavy syrup. Then remove the meat, lay it down in another casserole, and take from the first one all the fat that remains [i.e., skim off the fat from the juices in the original casserole]. Take some *jus* or *coulis* (see Note) and [1 tablespoon] lemon juice, bring to a boil, strain through a hair [fine] sieve over the meat, then allow to cook for another half hour and serve immediately."

NOTE: *Jus* or *coulis* is also known as *Fleischsauce,* beef broth mixed with flour that has been lightly browned in butter, considerably reduced to make a thick gravy. Use the well-skimmed cooking broth to make the *jus.*

MAKES 6–8 SERVINGS

2 pounds round steak
1 teaspoon salt
2 teaspoons freshly
  ground pepper
  Pinch of ground cloves
4 tablespoons finely
  chopped shallots
1 teaspoon finely
  chopped thyme
1 pound sliced bacon
  (use ½–¾ pound to
  wrap roast)
½ pound ham cut in ⅛"
  slices
1 medium onion, finely
  chopped
4 tablespoons butter
3–4 cups rich beef stock
2 tablespoons flour
1 tablespoon lemon juice

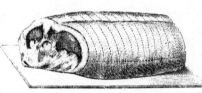

RHINELAND

Rheinischer Sauerbraten

Here is one version of a dish that's very popular throughout Germany, and indeed all over the world. The raisins are often omitted, though they're one of the main things that distinguish this "Rhenish" sauerbraten from other varieties. The original point of the marinade, of course, was to make the

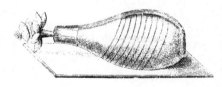

MARINADE:
1 carrot, peeled and
    finely chopped
1 celery stalk, finely
    chopped
½ leek, finely chopped
1 onion, finely chopped
2 whole cloves
1 bay leaf
6 peppercorns
6 juniper berries
1½ cups red wine
¼ cup wine vinegar

BEEF:
1¾ pounds beef shoulder
    or rump
    Salt and freshly
    ground black pepper
1 tablespoon butter
3 tablespoons raisins

GRAVY:
1 tablespoon lard
1 tablespoon flour

dish stay fresh longer, though nowadays we're more concerned with the taste. Sophisticated shoppers need hardly be told that the sauerbraten sold in butcher shops, already marinated, normally starts out with beef that is very tough indeed.

Sauerbraten is customarily accompanied by potato dumplings or by a kind of crispy potato pancake called *Reibekuchen*, or *Rievekooche*.

•   •   •   •   •   •   •   •   •

In a stainless steel or non-reactive pot combine all the marinade ingredients. Bring the marinade to a boil; allow it to cool.

Wash the beef and place it in a bowl small enough that the meat is totally immersed when you pour the liquid (including the spices and chopped vegetables) over it. Marinate for 3 to 5 days, turning the meat occasionally in the marinade.

Remove the beef from the marinade, dry off with paper towels, and sprinkle with salt and pepper. Melt the butter in a large casserole pot and brown the beef on all sides. Pour in the marinade (still including the solid ingredients), cover, and stew over low heat for 1½ hours. Then remove the beef from the casserole and pour the sauce through a fine strainer. Return both beef and sauce to the casserole. Wash the raisins and add these to the casserole.

Melt the lard in a small skillet saucepan; add the flour and cook the roux until brown; stir in 1 cup of the cooking liquid to make a smooth sauce. Pour this sauce back in with the beef, mixing it with any remaining cooking liquid in the casserole. Cook over low heat for an additional 15 minutes. Cut the beef into slices and serve on a platter with a little of the sauce poured over it; serve the rest of the sauce in a gravy boat or a separate bowl.

MAKES 6 SERVINGS

WESTPHALIA

Beef Hot Pot with Pepper   Pfeffer-Potthast

This is a traditional Westphalian specialty of very long standing; it made its first recorded appearance in an inventory of foodstuffs sold by vendors in the Dortmund market square some time during the thirteenth century and is still served at municipal banquets and other official functions in Dortmund. *Potthast* means "fleshpot." As with most traditional specialties, there are a great many different recipes to choose from. In this one, the beef is not seared in the skillet beforehand, which is the usual practice nowadays though not strictly authentic. Serve with potatoes boiled in salted water, half-sour pickles, dills, or spicy gherkins, and pickled beets. Also, nothing brings out the flavor of *Potthast* like a good German beer.

•   •   •   •   •   •   •   •   •   •

Place the beef cubes, onions, spices, and lemon slices in a large heavy-bottomed pot; the pepper should be as coarsely ground as you can manage and applied with a liberal hand. Add the water or stock until the beef cubes are well covered. Mix well and cook over low heat for 1 hour, stirring frequently and adding more liquid if necessary.

Add the bread crumbs and zwieback crumbs and cook for an additional 20 minutes. Remove the bay leaves and lemon slices. Taste for seasoning. The gravy should be thick and very spicy; add more lemon juice, salt, or allspice if desired.

VARIATIONS: Feel free to toss a (modest) handful of capers into the stewpot—another inauthentic but otherwise commendable innovation. Likewise, browning the beef in the skillet before it goes into the stew results in a more flavorful "twice-cooked *Potthast*."

On the other hand, using flour instead of bread crumbs to thicken the gravy, which is also more in line with contemporary practice, is not recommended. You can leave out the zwieback crumbs, however, and just add more bread crumbs plus a pinch of sugar.

Many cooks like to use a mixture of beef and pork for the

1¾ pounds well-marbled beef, cut into ¾"–1" cubes
3 medium onions, half thinly sliced and half finely chopped or grated
1 level teaspoon salt
2–3 tablespoons coarsely ground (or cracked) black pepper
⅓ teaspoon allspice
2 bay leaves
3–4 lemon slices, including peel
2–3 cups water or beef stock
1 tablespoon bread crumbs
2 tablespoons zwieback crumbs (see Variations)
Lemon juice (optional)

stewing meat, which makes good sense from a historical standpoint, since the old-time Westphalians undoubtedly went in more for raising hogs than beef cattle. More to the point, however, this provides a little textural variety, though of course the heartier flavor of the beef still tends to predominate.

Caraway seeds may also be added to the list of spices, though they tend to dominate the other flavors unless applied very sparingly.

MAKES 4–6 SERVINGS

Swiss Steak, Braised Sirloin
Mürbbraten auf Teutsch

2 pounds beef for pot roast
1 teaspoon minced fresh parsley
1 teaspoon dried basil "As much crushed sage as will fit on the point of a knife"
8 strips sliced bacon
Salt
2 tablespoons butter
½–1 cup cream
1–2 tablespoons capers

This recipe for German-style Braised Sirloin dates from 1790, but I have restored it to correspond closely to the standard modern method of preparing Swiss steak. This recipe is unusual in that the steak is larded and braised in its own drippings, a method that does not involve water or any additional cooking fat, so that all the cooking juices are retained for the gravy. In Germany, this dish would nowadays be prepared with a less formidable cut called the *Blume,* which—as can be seen from the picture of the cow on page 207—corresponds more closely to a rump steak.

•   •   •   •   •   •   •   •   •

Wash the meat and carefully trim all bits of skin, fat, and gristle. Do not discard the fat. Mix the herbs and dredge the bacon strips in this mixture, then use them to lard (wrap) the steak on all sides. If necessary, use a toothpick to secure them. Place the steak in a heavy iron skillet, salt lightly, and put the scraps and trimmings in with the steak so they will help to enrich the gravy.

Cover tightly and seal the lid shut with flour-and-water paste. (Owners of a pan with a tight-fitting lid will find it an easier alternative.) Set over a very low fire and cook for 4 hours. When you take off the lid, you will see how nicely the juices have accumulated in the pot.

Clarify the butter in a small saucepan (i.e., pour off the clear liquid and leave the milky residue). Add in the cream, capers, and the pot liquid, and stir. You may want to add a little salt and cook for a few minutes till heated through. Serve as a gravy for the steak.

MAKES 4 SERVINGS

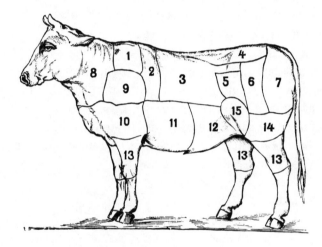

W E S T P H A L I A

1. *Mürbekamm* (boneless neck)
2. *Fehlrippe* (middle rib and chuck)
3. *Roastbeef* (short loin)
4. *Filet*
5. *Blume* (part of sirloin)
6. *Mittelschwanzstück, Schmorstück* (part of sirloin)
7. *Schwanzstück* (rump and top round)
8. *Kamm* (neck)
9. *Schaufelstück* (shoulder)
10. *Bug* (brisket)
11. *Nachbrust, Querrippe* (hind brisket or short plate)
12. *Flanke* (flank)
13. *Hesse* (shank)
14. *Unterschwanzstück* (bottom round)
15. *Nuss* (tip of steak); the *Oberschale* (British "top side") is underneath 6 and 7

Beef Braised in Beer   Ochsenfleisch in Bier

This dish should be made with Bavarian beer rather than a Pilsner-style (or American) beer, which would make the sauce too bitter. I've had good results with dark beer and a variety of top-fermented light beer from the Rhineland known as *Alt-Bier,* at least one brand of which should be available in a well-stocked market or delicatessen in North America. Braising in beer is another recommended technique when the tenderness of the meat is in doubt; even the toughest cuts can be successfully brought to heel with this method.

·   ·   ·   ·   ·   ·   ·   ·   ·   ·

2 pounds beef for pot
   roast (shoulder, chuck,
   rump, brisket)
4 slices medium-lean
   bacon
1 large onion, coarsely
   chopped
1 carrot, peeled and
   coarsely chopped
1 bay leaf
12 peppercorns
   Salt and freshly
   ground black pepper
2–3 bottles of beer
2–3 tablespoons vinegar
1 teaspoon corn or cane
   syrup
1–2 tablespoons flour
1 tablespoon butter
   (optional)

First, unless you have a great deal of confidence in your market or butcher, the meat should be pounded energetically to tenderize it. In a pot just large enough to hold the roast but not a great deal larger, lay out the bacon strips and place the meat on top, place the onion, carrot, bay leaf, and peppercorns all around it.

Sprinkle the roast with salt and pepper. Pour the beer (about a third of which can be replaced with water if you prefer) slowly into the pot until the steak is about half submerged. Mix the vinegar with the corn or cane syrup, add it to the pot, and stir until the liquid in the pot is well mixed. Cover the pot tightly and cook for about 2 hours.

Skim off the fat and transfer it to a saucepan. Brown the flour in the fat (add a little butter if the meat is fairly lean and the fat is insufficient for this task). Strain the cooking liquid from the pot and mix with the roux to make a light gravy. Cook for a few more minutes until heated through. Check for seasoning, pour the gravy over the sliced meat, and serve.

MAKES 4–6 SERVINGS

Stuffed Beef Rolls   Rindsrouladen

4 large (6-ounce)
   slices top or bottom
   round
2 teaspoons strong
   mustard
   Freshly ground
   black pepper
8 slices medium-lean
   bacon
2 large gherkins or
   dill pickles, halved
   lengthwise
   Salt
1–2 tablespoons flour

Here is a dish that's very popular all over Germany. There are many different recipes for the filling; this is one of the most common, and it has a very nice spicy tang to it.

·   ·   ·   ·   ·   ·   ·   ·   ·

Lay the beef slices out flat and thinly coat with mustard, then sprinkle them with a little pepper. Place 2 strips of bacon on each slice, then a pickle or gherkin, and roll it up tight. German cooks keep the *Rindsrouladen* from unrolling with little metal clips called *Rouladenklammer,* but ordinary poultry skewers or cooking twine will do as well. Sprinkle lightly with salt and pepper and coat beef rolls in the flour.

Heat the fat in a large stewpot; sauté the onions until trans-

Marketplace, Greifswald, small university town in East Germany (engraving by H. Winkles, after a drawing by Johann Poppel)

lucent; then add the beef rolls, browning them well on all sides. Pour in 1 cup of beef stock, add the carrot, cover, and braise over moderate heat for 2 hours. You may want to add a little more stock from time to time.

Remove the beef rolls from the broth. Stir the cornstarch in a little cold water; add this to the cooking liquid and bring to a boil. You can strain the gravy if you choose, but I prefer to leave the diced vegetables in there.

MAKES 4 SERVINGS

> 2 tablespoons lard,
>   clarified butter, or
>   vegetable oil
> 2 medium onions,
>   finely chopped
> 1–1½ cups beef stock
> 1 large carrot, peeled
>   and diced
> 1 teaspoon cornstarch

WÜRTTEMBERG

Pan-Fried Steak with Onions, Swabian-Style
Schwäbischer Rostbraten

This is a traditional Swabian festive dish, though even in Swabia, not every steak smothered in onions is a bona fide *Schwäbischer Rostbraten.*

·   ·   ·   ·   ·   ·   ·   ·   ·   ·   ·

Tübingen, famous university
town near Stuttgart, Swabia

*4 9-ounce steaks (sirloin,
porterhouse, or
rumpsteak), not too
thickly sliced
Freshly ground black
pepper*
10 slices bacon
*1 tablespoon clarified
butter*
*4 medium onions, thinly
sliced
Salt*
1 tablespoon butter
*1 tablespoon flour
(optional)
Cooked sauerkraut
Cooked spätzle
(page 318)*

Score the edges of the steak all around to keep them from curling up. Sprinkle with pepper on both sides. Cook the bacon in a skillet until quite translucent; remove it from the skillet and set aside. Add the clarified butter to the bacon fat in the pan; fry the onion rings until well browned. Remove them from the skillet and set aside.

Pan-fry the steaks in the remaining fat for about 3 minutes on each side. Sprinkle with salt. Add butter to the skillet and fry for another minute on each side. Arrange the steaks on a heated platter. Return the onion rings and the bacon strips to the skillet and heat them, keeping them separate.

Serve heated sauerkraut on one side of the steak slices and arrange the bacon strips over it; on the other side, serve the warm spätzle and pour the remaining fat from the skillet over it. Place the onion rings on top of the steak slices.

NOTE: Some of the older recipes also suggest that you add a little flour and stock to the pan juices in order to make a brown gravy for the *Rostbraten*.

MAKES 4 SERVINGS

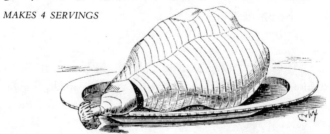

HUNSRÜCK (PALATINATE)

August Görg's Grilled Steak
Spiessbraten August Görg

This recipe originated in the town of Idar-Oberstein during the last century, where the nonculinary specialties of the region were gems and precious stones. Hunsrück prospectors, returning from South America, had already created their own version of gaucho-style grilled steaks, which had become a local specialty. This dish was further refined by my friend and mentor, the late August Görg, into a gourmet delicacy (which, according to his typically exacting specifications, should be made only with steaks cut from a heifer and then hung for at least 3 weeks before being roasted on a spit). Even ordinary steaks prepared by this method taste perfectly delicious, and I have seen otherwise normal individuals put away 3 of them at a sitting with every appearance of pleasure (and with no subsequent regrets). In their native Hunsrück district, the grilled steaks are customarily served with *Bauernbrot* and White Radish Salad (page 211).

PER PERSON:
*1 shallot or small onion,
cut into small pieces
Freshly ground black
pepper
Pinch of mace*
*1 large steak (just over 1
pound), at least 1¼"
thick, trimmed*

· · · · · · · ·

Mix together the shallot or onion with the pepper and mace. Insert a few shallot pieces into the steak using the point of a small knife. Coat the steak with the shallot mixture, pressing it in so it will adhere.

Remove the loose shallot pieces and grill the steak (over a fire of oak logs, says August Görg, from which the bark has been removed).★ Take the steaks off the grill while they are still pink inside. Sprinkle them with salt.

★ NOTE: A special grill is used, suspended with 3 chains from an iron tripod and constantly swinging through the flames.

To Cook a Nice Juicy Steak
Ochsenfleisch Sehr Saftig zu Kochen

1½ pounds rib steak
1 cup vinegar
½ pound caul fat
  Salt
1 tablespoon chopped
  onion
1 tablespoon chopped
  parsley
¼ teaspoon grated lemon
  peel
1 bay leaf
¼ teaspoon marjoram
1 tablespoon olive oil
2 tablespoons beef broth
  Juice of 1 lemon

The title page of my copy of the cookbook from which this recipe is taken is so badly damaged that the title itself is totally undecipherable and the date of publication, 1844, just barely so. This stratagem for tenderizing a tough rib steak is so effective that it is certainly worth all the extra work involved. I give the old text:

. . . .

"Take a piece of ribsteak [1½ pounds] and pull the meat a little away from the bone with a knife, pour warmed vinegar over it, and let it stand overnight. The next morning take the caul fat from a calf (or 2 pieces of caul fat from a hog laid overlapping) and place the steak on top of it, rub the steak all over with salt, cover with chopped onion, parsley, a little lemon peel, a bay leaf, and a little marjoram, pour a spoonful of oil of Provence [olive oil] over it, and wrap the caul fat all the way around the steak.

"Place the steak on a platter, baste with 2 tablespoons of beef broth, and broil slowly in an oven, turning diligently. Before the meat gets too soft, remove the caul fat, squeeze rather a lot of lemon juice over the steak, and bring it in its good *jus* to the table."

NOTE: The point of separating the meat from the bone is to make sure that the steak cooks evenly. Caul fat *(Schweinenetz, crêpine)* is the delicate fatty lining of the abdominal cavity of a hog (less frequently of a calf nowadays); it may be available in European-style and will certainly be available in Chinese-style butcher shops in North America.

MAKES 2 SERVINGS

Roast Beef Hash   Haschee von Rindfleisch

This dish, which figures in the happy childhood memories of a great many of my contemporaries, has practically become extinct in the land of its birth; perhaps this is another reflection of postwar abundance and prosperity—or merely of postwar cynicism and suspiciousness, since I admit I might hesitate to order a dish that shows so little of its pedigree on its face in an unfamiliar restaurant.

· · · · · · · · ·

Heat the lard or butter in a skillet and fry the onion with the flour to make a dark roux. Add the stock (which can be mixed with any leftover beef gravy that might be on hand) and then stir in the ground beef. Season to taste with salt, pepper, and lemon juice. Cook for about 5 minutes more. Garnish with fried egg and pickle. This dish must have the consistency of a very thick soup.

MAKES 4 SERVINGS

2 tablespoons lard or clarified butter
1 large onion, finely diced
1 tablespoon flour
1 cup concentrated beef stock
2–3 cups leftover roast or stew meat, coarsely ground
Salt and freshly ground black pepper
Lemon juice
4 eggs, fried
4 dill pickles or gherkins

EAST   FRIESLAND

Corned Beef   Pökelfleisch

East Friesland was noted for the quality of its beef cattle, which grazed in the grassy meadows during the summer but most of which had to be slaughtered by the beginning of winter. Before the days of walk-in freezers and government price supports, corned beef was the obvious solution to the winter storage problem: a side of beef was left at the butcher's to be cured, or corned for about 10 days in brine, to which sugar and saltpeter (a preservative) had also been added. Since the preparation of this dish is entirely straightforward, the real

13 pounds corned beef
4 onions
4 bay leaves
8 cloves

CONDIMENTS:
Grated horseradish
Mustard
Pickled beets
Pickles of various sorts (see
Headnote)
Pearl onions
Cranberry preserves (or
cranberry sauce)
Applesauce

challenge to the culinary imagination of the countryfolk of East Friesland was in devising and assembling the full panoply of condiments and garnishes to suit this noble dish.

If the night is chilly, the fire cozy, the guests numerous (at least a dozen) and convivial, the beer free-flowing and plentiful, with plenty of *Doornkaat* (corn whiskey) as a pleasant lubricant, then there should be no problem in disposing of the suggested quantity of this old East Frisian specialty. Pickles, chowchow, watermelon pickles, or whatever else appeals to you can be freely substituted for such local favorites as *Süss-Säure Kürbis* (Sweet-and-Sour Pumpkin Relish) and *Essigpflaumen* (sweet-and-sour plums preserved in vinegar with sugar and cinnamon). Boiled potatoes and pickled beets are practically obligatory, but everything else is at the option of the individual diner.

•   •   •   •   •   •   •   •   •   •

Wash the corned beef thoroughly and simmer, along with the onions, bay leaves, and cloves, in a generous amount of water for 2½ to 3½ hours. The corned beef is brought to the table on a large platter, with all the condiments.

MAKES 15 SERVINGS

LOWER   SAXONY

Shoulder of Veal, Hanoverian-Style
Kalbsschulter auf Hannoverische Art

This comes from a booklet illustrating the traditional recipes from the various *Länder* (states) that make up the Federal Republic, prepared by the West German Farm Marketing Board for the Munich Olympics of 1972. It is best served with buttered noodles that have been sprinkled with a little nutmeg, plus green salad with sour cream dressing.

Insert the bacon into the inside of the boned veal shoulder, then roll it up and secure with twine or skewers. Brown it slowly in butter, then add the carrots or turnips and bacon rind and continue to brown the veal. After 15 minutes add the cream and vinegar, and braise the veal for 2 to 2½ hours, until it is cooked through and tender.

Remove the veal from the pan, add the broth to the pan, and heat thoroughly with the braising liquid before adding the cornstarch mixed with a little cold water. Bring the sauce to a boil. (In the old days, they would have used a little grated potato for this purpose.) Stir the anchovies or herring in the sauce to give it a little extra flavor.

Cut the veal into serving slices, cover with the sauce, and serve.

MAKES 8–10 SERVINGS

10 *slices bacon or 5½ ounces slab bacon, cut into pieces for larding*
5½ *pounds boneless shoulder of veal*
5 *tablespoons butter*
2 *cups peeled and diced carrots or turnips*
Rind of the slab bacon, if available, diced
5 *cups heavy cream*
⅓ *cup vinegar*
1 *cup concentrated veal stock*
1 *tablespoon cornstarch*
15 *anchovies or 3 herring fillets, soaked in water, then minced*

BADEN

Black Forest Veal Cutlets
Schwarzwälder Hochzeitsfleisch

At the Black Forest wedding feasts for which this dish was devised, the *Hochzeitsfleisch* was customarily accompanied by flat egg noodles.

In a large pot place the veal, vegetables, seasonings, and enough water to cover. Cook over low heat until the veal is tender, at least 1 hour.

Melt the butter in a large saucepan. Add the flour and cook the roux till golden brown. Add a ladleful of veal broth plus the white wine and lemon juice into the roux. Mix thoroughly, then stir in the cream with a whisk; you may want to add more broth to make a lighter sauce. Cook for another 15 minutes, then season it with salt and pepper. Remove from heat, then add the egg yolks to thicken the sauce.

2½ *pounds boneless veal roast (loin end roast)*
1 *carrot, peeled and diced*
1 *stalk celery, diced*
1 *leek, diced*
3 *sprigs of parsley*
10 *peppercorns*
2 *bay leaves*
6 *allspice berries*
Salt
2 *tablespoons butter*
3 *tablespoons flour*
1 *cup white wine*
Juice of 1 lemon
1 *cup heavy cream*
Freshly ground white pepper
6 *egg yolks*

Cut the veal into slices and serve on a deep platter; pour part of the sauce over the veal and the rest into a sauceboat.

MAKES 8–10 SERVINGS

B E R L I N

Veal Cutlet Holstein   Schnitzel Holstein

PER PERSON:
1 veal cutlet, not too thin
Butter for frying
Salt and freshly ground
white pepper
1 egg
1 tablespoon capers

APPETIZERS:
2–3 toast points
Boned anchovies
Smoked salmon
1 sardine (packed in oil)
Gherkins
Marinated green beans
Caviar, lobster tails,
or what you will

The Holstein in question is not the place up near Denmark where the cows come from but rather *Geheimrat* Friedrich von Holstein (1837–1909), who served for many years as a diplomat to the imperial foreign office on the Wilhelmstrasse under Count Bismarck. Holstein ate his breakfast (then a rather substantial meal served in the late morning) every day at Borchard's Café. Since he preferred to be disturbed as little as possible as he pondered the morning's dispatches and ate his morning cutlet, he asked to be served the cutlet and the appetizer platter at the same time—hence, *Schnitzel Holstein.*

Note that although *Geheimrat* von Holstein had a reputation as something of an eccentric, he was quite orthodox in the matter of potatoes—he preferred ordinary fried potatoes to the infamous *pommes frites.* So be it.

•   •   •   •   •   •   •   •   •   •

Pan-fry the cutlet in butter, season it with salt and pepper. Fry an egg in butter and place it on top of the cutlet. Sprinkle this with capers and serve the cutlet and the egg in the midst of a large platter surrounded by the appetizers.

SCHLESWIG-HOLSTEIN

Stuffed Breast of Veal   Gefüllte Kalbsbrust

This recipe was recorded around the turn of the century by Frau Luise Keck. It is still very popular in southern Germany.

•   •   •   •   •   •   •   •   •

"The breast should be thoroughly pounded and the bone taken out; the ribs can be removed as well by making a cut along the underside of each of them. Wash the veal and dry it, then put the following dressing into the opening: [1 pound] veal, [¼ pound] bacon or suet, both of which should be cut up into little cubes, and then chopped up very small [or coarsely chopped in food processor], [plus] salt according to taste, a little mace and some white pepper, 1 loaf of white bread with the crust taken off and then grated, 3 eggs, and, if you choose, a stick of butter, then knead it all together with clean hands. Roll some of the dressing into a little ball and boil to test it. If it is too firm, add a little of the soup in which the sinews [tendons and other trimmings from the veal] have been cooked [or water]. If it is too soft, add a little spoon [teaspoon] of flour. The forcemeat is inserted into the opening, though not too tightly or it might expand too much in the oven. The opening should be sewed up, and if the breast of veal is to go into the oven, it should be larded [wrapped in bacon] and placed in browned butter or cooking fat, then roasted for 2 hours, and basted frequently with sour cream or milk, until well browned."

NOTE: Replace 1 loaf of white bread with 2 stale kaiser rolls grated in a food processor. Apart from being much easier to come by nowadays, bacon also tastes better than suet.

I'd advise using clarified butter instead of "browned butter or cooking fat." You can also make pan gravy by adding a little stock, flour, and butter to the pan juices. And it won't do the breast of veal any harm if you sprinkle it with a little salt and pepper while it is in the oven.

MAKES 8 SERVINGS

1 boneless veal breast
1 pound stew veal
¼ pound bacon or suet
¼ teaspoon salt
  Pinch of mace
½ teaspoon freshly ground
  white pepper
1 uncut loaf white bread
3 eggs
½ cup butter
¼ pound bacon for larding
3 tablespoons browned
  butter or cooking fat
1 cup milk or sour cream

SOUTHWESTERN   GERMANY

Stuffed Breast of Veal   Gefüllte Kalbsbrust

1 3-pound breast of veal
   (including bone)
   Salt and freshly
   ground white pepper
4 stale or dry-baked
   dinner-size rolls
2 onions
1 teaspoon butter
1 small bunch of
   parsley, washed and
   finely chopped
4 eggs
   Grated nutmeg
2 tablespoons clarified
   butter
1 carrot
1½ cups water or stock
   (veal or beef)
½ cup sour cream

Serve this dish with a salad, egg noodles, or *glitschige* potato salad.

•   •   •   •   •   •   •   •   •   •

Remove the bones from the veal breast—or you might care to have the butcher do this for you, since he has sharper implements and a bit more practice. He can also cut out a pocket in the veal, which has to be washed thoroughly and then dried off before the stuffing is inserted. Rub the veal with salt and pepper inside and out and let it sit for a little while.

In the meantime, coarsely chop the rolls and soak them in water to soften. Dice 1 onion and sauté it in 1 teaspoon butter until golden. Transfer the onion to a mixing bowl; squeeze as much water from the rolls as possible, and combine with the onion in the bowl. Add the parsley and eggs. Mix the stuffing thoroughly and season it with salt, pepper, and nutmeg. Insert the stuffing into the pocket in the breast of veal (do not stuff too tightly) and sew up the pocket with cooking twine. Gently press it flat and sear the veal on both sides in the clarified butter.

Preheat the oven to 425°F. Peel the other onion, peel and

1. *Hals* (neck and shoulder)
2. *Rücken* (rib and loin)
3. *Keule* (including *Frikandeaux* and *Schnitzel*) (leg of lamb)
4. *Brust* (arm and breast)
5. *Hesse* (shank)

wash the carrot, and cut both into thick slices. Place these in the skillet next to the veal; add water or stock to the skillet. Slide the skillet into the oven and roast the veal, with the bone side facing downward, for about 1½ hours. The veal should be basted a number of times, and after the first 30 minutes, the heat can be reduced to 350°.

When the veal breast is well browned, remove it from the pan and keep warm. Deglaze (scrape the sides and bottom of) the skillet with a few tablespoons of water and strain out the onion and carrot pieces from the pan juices. Combine the juices from the pan with the sour cream, mix well, heat thoroughly, and serve as a sauce for the veal, which should be cut into serving slices and overlapped when arranged on a platter.

VARIATIONS: Over the years, cooks have exercised considerable ingenuity in coming up with new ingredients for *Kalbsbrust* stuffing in order to make it more attractive and different from anybody else's. As additives and coloring agents, chopped spinach or pistachio nuts are both very much in accordance with contemporary tastes; some cooks like to insert a central core of whole hard-boiled egg inside the rest of the stuffing, whereas the spinach and pistachio nuts (along with other fortifying ingredients such as finely chopped pickled tongue or chopped ham) should be added directly to the stuffing mixture.

MAKES 6–8 SERVINGS

BADEN-WÜRTTEMBERG

Marinated Breast of Veal   Eingemachtes Kalbfleisch

Serve with egg noodles, spätzle, or *Schupfnudeln,* perhaps a green salad as well, and most definitely a dry white wine. In Baden, this and other meat dishes are often served with the famous semisweet pastry known as *Gugelhupf.*

·   ·   ·   ·   ·   ·   ·   ·   ·

1 3-pound breast of
    veal, washed and cut
    into bite-size pieces
1 onion, quartered
3 cups white wine
2 cloves
1 bay leaf
1 tablespoon vinegar
2 tablespoons butter
6 tablespoons flour
2–3 egg yolks
    Chopped parsley

Place the veal and onion in 2 cups of the white wine with the cloves, bay leaf, and vinegar, and marinate for 24 hours, turning the veal several times in the marinade. In a non-reactive pot, simmer the veal in the marinade (to which salted water may be added if necessary) until tender, about 30 minutes. Pour off the broth, strain, and reserve it. Remove any vegetable pieces from the veal and keep the veal warm.

In a medium non-reactive saucepan melt the butter, stir in the flour, and cook without browning. Stir in 1 cup white wine and enough marinade to make a smooth sauce. Simmer for 15 minutes, then remove from heat and stir in the egg yolks. Add the veal pieces and gently heat them in the sauce without letting it come to a boil. Garnish with parsley.

MAKES 6 SERVINGS

Breaded Calves' Feet   Gebackene Kalbsfüsse im Teig

2–3 calves' feet
1 carrot, peeled and
    coarsely chopped
1 stalk celery, coarsely
    chopped
1 leek, coarsely chopped
3 sprigs of parsley
1 bay leaf
10 peppercorns
    Salt and freshly
    ground black pepper
1 cup dry white wine
½ cup flour
½ cup light (as opposed
    to dark) beer
1 tablespoon vegetable
    oil
    Very small pinch of
    sugar
2 egg whites
    Flour for dredging
    meat
    Oil for deep-frying
    Sprigs of parsley

In our disposable society, a great many things get thrown away before they've been used even once, whereas in our grandmothers' day, calves' feet were used twice—first as a source of calf's foot jelly, another of those foods that was thought to be especially good for invalids and convalescents, and second, as the source of a delicious gourmet delicacy (not very plentiful, admittedly, but that's one of the things that makes it such a delicacy). Breaded calves' feet are especially good with a sauce remoulade or Chive Sauce (*Schnittlauchsauce*). Serve these with potato salad.

•   •   •   •   •   •   •

Wash and scrape off the calves' feet thoroughly, then split them (something you may prefer to have the butcher do for you). Place the calves' feet, vegetables, parsley, bay leaf, peppercorns, and 1 teaspoon salt in a large pot with enough water to cover the ingredients and cook on low to medium for at least 2 hours. Before the calves' feet have a chance to completely cool, separate the fleshy skin from the bone, divide this into 2″ or 3″ pieces, and sprinkle with pepper, then immediately press these between two boards with a heavy weight on top of them. (Meanwhile, proceed with the batter, below.) After about an hour, take the pieces of calves' feet and marinate in wine for yet another hour, turning them occasionally. Remove the pieces from the marinade and pat dry.

Mix the flour and beer into a smooth paste. Add a little more beer if needed for a smooth batter. Add the vegetable oil, season with salt and sugar, and stir vigorously with a whisk. Let the batter sit for about 1 hour. Beat the egg whites into stiff peaks and fold them into the beer batter.

Dredge the dried pieces of meat first in the flour, then in the batter; the coating should not be too thin. Heat the oil to 350°F. and deep-fry the meat until golden brown and crispy on the outside. Deep-fry a couple of sprigs of parsley, which makes a tasteful as well as a tasty garnish.

MAKES 4–6 SERVINGS

BAVARIA

Roast Shank of Veal Kalbshaxen

Over the years, Bavarian homemakers have learned how to transform a calf's hind leg into something that, in the words of one authority (Erna Horn), "you'd be willing to sell your birthright for." This dish can be prepared in a number of different ways: simmered ("seethed") in broth, which is by far the oldest way of doing it; *eingemacht,* which normally means "marinated," but here just means cut up in pieces after it's cooked and served with a white sauce; *sauer,* cooked and served in vinegar; as well as broiled or roasted, as in the present recipe, which is undoubtedly the most popular. Serve the leg of veal with potato salad, green salad, and Bavarian Bread Dumplings *(Semmelknödel).*

1 shank of veal
Salt and freshly ground white pepper
2 tablespoons clarified butter or lard
2 large onions, thickly sliced
1 large carrot, peeled and sliced

Wash off the shank of veal, dry thoroughly, and trim off all the loose shreds of meat; larger loose pieces that you're not prepared to part with can be secured with cooking twine. Rub the shank vigorously with salt and pepper, and let sit for about 15 minutes.

Preheat the oven to 400°F. On the stove heat the butter or lard in a large roasting pan and sear the veal on all sides. Add 1–2 cups of water to the pan. Add the onions and carrot to the pan. Place the roasting pan in the oven. Baste the veal from time to time, for which you may have to add a little cold water. Total cooking time should be about 2 hours, and you may want to turn up the oven a bit during the last 15 minutes if the veal doesn't look browned enough on the outside; you may even need to use the broiler for a little while.

After the gravy makings have been scraped loose from the edges of the roasting pan, the pan juices can simply be strained and used as the gravy—this is one occasion in traditional German cookery, I'm glad to report, that flour is *not* used to bind the gravy. In any case, not very much gravy will be required.

A nicely roasted shank of veal is such an attractive sight that you wouldn't want to deprive your guests of this visual prelude to the actual experience of eating it; thus, the veal should be served as is, on a large platter, and carved into serving slices at the table.

MAKES 2–3 SERVINGS

SILESIA

Fresh Ham, Silesian-Style   Schwärtelbraten

Schwarte means "skin" or "rind." When it comes onto the table everybody knows it is Sunday. The bigger this roast, the more beautiful the Sunday. Accompany with *Semmelknödel,* even though they'd be called *Semmelklösse* in Silesia, and sauerkraut.

• • • • • • • • • •

Preheat the oven to 400°F. Combine the caraway seeds, salt, and pepper. Wash off and dry the ham thoroughly, and rub it all over with the seasonings. Put the ham in a large ovenproof frying pan; the skin side should be facing upward. Pour in the water, add the coarsely chopped onion and carrot, and place in the oven. Braise for a good 30 minutes, then take out the ham and cut a series of diamond-shape crosshatches in the skin with a very sharp knife; the cuts should penetrate into the fatty layer below the skin. Put the ham back in the oven, replenish liquid, and baste the ham every 10 minutes. The ham should cook for 2 to 2½ hours altogether.

During the last 20 minutes, you may want to wet the skin with cold salted water to make sure it attains the proper crispness. When the ham appears to be done, take it out of the oven; remove the ham from the pan; deglaze the pan (scrape particles off the bottom and sides and mix with the pan juices) and strain this to remove the vegetables. Stir the cornstarch into the sour cream with a whisk, and combine this mixture with the pan juices in a saucepan. Bring this to a boil and season to taste. Carve the ham into serving slices before bringing it to the table; serve the sauce separately.

MAKES 4–6 SERVINGS

1 teaspoon ground
   caraway seeds
½ teaspoon salt
1 teaspoon freshly
   ground black pepper
1 2–2½-pound boneless
   fresh ham (butt or
   shank portion,
   uncured, unsmoked,
   with the skin still
   on it)
1 onion
1½ cups water
1 large carrot
1–2 teaspoons cornstarch
½ cup sour cream

HUNSRÜCK

Grilled Steaks al Fresco   Spiessbraten Idar-Oberstein

As mentioned earlier in connection with my friend August Görg's wonderful recipe for grilled steaks, a great many young men from this area went off to seek their fortunes as emerald prospectors in South America during the last century. Most of the prospecting, of course, was done in remote, sparsely populated areas, where stray beef cattle might be plentiful but *Gasthäuser* and other amenities for travelers were

PER PERSON:
2 green forked sticks
1 thick steak, 10 ounces
   minimum
   Salt
1 sturdy jackknife or
   hunting knife

very few. This style of grilling steaks and other foodstuffs has become one of the most memorable tourist attractions of the Hunsrück district and remains one of the liveliest regional culinary traditions in West Germany today.

The original recipe, given below, is suitable for camping out in the pampas and is still used in Idar-Oberstein on family excursions.

. . . .

Everyone sits around an open fire, equipped with a steak and 2 forked sticks. The first stick is used to turn the meat over the fire, the second as a prop to rest the first one on. Each diner skewers his steak on the stick, grills it to taste, cuts off piece after piece, sprinkles it with a little salt, and eats it, perhaps accompanied by a thick slice of *Bauernbrot* but certainly nothing more.

Roast Suckling Pig   Spanferkel

1 suckling pig, not more than 2 or 3 weeks old
1–2 tablespoons salt
¾ cup plus 2 tablespoons butter

"Suckling pig" is a term that gladdens the heart of the serious German gourmet (and in German, of course, it's just one word—*Spanferkel*). Modern-day gourmets may have some difficulty in acting out their fantasies around this legendary delicacy, since experimental luaus and amateur "backyard blast furnace" attempts at barbecuing a whole pig, even a very small one, are unlikely to be successful. Also, a genuine suckling pig—as opposed to a half-grown adolescent porker—is not so easy to come by these days as it was 100 years ago. In this recipe, taken from Hedwig Heyl's *ABC's of Cooking,* the suckling pig is roasted in the more reliable cast-iron kitchen stove.

. . . .

"Fold the animal's legs underneath its body, rub it with salt on the inside and out, and place it in a pan on the roasting rack of the oven [the wooden equivalent of today's metal grill rack]; add about ⅛ of a [pint] of water to the pan, and brush the roast all over with salted water. Depending on the size of the roast, the oven should be at 365–400°F. The beads of moisture that appear on the surface of the skin should be wiped away with a cloth, and the animal should be brushed with melted butter every 5 or 10 minutes; prick the skin lightly with a larding pin every quarter of an hour or so to prevent it from blistering. The suckling pig should be roasted for 1¼ to 1½ hours. The drippings should not be allowed to burn in the pan; pour in a little liquid from time to time to prevent the roasting rack from taking fire [!]. Brushing the roast with butter will make the skin good and crispy. Serve with a sauce made of olives, tomatoes, capers, or truffles, or garnish with fried potatoes or pickled cabbage."

MAKES 10 SERVINGS

FRANCONIA

Pork Cutlets with Marjoram
Fränkisches Marjoranfilet

This recipe is courtesy of the chef of the Steigenberger Hotel in Kissingen. Serve with boiled or scalloped potatoes and green salad.

•   •   •   •   •   •   •   •   •

Cut the pork loin into 1¼"-thick cutlets, pound these very lightly, sprinkle each with a little salt and pepper, and finally spread a thin layer of mustard on them.

In a skillet heat 3 tablespoons lard or butter and start to brown the onion and apple slices. Add the rest of the butter, and brown the pork cutlets on both sides. Then reduce heat and cover; after 3 minutes, sprinkle the cutlets generously with marjoram. Cover and allow them to cook for another 2 minutes, or until the cutlets are thoroughly cooked.

MAKES 4 SERVINGS

1–1½ boneless pork
   loin(s)
   Salt and freshly
   ground black pepper
   Mustard
5 tablespoons lard or
   butter
1 large onion, sliced
1 large apple, peeled,
   cored, and sliced
1 tablespoon crushed
   marjoram

1. *Kopf mit Schnauze* (head, snout, and jowl)
2. *Rückstrang* (fatback)
3. *Kamm* (butt, shoulder, and hock)
4. *Koteletts, Karbonade, Rippenspeer, and Speck* (loin, spareribs, and bacon)
5. *Schinken, Keule* (ham and hind foot)
6. *Bauch* (belly)

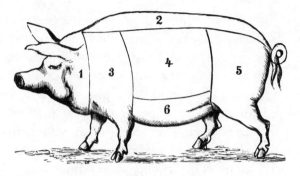

Butcher's Platter   Schlachtplatte

In farming country, hog-butchering day was (and to some extent still is) a day full of hard work and excitement, one that was naturally followed by an evening of hearty eating and celebration. Eventually, hog-butchering meals arrived in town in the form of *Schlachtplatten* or *Schlachtschlüssel,* the classic accompaniment for which, of course, was sauerkraut, perhaps assisted by potatoes, mashed potatoes, and diced pea puree.

Even the broth in which the wursts were cooked, accordingly known as *Wurstbrühe* or *Metzelsuppe,* was sold in the butcher shops in town up until the time of the Second World War. This was not much of a delicacy in its own right but served as the starting point for a great many recipes for thick soups and stews, and every self-respecting farmer made sure that the contents of a few of the sausage casings accidentally got punctured to add more body to the broth. All neighbors showed up with canteens to get their share of it. A much more substantial by-product was the sausage fat—known as *Wurstfett* and no longer available on the open market in this calorie-conscious era—notable for its slightly grayish-green color and its unforgettable aroma; *Wurstfett* was also sold prepackaged at the butcher shop, like lard, to be spread on bread or used for frying.

A typical *Schlachtplatte* might include a balanced selection of:

various cuts of pork and trimmings, boiled *(Kesselfleisch, Wellfleisch)* fresh liverwurst (see pages 197 and 238), blutwurst (blood sausage), bratwurst

fresh "belly bacon" *(Bauchspeck)*

liver dumplings *(Leberknödel)* (see pages 244 and 245)

boiled headmeat

black pudding *(Schwarzsauer)* (see page 228)

Weckeweck (see page 227) or some other dish made with the skin and other miscellanea

plus sauerkraut as the obligatory complement of all fleshy pleasures (of this particular type).

All of these might conceivably have been available in the kitchen of an especially industrious farm family on butchering day, and a short time later a number of other smoked and pickled by-products—such as Pigs' Knuckles (see page 229), spareribs, various kinds of bacon, fresh ham *(Haspel),* brine-cured "trimmings" *(Solber)*—would start turning up at the buffet, or the equivalent of the free-lunch counter, in the tavern in the nearest town.

NORTHERN HESSE

Weckeweck

Weckeweck and *Schwarzsauer* are two typical recipes for rural hog-slaughtering feasts.

· · · · · · · · ·

Soften the rolls by pouring the stock over them. Put the pork scraps and onions through the meat grinder twice (just once through the processor, however). Combine this with the rolls and mix thoroughly, then add the seasonings. The mixture should have a nice spicy tang to it. Bring the mixture to a boil and cook for about 30 minutes, stirring frequently. Serve hot.

MAKES 4–6 SERVINGS

1 quart beef stock (in lieu of Wurstbrühe)
4–5 stale or dry-baked hard rolls, sliced
1¾ pounds pork scraps and trimmings, including (but not necessarily limited to) the skin
3 onions
1 teaspoon each salt and freshly ground black pepper
¼ teaspoon ground caraway seeds
½ teaspoon crushed marjoram

SCHLESWIG-HOLSTEIN

Black Pudding   Schwarzsauer

1¼ pounds pork trimmings (from the snout, neck, trotters, or what you will), cut into small pieces
1 quart beef stock (if not actual Wurstbrühe)
2 bay leaves
Salt and freshly ground black pepper
1 onion, finely chopped
A few splashes of vinegar
2–3 cups fresh pigs' blood *

Not the least of the virtues of this dish is that the ingredients would all be available in abundance on butchering day. If the dish is served cold after the sauce has been allowed to gel (which is why it is called a pudding), accompany it with fried potatoes; if it is served warm, accompany it with boiled potatoes and stewed fruit (prunes, dried apricots, and apple rings).

•   •   •   •   •   •   •   •   •   •   •

Cook the pork scraps in the stock seasoned with bay leaves, salt, pepper, onion, and a generous splash of vinegar for 1½ to 2 hours. As soon as the meat is tender, remove it from the broth and place on a deep platter. The broth should be boiled down a little and as much of the pigs' blood added as is necessary to make it thick and creamy. Add a little more salt and pepper if you wish, and pour the broth over the platter.

MAKES 4 SERVINGS

* Blood is a very good thickener for sauces. It has to be ordered from a butcher. It can be stored in the refrigerator for 3 days. Mix with a splash of vinegar to prevent clotting. Substitute: blood sausage or *Boudin noir* (imported), pureed in a food processor.

Görlitz, Silesia, after a drawing by Borussia

BAVARIA

Pigs' Knuckles with Onion, Apple, and Sauerkraut   Schweinshaxen mit Kraut

Serve with potatoes that have been boiled in salted water, plus a little mustard or grated horseradish for the pigs' knuckles.

•   •   •   •   •   •   •   •   •   •

Wash the pigs' knuckles and drain thoroughly. In a large enameled cast iron casserole sauté the onions and apples in the lard or other cooking fat; add the sauerkraut along with the bay leaves, white wine, and stock. Mix thoroughly.

Press the pigs' knuckles down into the sauerkraut, cover with a lid, and cook over low heat for about 45 minutes, or until the meat is tender.

MAKES 4 SERVINGS

4 small pigs' knuckles (smoked ham hocks can be used as well)
2 onions, chopped
2 small Granny Smith apples, peeled, cored, and finely chopped
2 tablespoons lard or other cooking fat
2 pounds sauerkraut
2 bay leaves
1 cup white wine
1 cup beef stock

MÜNSTER

Black Pudding with Pork
Schweinefleisch in Schwarz Gekocht

This is a very old recipe from the Münsterland region, dating from about 1800, which is given here in its original form as far as the instructions are concerned, though the language has been modernized somewhat.

•   •   •   •   •   •   •   •   •   •

Wash and dry off the pork shoulder and cut it into thin strips that are a little thicker and shorter than julienne potatoes *(pommes frites)*. Along with the seasonings cook the pork in a saucepan with just enough water to cover until it is tender (about 1 hour). Remove the pork from the water and set aside.

Strain out the herbs and spices from the liquid in which the

1½ pounds boned pork shoulder
1 teaspoon salt
2 bay leaves
12 peppercorns
6 allspice berries
1 cup pigs' blood (see Note)
A few splashes of vinegar
Salt and freshly ground black pepper
Pinch of ground allspice

pork was cooked and put the liquid back on the heat. Stir in the pigs' blood and add a few splashes of vinegar. Mix this thoroughly and return the pork to the saucepan. Season the pork with salt, pepper, and the ground allspice. Heat through for several minutes before serving.

NOTE: Pig's blood is no longer a standard ingredient in German cuisine, nor is it elsewhere, and I'm sure that many readers would just as soon avoid using it. My suggestion would be to get a couple of fresh *Blutwürste* (blood sausages) or the equivalent at a German-, Polish-, or Eastern European-style butcher shop, squeeze the stuffing out of them, mash them up a little, and use this to bind the sauce instead.

MAKES 4 SERVINGS

PALATINATE

Pork Maw, Palatine-Style   Pfälzer Saumagen

1 large kaiser-type roll or ¼ of a French bread
2 onions, coarsely chopped
¾ pound lean pork, cut into cubes
½ pound fatty pork (fresh pork belly, if available), cut into cubes
¾ pound lean beef, cut into cubes
3 eggs
1 tablespoon crushed marjoram
Salt and freshly ground black pepper
1 generous pinch of ground allspice
Grated nutmeg

Saumagen is the best-known regional specialty of the Palatinate, or Pfalz, which nowadays simply means that there are a lot of people who are familiar with the name but have never tasted the delicate yet far from unassuming flavor of pork maw. *Saumagen* was originally part of the fall butchering-day festivities, and though it may not be a great favorite with younger cooks, who tend to shy away from all the work involved, it can still be found on the menus of some of the old-time *Wertschafte* (Pfälzer colloquialism for *Wirstschaften*, "taverns") in the Palatinate.

The *Saumagen* should be served in thick slices, with sauerkraut (heated up in a little white wine) and nice thick slices of *Bauernbrot*. The *Saumagen* slices can also be fried individually to make so-called double *Saumagen,* which is what is invariably done with the leftovers. Connoisseurs insist that it tastes even better the second time around. There also happens to be a vineyard called Kallstadter Saumagen, near Bad Dürkheim, in the Palatinate. A nice dry white wine would do very well in this dish in either of these two incarnations, for those interested in investigating the possibilities of a triple *Saumagen*.

· · · · · · · · · ·

Soak the roll in water and press it dry. Combine the onions and roll with half of the pork and beef and put it through the finest setting of the meat grinder or in the food processor. Beat the eggs into the meat mixture and add the seasonings. Knead all these together.

Cut the cold potatoes into cubes; add them along with the bacon, remaining cubes of pork and beef, and 1 cup of beef stock to the mixture and knead thoroughly.

Wash the pork maw thoroughly and fill it up with stuffing —though not too full, since the stuffing will expand somewhat while cooking. Sew it up tight with cooking twine, and place the stuffed pork maw in a large pot with the vegetables and cold salted water; cook over moderate heat for about 1½ hours. Remove the pork maw from the water, drain, and pat dry. Heat the lard (or other cooking fat) in a skillet and sear the pork maw on all sides; there is still some danger of the maw bursting, however, so don't set the heat too high. Remove the pork maw from the skillet, add the remaining cup of stock, and stir it with the contents of the skillet to make a sauce.

MAKES 6–8 SERVINGS

2 medium potatoes, peeled, boiled, and cooled
3 slices fatty bacon (smoked)
2 cups beef stock
1 pork maw (stomach), which should be ordered from the butcher well in advance and soaked overnight in salted water before cooking
1 carrot, peeled and diced
1 celery stalk, diced
1 leek, diced
2 tablespoons lard or other cooking fat

EAST PRUSSIA

Ham with Sour Cream Schmantschinken

This dish is traditionally accompanied with mealy, boiled potatoes and with cucumber salad, which, needless to say, was also made with sour cream in East Prussia.

· · · · · · · · · ·

1½ *pounds very mild cured*
ham (see Note)
2 *cups milk*
2 *tablespoons butter*
1 *heaping tablespoon*
flour
1 *cup sour cream or*
crème fraîche
Salt and freshly
ground white pepper
1 *tablespoon lemon juice*
1 *teaspoon sugar*

Cut the ham into 4 thick slices and allow them to soak overnight in the milk, turn occasionally. Drain and pat dry.

In a large skillet heat the butter and sear the ham slices on both sides for about 3 minutes. Remove the ham from the skillet, but keep it warm. Stir the flour into the browned butter in the skillet and cook the roux until golden; add the sour cream or crème fraîche, and stir vigorously. Cook till heated through and season with salt and pepper (more pepper than salt), lemon juice, and sugar.

Just before serving, pour the sauce over the ham slices.

NOTE: The smoked ham used for this recipe should be very mild and not too salty. You can, of course, ask your butcher for an especially mild ham, in which case you'll probably end up buying a great deal more than you need for this recipe. Or try your luck with a canned ham from the supermarket. As far as this recipe is concerned, you'd be better off with the latter than with a more expensive ham that turns out to be too salty.

MAKES 4 SERVINGS

THURINGIA

"Pot Roast"   Topfbraten

Probably not even the oldest living Thuringian—or even the elves and hobgoblins that live on the slopes of the Inselberg—remembers why *Topfbraten* should be so called, when in fact it's a kind of stew made from a variety of butchering-day by-products and customarily serves up as part of the evening's festivities. In an especially good year, old-time Thuringians might get a taste of *Topfbraten* on one or two other days as well. The traditional side dish is *Watteklösse* (dumplings, see page 289).

•   •   •   •   •   •   •   •   •

Wash all the meat very thoroughly. Remove the bones from the head, cut open the heart and the kidneys, remove the veins and tough membranes, and soak these for 2 or 3 hours in cold water, changing the water occasionally. Parboil the tongue for 15 minutes in a large pan or stockpot, skimming off the impurities from the surface. Add the meat and organs and skim the impurities from the surface once again.

Peel the onions, insert the cloves into the onions, and add them along with the bay leaves to the broth. Season the broth with salt and pepper. Add the vinegar after 30 minutes and cook over a low flame until the meat is tender, 1–1½ hours. Remove the meat and organs from the broth. Cut them into bite-size pieces, set aside. Remove the tough outer covering from the tongue before cutting. Pour the broth through a strainer, add the gingerbread, and put this back on the heat to cook until the gingerbread has dissolved.

Strain the broth through a fine sieve and stir in the plum jam. Boil this down a little if necessary to make the sauce the thickness of heavy cream. Check the sauce for seasoning; it should have a very distinct sweet-and-sour taste. Return the meat to the broth (except for the fattiest pieces from the pig's head which should be discarded). Cook gently for another 10 minutes and serve in a tureen or deep platter. Total cooking time: 2 hours.

MAKES 6–8 SERVINGS

1 *piece of pig's head, about 2 pounds including bones*
1 *pork heart (½ pound pork liver may be substituted but shorter cooking time must be considered)*
2 *pork kidneys (or 1 calf kidney)*
1 *pork tongue*
½ *pound fatty pork (fresh pork belly)*
2 *onions*
4 *cloves*
2 *bay leaves Salt and freshly ground black pepper*
¼ *cup wine vinegar*
¾ *cup broken pieces of gingerbread*
2 *tablespoons plum jam*

BERLIN

Pork Chops in Aspic Sülzkotelett

This is a tasty German specialty that lends itself to an especially elegant presentation; these pork chops were once widely available as a prepared dish in butcher shops and taverns, though in recent years I've only come across them in Berlin, which can probably claim credit for their invention. There's another dish called *Casseler,* involving loin pork chops that have been lightly cured in brine, which is known for certain

2 calves' feet (or packaged
  gelatin, see Note)
4 center-cut bone-in pork
  chops in one piece,
  lightly marinated in
  brine
1 onion, quartered
1 carrot, peeled
2 bay leaves, halved
8 peppercorns
6 allspice berries
2 egg whites
½ cup vinegar
1 egg, hard-boiled and
  sliced
  A few gherkins, sliced
  lengthwise
  A few tarragon leaves

to have originated there. As an accompaniment for the chops, home-fried potatoes are *de rigueur.*

· · · · · · · · ·

Wash the calves' feet thoroughly, then split the calves' feet and put them into a large saucepan with the onion, carrot, bay leaves, peppercorns, allspice berries, and enough water to cover the feet, and simmer for a good hour. Add the pork chops, turn the heat down very low, and simmer for another hour. Remove the meat from the broth, separate the meat from the fat and bone, and set aside.

Retrieve the calves' feet from the broth and discard; skim off the fat and impurities from the broth and pour it through a fine strainer. Beat the egg whites to soft peaks, then add them to the broth while stirring continuously. Stop stirring. The egg whites will rise to the top and form a layer. Let this simmer for 5 minutes. Strain this mixture through a sieve lined with a double thickness of cheesecloth, then season with a splash or two of vinegar.

If you wish, you can cut the carrot that was cooked in the broth into matchstick strips or little shavings as a garnish. In the absence of individual *Sülzkotelett* molds that are available in Germany, you can use a shallow platter, just large enough to hold the chops, that has been well chilled in the refrigerator. Pour in a thin layer of the cool broth (the aspic) on the bottom of the platter and arrange the hard-boiled egg, gherkins, carrot, and tarragon leaves in an attractive pattern and set these firmly in place with a few drops of aspic "glue." Place in the refrigerator.

As soon as the aspic has gelled, pour on another thin layer of aspic, put the platter back in the refrigerator for a short time, and then set the chops down in it, side by side. Cover the chops with aspic and put back in the refrigerator to gel. Just before serving, immerse the platter with the aspic briefly in hot water and turn it over onto a clean flat platter. Either before or after you turn the platter over, you can cut around the edges of the chops with a knife that has been dipped in hot water; cut up the remaining aspic into cubes, and serve as additional garnish.

NOTE: Nontraditionalists will probably want to dispense with the calves' feet altogether, since aspic can much more easily be made by dissolving powdered gelatin or packaged gelatin leaves in clear beef broth that has been flavored with a little vinegar (about 1½ ounces powdered gelatin, or 16 to 18 gelatin leaves, to a quart of broth).

MAKES 4 SERVINGS

BERLIN

Bratwurst in Beer Sauce　Stolzer Heinrich

"Proud Heinrich" is the name by which this dish is generally known in its native city. Serve this dish with mashed potatoes and green salad.

• • • • • • • • •

Poke a few holes in the bratwurst with the tines of a fork to keep them from bursting. Dredge them in flour. In a skillet melt the butter and fry the wurst on both sides. Remove them from the skillet and set aside.

Pour the beer into the skillet and deglaze the skillet (scrape off the browned particles clinging to the sides and bottom). Sprinkle in the ginger cookie crumbs and grated onion and cook together for about 10 minutes. Season to taste with salt, pepper, a little beef stock, and lemon juice, and cook for 2 or 3 minutes more. Reduce heat, return the bratwurst to the skillet, and cook until heated through.

MAKES 2–4 SERVINGS

4 bratwursts or sweet
　Italian sausage
1–2 tablespoons flour
1–2 tablespoons butter
1½ cups dark beer
3–4 tablespoons ginger
　cookie (gingersnap)
　crumbs
1 tablespoon grated
　onion
　Salt and freshly
　ground black pepper
　Several tablespoons
　concentrated beef stock
1–2 tablespoons lemon
　juice

Blutwurst with Applesauce and Mashed Potatoes   Himmel on Ahd met Blootwoosch

2 pounds potatoes,
   peeled and washed
2 pounds Granny Smith
   apples, peeled, cored,
   and sliced ½" thick
   Juice of 1 lemon
   Sugar
2 tablespoons butter
2 cups hot milk
   Salt and freshly
   ground pepper
2–3 tablespoons lard
   (butter, etc.)
4 large onions, halved,
   cut into thin rounds
4 large, thick pieces of
   blutwurst (blood
   sausage)

The name *Himmel on Ahd,* which means "heaven and earth," is used in and around Cologne. Nevertheless, this is a favorite dish in a number of other regions as well, including Hesse, Rhenish Hesse, Lower Saxony, and Mecklenburg (where they use pears instead of apples). The type of blutwurst customarily used is a very simple one called a *Blunz,* containing very few bits of bacon if any at all.

. . . .

Cook the potatoes in salted water. Cut the apple slices in half and cook with a few tablespoons of water, the lemon juice, and sugar until they almost have the consistency of applesauce. Drain the potatoes and mash coarsely with the butter and hot milk, then mix the applesauce (which should have little bits of apple, somewhat firmer in consistency, mixed in with it) with the potatoes, add a little salt and pepper, and keep warm.

Xanten, lower Rhine

In a large skillet heat the lard and sauté the onions until golden brown. Remove from the skillet and set aside. Quickly sear the blutwurst pieces in the same skillet (adding a little more fat if necessary), then stack them on top of one another on the side in the skillet, and briefly reheat the onion rings in the skillet. Season with a little salt and pepper. Serve the blutwurst on a platter with the mashed potatoes-and-apple mixture, garnished with the onion rings (and the remaining contents of the skillet if you wish).

MAKES 4 SERVINGS

B A V A R I A

Bratwurst Cooked in Champagne
Bratwürste mit Champagnerwein

This is an interesting example of high-style regional cuisine, featuring the lowly bratwurst in unaccustomed court finery—glamorized with truffles and practically drenched in champagne. This dish was invented by Herr Rottenhöfer, personal chef and court chamberlain to King Maximilian of Bavaria during the latter half of the nineteenth century, and presented at court in silver tureens.

The recipe is a lavish variation of *Blaue Zipfel,* or "Blue Points," which "was greatly prized as a between-meal tidbit." Readers lacking the jaded appetites (and grocery allowances) of Middle European monarchs of that era, but still interested in re-creating this historic dish, may want to make some judicious substitutions as far as the secondary ingredients are concerned.

2–3 pounds bratwurst
3 tablespoons butter
½–¾ pound truffles
½–¾ pound mushrooms
1 cup glâce de viande
1 cup rich veal stock
½ bottle champagne

•   •   •   •   •   •   •   •   •

"Take as many as required of well-prepared bratwurst and brown lightly in fresh butter, remove the skins while still hot, cut into [1″] sections, and place in a shallow baking dish with a tight-fitting lid. Take [½–¾ pound] truffles, peel, slice thinly, and scatter over the bratwurst slices, along with an equivalent amount of mushrooms. Also, take *glâce de viande* [jellied beef consommé] and about [1 cup] of good veal broth and pour this into the baking dish, along with a half-bottle of champagne, and cook, well covered, until the sauce is reduced by half and the bratwurst have absorbed all the juices and acquired a taste that is both robust and highly agreeable."

MAKES 4–6 SERVINGS

Liverwurst, Lower Rhineland-Style
Niederrheinische Leberwurst

This is the most characteristically German of all the German *Würste*. The nineteenth-century gastronome Carl Friedrich von Rumohr, who tried to do for the art of fine cooking in Germany what Brillat-Savarin was later to do for the French *haute cuisine,* was not much of one for simple and unpretentious fare. However, his book *The Spirit of the Art of Cooking,* published in 1822, does contain a recipe for a particularly delicious variety of liverwurst he had encountered in several households in the Lower Rhineland. Any cook who is willing to invest a little time and trouble in return for a guaranteed culinary success would do well to take note of von Rumohr's recipe:

. . . .

"Take one part each of fresh calves' liver, hogs' liver, and white bread that has been steeped in bouillon to soften it. The liver should be washed and finely chopped, and everything should be well mixed together, salted, and sprinkled with spices and fine herbs. Take about half again as much unsmoked bacon as you already have of all the rest, and cut it into little cubes, then mix it all together very well. Take this mixture and put it into sausage casings that have been thoroughly cleaned, tie off the ends, and put them to soak in hot water. Finally, take them out, let them cool, and hang them up to smoke until they are quite firm."

NOTE: I'd suggest you use as much bacon as calves' liver, since von Rumohr is a little vague on this point. Nowadays, you may want to put the liver through a meat grinder (or food mill, processor, et cetera) instead of chopping it up; it turns out a bit better if the calves' liver is finely ground, the pork liver a little more coarsely ground. As for "spices and fine herbs," I'd suggest allspice, pepper, some nutmeg, ground coriander, a generous amount of marjoram, and a somewhat less generous amount of thyme.

Unless you're one of those privileged few who has his or her own smokebox, smokehouse, or similar facility, you'll undoubtedly find it easier to put the liverwurst up in small mason jars or jars with screw-on caps. To sterilize the jars, leave them in the upper compartment of the pressure cooker for about 1 hour, or put them in a pan full of water (the water level should come right up to the lid of the jar) and leave the pan in the oven for 2 hours; the oven should be set to at least 212°F., the boiling point of water.

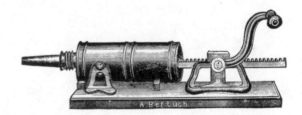

THURINGIA

Liverwurst, Thuringian-Style
Thüringer Leberwurst

This recipe dates from the 1920s, about 100 years later than von Rumohr's.

• • • • • • • • •

Gently simmer the pork belly (the whole piece) in a little water until it is almost thoroughly cooked, skimming the impurities from the surface frequently; the bacon can be

4½ pounds fairly fatty
  pork (fresh pork belly)
2 pounds farm fresh
  bacon (unsmoked)
4½ pounds pork liver
1 cup beef stock
1 large onion, grated
1 tablespoon crushed
  thyme
2 teaspoons crushed
  marjoram
1 teaspoon freshly
  ground white pepper
½ cup salt

cooked in the same way (and in the same pot). Cut the pork liver into cubes about an inch square, put in a sieve, and immerse in boiling water until it seems firm in consistency and there is no trace of blood. After the pork belly and the liver have had a chance to cool off, put both through the meat grinder or food mill—one half of it only once, the other half twice. Cut the bacon into little cubes.

Combine all 3 with the beef stock, onion, herbs, pepper, and salt. Mix thoroughly, then put into mason jars; the jars should be no more than three-quarters full. Seal the mouths of the jars with the rubber rings and close firmly. The rule is that jars should be sterilized for 100 minutes at 100°C. (212°F.), in other words, in a pressure cooker or in a bath of boiling water. The water can be brought to a boil in the oven as described in the preceding recipe. (In Europe, there is a special device, a sort of home autoclave unit, called a Weck-apparat, that is especially available for this purpose.) For longer storage the jars should be resterilized for another 10 minutes at 100°C./212°F. one or two days later; this last step is not strictly necessary, but my informant in these matters absolutely swears by it and insists that the liverwurst keeps much better that way.

MAKES 12 POUNDS

The Chapel, Wartburg Castle where Martin Luther translated the Bible

SOUTHWESTERN GERMANY

Veal Kidneys with Vinegar   Saure Nierle

In rural districts, this dish is still served (just with bread) after church on Sundays as a sort of delayed breakfast or as a curtain-raiser for the main Sunday dinner, which comes a bit later. Under different circumstances, it could also be accompanied by mashed potatoes or, nowadays, by rice or noodles.

.   .   .   .

Wash the kidneys thoroughly, cut them in half, cut out all blood vessels, and any fat that has not already been removed. Soak the kidneys in cool water for 1 hour, changing the water several times, dry off, and cut into crosswise slices.

In a large stainless or enameled skillet melt the butter and sauté the onion until it turns translucent. Push the onion to one side of the skillet, put in the kidney slices, and sauté these for a couple of minutes, turning very frequently and making sure they don't burn. Season with salt and pepper, then remove the kidney slices from the skillet and set aside. Sprinkle the flour into the skillet, brown it, then pour in the gravy mixture and the red wine, and stir vigorously.

Add the bay leaf and 1 tablespoon vinegar; cook for another 10 minutes over low heat. Remove the bay leaf and stir in the sour cream; season with salt, pepper, and more vinegar and allow the sauce to cook for a few more minutes. Return the kidneys to the pan, reduce heat still further, and cook until everything is heated through.

MAKES 4 SERVINGS AS AN APPETIZER

1½ pounds veal kidneys (preferably, though others are acceptable as well)
2 tablespoons butter
1 medium onion, finely chopped
Salt and freshly ground black pepper
1 tablespoon flour
1 cup veal gravy (or mixture of broth and canned beef gravy, Gravy Master, etc.)
¼ cup hearty red wine
1 bay leaf
1–2 tablespoons wine vinegar
2 tablespoons sour cream

LOWER SAXONY

Beef Liver with Herbs Leberragout mit Kräutern

1¾ pounds beef liver
(calves' or pork liver
for more subtle taste)
2–4 tablespoons butter
4–5 tablespoons finely
chopped fresh herbs
(a mixture of
parsley, thyme,
tarragon, and
shallots)
Salt and freshly
ground black pepper
¼ cup fresh bread
crumbs (from a loaf
of white bread
without the crust)
½–1 cup rich beef stock
½ cup white wine

First published in Henriette Davidis-Holle's famous *Practical Cookbook* (1844), this dish is best served with mashed potatoes.

• • • • • • • • •

Wash the liver and dry it off; remove all blood vessels and membranes and cut it into strips. Melt the butter and sauté the herbs briefly, then add the strips of liver and sauté while turning frequently; sprinkle in the salt and pepper. Add the bread crumbs, beef stock, and white wine, mix everything together thoroughly, and cook until the sauce begins to bind a little bit.

MAKES 4 SERVINGS

Holzminden on the Weser
River

BERLIN

Liver with Apples and Onions, Berlin-Style
Leber Berlinerart

The former national capital is still credited with the invention of this dish on menus all over Germany. Note that while this recipe is usually made with calves' liver, beef liver and pork liver (which are both somewhat cheaper) taste best when prepared according to this method.

· · · · · · · · ·

Carefully remove all membranes and connective tissue from the liver slices and lightly sprinkle them with flour on both sides. In a large skillet melt 1 tablespoon butter and fry the apple slices on both sides until they are tender (but not about to disintegrate). Set these aside and keep warm.

Add the remaining 3 tablespoons butter and fry the liver slices, while sprinkling salt and pepper on both sides, cook for no more than 5 minutes altogether, or until they are tender but well before they start to get tough and leathery.

If there's enough room in the skillet, spread the onions out around the outside and sprinkle with salt and pepper while the liver slices are just starting to cook. Remove the liver slices to a platter when they're done and keep them warm; allow the onion rings to continue cooking until golden brown. Place these and the apple slices (and the remaining contents of the skillet if you wish) on top of the liver slices and serve.

MAKES 4 SERVINGS

4 large (¼–½ pound each) slices of calves' liver
1 tablespoon flour
4 tablespoons butter
3 Granny Smith apples, peeled, cored, and sliced
Salt and freshly ground black pepper
4 medium onions, halved, cut into slices

The Michelangelo of the Kitchen, pastry chef to the royal household before the kings of Prussia became German emperors, Berlin

Liver Dumplings   Leberknödel

4 *stale or dry-baked*
  breakfast rolls
  (Semmel), *kaiser, or*
  large-size hard rolls
1 *cup hot milk*
  Salt
1 *medium onion,*
  quartered
½ *pound beef liver,*
  coarsely chopped
2 *eggs*
  Grated peel of ½
  lemon
  Pinch of crushed
  marjoram
1–2 *tablespoons butter*
1 *small bunch of*
  parsley, finely
  chopped
1 *quart clear beef broth*
  Chopped fresh chives

The controversy is still raging among devotees of this quint—essential South German specialty as to whether *Leberknödel* are properly to be regarded as soup dumplings pure and simple, or as a free-standing, independent entity in their own right, needing only a bit of broth to bring out the full flavor of the dumplings. On occasion, they're even served without the broth (with sauerkraut, for example), and they come in many different sizes, some of them as big as pigeon eggs or even tennis balls. Real Bavarian *Leberknödel* tend to have a little chopped spleen mixed in with the liver (in a ratio of about 1 to 4), and the larger ones tend to have a correspondingly heartier taste. Without *Leberknödel,* Bavarians could not be Bavarians anymore.

The impact of *Leberknödel* as a cultural force, however, has always been totally disproportionate to their size. The story is told, for example, that the only amicable encounter between the nineteenth-century composers Anton Bruckner and Johannes Brahms occurred at some sort of celebrity *Leberknö-delabend* somewhere; there, at least, they agreed there was nothing quite like *Leberknödel,* and, for just that once, a spirit of perfect harmony prevailed between them.

·   ·   ·   ·   ·   ·   ·   ·   ·

Remove the crusts from the rolls and cut into very thin slices; pour the milk over them, sprinkle with salt, and let sit for about 10 minutes, or until they have soaked up all the milk.

Put the onion and liver through a meat grinder (or food mill, processor, et cetera). With the meat grinder, you may want to put a little bit of dry bread through at the very end to make sure that all the liver has actually come out the other side. Knead this mixture together with the roll slices soaked in milk, then mix in the eggs, and season with salt, grated lemon peel, and marjoram.

Melt the butter in a skillet and briefly sauté the parsley, then allow it to cool, and stir it into the dumpling mixture. Chill this mixture in the refrigerator for about 10 minutes. Then make up a few small trial *Klösschen* and drop them into some simmering broth to see if they hold together. If the experiment is a success, then make the rest of the batch into 4 large meatballs (or as many small ones as you'd care to) and simmer in clear broth for 12 to 25 minutes, or until they're done. Serve the completed *Knödel* in the broth and garnish with chopped chives.

MAKES 4 SERVINGS

Marbach, Swabia

EAST PRUSSIA

Tripe, Königsberg-Style Königsberger Fleck

The former German (now Soviet) city of Königsberg, birthplace of the philosopher Immanuel Kant, is probably better known in culinary circles for having given birth to a delicious recipe for tripe, a meatball, and a kind of marzipan. Admittedly, tripe *(Kuttelfleck)* is nothing more or less than the linings of the first two of the cow's (though more frequently an ox's) stomachs, and of course there are a great many of our contemporaries who would hesitate to feed something like that to their dogs.

To these skeptics I can only reply that tripe is very highly

1½ pounds soup bones
2 pounds beef tripe,
   precooked and cut into
   2" squares
2 carrots, peeled and
   halved
3 stalks celery, halved
2 onions, halved
   Salt
2 bay leaves
6 allspice berries
12 peppercorns
   Several sprigs of
   parsley
1 leek, white part only,
   left whole
   Plus *coarse salt, fresh
   pepper, mustard, and
   crushed marjoram for
   the table*

regarded as a culinary specialty item not only in many parts of Germany but in several other countries as well (notably France and Italy) and has practically made the reputations of a couple of otherwise only moderately distinguished provincial cities (e.g., *tripe à la mode de Caen*), which brings us to the subject of *Königsberger Fleck.* In prewar days, a truly memorable *Fleck* was cooked and sold at stands on the market square by so-called *Fleckwiewerchen,* "little tripe ladies," though actually I've been told that the variety served to late-night pub-crawlers and early-morning revelers in the small taverns in the old city (comparable to the Parisian after-hours tradition of eating onion soup at a stall in the great central market of Les Halles) was even better; unfortunately, in those days I was still too young for that sort of night-reveling experience.

In the old days, tripe had to be soaked overnight, repeatedly washed, and seethed in boiling water for many hours before it was ready to cook. Nowadays, tripe is sold prepackaged at the butcher shop and even occasionally at the supermarket; the only preparation that's necessary is to cut the tripe into bite-size pieces.

.   .   .   .

Wash the soup bones thoroughly and simmer them in a generous amount of water for at least 1 hour, skimming off the impurities from the surface often. Those who prefer a very clear broth will want to let the water come to a boil and the soup bones cook for a little while, then discard the first batch of water and start all over again. Pour some of the broth through a strainer into the pot, put in the tripe, and keep adding stock until the tripe is well covered. Add the carrot, celery, and onion to the stockpot with salt. Put the spices, including parsley, into a tea ball or tie up in a little cheesecloth bundle, add to the stockpot, and cook for a good 30 minutes. After these have been in the stock about 15 minutes, add the white part of the leek to the stock. Skim the stock as necessary.

Remove the vegetables and dice them. Set aside. Remove the bundle of spices. Then pour the broth into a large tureen with the tripe and vegetables, and serve with crispy rolls. The diners should be provided with salt, a pepper mill, a generous supply of mustard, and some crushed marjoram so they can season their *Fleck* according to their individual inclinations. (In German-speaking circles, the exact linguistic connection between the word *Fleck,* meaning tripe, and *Fleck,* meaning a spot [such as a careless eater might happen to get on his or her clothes] is still unclear but almost certain to be discussed on these occasions.)

MAKES 4 SERVINGS

SWABIA

Tripe Cooked in Vinegar Saure Kutteln

Here is another dish that started out as a kind of savory curtain-raiser for an elaborate Sunday dinner after church and is likely to be served nowadays as a party treat or for late-afternoon "vespers" ("meat tea" in British terminology). The tomato paste is not strictly traditional but seems like a good idea in other respects. Accompany with bread or fried potatoes.

· · · · · · · · ·

In a large skillet heat the lard, add the flour, and brown the roux. Then pour in the beef stock and stir into a smooth sauce. Add all the remaining ingredients except the tripe. Stir together and cook for 5 minutes. Add the tripe to the skillet. Stir once more and simmer over low heat for just about 30 minutes. Test the seasoning and remove the bay leaves before serving.

MAKES 4 SERVINGS

1 tablespoon lard or
   cooking fat
1 tablespoon flour
1 good cup beef stock
2 bay leaves
1–2 tablespoons finely
   chopped onion
   "As much ground
   clove as will fit on the
   point of a knife"
1–2 tablespoons vinegar
   Salt and freshly
   ground black pepper
½ teaspoon sugar
1 tablespoon tomato
   paste
1½ pounds beef tripe,
   precooked, cut into
   small strips

EAST PRUSSIA

Meatballs, Königsberg-Style   Königsberger Klopse

2 thick slices of white
   bread, without the
   crust
½ pound ground beef
½ pound ground veal (or
   pork, though veal is
   preferable)
1 egg
   Salt and freshly
   ground black pepper
1 small onion, grated
2 anchovy fillets, finely
   chopped, or 2
   tablespoons anchovy
   paste
1 bay leaf
½ onion or the white
   part of a leek
6 allspice berries
4–6 peppercorns
3 cups beef stock
1 tablespoon butter
1 tablespoon flour
1 small jar of capers
   Juice of 1 lemon
2 egg yolks

Another of this Baltic city's notable culinary contributions first became known during the eighteenth century. The name is undoubtedly related to the northern German dialect word *kloppen,* "to beat, pound, thrash," and the dish itself was a favorite for Sunday dinners in Königsberg and the surrounding rural areas, where—just as French fries are simply called "fries" in America—it was known simply as *saure Klopse* (sour meatballs).★ Serve with pickled beets or dill pickles.

•   •   •   •   •   •   •   •

Soak the 2 slices of bread in water and press to remove excess moisture. Combine the ground meat, egg, salt and pepper. Add to this the bread, onion, and anchovies, and knead together thoroughly. Then use this mixture to make a number of good-size meatballs (about as big as an egg).

Add the bay leaf, onion or leek, allspice berries, and peppercorns to the beef stock and bring to a boil. Let this cook for at least 15 minutes. Add the *Klopse* and cook in the simmering broth for at least 10 minutes, then remove and keep warm.

Pour the broth through a fine strainer. Melt the butter in a large skillet, add the flour and cook to make a light roux, add the broth, stir well; add the capers along with the pickling liquid from the jar. Season with the lemon juice, salt and pepper to taste. Remove from heat, beat the 2 egg yolks, and stir these into the sauce. Put the meatballs in the sauce, put back on the stove until both are heated through, but do not boil. Serve.

VARIATIONS: The most basic principle of East Prussian cuisine, namely that everything tastes better with a little sour cream, can easily be applied here by stirring a few tablespoons of

★ In some American cookbooks, this recipe is presented under the name of German meatballs.

Aug. Müller. sc   Bernhard Mörlins

Schmant (sour cream) into the sauce at the very end. On the other hand, you might prefer to add a splash of white wine and a couple of teaspoons of sugar, which should result in a distinct sweet-and-sour taste.

MAKES 4 SERVINGS

Meat Patties   Buletten

1½ *pounds chopped meat
(half beef, half pork)*
1–2 *stale or dry-baked
rolls, dinner roll size*
2 *tablespoons clarified
butter*
2 *onions, finely chopped*
1 *egg
Salt and freshly
ground black pepper*
1 *tablespoon finely
chopped fresh parsley*

These are referred to by menu writers and other prestige-conscious persons as *Boulettes,* which seems fairly silly, since a foodstuff so insecure in its identity that its contents have had to be strictly regulated by law (no less than 70 percent beef or pork, at least within the confines of the Federal Republic) is not really what you'd call a high-status item. According to a popular saying among Berliners, one might assume that *Buletten* are a favorite dog food. If someone is trying very hard to accomplish something, Berliners will say: "He goes after it like Hektor after *Buletten.*" Hektor is the German equivalent of Fido or Bowser.

Serve hot with potato salad, or cold, spread on buttered bread with a little mustard. This is also a popular item at high-life cocktail parties and low-life bars, generally served on a *Schrippe,* or French roll, in either case.

•   •   •   •   •   •   •   •   •

Put the chopped meat in a mixing bowl. Coarsely chop the stale rolls and soak in water; press out the moisture and add to the mixing bowl. Heat the clarified butter in a skillet and sauté the onions until they turn translucent, then add these to the contents of the mixing bowl, followed by the egg, salt and pepper, and parsley. Knead all the ingredients together. Form into 8 meatballs, press flat, and fry on both sides over medium-high heat.

MAKES 4 SERVINGS

BERLIN

Mock Hare (Meatloaf) Falscher Hase

The credit for the invention of the nickname—and possibly of the dish itself, which is now popular all over Germany—belongs, once again, to the Berliners. Serve with red cabbage and potatoes boiled in salted water.

. . . .

Mix the ground beef with the ground pork; soak the roll and press out the moisture, and add it to the ground meat. Dice 2 onions. Cut the bacon into tiny squares; heat up 1 tablespoon lard or other cooking fat in a small skillet and fry the bacon and onions until both turn translucent. Add bacon and onions to the chopped meat and mix together; add the eggs and knead all the ingredients together, then season with salt and pepper, coriander, and marjoram.

Preheat the oven to 425°F. Heat the remaining 1 or 2 table-spoons lard in a large ovenproof skillet or baking dish. Form the chopped meat mixture into a loaf and place in the skillet, then slide the skillet into the oven and bake for a good 10 minutes. Peel the remaining onion and slice into rings; arrange these around the "mock hare" in the skillet, pour ¾ cup of the beef stock over it, and bake for another 45 minutes, basting frequently with the remaining stock. Remove from the oven; remove the loaf and deglaze the pan (scrape the browned particles from the sides and bottom) with any remaining stock, stir up the pan juices with the sour cream to make a sauce for the "hare," and taste for seasoning.

MAKES 4 SERVINGS

¾ *pound ground beef*
¾ *pound ground pork*
1 *large kaiser roll*
3 *onions*
6 *slices fatty bacon (smoked)*
2–3 *tablespoons lard or other cooking fat*
2 *eggs*
Salt and freshly ground black pepper
Small pinch of ground coriander
Pinch of crushed marjoram
½–1 *cup beef stock*
½ *cup sour cream*

Game

.   .   .   .

In the early medieval period, under the Carolingian emperors (800–918), the fields and forests of Germany were swarming with wild game—not just hares and partridges, but much more formidable big-game animals such as elk (the same creature that would be called a moose in North America), bison, wild oxen (Auerochsen), wild boar, wolves, and bears. In the early days, the only limitations on hunting were the speed and cunning of the hunter's quarry, but during the later Middle Ages, legal restrictions were introduced, and, at least technically, all wild game became the property of the owner of the land, which was generally either the church or the local squire.

Certainly the aristocracy devoted a large portion of their waking hours to pursuing the pleasures of the table and the pleasures of the chase; the surviving game diary of one sixteenth-century Saxon princeling, carefully maintained over a twenty-year period, winds up with a career total of 795,400 wild animals of various kinds. Many of these princes raised wild game in fenced-in parks, even in the moat around the castle of Nuremberg, thereby being able to indulge in the "joys of hunting" without any effort. Virtually all of the larger game animals were exterminated during the early modern period. The very last German bear, for example, was dispatched in the hills of Thuringia in 1686.

The medieval practice of hanging game birds, hares, and other creatures in a shed until their flesh was deemed to be sufficiently "high" (i.e., rotten) and then masking this aroma in the kitchen with heavy doses of condiments did manage to survive until fairly recent times but is decidedly not to be encountered in any of the recipes in this book. There are also

Der Jäger.

Die Wollust macht Wunder gleich beyssenden Hunden.

Der Teuffel spannet Garnen auff;
Der Tod zielt stets mit scharffen Pfeilen,
und der Versuchung schneller Hauff
ist frisch ein Wildpret zuzereilen
Wer hie will frey und sicher seyn:
kriech in die Wunden Hölen ein

a great many recipes in the older cookbooks for game birds that are now protected or very rare (the hazel hen, the swan, and the black grouse, for example), and it seemed pointless to include them. Even the hare is hardly able to make a home for itself in what remains of the countryside in Germany today.★ The chief ingredient of most of the *Hasenpfeffer* that is eaten by urban game fanciers has to be imported from eastern Europe.

Because of very limited availability of venison in the United States, only a small selection of the numerous German game recipes is given in this book.

★ Industrialization has left very little living space for wild animals. There are more automobiles than deer in Germany's forests. Fortunately, game can still be bought everywhere between the North Sea and the Alps.

Marinated Saddle of Venison
Rehrücken Baden-Baden

A recipe that originated in the elegant southwestern German resort city of Baden-Baden was clearly more at home in the grand hotel than the farmhouse kitchen. In fact, this is another one of the handful of German regional specialties that is genuinely entitled to a placecard of its own at the great banquet table of international gastronomy. The venison is customarily accompanied with spätzle (or with an alternate choice of potato croquettes on very festive occasions) and forest mushrooms (chanterelles) sautéed in butter.

. . . .

Remove the skin from the venison and marinate with the wine, 1 onion, 8 whole juniper berries, and peppercorns for at least a day, preferably two. Remove the venison from the marinade (strain the marinade and save the red wine), dry off, and make incisions, not too deep, on both sides, along the backbone. Dredge the strips of bacon in some of the crushed juniper berries and insert the bacon in the incisions. Next, mix the remaining crushed juniper berries with coarsely ground pepper and rub this lightly and sparingly over the outside of the venison. Let stand for another hour.

In the meantime, in a large non-reactive pot, heat the clarified butter and briskly sauté the remaining onion, carrot, and bones until well browned. Sprinkle the flour over the contents of the pot and allow to brown, stirring constantly. Pour in the water, deglaze (scrape off burned particles from the sides and bottom of the pot), and bring this to a boil; pour in one half of the red wine from the marinade (save the rest for later on) and reduce until you have half a cup of rich game sauce. Strain the sauce into a medium saucepan. Season with salt and pepper. Preheat the oven to 475°F.

Baste the saddle of venison with the melted butter and place in the hot oven; reduce the heat to 400° and roast the venison for about 35 minutes, basting repeatedly with butter. Next, remove the bacon strips and keep the venison warm. Pour off

1 saddle of venison
3 cups red Burgundy (e.g., Badener Spätburgunder, French red Burgundy, California Pinot Noir)
2 medium onions, sliced
13 juniper berries, 5 crushed
10 peppercorns
2–3 bacon slices
Coarsely ground black pepper
2 tablespoons clarified butter
1 carrot, peeled and sliced
1–2 pounds venison bones with a few scraps of flesh adhering to them, chopped into small pieces (you may use beef bones as a substitute)
1 teaspoon flour
1½ cups water
Salt and freshly ground white pepper
¼ cup butter, melted
½ cup sour cream
4 pears, halved and seeded
2 cups white wine
Red currant jelly

the fat from the roasting pan and deglaze the pan with the remaining marinade. Strain this pan gravy and combine with the reduced game sauce, then stir in the sour cream. Taste for seasoning.

Parboil the pear halves in the white wine. Fill each with a little currant jelly.

Detach the venison from the backbone on both sides, carve against the grain into thick serving slices, and replace the slices at both sides of the backbone to give the saddle its original appearance. Garnish with the pear halves. Serve the sauce separately.

NOTE: Originally, the pears would have been peeled, halved, cored, and briefly cooked up in lemon juice with ½ cinnamon stick to make a pear compote, but the halved pears and currant jelly seem to make a more attractive garnish.

MAKES 8 SERVINGS

1. *Rücken, Ziemer* (saddle, loin)
2. *Blatt* (shoulder)
3. *Bauch* (belly)
4. *Keule* (haunch); the fat of a stag is called the *Weiss*

Jugged Hare Hasentopf/Hasenpfeffer

This most famous of traditional German game dishes presents certain problems for those who have difficulty getting hold of fresh hare's blood, which the traditional recipes call for; any other kind of blood would do as well, to be sure, but many of us would just as soon not pursue the matter any further. Luckily, a solution is at hand—a fresh, smooth blutwurst can provide the same rich flavor and sufficient binding without disturbing our contemporary sensibilities too much. (Just puree it with some beef broth in a food processor.)

Hasenpfeffer is the name by which this dish is best known outside Germany, as well as in most German country inns that specialize in wild game and in hunters' households. In Rhenish Hesse, the Palatinate, and the Rhineland, where this has long been the most popular (and certainly the cheapest) of all game dishes, it was originally called *Dippehas,* which means more or less the same thing as the English expression "jugged hare," since a *Dippe* is a pot or crock in dialect.

Originally, only the forelegs, head, neck, belly, and innards were used to make *Hasenpfeffer,* which is the way it is still made by some hunting families; the forelegs are considered to be the tastiest part, and a special cordon bleu *Hasenpfeffer* is sometimes prepared using these alone. Otherwise venison may be substituted for hare.

SOUTHWESTERN GERMANY

Braised, or "Jugged," Hare Hasenpfeffer/Dippehas

Serve with egg noodles, Potato or Mushroom Dumplings, or spätzle, and red cabbage salad.

•   •   •   •   •   •   •   •

1 hare (or the equivalent
in selected pieces,
e.g., forelegs, see
above)
8 strips lean bacon,
sliced, without the
rind
1 tablespoon lard
¾ pound lean pork, cut
into 1" cubes
½ pound fatty pork
(originally, fresh pork
belly, without the
skin), cut into 1"
cubes
3 medium onions, finely
chopped
1 carrot, peeled and
julienned
1 small celery root or 2
stalks celery,
julienned
1 cup sturdy red wine
½ cup beef stock
2–3 tablespoons vinegar
3–4 fresh (uncooked)
blutwursts, casings
removed
Pinch of ground
allspice
Crushed bay leaf
1 tablespoon flour
Salt and freshly
ground black pepper
2 tablespoons red currant
jelly
Crushed marjoram
(optional)

Skin the hare and cut it into 10 or 12 serving pieces. Cut the lean bacon into postage stamp–size squares. Heat the lard in a large enameled cast-iron casserole or a stewpot. (The pot should be large enough to hold all the ingredients for this recipe, presentable enough to serve the *Hasenpfeffer* to your guests or family in, and equipped with a tight-fitting lid.) Sauté the bacon and pork cubes until the fat has all been rendered, remove from the pan, and place on paper towels to drain. Sauté the onions, carrot, and celery root or celery in the fat remaining in the casserole until the onions are golden yellow.

Preheat the oven to 350°F. In a non-reactive saucepan combine the red wine, stock, vinegar, fresh blutwursts (without the skin, to be sure), plus the allspice and bay leaf, and bring to a boil while stirring. Now add the hare and pork belly to the onions and vegetables in the casserole and sprinkle with flour, salt, and a generous amount of pepper. Cook the pieces until they are just barely browned, turning continually, then return the bacon and pork cubes to the casserole. Pour in the wine mixture and stir until the ingredients are blended.

Stir in the currant jelly and test for seasoning; if the blutwurst stuffing was not too heavily spiced to begin with, for example, you may want to add a little crushed marjoram. Put the lid on the casserole, make a paste of some flour and water, and use this, in effect, to caulk the seam between the casserole and the lid. Set the casserole in the oven and cook for a good 1½ hours. You can also transfer the ingredients from the pot to a terrine or similar earthenware vessel (the original "jug" or *Dippe* that was used in such cases) before placing it in the oven.

It's best not to break the seal on the lid until the casserole or terrine has been brought to the table, since in either case the highly concentrated essence of *Hasenpfeffer* that comes billowing out from under the lid is one of the most wonderful aromas that it is possible to experience or imagine.

MAKES 4–6 SERVINGS

SCHWARZWALD

Marinated Rabbit   Eingemachter Haas

Even in the Schwarzwald, rabbits are a lot easier to come by these days than wild hares and are often used in this recipe, which originated in the town of Villingen and was communicated to me by my friend Heiner Flaig. Serve the rabbit with flat egg noodles.

. . . .

Cut the rabbit into at least 8 serving pieces. Combine alcoholic cider or white wine with the onion, cloves, and bay leaf to make the marinade, and set the rabbit pieces to marinate for at least 24 hours.

In a non-reactive pot, bring the water and salt to a boil and add the rabbit pieces; strain out the onion and spices from the marinade and pour the liquid into the pot. Simmer for about 1 hour.

Heat the butter in a saucepan, stir in the flour, and cook to make a light roux. Then pour in about 3 cups of the broth that the rabbit has been cooking in and stir until you have a smooth sauce. Stir in the cream with a whisk, and season with an additional hearty splash of white wine and a little vinegar, plus salt and white pepper. Place the rabbit pieces in the sauce, and after a few more minutes, remove from the heat and stir in the egg yolk to thicken the sauce.

MAKES 4 SERVINGS

1 rabbit (a deep-frozen one is perfectly all right)
2 cups hard cider or dry white wine
1 large onion, chopped
2 cloves
1 bay leaf
2 cups water with ½ teaspoon salt
Scant ¼ cup butter
⅓ cup flour
½ cup cream
Splash of white wine
Vinegar
Salt and freshly ground white pepper
1 egg yolk

LOWER SAXONY

Cold Saddle of Hare   Kalter Hasenrücken

Backs and sides
(saddles) of 2 hares
½–1 cup oil
Salt and freshly
ground black pepper
2 medium onions, 1
sliced into thin
rounds
1 tablespoon flour
1 cup red wine
2 bay leaves
Juice of 1 lemon
About 1 teaspoon
sugar

This particular recipe was given to me by a family that now lives in Stuttgart. It was a much appreciated legacy of an old great-aunt who had spent the best part of her life on a farm in Lower Saxony. This dish tastes especially good with a light *Bauernbrot*. The present custodians of *Grosstante*'s original recipe have introduced certain refinements that are worth passing on. The first is to add 2 tablespoons tomato paste to the sauce; the second is to garnish the completed *Hasenrücken* with sliced black olives.

. . . .

Skin the saddles of 2 hares and cook over low heat with 1 onion in lightly salted water until the meat is almost fully cooked (about 25 minutes). Allow to cool for a little while, then take the meat off the bones, but leave it in whole pieces. Heat the oil and brown the meat well on all sides. Season with salt and pepper, reduce heat, remove the pieces from the pan as soon as they're ready, and allow them to cool.

Preheat the oven to 350°F. Fry the onion rings in the oil remaining in the pan until golden brown, then sprinkle with flour and allow the flour to brown. Pour in the red wine and add the bay leaves, lemon juice, and pepper to taste. Stir together and allow to cook for 15 minutes. Season with salt and the sugar, and then set the pan in the oven until the oil comes to the surface, 15 to 20 minutes. Skim the fat from the sauce.

Press the sauce through a fine-meshed strainer and allow to cool. Cut the cold hare meat into not-too-thick slices, serve these on a plate in an overlapping arrangement, and pour the sauce over them.

MAKES 8 SERVINGS

MANNHEIM

Palatine-Style Game Pie   Kurpfälzer Jagdpastete

The following recipe was devised by the chief pastry chef of the Elector Prince in Mannheim (the ruler of the Palatinate was so called because he was one of about half a dozen German princes who had the right to elect the Holy Roman Emperor). A descendant of this chef, Eugen Kettemann, who still runs a café and confectionary shop near Mannheim's main station, more or less by prescriptive right, has preserved this family recipe, which is lovingly re-created on very special occasions.

·   ·   ·   ·   ·   ·   ·   ·   ·

Stir into the flour the salt, water, and fine herbs. Melt the shortening, combine with the previous ingredients, and knead thoroughly. Let stand in the refrigerator overnight; the pastry dough will actually keep safely in the refrigerator for at least a week.

Next, marinate the venison overnight in red wine that has been seasoned with the bay leaf, 6 crushed juniper berries, and the onion.

Cook the pork liver in boiling water for about 5 minutes, until it is quite firm in consistency. Remove it from the water and cut into strips like the venison. Heat the clarified butter in a skillet and briefly sauté the chanterelles (without the liquid from the jar!), then drench these with the jigger of brandy and flambé. Allow to cool and mix in the sausage stuffing.

Crush the peppercorns, remaining 4 juniper berries, rosemary, allspice berries, and coriander seeds in a mortar and mix together to make a savory game seasoning.

To make the crust, grease a 10″ x 3″ rectangular terrine with lard, and roll out the dough into a large sheet and a small sheet. Cover the bottom of the terrine with the large sheet of dough, smoothing out the bulges in the corners and allowing the edges of the dough sheet to hang over the brim of the pan, perhaps by a considerable margin; later on, these will be folded over as part of the top crust of the game pie.

PASTRY DOUGH:
3½ *cups flour*
Pinch of salt
4 *tablespoons water*
1 *teaspoon fine herbs (blend of tarragon, parsley, chervil, and chives)*
¾ *cup vegetable shortening*

MARINADE AND FILLING:
1 *pound venison (any kind, or beef tenderloin as substitute), cut into thin strips*
2 *cups red wine*
1 *bay leaf*
10 *juniper berries*
1 *medium onion, coarsely chopped*
¼ *pound pork liver*
1 *tablespoon clarified butter*
1 *small jar of chanterelles*
1 *jigger of brandy*
1 *pound uncooked, coarsely ground sausage (bratwurst or sweet Italian sausage) stuffing*
8 *peppercorns, crushed*
Pinch of rosemary
2 *allspice berries*
¼ *teaspoon crushed coriander seeds*
1 *tablespoon lard*
2 *tablespoons very thick cranberry sauce*

1 *egg yolk*
1 *teaspoon powdered gelatin (aspic)*

Drain the marinated venison (do not discard the marinade) and lay strips of venison and pork liver on the dough, then sprinkle with a little of the game seasoning you mixed earlier. Spread half the sausage stuffing on top, then make a little trench down the middle (lengthwise) and fill with the cranberry sauce. Cover with the rest of the liver and venison strips and then the rest of the sausage stuffing. Smooth off the surface of the game-pie filling and fold the edges of the bottom crust up around the filling, as if to enclose a packet; brush the surface with egg yolk. Trim the smaller sheet of dough until it's the right size to cover the whole top of the pie, set in place, and press around the edges, making sure the corners are completely sealed. Trim off the edges of the pie crust cleanly, make a (small) round ventilation hole in the center of the crust, and insert a piece of rolled-up aluminum foil to make a "chimney."

Preheat the oven to 400°F. Decorate the top crust of the pie by scratching a design into it with a fork or molding bits of leftover dough into little ornaments and setting these firmly in place with egg yolk. Then brush the entire surface of the crust with egg yolk and bake the pie for at least 1 hour, or until the crust is golden brown. Pour the red-wine marinade through a fine strainer. Soak the gelatin powder in a little water and dissolve in the marinade which has been heated.

"The Long Wall," near
Weltenberg, Bavaria

Remove the aluminum-foil chimney from the pie, allow the pie to cool, then put in the refrigerator until it's quite cold. Pour the dissolved, but cooled, gelatin mixture into the hole in the middle of the crust and put back in the refrigerator to set, about 6 hours or overnight. Use a knife with a serrated edge to cut (about a finger's breadth) serving slices from the unmolded pie.

MAKES 4–10 SERVINGS

BADEN

Hare Terrine   Hasenkuchen

Another very simple way of making a game terrine, this is authentically "popular" rather than *bürgerlich* (or even princely) in its origins. Beef or lamb can be used as well with an addition of 10 crushed juniper berries. This dish can be served cold.

. . . .

Preheat the oven to 350°F. Combine the hare meat (leftover roast or stew) with the anchovies, capers, onion, and parsley. Put all these ingredients through the finest setting of the meat grinder (or food mill, processor, et cetera). Beat 4 tablespoons butter till creamy and mix with the flour; beat the eggs and work these into the flour-butter mixture quite thoroughly, then mix this with the ground hare meat. Add the sour cream and season with salt and pepper.

Grease a cake pan (ideally a small 8″ or 9″ springform) with the remaining 1 tablespoon butter, sprinkle the bottom with bread crumbs, fill with the mixture, and bake 45 to 50 minutes, until golden brown. Now it's time to perform the famous toothpick test *(Stäbchenprobe!).* Insert a wooden toothpick into the interior of the terrine. If it comes out with no moist particles adhering to it, the terrine is cooked all the way through. Do not overcook.

MAKES 8–10 SERVINGS

1¼ *pounds leftover roast (or stewed) hare*
4 *anchovy fillets, chopped*
1 *heaping teaspoon capers*
1 *onion, coarsely chopped*
1 *small bunch of parsley, coarsely chopped (stems removed)*
5 *tablespoons butter*
1 *tablespoon flour*
3 *eggs*
2–3 *tablespoons sour cream*
Salt and freshly ground black pepper
2–3 *tablespoons bread crumbs*

Sauces

· · · · · · · · ·

Recipes for rich and complicated sauces abound in the earliest German cookbooks, as in other European cookbooks, since these were about the only available means of combating the two great scourges of the late medieval dinner table—spoilage and monotony. The medieval cook was often tempted to pour on a pungent, spicy sauce to disguise or overpower, rather than to enhance, the natural flavor of the prepared foodstuff.

In the modern period, these complicated formulas were adapted for mass consumption so that bland and tasteless dishes—something of a nineteenth-century specialty—could be made, if not palatable, then at least recognizable by pouring on a variety of spicy bottled sauces, catsups, chutneys, and other condiments. In other parts of Europe, the English were held to be chiefly responsible for this trend.

In the meantime, German homemakers and restaurateurs had discovered that all the elaborate sauces and savories devised by their Renaissance forebears could be replaced with a floury, viscous substance of almost limitless utility, referred to in cookbooks and contemporary treatises on domestic science as "gravy base" *(Grundsauce)*. German cooking has gotten itself into a very sorry state as a result of this crippling dependence on a single, not very satisfactory, sauce. In the following section, I would like to forget about "gravy base" for a moment and introduce you to several happier inspirations of the German sauce tradition.

Sour-Cherry Sauce   Amerellen Salsen

This is from one of the earliest German cookbooks, a volume entitled *Master of the Cellar and Kitchen,* which was first published in Frankfurt in 1581. An *amerelle* is a kind of sour cherry, not quite the same thing as a morello but very similar.

• • • • • • • • • •

"Pound them in a mortar, pits and all, then crumble up some gingerbread, and press this [mixture] through a cloth with some good wine and catch it in a glazed crock. Grind in some cloves and all manner of strong spices, and add a bit of salt as well. Set by the fire and bring to the boil, then pour it into a basin and let stand for a while."

Sour-Cherry Sauce   Sauerkirsch Sauce

A modern descendant of the above, usually served with game.

• • • • • • • • • •

Melt the butter in a skillet and briskly sauté the venison bones and trimmings (scraps of meat, gristle, et cetera) as well as the diced vegetables. Sprinkle the flour into the pan and continue cooking until the flour is well browned. Pour in 1 cup of the hot water, deglaze the pan (detach browned particles from the sides and bottom and stir), then add more 3 cups water, the juniper berries, pepper, and perhaps a little pinch of cinnamon as well.

Cook for 30 minutes, stirring frequently, then pour in 2 more cups water and allow to simmer briskly for another 30 minutes. The sauce should have boiled down until there is barely 1 cup of liquid remaining. Pour this through a fine strainer, then add the red currant jelly and the sour cherries along with their juice. Addition of 1 more pinch of ground cinnamon enhances the flavor. Season to taste with salt.

MAKES 1½–2 CUPS

2 tablespoons butter
1–2 pounds bones and scraps of venison or other game
1 onion, diced
1 carrot, peeled and diced
3 stalks of celery, diced
1–2 tablespoons flour
1½ quarts hot water
6 juniper berries, crushed
Ground cinnamon (optional)
2–3 tablespoons red currant jelly
½ pound sour cherries, pitted and briefly parboiled (canned will do)
Salt and freshly ground black pepper

Warm Horseradish Sauce   Warme Meerrettichsauce

*1 fresh horseradish root
(prepared horseradish
may be substituted)
3 heaping tablespoons
finely grated bread
crumbs, preferably
fresh
3–4 tablespoons butter
Pinch of grated nutmeg
Freshly ground white
pepper
Generous pinch of salt
1 cup real beef stock*

Horseradish sauce is traditionally served with boiled beef.

•   •   •   •   •   •   •   •   •   •

Wash the horseradish thoroughly, finely grate, and combine with the other ingredients. Bring this to a boil while stirring continually. If the sauce is too thick, you can stir in a little beef stock or cream; if too thin, throw in another handful of bread crumbs.

MAKES 2 CUPS

BAVARIA

Apple-Horseradish Sauce   Apfelkren

*4–5 heaping tablespoons
freshly grated
horseradish (prepared
horseradish may be
substituted)
4 tablespoons grated
Granny Smith apple
2 tablespoons lemon
juice
Sugar
Salt
2–3 tablespoons sour cream
or crème fraîche*

Kren is *"bajuwarisch"* (Bavarian dialect) for horseradish. This sauce is traditionally served with boiled beef or hot wurst.

•   •   •   •   •   •   •   •

Put the ground horseradish in a small mixing bowl, add the grated apple and lemon juice, and mix thoroughly. Season with a little sugar and a very little bit of salt. Let stand for about 15 minutes before adding the sour cream. If you'd like a milder sauce, you can add a handful of freshly grated bread crumbs in addition to increasing the proportion of sour cream.

MAKES ¾ CUP

Frankfurt am Main (engraving
by W. Lacey, after a drawing
by W. Tombelson)

FRANKFURT, HESSE

Green Sauce Frankfurter Grüne Sauce

One of the star performers in this section, this unpretentious
regional specialty has finally begun to make an appearance on
the banquet circuit. It has long been known in Hesse and
Rhenish Hesse under the sonorous dialect name *grieh Soos,* and
because of all the chopped-up greenery that goes into it, it was
traditionally served with eggs on Maundy Thursday (*Grüner
Donnerstag,* the Thursday before Easter) to help celebrate the
approach of spring. Nowadays, in the region around Frankfurt, little bundles of "saucegreens," grown in greenhouses
during the colder months, are available all year round.

The earliest published green-sauce recipe, from W. Schüne-
mann's *Frankfurter Kochbuch* (1842), is rather rudimentary:
"Take a handful each of chervil, sorrel, tarragon leaves, and
about half as much of finely chopped parsley, squeeze dry in
a napkin, press through a sieve, and stir up with mayonnaise."

The following recipe is taken from a handwritten collection
assembled by a patrician Frankfurt lady known as "Tante
Schlosser," the wife of an alderman and an acquaintance of
Goethe's mother. It corresponds much more closely to certain

*3 cups mixed herbs
(parsley, chives,
chervil, borage, dill,
spinach greens,
watercress, tarragon,
basil, pimpernel)*
*1 cup sour cream or
plain yogurt*
*2 small onions, coarsely
chopped*
2 tablespoons cream
*2 tablespoons
mayonnaise*
*¾ cup low-fat cottage
cheese (pressed
through a fine sieve in
order to smooth curds)
Salt and freshly
ground white pepper
Small pinch of sugar*
*1–2 eggs, hard-boiled and
coarsely chopped*

modern notions of *Grüne Sauce,* especially where the hard-boiled eggs are concerned, though it most probably dates from a slightly earlier period than the previous recipe.

To make enough for 3 people, take 3 hard-boiled eggs. The yolks should be thoroughly crushed, then seasoned with salt and pepper, 1½ tablespoons oil and 1 tablespoon vinegar all mixed up together. Then parsley, borage, pimpernel, estragon [tarragon], mince very fine, and mix with the preceding. Depending on the consistency of the sour cream, add either 3 or 4 tablespoons. Press the sauce through a sieve, and discard any of the greens that will not pass through the sieve.

The modern version of *Grüne Sauce* is a composite of several different recipes, including the one I learned in my parents' house in Frankfurt. (Residents of North America should not be too disappointed if they can't locate any fresh borage or pimpernel.) *Grieh Soos* is traditionally served with boiled beef or poached fish, hard-boiled or poached eggs, baked potatoes or potatoes that have been boiled in their jackets.

•   •   •   •   •   •   •   •   •

Choose all or merely a selection of the herbs and greens mentioned in the list of ingredients (using the tarragon more sparingly than the others). Wash them thoroughly and drain on paper towels. Coarsely chop the greens; loosely packed, they should amount to about 3 cups altogether. Take 2 cups of the greens, combine with the sour cream or yogurt and the onions, and puree in the blender or processor; add a few tablespoons of cream if it doesn't seem to be fluid enough. The rest of the greens should just be finely chopped and stirred in a mixing bowl with the puree in order to give the sauce a little bite. Stir in as much mayonnaise and low-fat cottage cheese as it takes to produce a smooth, creamy sauce.

Season with salt, pepper, and a very little sugar. The hard-boiled eggs can either be mixed in with the sauce or strewn over it as a garnish.

MAKES 2–3 CUPS

BALTIC COAST

Cream Sauce for Fish   Sahnen Sauce

Here is a handwritten recipe, originally written down in about 1840 and preserved by a family from the old Hanseatic seaport of Rostock.

1 tablespoon butter
1 tablespoon flour
4 egg yolks
1 teaspoon grated lemon
  peel
  Grated nutmeg
1 cup cream (see Note)

•   •   •   •   •   •   •   •   •

"Heat a little bit of butter and a little flour, add a couple of egg yolks, grated lemon peel and nutmeg, and stir with the cream to make a smooth, creamy sauce. If you are going to serve this sauce with stockfish, use chopped shallot in place of the grated lemon peel."

NOTE: This sauce is also quite good with poached fish or baked fillets. Heat the cream separately; combine the other ingredients, then stir in the cream a little bit at a time. Do not heat the sauce itself; just keep stirring and adding a little cream each time until it reaches the desired consistency. Taste once again for seasoning before serving.

MAKES 1½–2 CUPS

Sorrel Sauce   Sauerampfersauce

This sauce was enjoyed in middle-class Berlin households at around the turn of the century. Sorrel sauce is recommended for fish, pork, veal, lamb, or fowl.

2 tablespoons butter
2 tablespoons finely
  chopped onion
1 tablespoon flour
1 cup veal or chicken stock
2 or 3 handfuls fresh sorrel
  (approx. 5 cups, packed)
2 tablespoons cream
2 egg yolks
  Small pinch of cayenne
  pepper
  Salt

•   •   •   •   •   •   •   •   •

In a medium saucepan melt 1 tablespoon butter and fry the onion until translucent, sprinkle with the flour, then cook until the mixture is golden. Pour in the stock, stir, and simmer gently for about 15 minutes. Pour through a strainer.

In the meantime, wash the sorrel leaves and lightly sauté in 1 tablespoon butter for several minutes, then mince the sorrel or press through a food mill. Add both the sorrel and whatever liquid is released during this process to the strained sauce. Stir in the cream and beat the sauce with a whisk or an egg-beater. Bring once more to a boil, then take off the heat, thicken with the egg yolks, and season with cayenne pepper and salt.

MAKES 2½ CUPS

Mustard Sauce   Senfsauce

1 cup wine vinegar
1 bay leaf
  Grated peel of ½
  lemon
4 whole cloves
  Freshly ground black
  pepper
1–2 tablespoons sugar
  Generous pinch of salt
1 cup beef stock
1 tablespoon cornstarch
3 tablespoons mustard
3–4 boneless anchovies,
  finely chopped, or 2
  teaspoons anchovy
  paste
1 tablespoon butter
3 egg yolks

This sauce goes well with any kind of fish.

. . . .

Combine the wine vinegar with the bay leaf, grated lemon peel, cloves, pepper, sugar, salt, and beef stock and bring to a boil in a non-reactive saucepan while stirring vigorously with a whisk. Stir the cornstarch with several tablespoons water and, together with the mustard, stir into the sauce mixture with a whisk. Simmer gently for just 2 or 3 minutes, then press the sauce through a strainer.

Season with anchovies. Add the butter, heat thoroughly, then remove from the heat and thicken with the egg yolks.

MAKES ABOUT 2 CUPS

CENTRAL GERMANY

Caraway Sauce   Kümmelsauce

This sauce is frequently served with lamb or mutton stew and is especially good with breast of lamb.

. . . .

Heat the butter in a skillet and fry the onion until translucent. Sprinkle the flour over this and continue cooking until the flour is golden brown. Pour in the beef stock a little at a time, stir into a smooth sauce, add caraway seeds, and simmer over low heat for about 15 minutes.

Press the sauce through a sieve, or puree in a processor, heat once again, and test for seasoning; normally the beef stock will be salty and flavorful enough so that no salt or pepper will be necessary.

MAKES 2½ CUPS

¼ cup (4 tablespoons) butter
1 large onion, cut into large cubes
2 tablespoons flour
2 cups beef stock
1 tablespoon caraway seeds
Salt and freshly ground black pepper (optional)

Caper Sauce   Kapernsauce

Serve with salmon or pike.

• • • • • • • • • •

In a saucepan stir the flour with a little of the stock to make a paste, then stir in the rest of the stock; add the lemon slices and mace. Bring to a boil while continually stirring; cook vigorously for several more minutes, then remove from the heat, remove the lemon slices, and add the egg yolks to thicken the sauce. Add the butter gradually while continually stirring over low heat, until the sauce is nice and smooth. Add the capers and season with salt and pepper.

MAKES 2½ CUPS

1 tablespoon flour
2 cups beef stock
4 lemon slices, without seeds
Pinch of ground mace
3 egg yolks, beaten
10 tablespoons chilled butter cut into pats
½ cup capers
Salt and freshly ground pepper

The Cathedral, Erfurt, Thuringia

Chive Sauce   Schnittlauchsauce

3 tablespoons butter
2 tablespoons flour
1 cup beef stock
2 tablespoons lemon
  juice
  Salt and freshly
  ground white pepper
½ cup heavy cream or
  crème fraîche
  Small pinch of sugar
6–8 heaping tablespoons
  chopped fresh chives

This sauce goes particularly well with boiled beef of any kind (including brisket, corned beef, and so on).

•   •   •   •   •   •   •   •   •

Melt the butter in a medium saucepan, sprinkle the flour into the pan, and cook to make a light roux. Pour in the cold beef stock and stir into a smooth sauce. Add the lemon juice, salt, and some pepper; simmer for 15 minutes before stirring in the cream and a very little sugar. Remove from the heat and stir in the chopped chives.

MAKES 1½ CUPS

CENTRAL   GERMANY

Thuringian Onion Sauce   Thüringer Zwiebelsauce

1 medium onion, cut into
  half rings
3 strips fatty bacon,
  diced
¾ cup pork or goose
  cracklings (Grieben),
  see page 125
2 tablespoons butter
½ apple, peeled and grated
  (optional)

This sauce is almost unique among German sauces, since it does not have any flour in it. Try it especially with boiled or baked potatoes.

•   •   •   •   •   •   •   •   •

Fry the onion, along with the cracklings and bacon bits, over moderate heat until the onions are lightly browned. (Add 1 teaspoon oil if the mixture is too dry.) Reduce heat sharply —"Push the pan over to a corner of the hearth," as they put it in the older recipes. Add the butter and apple, and stir all the ingredients together. Serve the sauce in a deep, medium-sized ceramic vessel.

In the old days, the cracklings would have been made by rendering goose fat to which bits of apple had been added to provide a little flavoring; if you like, the apple can still be added and fried up along with the onions, cracklings, and bacon to provide the same effect.

MAKES 1 CUP

RHINELAND

Hearty Bacon Sauce Deftige Specksauce

Best with boiled or baked potatoes.

• • • • • • • • •

Fry the bacon in a heavy-bottomed skillet over moderate heat, until translucent. Add the onions to the bacon and fry these until golden. Sprinkle the flour into the pan and cook, stirring continually, until lightly browned.

Pour in the beef stock and stir into a smooth sauce. Add the bay leaf and season with the remaining ingredients, then simmer for about 20 minutes over low heat. Remove the bay leaf and serve the sauce, while it is still hot.

MAKES 2½ CUPS

4 strips fatty bacon
  (smoked), cut into
  thin little strips
3–4 onions, halved and
  sliced thinly
1 tablespoon flour
2 cups beef stock
1 bay leaf
  Salt and freshly
  ground white pepper
  Vinegar
  Small pinch of sugar

Morel Sauce Morchelsauce

A few decades ago these delicious mushrooms were a lot more common than they are today and thus cheap enough to use in sauces for veal, lamb, and the more delicate meat dishes in what now is considered incredibly profligate quantities.

• • • • • • • • •

Wash the morels thoroughly, drain, squeeze lightly to remove additional moisture, and cut into little pieces. Melt the tablespoon of butter in a heavy-bottomed saucepan, and thoroughly sauté the morels along with the parsley and chopped chives, turning frequently. Sprinkle with pepper; then sprinkle the flour over the mushrooms and brown lightly. Pour in the beef stock, mix all the ingredients thoroughly, and simmer for about 15 minutes over low heat.

Stir in the sour cream and remove the sauce from the heat after a moment or two. Thicken with the egg yolks, season to taste with salt and pepper, and add a little butter just before

1½ cups fresh morels (see
  Note)
1 tablespoon butter
1 tablespoon finely
  chopped fresh parsley
1 teaspoon finely
  chopped fresh chives
  Salt and freshly
  ground white pepper
1 tablespoon flour
1 cup beef stock
½ cup sour cream
2 egg yolks, beaten
1 teaspoon butter

serving. As noted, this makes an exquisite sauce for light meat dishes, whether stewed or roasted.

NOTE: Since fresh morels are not easy to come by nowadays (and are currently retailing at over $15 a pound), you may have to substitute 2 heaping tablespoons dried morels that have been soaked in water for 20 minutes or so.

MAKES 3 CUPS

Herring Sauce   Häringsauce

Häringsauce (the first two syllables would nowadays be spelled *Hering,* by the way) was greatly prized before the First World War as a cheap, simple, and effective means of adding a little flavor to plain poached fish or boiled beef. The sauce was pungent and flavorful enough in its own right that it was sometimes used as a soup base to which water could be added as desired.

•   •   •   •   •   •   •   •

1 salt herring
½ onion
1–2 tablespoons chopped
   fresh parsley
1 slice lemon peel
2 tablespoons butter or
   margarine
2 tablespoons flour
2 cups beef stock
1–2 tablespoons vinegar

Soak the salt herring in water for about 30 minutes, dry off, pound lightly, remove the skin, split, and fillet. Mince the herring along with the onion, parsley, and lemon peel (from which the white inner surface has been removed).

Melt the butter in a heavy-bottomed, non-reactive saucepan, sprinkle with the flour, and cook the roux until lightly browned. Pour in the beef stock and stir until smooth, then add the vinegar and simmer gently for about 15 minutes. Add the chopped herring and other ingredients and cook for an additional 5 minutes. You may want to pour the sauce through a strainer before serving (or smooth it in a food processor).

MAKES 2½–3 CUPS

NORTHERN GERMANY

Holstein Fish Sauce   Holsteiner Fischsauce

This sauce is customarily served with steamed or poached fish.

• • • • • • • • •

Melt the butter in a skillet and fry the onion until golden, then reduce heat and stir in the mustard. Add the fish stock, raise heat again, and allow all the ingredients to cook together for several minutes. Just before serving, season with salt, pepper, and lemon juice.

MAKES ¾ CUP

¼ cup (4 tablespoons) butter
1 large onion, diced
3 tablespoons mustard
4–6 tablespoons concentrated fish stock
Salt and freshly ground white pepper
½ teaspoon lemon juice

Wine Custard Sauce   Weinschaumsauce

Similar to the Italian *zabaglione* or the French *sabayon,* this "wine-foam sauce" recipe, common in many countries, has also become the indispensable accompaniment of a number of characteristically German foodstuffs—most notably sweet dumplings, or *Dampfnudeln* (see "Desserts" chapter).

Weinschaumsauce can be served hot or cold as a sauce for baked desserts or, as in former days, for boiled puddings. It is still enrolled on the active list of German dessert sauces, and a number of different recipes are current—none of which, in my opinion, gives as good results as this one, but all of which are just as typically German.

• • • • • • • • •

Set the mixing bowl in a pan full of hot but not simmering water, add the sugar to the egg yolks, and beat into a light foam. Add the lemon juice and peel. Gradually pour in the white wine while continuing to mix vigorously with a whisk (or electric beater) until stiff peaks are just beginning to form on the surface.

MAKES 2 CUPS

4–5 tablespoons sugar
5 egg yolks
Juice of 1 lemon
Peel of 1 lemon, finely chopped
1 cup full-bodied white wine (aromatic varietals like the Morio Muskat or Gewürztraminer are best)

A Simple Wine Sauce   Einfache Weinsauce

2 cups dry white wine
  (preferably an aromatic
  one)
¼ cup sugar
1 tablespoon cornstarch
¼ cup sour cream
  Peel of 1 lemon, outer
  yellow skin only
2 eggs, separated, yolks
  beaten

This sauce can be made without the sour cream, or flavored with a stick of cinnamon. And in rural districts, as with most wine sauces, it was frequently made in the old days with apple wine or *Most* (hard cider). Nowadays, like rice pudding, it has practically been superseded by various prepackaged supermarket dessert sauce mixes.

•   •   •   •   •   •   •   •   •   •   •

Combine the wine, sugar, cornstarch, and sour cream, and stir well until the sugar has dissolved and the mixture takes on a smooth consistency. Add the lemon peel and heat while still stirring; allow the sauce to come to a boil at least once before removing from the heat, removing the lemon peel, and thickening with beaten egg yolks.

The sauce can be served hot as a topping for rice pudding or other desserts or allowed to cool, in which case the whites of the eggs, beaten into stiff peaks, can be folded in as an added refinement.

MAKES 2½ CUPS

Rum Sauce   Rumsauce

  Grated peel of 1 lemon
½ cup granulated sugar
  (to be used in place of
  sugar loaf)
1 egg
4 egg yolks
  Juice of 1 lemon
⅔ cup white wine
4–5 tablespoons rum

This is an old-fashioned dessert sauce that can be freely substituted for wine sauce and tastes especially good with any kind of boiled pudding (i.e., one that is placed in a pan of water and then baked in the oven), bread pudding in particular. This recipe is borrowed from master pastry chef L. Kurth's *Illustriertes Kochbuch,* published in 1858.

•   •   •   •   •   •   •   •   •   •   •

"Grate the yellow peel of a lemon over a quarter-pound sugar loaf, pound the sugar into fine grains, stir together with

1 whole egg and 4 yellow eggs [egg yolks] and the clear [strained] juice of a whole lemon, then pour in ⅕ bottle [⅔ cup] of white wine as well as 4 to 5 tablespoons rum and, while heating over a slow fire, beat into a thick foam with a wooden or wire whisk. As soon as the sauce starts to bubble [literally, 'starts to belch'!], it is ready to serve and should be taken off the heat immediately. If the sauce is to be served over a cold pudding, it can later be mixed with a little whipped cream as well.''

MAKES 1½ CUPS

Chocolate Sauce Chokoladesauce

This homemade chocolate sauce *(Schokoladensauce* is the way we would spell it nowadays) is extremely easy to make. The recipe comes to us courtesy of Maria Schandri, who was cook at the Golden Crown in Regensburg for forty years and published her culinary reminiscences in 1876.

4 ounces semi-sweet chocolate, grated
2 cups milk
1 tablespoon cold milk
3 egg yolks

• • • • • • • • •

"Grate [4 ounces] chocolate into a pint of milk that is boiling nicely and allow to come to a second boil. [You may very well want to stir in some sugar at this point as well.] Stir 1 tablespoon cold milk with the 3 egg yolks, pour the hot chocolate over the egg yolks, and swirl [whisk; *Strudeln* in the original] everything around quite vigorously until the sauce is foamy on top.''

MAKES ABOUT 2½ CUPS

Vanilla Sauce   Vanillesauce

2 cups milk
1 vanilla bean, split
6 egg yolks
1–2 tablespoons sugar
  Very small pinch of
  salt

This once-popular topping for many different kinds of puddings has been superseded by a prepackaged mix; in this case, however, the extra effort involved in mixing up the real thing is very slight, and the improvement in taste considerable.

•   •   •   •   •   •   •   •   •

Bring the milk to a boil with the vanilla bean, remove from heat, and let stand for about 15 minutes so the milk can absorb the vanilla flavor. Remove the vanilla bean.

Combine the egg yolks with the sugar and just a very few grains of salt in a mixing bowl; stir until the salt and sugar are dissolved and the yolks are light in color. Pour the milk into the mixing bowl very slowly, while stirring continually. Return the sauce to the pot. Heat the sauce, continuously stirring until it has thickened, but do not allow it to come to a boil. Remove from heat and whisk lightly.

MAKES 2½ CUPS

Cold Red Currant Sauce for Game
Kalte Johannisbeersauce

4 heaping tablespoons
  currant jelly
2 tablespoons mustard
  (Düsseldorf or Dijon-
  type)
½ cup dry red wine
  Salt
  Juice of 1 lemon
  Peel of 1 orange

This recipe was provided by an old woman whose grandfather was a high official in the Bavarian forest service; the sauce can be served with ham as well as roast wild boar and other game. It is very similar to the English Cumberland sauce, which is not named for the English county but for the Duke of Cumberland, a courtesy title borne by the younger sons of the Hanoverian kings of England; since Hannover is in Lower Saxony, it is possible that the sauce, like the dukes, also originated in Germany.

•   •   •   •   •   •   •   •   •

Combine the currant jelly, mustard, red wine, salt, and lemon juice, and mix quite thoroughly. Carefully remove all the white inner surface of the orange peel, then cut the thin orange skin into fine slivers, blanch these for a few minutes in a little water, drain, add to the currant mixture, then mix thoroughly once again.

MAKES 1 CUP

*D*umplings, Spätzle, and Other Side Dishes

.   .   .   .

"*Klösse, Knöpflein,* or *Knötlein,* also called *Klümpe* in Lower Saxony, are little round balls or spheres made in various sizes out of whatever sort of meat, fish, bread crumbs, flour, leavening, and spices are available and then prepared by boiling in water or cooking in butter, and then served up in a broth, or with various sorts of food, or as a pottage, and so forth."

This definition was provided by the authors of *The Young Lady's Encyclopedia of Useful, Elegant, and Curious Knowledge,* published in Leipzig in 1773. In those days, the potato dumpling was still unheard of, though it would be just a couple of years before the exotic "earth apple" would gain a permanent foothold in the German pantry. Other potato side dishes will be dealt with in the following section, and we have already encountered a number of other dumpling subspecies—fish, meat, and soup dumplings—in their respective sections; in this one, I would like to restrict myself to dumplings made with raw or cooked potatoes, flour, rolls or bread crumbs, and cottage cheese.

Even so, there are many hundreds of regional and traditional dumpling recipes, enough to fill several volumes (as indeed they have on one or two occasions), and almost as many regional and dialect names for the end results—some of which we have also encountered earlier. These names range from the frankly descriptive (*Knöpf,* "buttons," *Klump,* "clods" or "lumps," and *Keilchen,* "little wedges") to the picturesquely libelous (in the Palatinate, they're sometimes called

Herzdricker, or "heartsqueezers"). The word *Knödel,* like the English *noodle,* the French *quenelle,* the Italian *gnocchi,* and the Yiddish and Slavic *knedlakh,* derives ultimately from the Latin *nodulus,* "little knot," and is the favored term for dumplings in southern and southwestern Germany, as is a *Kloss* (plural *Klösse*) or *Klotz* in northern, eastern, and central Germany— where the sort of person who might be called a wet blanket in English is known as a *Trauerkloss,* a "doleful dumpling," and an exceptionally stupid person is likely to be called a *Klosskopp,* or, roughly, "meathead."

A word about fried dumplings: Such an abundance of dumplings has been produced in every part of Germany that the surplus has always been available for frying—after they've been cut into slices—on some future occasion. This is more than just another way of recycling leftovers; I personally would much rather eat fried potato dumplings (*Watteklösse,* for example) than the original article, and if they have been fried in butter, which gives them an especially tasty little crust, then all you need is a green salad to make a quite respectable meal.

It might be best for us to begin with the latest and largest entrants in the field—potato dumplings, more specifically, *Thüringer Klösse,* which are also known by a variety of different names, including "green" or "woolen" dumplings, as well as "hairy buttons" (*Hoorische Knepp,* in the Palatinate).

Schleusingen, Thuringia

Dumplings Made with Raw Potatoes
Klösse aus Rohen Kartoffeln

Thuringian Potato Dumplings   Thüringer Klösse

I have happy childhood memories of these particular *Klösse,* even though, at a somewhat earlier point in time, they had almost prevented my mother, who was from Frankfurt, from marrying my father, who was from Ilmenau in Thuringia. When he brought his future bride back home to meet his family, this naturally entailed a whole series of festive dinners at the homes of relatives and friends, all of which featured *Thüringer Klösse.* A steady intake of these *Klösse* came to produce a violent pang in the region of her heart, which she realized had nothing to do with her approaching nuptials. Eventually, however, love triumphed over culture shock and gastric distress, and my mother even learned to make first-rate *Thüringer Klösse*—from her mother-in-law, of course, who had this recipe from her grandmother, the ultimate source of which is lost in the mists of culinary prehistory.

Father, by the way, was responsible for squeezing all the water out of the grated potatoes—men's work.

Thüringer Klösse are especially good with roast beef, pork, goose,★ or with game, provided that the sauce or gravy is rich and plentiful (*"Klösse wollen schwimmen,"* as they say in Thuringia—"dumplings like to swim").

.   .   .   .

5 pounds raw potatoes
(the larger ones being
easier to grate), peeled
⅓ cup semolina (farina)
2 cups milk
1–2 teaspoons salt
1 medium-size stale or
dry-baked roll
1 tablespoon butter,
margarine, or lard

Peel the potatoes and grate them into a bowl of cold water. (Food processors, blenders, and other electrical marvels may have their uses but grating potatoes is not one of them; use the surface of the hand-powered metal grater that is covered with little round holes surrounded by a sharp metal burr, as if a fat nail had been driven through it from the other side.) Keep the grated potatoes in fresh water for a while to prevent them from becoming discolored, then transfer them to a coarse muslin (cheesecloth) bag (or perhaps wrap them carefully in a dish towel), press vigorously, and twist the bag or towel around to wring them out. (Thuringian kitchens have a special potato press for this purpose.) The grated potato should be very dry, almost floury in consistency; place it in a mixing bowl, but, once again, it should not be allowed to come into contact with the air for very long.

In the meantime, cook the semolina about 10–15 minutes in the milk, stirring frequently, until you have a sort of thin porridge, which should be poured over the grated potatoes in the mixing bowl while it is still hot. Sprinkle with salt and mix very well with a sturdy wooden spoon; work this mixture around vigorously with the spoon and finally knead it by hand. Moisten your fingers and shape the dumpling dough into large round *Klösse* at least the size of a lumberman's fist. (Today the *Klösse* are frequently reduced to the size of a lady's fist . . . especially outside of Thuringia.) Cut up the stale (or dry) roll into cubes and fry these in butter until crispy to make

---

★ "Fünf Klösse und 'ne Gans/fünf Kilo im Gewicht/das ist dem Thüringer sein Leibgericht." An inspirational folk rhyme, the gist of which is that five *Klösse* and an eleven-pound goose is every Thuringian's favorite dish. Note that the poem does not specify the weight of the dumplings.

little croutons. Make an indentation in the middle of each of the *Klösse* with 2 fingers, and insert 3 to 6 of the croutons, then smooth over the dough again to cover them up.

Very carefully slide the *Klösse* into boiling salted water; they won't tolerate much in the way of jostling or overcrowding, and the water should be simmering smoothly and evenly. If the water is bubbling and sputtering, then even the sturdiest and shapeliest *Klösse* will either dissolve into their fundamental components or coagulate into a single claylike lump about the size of a tennis ball at the bottom of the pot. (If the *Klösse* merely stick together lightly, this is no great tragedy, however, since they can easily be separated with 2 forks either on the serving dish or while still in the pot.) If all goes well, the *Klösse* should be ready in 30 minutes.

No matter how severe the current energy crisis, the pot should not be covered, and even the most experienced cooks like to protect themselves by floating a couple of trial *Klösse* to make sure that the current batch is not going to turn out either rock-hard or overcooked and soggy. The ultimate test of quality has been well described by the writer Rudolf Hagelstrange: "It is a firmly held belief among connoisseurs that it is impossible, if the *Klösse* are real Thuringian *Klösse,* to eat too many of them."

In the old days in Thuringia and Bavaria, the prospective bride was generally called upon to stage a demonstration of her *Klösse-* or *Knödel-*making abilities—a kind of culinary survival of the medieval ordeal by boiling water. We may presume that many a village maid (or rather, *Maid*) had her expectations dashed, dissolved, or simply sunk in this cruel and unexpected fashion, which simply underscores the point that first-rate *Klösse* are not so much the product of memorized instructions or careful measurements but of sound instincts and long experience.

Since the dumplings are on the dry side, it helps if the gravy is a little fatty (and if the gravy is very fatty, then so much the better as far as the dumplings are concerned). This is very likely the origin of the besetting national sin of German cookery, namely, the tendency to make the gravy stretch a little

further than it really ought to—so we'll be sure to have plenty to go with our *Klösse*.

In the old days, poor families had to make do with an improvised "gravy base" of flour and bacon, and families with growing children would try to slow them down with a *Vorspeise* (appetizer) of a single dry dumpling—that way, they'd only be able to put away about 4 or 5 more of the things, each about the size of a large man's fist, with gravy and a little piece of meat during the rest of the meal. Thrifty Thuringian housewives also saved the potato starch that was released when the grated *Klösse* potatoes were wrung dry, to be used in lieu of cornstarch as a thickening agent, and so on. When the potato starch has not separated out—at least in part—the *Klösse* tend to turn out rather sticky and grayish, so this is an essential phase of the operation, even if there is no great demand for potato starch in your household.

VARIATIONS: The semolina (farina) may be replaced either with a combination of mashed potatoes and milk or with hot milk all by itself.

Some authorities recommend that the croutons be uniformly distributed throughout the dumpling dough before the dumplings are formed.

MAKES 4–6 SERVINGS

EAST   PRUSSIA

Potato Dumplings   Kartoffelkeilchen

2 pounds potatoes,
  peeled
1 egg
  Salt
1–2 kaiser or hard rolls,
  without the crusts
1 tablespoon butter

These "little potato wedges" are considerably smaller than *Thüringer Klösse* and often made in the shape of slightly elongated ovals, known in their native region also as *Flutschkeilchen*, because they *flutschen* (slither, slide) so smoothly off your fork or spoon. As with the *Klösse*, the East Prussian *Keilchen* may be served with any kind of roast that has a rich and abundant sauce or gravy.

Grate the potatoes into a bowl filled with water. As in the previous recipe, place the grated potato in a coarse muslin bag (or perhaps wrap in a dish towel or the like), wring out as much of the starchy liquid as possible, and let the water drip into a wide bowl; before long (5 minutes), the starch will have collected at its bottom. Pour off the water and take half the starch and return it to the grated potato, stir in the egg, and sprinkle in some salt. Stir this mixture very thoroughly, moisten your hands, and form the dough into wedge-shape or elongated oval dumplings.

Cut the roll(s) into cubes small enough to fit inside the dumplings. Sauté these in the butter until crispy. Press the croutons into the dumplings, then bring a generous amount of salted water to boil in a large pot and cook the dumplings in the simmering water for about 20 minutes.

VARIATION: If you make your dumpling dough with 2 parts grated raw potato, as above, with 1 part boiled potato that has been pressed through a strainer, then you have *Kartoffel-keilchen halb und halb* (. . . half and half), which is traditionally served with little bits of onion and bacon that have been fried in butter and then poured over the dumplings (along, of course, with whatever remains of the butter).

MAKES 4 SERVINGS

Gotha, Thuringia

Dumplings Made with Boiled Potatoes
Klösse aus Gekochten Kartoffeln

FRANCONIA

Cotton Dumplings   Baumwollene Klösse

1¾ pounds or 4 medium
   potatoes (the mealier
   the better)
½ cup warm water
1¾ cups cornstarch
Salt
1–2 small stale or dry-
   baked rolls, cut into
   small cubes (½ cup)
1 tablespoon butter

As opposed to the "woolen dumplings" mentioned earlier, these originated in Franconia, which is in Upper Bavaria, just south of Thuringia. The Franconian seems to have introduced potato *Klösse* into the rest of Bavaria, where *Knödel* made from flour or bread crumbs had previously reigned supreme. Every Franconian city has its own traditional dumpling recipe, and in general it seems fair to say that Franconians are hardly less fanatical about their *Klösse* than the Thuringians.

.   .   .   .

Boil, peel, and grate the potatoes (or "press in the potato press," according to later recipes; grating is actually the more traditional method). Mix the warm water with the grated potatoes, then knead in the cornstarch. Season with salt, then form the dough into dumplings about as big as a child's fist. Fry the bread cubes in butter to make croutons. Press the croutons into the center of each of the dumplings. Cook in barely simmering salted water for about 20 minutes, or until done (floating on the surface).

NOTE: Here again, the *Klösse* really don't amount to much without sauce or gravy to eat them with, though in this case what's more important is not the richness (i.e., fattiness) or sheer abundance but rather the genuine meaty flavor of the gravy.

VARIATIONS: The addition of an egg or a little baking powder is suggested in some recipes. Traditional peasant *Klösse* dough might have been spiced up with a little crushed marjoram— for which grated nutmeg would have been the citified, or *bürgerlich,* equivalent.

MAKES 4 SERVINGS

THURINGIA

Cotton Dumplings Wattteklösse

The name of this popular dumpling also means "cotton dumplings," the implication being once again that they're something of a poor man's version of the "real" Thuringian "woolen dumplings."

These dumplings are traditionally served with *Topfbraten,* (see the recipe in the chapter "Beef, Veal, and Pork"), which means "pot roast," but is actually a sweet-and-sour stew made with pork kidneys and other variety meats (including the pig's head on butchering day and other especially festive occasions); the sweet taste is provided by plum jam and gingerbread.

· ·   ·   ·   ·   ·   ·   ·   ·   ·   ·

Wash and boil the potatoes. Peel while lukewarm and grate them (or press in the potato press where applicable). Mix in the cornstarch and salt, then add the boiling milk, while stirring constantly, until you have a workable dumpling dough. Here again, the *Klösse* should be about the size of a baby's fist.

Briefly sauté the bread cubes in butter, and press a small amount of these into the center of each dumpling, then seal up the opening once more. Dredge lightly in flour and cook in simmering water for about 10 to 15 minutes.

MAKES 4–6 SERVINGS

2½ *pounds potatoes*
1¼ *cups cornstarch*
   Salt
2 *cups boiling milk*
3–4 *tablespoons bread cubes*
1 *tablespoon butter*
   Flour for dredging

SAXONY, HARZ MOUNTAINS

Rolled Dumplings Wickelklösse

These dumplings are traditionally served with sauerkraut and corned beef *(Pökelfleisch),* and the dumplings are sometimes cooked in the broth in which the corned beef has already been boiled.

2 pounds potatoes
1¾ cups flour
1–2 eggs
    Salt
  1 teaspoon baking
    powder
1–2 tablespoons butter
  5 tablespoons bread
    crumbs
 10 strips medium-lean
    bacon, diced
    Beef stock

Boil the potatoes in their jackets; peel and let stand overnight, then grate (or press) them and knead together with the flour, egg(s), salt, and baking powder. Melt the butter in a small skillet and briefly sauté the bread crumbs; quickly fry the bacon squares in a separate skillet. Drain.

Place the potato dough on wax paper or a smooth cloth and roll it out into a thin sheet. Sprinkle the dough with the bread crumbs and cooked bacon squares, then, by lifting the paper, roll up the sheet of dough as for a jellyroll. Cut this sausage of dough, on the bias, into finger-length sections; try to press together the outer layer of dough on both cut edges so the filling is covered. Cook for about 15 minutes in boiling beef stock; remove from the pot and drain before serving.

MAKES 4 SERVINGS

BADEN

Rolled Noodles Schupfnudeln

2 pounds potatoes
  1 egg
    Salt
    Grated nutmeg
4–6 heaping tablespoons
    flour
2–3 tablespoons clarified
    butter, lard, or
    vegetable shortening

These dumplings are rolled in shapes like breakfast sausages with pointed ends. They haven't been phased out by deep-fried, deep-frozen French fries and are still enjoyed in several different regions—and accordingly under several different names. These are the very dumplings that are affectionately known as "belly-pokers" in the southwest (*Bauchstecherle* or *Ranzenstecher* in Württemberg, *Buwespitze* in Baden), also, less controversially, as "potato spätzle" *(Potatoespatzn)* in Franconia.

In Swabia, the *Bauchstecherle* are sometimes dipped in fried bread crumbs just before serving. In most regions where they are popular, "rolled dumplings" are served with sauerkraut and bratwurst.

Boil the potatoes in their jackets, allow to cool somewhat, and peel, then let stand overnight. Sometime the next day, grate (or press) them. Mix in the egg and season with salt and nutmeg. Start adding flour to this mixture a little at a time until you have a workable dumpling dough. Shape the dough into little cylinders that are pointed on both ends (hence, "belly-pokers"), about ½″ in the middle, and 3″ to 4″ long. Cook in a generous amount of simmering water, then remove from the pot as soon as they come bobbing back up to the surface. Put on a paper towel to drain. Then brown lightly on both sides in hot butter or lard.

VARIATION: If you make the dumplings a little thinner, they can be fried right away without cooking them in hot water.

MAKES 4 SERVINGS

BERLIN

Fancy Potato Dumplings Feinere Kartoffelklösse

This is top-of-the-line *Klösse* for the scientific homemaker, as prepared at the Berlin School of Domestic Economy in 1912 and based on handwritten notes preserved by Frau Erna Frickert (née Scharfenberg). These dumplings are served most often with stewed fruit or with stewed pears and plum compote, or occasionally with an improvised "gravy" *(Speckstippe)* made of bacon and onions sautéed in butter.

1¾ pounds potatoes,
boiled, then peeled
7 tablespoons butter
¾ cup flour
2 eggs
4 egg yolks
2 tablespoons salt
Pinch of grated nutmeg
2 teaspoons sugar
4–6 tablespoons milk
1 large kaiser roll or a
4″ piece of French
bread, without crust,
cut into cubes
2 tablespoons butter
⅓ cup flour

• • • • • • • • • • •

Grate the peeled potatoes. Whip the butter until creamy and combine with the grated potato, flour, eggs, egg yolks, salt, grated nutmeg, sugar, and milk. Fry the bread cubes in the butter until crispy. Add these to the dumpling ingredients and knead together thoroughly. Coat your fingers with a little flour, form the dough into *Klösse* about the size of an egg, and cook in boiling salted water for 20 minutes.

MAKES 4 SERVINGS

Vogtland-Style Potato Dumplings
Kartoffelklösse aus dem Vogtland

2 pounds potatoes
2 tablespoons flour
1 egg
3–5 tablespoons sour cream
   Salt
   Grated nutmeg
1 stale or dry-baked
   roll, cut into cubes
   (½ cup)
1 tablespoon butter

The Vogtländer yield to no one in their fondness for potato dumplings, though, unlike their neighbors the Thuringians, they prefer the variety that bears their name to be made from cooked rather than raw potatoes.

•   •   •   •   •   •   •   •   •   •

Boil the potatoes in their jackets. Allow to cool off, peel, and grate (or press) them. Mix the flour with the grated potato, stir in the egg, then add as much sour cream as the dumpling dough mixture can still accommodate after the egg has been added. Season with salt and grated nutmeg. With wet hands, shape the dough into dumplings the size of a small child's fist.

Fry the bread cubes in butter until crispy, then press a crouton into the middle of each dumpling. Cook for about 15 minutes in boiling salted water.

VARIATION: To make *Speckklösse,* the Saxon version of the above, take about 3 ounces diced medium-lean bacon and a finely chopped onion, sauté together, drain, and add to the dumpling dough.

MAKES 4 SERVINGS

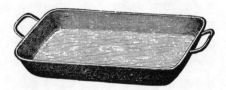

Dumplings Made from Both Raw and Cooked Potatoes
Kartoffelklösse Halb und Halb

H E S S E

Glitscher

So called from their well-known propensity to slip *(glitschen)* off one's plate, *Glitscher* are also called *Wetzsteine* (whetstones) because they are more or less the same shape (although shorter) as the old-fashioned sharpening stone used for a sickle or a scythe blade.

⋅   ⋅   ⋅   ⋅   ⋅   ⋅   ⋅   ⋅   ⋅

3 medium raw potatoes
1¾ pounds potatoes, boiled in their jackets a day ahead
3–4 heaping tablespoons flour
2 eggs
¼ cup water
Salt

Grate the raw potatoes into a bowl full of water, then place in a coarse muslin bag or wrap in a rolled-up dish towel, and wring out thoroughly. The boiled potatoes should be cooked a day in advance, then peeled and grated on the following day. Combine the two, along with the flour, eggs, and water, and mix thoroughly; season with salt. Shape the dumplings with wet hands. The dumplings should be fairly long and pointed at both ends. Cook in simmering salted water for about 20 minutes.

MAKES 4–6 SERVINGS

V O G T L A N D

Klump

The dumplings themselves are made just the same way as in the previous recipe, except that equal amounts of raw and cooked potatoes are occasionally used—in this case about 1 pound of each. The main difference is that the Vogtländer

1¼ pounds white cabbage
1¼ pounds pork belly
½ pound (2–3) small, tart pears
Dash of vinegar
2 teaspoons sugar

dumplings are cooked and served in a vegetable stew, called *Krautklump,* which is made in the following way:

Take 1¼ pounds finely chopped white cabbage and cook in a generous amount of water with an equal amount of fresh pork belly. A little later, add about ½ pound (2–3) small tart pears to the pot. When all ingredients are thoroughly cooked, cut the pork into bite-size pieces, season the broth with vinegar and a little sugar, and cook the *Klump* in the broth for about 20 minutes. Serve all the ingredients together as a stew *(Eintopf).*

MAKES 4 SERVINGS

FRANCONIA

Franconian Potato Dumplings Fränkische Klösse

3⅓ *pounds raw potatoes, peeled*
1¼ *pounds potatoes, boiled the day before*
1 *cup hot milk*
Salt
1 *cup homemade white-bread croutons*

Franconian potato dumplings are also claimed as their very own by the upstart town of Guben on the Polish border, where *Gubener Klösse* are served with corned beef and horseradish sauce. Note that the cooked potatoes should be made a day ahead of time.

•   •   •   •   •   •   •   •   •

Grate the raw potatoes into a bowl full of cold water. Place the potatoes in a coarse muslin bag (or wrap in a dish towel) and wring out thoroughly. Peel and in another bowl likewise grate the boiled potatoes, stir together with the hot milk, then mix the raw and cooked potatoes together and add salt. Wet your hands and form the dough into dumplings, inserting a homemade white-bread crouton into the middle of each one. Cook in boiling water for about 20 minutes.

VARIATION: If equal amounts of raw and boiled potatoes are used (i.e., 2 pounds), then you have so-called *Halbseidene,* or "poplin," *Klösse,* possibly so called because the German word for *poplin* literally means "half-silken" and thus expresses the idea of "half and half," or "partly smooth and partly rough" (this also ties in very nicely with the prevailing textile motif of "woolen" and "cotton" *Klösse*). Also, the quantity of hot milk that is added to the boiled potatoes should be somewhat increased. In Franconia, these dumplings are served with roast pork and red or white cabbage; the "poplin" variety is specifically intended to be served with game.

MAKES 6 SERVINGS

NORTHERN HESSE

Diebchen

The name sounds like "little thieves," but possibly derives from an unknown dialect word. This and the following recipe reflect a highly individualized Hessian approach to *Klösse*-making. The *Diebchen* are customarily served with a special sauce, locally known as *Duckefett,* which consists of the standard bacon-and-fried-onion garnish thickened with sour cream.

1¼ pounds potatoes boiled in their jackets the day before
1¼ pounds raw potatoes, peeled
Vinegar
½ cup hot milk
2–3 eggs
Salt
Generous pinch of crushed marjoram
2–4 tablespoons flour
½ pound hard smoked sausage (bauernmettwurst) or hard salami

. . . .

Peel and grate the boiled potatoes. Set aside. Grate the raw potatoes into a bowl full of water to which a few drops of vinegar have been added. Place these in a coarse muslin bag (or wrap up in a dish towel) and wring out thoroughly. Combine the two kinds of grated potatoes, add the hot milk, eggs, a little salt, and marjoram, and mix well. Gradually add the flour until you have a workable dumpling dough.

Cut part of the hard sausage into 8 fairly large cubes and dice up the rest into much smaller cubes, which should be mixed in with the dumpling dough. Shape the dough around each of the larger cubes to form a *Kloss,* and cook in boiling salted water for 15 minutes.

MAKES 4–6 SERVINGS

VOGELSBERG   (HESSE)

Kartoffelsäck/Beulches

2 pounds raw potatoes
½ pound potatoes, boiled
  in their jackets the day
  before
  Salt and a little freshly
  ground white pepper
1 medium onion, diced
1 teaspoon lard
1 pound salt pork, boiled,
  finely chopped (cooked
  ham can be substituted)

Here you have your choice of only two different dialect names. These little "potato sacks" or "lumps" are the culinary specialty of a very small area—the mountainous region known as the Vogelsberg, where they still enjoy the status of a beloved national dish. They have never caught on in other parts of Hesse, perhaps because of the rather special equipment—a number of little cheesecloth bags, about 3″ × 8″, that can be tied off at the top—that are required to cook the dumplings in. Accompany these with onion sauce or bacon-and-onion sauce or (especially if the salt pork has been added) sauerkraut.

.   .   .   .

Grate both the raw and boiled potatoes (peeled) and mix together right away, along with a little salt and pepper. Sauté the onion in the lard until translucent, and add to the dumpling dough. In the Vogelsberg, a substantial quantity of finely diced boiled salt pork *(Solberfleisch)* is often added to the dough.

Rinse the linen bags in hot water and then wring dry before filling with the dumpling dough, then tie them off at the ends. Place the bags in boiling salted water and cook the dough for about 1 hour. Afterwards, briefly immerse the bags in a bowl full of cold water, which should make it a little easier to squeeze the dumplings out of the bags, like an ice pop. The *Beulches* are served whole, then are cut up by each diner with knife and fork.

MAKES 4–6 SERVINGS

PALATINATE

Dumplings with Meat Filling Gefillte Knepp

This is a specialty of the region around Zweibrücken and Pirmasens, near the French border. The *Gefillte Knepp* can be garnished with little bits of cooked bacon or sour cream that has been warmed up on the stove, and served with a green salad. In the old days, families with a large number of children would foster competitive eating habits by inserting a small onion into one of the *Knepp* instead of the usual filling; the discoverer of the counterfeit dumpling would receive a small reward, possibly a 10-pfennig piece (a nickel).

•   •   •   •   •   •   •   •   •   •

Grate the raw potatoes into a bowl full of water, then place the grated potatoes in a coarse linen bag (or wrap in a dish towel), and wring dry. Grate the boiled potatoes, combine with the raw ones, then stir in the hot milk. Mix in the egg and as much flour as it takes to produce a workable dumpling dough; season with salt and very finely chopped leek. Shape the dough into round, thick, flat cakes by pressing it against the palm of one hand.

To make the filling, combine all the ingredients. Sometimes a roll that has been soaked in water or milk and then pressed dry is added to bind the filling. Place a dab of filling (*Gefillsel*, as it's called) in the center of one cake, then press the edges of the cake together to surround the filling and form it into a ball. Repeat for each dumpling. Cook for about 25 minutes in simmering water.

MAKES 4–6 SERVINGS

DOUGH:

1¾ pounds raw potatoes, peeled
¾ pound potatoes, boiled in their jackets the day before
½ cup hot milk
1 egg
2 tablespoons flour
Salt
2 tablespoons very finely chopped leek (white and yellow parts, not the green)

FILLING:

½ pound uncooked bratwurst filling or mild Italian sausage, or cooked beef of any kind, minced or ground
1 medium onion, diced and lightly sautéed in 1 teaspoon lard
Salt and freshly ground black pepper

Dumplings Made with Dry Rolls
Knödel aus Semmeln

BAVARIA

Bread Dumplings   Semmelknödel

10 stale or dry-baked,
    small-size kaiser rolls
1 cup hot milk
1 medium onion, finely
    chopped
1 small bunch of Italian
    parsley, 8–10 sprigs
1 tablespoon butter
2 eggs, beaten
    Salt and freshly ground
    white pepper
    A very small amount of
    grated lemon peel or
    nutmeg

Semmel (called *Wecken* in other parts of Germany) are crusty breakfast rolls that may be dried out in the oven or simply allowed to get stale, then cut into thin slices and soaked in milk (as in the following recipe) to provide the raw material for the *Knödel*. Kaiser rolls most closely approximate these. This dish is so closely associated with the cuisine and popular culture of Bavaria that the citizens of that ancient kingdom are sometimes known as *Knödel-bayern,* or *"Knödel*-Bavarians." Anyone tempted to interpret this as a term of disparagement has clearly never tasted real Bavarian *Knödel.*

· · · · · · · · ·

Cut the small rolls into ¼" slices, place in a bowl, and cover with hot milk. Cover and let them soak for about 30 minutes to give them time to absorb the milk. Sauté the onion and parsley in butter for a short while, until the onions are just translucent or lightly golden, then combine with the *Semmeln* (roll slices).

Mix the eggs in with the dumpling dough, along with a little salt and pepper and either a very little bit of grated lemon peel or grated nutmeg. The dough should under no circumstances be kneaded, or the *Knödel* won't turn out well at all. Wet your hands and form the dough into 8 *Knödel* and cook in simmering water for about 15 minutes. (Bread dumplings won't disintegrate while boiling if they've been slightly coated with flour before.)

VARIATIONS: Leftover dumplings can readily be sliced and pan-fried; sometimes an egg or two is added to the pan as well. Serve with a salad in either case. They can become—thinly cut—a salad themselves. Freshly made *Semmelknödel* go very well with sautéed forest mushrooms *(Pilze),* not to mention roast beef and goose, with ample amounts of gravy.

You can also sauté some bread crumbs in butter to make a garnish for the *Knödel,* which tastes very good indeed. In Bavaria, special sliced *Knödel*-bread is widely available, so that people will be spared the distasteful task of cutting up perfectly good breakfast *Semmeln.*

MAKES 8 DUMPLINGS

Bread Dumplings with Bacon   Speckknödel

Undoubtedly, these are the sturdiest members of the *Knödel* family; their hearty flavor enables them to stand practically by themselves (perhaps in a little beef broth) as an appetizer, a light snack, even a modest meal. Strictly speaking, this dish is thought to have originated in the Austrian Tyrol, but it has been part of the Bavarian folk tradition for long enough to qualify as a German regional specialty in its own right.

• • • • • • • • •

6 crusty stale or dry-
baked kaiser rolls
(Semmel), or possibly
7 or 8 if they're very
small ones, or an
equivalent amount of
Italian bread
1 cup milk
6 slices medium-lean
bacon, without the rind,
sliced into little strips
⅛ pound salami, sliced
into little strips
2 eggs
A little salt
Flour

Slice the rolls thinly and evenly. Bring the milk to a boil and pour it over the sliced rolls; put a cover on the mixing bowl so the steam will help to soften the roll slices. Cut the bacon and the salami into little strips or just into very small pieces. Fry together in a skillet until the bacon is quite translucent; pour the entire contents of the skillet in with the roll slices. Allow the mixture to cool, then beat in the eggs, add salt cautiously, and mix thoroughly; once again, do not knead the dumpling dough, since no good ever comes of it.

If you choose, you can sprinkle in up to 1 tablespoon flour or add a little more milk according to the texture of the dough. A good bread dumpling dough should be a little coarse-grained and crumbly, though you should be able to roll it into a ball. If the dough seems to be too moist, it's actually better to add bread crumbs than to put in too much wheat flour. Moisten your hands and shape the dough into not-too-large *Knödel,* then cook for about 10 minutes in boiling water that should be "smiling," as the Germans say—that is, bubbling smoothly and evenly rather than seething and blustering. . . .

VARIATIONS: Folklorists will note that the original version of this dish was just made with bacon and no salami. If you substitute about ¼ pound or so of raw or cooked ham, then you have *Schinkenknödel,* sometimes called *Bauernknödel* on restaurant menus; cooked corned beef (called *G'selchtes* in these parts) is also sometimes added to the dumpling dough, and each of these variants can readily accommodate a finely chopped onion that has been lightly sautéed till light golden, or golden brown at most.

CULTURAL NOTE: The world speed record for dumpling consumption—1 *Knödel* per second—was undoubtedly set by a little mechanical man on a Black Forest cuckoo clock, currently on view in the clock museum in Furtwangen.

MAKES 4 SERVINGS

SILESIA,   ERZGEBIRGE

Pan-Fried Dumplings with Mushrooms
Brotklias mit Pilzen

1 medium-size unsliced
loaf white bread, with
the crusts removed
2 cups hot milk
1 small onion, finely
chopped
1 teaspoon butter
2 tablespoons chopped
fresh parsley, plus
extra for garnish
2 eggs
Salt
3 tablespoons butter,
melted

Cut the rolls into thin slices, and pour the hot milk over them. Put a cover on the mixing bowl to trap the steam.

Sauté the onion in butter until translucent. Remove the onion from the skillet but reserve the fat. Mix the onion together with the parsley, eggs, salt, and the bread slices. Form this mixture into medium-size *Klösse* and cook in boiling salted water for at least 15 minutes. Allow to cool, cut into slices, and fry until crisp in melted butter.

Lightly sauté the mushrooms in the fat in which the dumplings have already been cooked, then add a few tablespoons of stock and a little cornstarch or a mixture of flour and butter to bind the sauce. Season with salt, white pepper, and lemon juice (the original recipe calls for vinegar, but lemon juice tastes a bit better) and cook for 5 minutes. Serve the mushrooms over the pan-fried dumpling slices and garnish with coarsely chopped parsley.

MAKES 4–5 SERVINGS

BAVARIA

Wedding Dumplings   Hochzeitsknödel

The name of this dish might be freely translated as "country-style dumpling deluxe," since any rural specialty that is traditionally served at weddings *(Hochzeiten)* is bound to be the tastiest, showiest, and costliest of its kind.

• • • • • • • • •

Whip the butter until foamy, add the eggs, and stir until this mixture is smooth and creamy. Season with nutmeg, pepper, and just a little salt (since some of the other ingredients are very salty). Add the ham and bacon along with the cheese (purists will insist on Allgäuer Emmentaler) and sauerkraut, to the butter-and-egg mixture and stir well. Cut the rolls into very thin, even slices and combine with the above mixture, then let soak for a little while, 15 to 20 minutes.

Form the dough into a single large dumpling, somewhat longer than it is wide; loosely wrap the dumpling in a cloth napkin that has been moistened with boiling water. Tie the ends of the napkin together to make a loop; insert a long-handled spoon or ladle into the loop so that the dumpling can be balanced in a kettle of boiling salted water; in about 35 minutes it should be done. Remove from the cloth and transfer to a heated platter.

When serving the dumpling, cut open the top so that everyone can savor the wonderful steamy aromas that are billowing out from inside; garnish, if you wish, with bread crumbs that have been lightly sautéed in butter. Cut into thick slices.

MAKES 4–6 SERVINGS

¼ *pound dried mixed forest mushrooms* (Waldpilze), *soaked in water for several hours*
3 *tablespoons beef stock*
1 *teaspoon cornstarch or 1 tablespoon butter mixed with 1 teaspoon flour*
Freshly ground white pepper
1 *tablespoon lemon juice*

2 *tablespoons butter*
4 *eggs*
Grated nutmeg
Freshly ground white pepper
Salt
¼ *pound cooked ham, diced*
3 *strips medium-lean bacon, diced*
1 *cup loosely packed, grated Swiss cheese*
⅔ *cup finely chopped, drained sauerkraut*
5 *stale or dry-baked kaiser rolls, without crusts*
Bread crumbs and butter (optional)

Kiensburg, Silesia

WESTPHALIA

Apple Dumplings   Apfelklösse

Here the *Klösse* are made from bread crumbs rather than rolls. The following admirably succinct recipe is taken from Henriette Davidis's *Practical Cookbook,* published in 1844.

•   •   •   •   •   •   •   •   •   •   •

"1 soup plate full of diced cooking apple
1 cup milk
Sugar
Lemon peel
Enough grated white bread to make a good dough (about 375 grams [¾ pound])
A piece of [softened] butter about the size of an egg
When all the ingredients have been well mixed, form into dumplings, cook in salted water, sprinkle with sugar, and serve with a wine sauce."

MAKES 4 SERVINGS

WESTERN AND SOUTHWESTERN GERMANY

Carthusian Dumplings Kartäuserklösse

Nowadays the Carthusians may be better known as distillers and purveyors of fine liqueurs (Grande Chartreuse, etc.), but in the old days the members of this monastic order were famous for their strict observance of meatless days and fasts, which is probably why these little pastries—which are not really *Klösse* in the usual sense of the term—were named for them. When I was a boy, they were often served after a soup as a light Saturday dinner, with fruit preserves or *Weinschaumsauce* (see "Sauces" chapter).

4 stale or dry-baked kaiser rolls, as large as you can find
2 eggs
1 cup milk
2–3 tablespoons sugar
Lard for frying
2–3 tablespoons ground cinnamon and sugar (mixture)

. . . .

Remove the crusts from the dry-baked rolls, then carefully cut the rolls in half and trim off the outsides so the two halves are as round as you can make them. (Do not discard the crumbs produced by this procedure.) Combine the eggs, milk, and sugar, and stir together. Soak the roll halves in this mixture; press very lightly to remove some of the moisture, then press the roll halves into *Klösse*-shape dough balls and dredge in the leftover bread crumbs. Deep-fry in hot fat, then turn them in the cinnamon and sugar mixture.

MAKES 8 DUMPLINGS (4 SERVINGS)

Carthusian Dumplings with Fruit Filling
Gefüllte Kartäuserklösse

This published recipe was written in 1890 by Marie Schandri, a professional cook from Regensburg.

. . . .

"Remove the crusts from several stale French rolls, cut a little piece out of the top (which need not be retained) and hollow out each one before dunking in cold milk, then lay out on a plate for a little while until they have softened somewhat. Stir up some eggs with sugar, turn the bread in this, and then deep-fry in hot schmalz until brown. Fill the insides of the *Klösse* with fruit preserves, place in boiling red wine with a cinnamon stick, and bring to a second boil. Or you can simply sprinkle them with cinnamon and sugar as they come out of the schmalz, and then you can dispense with the wine altogether. Serve with cherry sauce.''

Flour Dumplings   Klösse und Knödel aus Mehl

SCHLESWIG-HOLSTEIN

Mehlbeutel/Grosser Hans

Whether large or small, sweet or savory, flour dumplings have always been a favorite dish in all regions of Germany, particularly, it seems, in the north. This recipe may very well result in the biggest dumpling of its kind.

These giant-size flour dumplings, known as ''floursacks'' or *Grosser Hans* (freely translatable as ''Big John''), have been popular in the northernmost region of Germany for at least 250 years. Before that, there are stray references to ''English puddings,'' which suggests that the ancestral *Mehlbeutel* had been brought over the North Sea by merchants or mariners. If so, the Schleswig *Mehlbeutel*—conventionally described as being ''as big as a baby's head''—has easily outstripped its famous ancestor in size and has long since become a naturalized North German specialty, most closely identified with the (formerly) large tract of cultivated fenland along the North Sea coast that is known as Dithmarschen, from which the Germanic tribe of the ''Angeln'' set out for the land named after them, ''Angle land'' or ''England.''

. . . .

Combine the egg yolks with the milk and melted butter; stir well. Combine the flour, baking powder, salt, and the grated lemon peel and stir together with the previous mixture until you have a smooth dough. Beat the egg whites until stiff peaks start to form, then fold the egg whites into the dough.

Rinse a large cloth napkin in boiling water, wring dry, and spread out on the kitchen table or counter. Sprinkle a little flour in the center of the napkin, place the pitted prunes (or raisins or sultanas) on top of it, then form the dough into a very large dumpling, and place this on top of the fruit. Knot the four corners of the napkin together, leaving a fair amount of "breathing space" above the dumpling; stick a long-handled ladle or stirring spoon (or two, just to be on the safe side) through the loop and lay it across the rim of a large pot in which the smoked pork or bacon (the original recipe calls for an equivalent amount of hog jowl, by the way) has already been briefly parboiled; adjust the water level so that about half of the dumpling is submerged. Now, without removing the bacon from the water, put a cover on the pot and poach/steam the dumpling for a good 1½ hours, adding a little hot water from time to time if necessary.

Remove the dumpling and the pork from the pot. Untie the napkin; the dumpling should be allowed to sit and "blow off steam" for about 5 minutes before serving. Cut the dumpling into serving wedges, like a torte or pie, which can be eaten with butter or sugar or with fruit compote (dried fruit that has been reconstituted and stewed in water) or, failing that, with a simple sauce made by heating some fruit juice and thickening with cornstarch. Together with fruit, serve the sliced bacon or ham hock. Without the fruit, the *Mehlbeutel* can be served with bacon, mustard sauce, and boiled potatoes.

VARIATIONS: Nowadays, a *Mehlbeutel* is frequently boiled or steamed or cooked in a spring-lock pudding mold, but without the pork—which deprives it of the distinctive smoky flavor that would seem to be the main point of eating *Mehlbeutel.*

Yeast or bread that has been soaked in milk is sometimes added to the dough, and in Schleswig, the owners of a cow that had just given birth to a calf would add a little of the rich

6 *eggs, separated*
2 *cups milk*
9 *tablespoons butter, melted*
4 *cups flour*
½ *teaspoon baking powder*
Generous pinch of salt
Grated lemon peel
½ *pound pitted prunes (or raisins or sultanas)*
1¾ *pounds medium-lean bacon (in one-piece "slab," if possible) or smoked ham hocks, briefly parboiled*

Butter, sugar, stewed fruit, or fruit juice thickened with cornstarch

colostrum milk (known locally as *Beestmilch*), another rural delicacy that is not available in any store.

As another refinement that is more in accordance with old-timey than contemporary tastes, blood could be substituted for the milk to make a *Mehlbeutel* black pudding *(Schwarzer Mehlbeutel)*, seasoned with cardamom and cloves and sweetened with sugar-beet syrup or fruit syrup.

MAKES 6 SERVINGS

SILESIA, BERLIN

Yeast Dumplings Hefeklösse

2½ *teaspoons yeast*
  1 *cup milk, 3*
    tablespoons of which
    should be lukewarm
3½ *cups flour*
1–2 *tablespoons sugar*
    Small pinch of salt
1–2 *eggs*
  3 *tablespoons soft butter*

This regional specialty is known to have been appropriated by the Berliners (many of whom were of Silesian origin) and shortly afterwards by cooks all over Germany, at around the turn of the century. The original Silesian *Klösse*, though not quite as supercolossal as the Schleswig *Mehlbeutel*, were still quite respectably sized—1 to a person was the rule, and the quantities suggested for this recipe would be enough to make just 4 authentic Silesian-size dumplings. Incidentally, someone who has suddenly put on a great deal of weight is still said to have "puffed up [*aufgegangen*] like a *Hefekloss*"—a folk memory of these original giant dumplings that has apparently been retained to this day.

. . . .

Sprinkle the yeast over 3 tablespoons lukewarm milk and allow it to dissolve, 5 to 10 minutes. Stir together the flour, sugar, and salt in a bowl. Heap into a little mound and make a well in the center, pour in the yeast mixture, sprinkle with flour, and give the yeast a little time to foam, about 15 minutes. Then stir in the eggs, remaining milk, and soft butter, and beat the dough vigorously. Cover and let the dough rise for 15 to 20 minutes. Then knead it once more; form the dough into 10 or 12 *Klösse,* place on a clean surface that has been dusted with flour, and let stand 1 hour.

To steam the dumplings in the traditional manner, you will need a large (wide) pot, possibly two. Fill the pot about half full with salted water, and bring to a boil. Stretch a cloth napkin—or better yet a piece of muslin—that has been rinsed in boiling water over the mouth of the pot, fasten it so that it will stay reasonably taut, and arrange the *Klösse* on the cloth. They should be touching one another, but since they are supposed to be steaming rather than boiling, they obviously should not be allowed to dip down into the water. Cover the pot with an upturned bowl, and steam the *Klösse* for 15 minutes.

When you bring them to the table, cut open the tops and let the steam escape.

NOTE: *Hefeklösse* are customarily served with stewed prunes that have been heavily sweetened or with stewed fruit in its own juice. You may be tempted to anoint the cut-open tops with melted butter, like a baked potato, which is not such a bad idea.

Alternatively, the *Klösse* can be garnished with bread crumbs that have been lightly sautéed in butter, along with a little melted butter—though if you're planning on doing this, you should add a little extra sugar to the dumpling dough, and perhaps some drops of vanilla extract as well.

Hefeklösse are also sometimes served as a side dish with boiled corned beef, in which case only a pinch of sugar goes into the dumpling dough.

MAKES 10–12 DUMPLINGS (4–6 SERVINGS)

Pear Dumplings Schnitzelklösse

1 recipe for Hefeklösse
  (see above)
1¾ pounds pears (or more
  if they're small),
  peeled and cored
3–4 tablespoons sugar
2 whole cloves
1 cinnamon stick

An interesting dish that I've only come across in a couple of isolated villages in the Spessart Mountains of Franconia, this dumpling is often cooked in a ceramic crock, in which it can also be brought to the table. Clearly, this dish is substantial enough to be enjoyed as a main course rather than just a dessert, and is generally preceded only by a soup course (potato or vegetable soup).

. . . .

Make the dough in the same way as with *Hefeklösse* (above), roll into a big ball, and let stand while the dough rises.

In the meantime, preheat the oven to 350°F. Cut the pears into pieces (which is what *Schnitzel* means, in this particular case). Mix sugar and spices with pear pieces. Place the pears in a small amount of water ¾" high in a large pot; heat until the water is lukewarm, then place the *Hefeklösse* on top of the pears, cover, and bake for about 45 minutes. Take off the cover so that the *Klösse* will end up with a nice brownish crust on top and bake for 10 more minutes. Pour in a little hot water if necessary; test for doneness with a toothpick.

VARIATION: Bread dumplings *(Semmelknödel)* are sometimes used as the point of departure for this dish, which, in my experience, is not nearly as good as the *Hefeklösse* method.

MAKES 10–12 DUMPLINGS (4–6 SERVINGS)

EAST FRIESLAND

Jan in Hemd

If you make a single giant-size dumpling out of yeast dough (see *Hefeklösse* recipe above) and steam it according to the *Mehlbeutel* technique (see page 304), then you have *Jan in Hemd,* "Johnny with a Shirt On," which is customarily served with a pear compote.

Miscellaneous Dumplings
Allerlei Klösse und Knödel

These are the poor relations and eccentric distant cousins of the *Klösse* and *Knödel* nobility; they may not always be acknowledged or given their due by the older and more conventional family members, but they still have an equally valid claim to culinary legitimacy.

Semolina Dumplings   Griessklösse

These *Klösse* are customarily served with fruit compote (in which case a little more sugar may be added to the dough) or flavored with sugar and cinnamon and garnished with fried bread crumbs. Dumplings cooked in beef stock have a heartier taste and may be sprinkled with chopped chives, scallions, or other greens and served with a green salad. In Hannover, somewhat smaller groat dumplings are heated up and served in pea soup.

•   •   •   •   •   •   •   •   •   •

2 cups milk
5–6 tablespoons butter
½ teaspoon salt
1 teaspoon sugar
¾ cup uncooked semolina
    (farina)
3–4 eggs
    Beef stock (optional)

In a pot combine the milk, butter, salt, and sugar, and bring to a boil while stirring constantly. Slowly add the semolina and continue stirring until the grains have absorbed the full amount of moisture. Remove from the heat and stir in the eggs, one after the other, then allow the mixture to stand about 1 hour, until it is quite cool. Take a wooden spoon that has been dipped in cold water or scoop out enough dough with wet hands to form a medium-size dumpling; the semolina dumplings can be cooked in simmering salted water or in beef stock.

MAKES 4 SERVINGS

SILESIA

Pasta Shells   Schälklösse

Less formally known as *Schlitzchen,* "little slots," these little dumplings have plenty of butter and egg in them and are quite a bit less austere than some of the other Silesian specialties— *Assen für arme Leut,* "poor folks' vittles," as they say—that we've encountered so far.

Altona, part of the city of Hamburg

In the old days, these *Klösse* would probably have been cooked in mutton broth, since mutton was the great favorite in Silesia, but nowadays people prefer to cook and serve them in beef stock with cooked (but not overcooked) soup greens that have been cut up into thin strips.

2¾ *cups flour*
½ *teaspoon salt*
4 *eggs*
9 *tablespoons butter, melted*
4–5 *heaping tablespoons bread crumbs*
Beef or mutton stock

·   ·   ·   ·   ·   ·   ·   ·   ·

Combine the flour, salt, and eggs to make a firm egg noodle dough; let stand for 1 hour. Roll the dough into thin rectangular sheets (about 8″ × 12″), brush with melted butter, and sprinkle with bread crumbs, then roll the sheets like a jellyroll, and afterwards flatten these into logs about 2″ wide × 12″ long. Cut each of these logs of dough into rhombic shapes and press the cut edges together. Put into a wide pot with boiling stock. Let simmer for about 8 minutes.

VARIATIONS: The bread crumbs in this recipe may be replaced with 1 bunch of parsley, washed and finely chopped, then sprinkled over the buttered sheets of dough.

These *Schälklösse* can also be cooked and served with beef-vegetable broth; needless to say, the beef and the vegetables need to cook somewhat longer than the *Klösse.*

MAKES 4 SERVINGS

SILESIA, BERLIN

Poppyseed Christmas Pastry   Mohnklösse

This cold dessert has a rather tenuous claim to membership in the *Klösse* family; in Berlin, their naturalized second home, they're called *Mohnspielen* rather than *Mohnklösse* (poppyseed dumplings), though when the *Mohnkliessla (Mohnklösse)* is scooped out into individual portions, they do bear some resemblance to elongated dumplings. This dish is customarily served at midnight on Christmas Day or New Year's Eve and is incredibly rich—thus best washed down with a glass or two

5 tablespoons sugar

2 cups milk

2 cups crushed poppyseeds (or prepared, canned poppyseed filling)

⅓ cup sultanas or raisins

5 tablespoons rum

1 teaspoon ground cinnamon

2 drops almond extract, or 3 crushed bitter almonds

12–16 zwiebacks (more or fewer according to size)

¾ cup slivered almonds (optional)

of Christmas punch, mulled wine, or the like. This recipe comes courtesy of my friend Heinz Schwarz, who has initiated me into many of the mysteries of traditional Silesian cuisine.

•   •   •   •   •   •   •   •   •

First dissolve the sugar in 1 cup of boiling milk, then pour the milk over the crushed poppyseeds and allow a little time for them to absorb the liquid before stirring. Wash and dry the raisins and soak them in the rum for a while, then add them with the rum, cinnamon, and the almond extract to the poppyseed mixture and stir well. Soak the zwiebacks very briefly in the remaining cup of milk; they should not be allowed to get soggy.

In a glass baking dish, lay down alternate layers of poppyseed filling and zwieback until all the ingredients have been used up—the bottom and top layers should be poppyseed. If you like, you can decorate the top of the *Mohnkliessla* with slivered almonds. Let stand overnight, at least, to give the various flavors some time to blend properly.

MAKES 8 SERVINGS

Puttsbus Castle on the Baltic Sea island Ruegen (engraving by H. Winkles, after a drawing by B. Peters)

EAST PRUSSIA

Farmer Cheese Dumplings   Glumskeilchen

These are like potato dumplings in which the main ingredient has been overshadowed though not entirely replaced by the East Prussian staple *Glumse* (farmer cheese). These dumplings are customarily served with browned butter and a mixture of sugar and cinnamon.

· · · · · · · · ·

Soak the currants in water. Combine the farmer cheese, sugar, salt, and eggs and stir; depending on how moist this mixture is, stir in more or less of the indicated quantities of flour and cornstarch. Mix the potatoes and currants into the dumpling dough.

Wet your hands and form the dough into little wedge-shape *Keilchen* and cook for about 10 minutes in simmering water. Remove from the water and drain.

VARIATIONS: Cooled melted butter and 1 teaspoon baking powder are occasionally added to the dumpling dough.

In Saxony, *Quarkkeulchen* are made with the same ingredients (here the baking powder is a necessity), then the dough is smoothed out flat, insofar as possible, cut into little strips about ½″ × 3″, and deep-fried. These are served with applesauce, stewed fruit, or just with sugar and cinnamon.

MAKES 6 SERVINGS

½ *cup currants*
1 *pound farmer cheese*
   (or cottage cheese put
   through a sieve)
2–3 *tablespoons sugar*
   Small pinch of salt
2 *eggs*
2 *tablespoons flour*
2 *tablespoons cornstarch*
3 *medium potatoes,*
   boiled, peeled, pressed
   through a strainer

BAVARIA

Plum Dumplings   Zwetschgenknödel

3 medium potatoes,
   boiled the previous
   day
1 tablespoon butter,
   melted and cooled
2 egg yolks
   Pinch of salt
2–3 heaping tablespoons
   flour
1–1¼ pounds damson
   plums
1 sugar cube for each
   plum
¼ cup bread crumbs
3 tablespoons butter
2 tablespoons sugar
   and 1 teaspoon
   ground cinnamon
   (optional)

This dish originated in Bohemia and was, understandably, appropriated by Bavarians many years ago. The best plums to use are late damsons, firm-fleshed and not very juicy.

•   •   •   •   •   •   •   •   •   •

Grate (or press) the boiled (peeled) potatoes and mix with the cool melted butter, egg yolks, and salt, then add as much flour as it takes to produce a slightly adhesive dough that can be easily rolled out. Roll out into thickish flat sheets (about ½" thick), then cut the sheets into squares large enough to cover a plum.

Wash the plums, wipe dry, remove the stones, and insert a sugar cube into the center of each plum. Wrap the dough squares around the plums and carefully press the edges together to make a continuous covering. Cook the dumplings in salted water that is simmering evenly and gently; remove from the pot, drain, and sprinkle with bread crumbs that have been fried in butter or with sugar and cinnamon.

MAKES 6 SERVINGS

CENTRAL GERMANY

Cabbage Dumplings   Kohlklösse

Here is an old recipe from Saxony and Thuringia; these dumplings were traditionally served with roast duck, but they taste
awfully good with a roast of any kind. In the more frugal
Saxon and Thuringian households, they might have been
served as a main dish with a little flour-and-bacon gravy to
sop them in. Depending on the size of the cabbage, the indicated quantities should be enough for 4 portions.

· · · · · · · · · · · ·

Cook the cabbage in salted water until it is not quite tender,
which should take about 45 minutes. Set in a colander to
drain, squeeze out the remaining moisture, and finely chop.
Melt the butter in a large skillet or stewpot; sauté the onion
for a few minutes, then add the chopped cabbage, sprinkle
with salt and pepper, and allow to cook for about 10 minutes
over medium high heat while stirring constantly.

Remove the cabbage from the heat and allow to cool. Mix
in the egg yolks (do not discard the whites!) and sour cream;
gradually add the flour and bread crumbs, in equal proportions, until the dough is firm yet pliable enough to be
kneaded. Season with nutmeg, plus additional salt and pepper
if necessary. Beat the egg whites until stiff peaks begin to
form, then fold into the dumpling dough.

Moisten the bowls of 2 wooden spoons and scoop out
enough dough to make *Klösse,* which should be about as big
as medium-size potatoes in this case. Cook for 10 to 15 minutes in salted water that is simmering smoothly and evenly.

MAKES 4 SERVINGS

1 small head of white
 cabbage, cleaned and
 quartered
¼ cup butter
1 large onion, finely
 chopped
 Salt and freshly ground
 black pepper
4 eggs, separated
¼ cup sour cream
¾ cup flour
¾ cup bread crumbs
 Grated nutmeg

Both Ends of the Loaf

Perhaps at this point a word should be said on behalf of an enormously popular German specialty (of a sort), one that fulfills much the same function as more substantial side dishes such as dumplings and potatoes. That function, of course, is soaking up the gravy, and I refer to the humble, necessary *Kanten,* which is the commonest German word for the heel of a loaf of bread. The Germans have about as many different kinds of bread as the French have cheese—somewhere in the neighborhood of two hundred, give or take a few—and, as with most of the homier and more intimate aspects of daily life, almost every region of the country has its own special dialect term for the heel of the loaf. Since all of these may soon be in some danger of extinction because of the advent of sliced and packaged bread, I would like to provide a brief glossary, if only for the record:

Kneisle, Riebele—Swabia
Knäppchen, "knaves"— Westphalia
Knust—North Germany
Knüstchen or *Krüstchen*— Hesse
Rämpfchen—Thuringia
Ränftel—Silesia
Reifle—Allgäu
Scherzel—Bavaria and Austria

The *Kanten* was always supposed to be especially good for you, though the nutritionists that I've asked to substantiate this article of parental faith were unable to do so from a merely scientific point of view. Obviously, it does provide some exercise for the teeth and jaw muscles, but beyond that, the benefits are purely psychological. I remember being told as a child that if you always ate your crusts, you would learn to whistle beautifully; suffice it to say that I crunched the heels of all loaves I could get hold of, but—I never learned to whistle. Since then, sorely disillusioned, I've given up on them altogether—having learned, as the Germans say, "to whistle at them" (to pay them no mind, to hold them in lofty contempt) and to leave the *Kanten* to those who truly appreciate them.

SWABIA

Spätzle

Now that the fame of this quintessential Swabian delicacy has spread not just to every region of Germany but over most of the rest of the world as well, there has come to be a problem with quality control. Cellophane packages of ready-made spätzle (some of them actually manufactured in Swabia) are available almost everywhere, but obviously even the best of these are but a pale simulation of the original article, made by hand in *Oma*'s (Grandma's) Swabian kitchen. Nowadays, most of Oma's granddaughters and grandnieces very seldom scrape their spätzle from a board, and they wouldn't do without their shiny new "spätzle presses" and "spätzle slicers," even though the dough is still likely to be handmade.

In 1966, my colleague Dr. Karl Lerch published a little book entitled *Spätzle-Breviary* (roughly, "The Spätzle-Lover's Bible"), though even he was unable to clear up the fundamental confusion surrounding the origin of the word itself. Some say that these dumplings reminded someone of fat-bodied little sparrows (*Spatzen* in South German dialect); others derive the word from the Italian *spezzare,* "to cut into pieces." I tend to prefer this second explanation: having observed the Italian "guest workers" in Germany and the tenacity with which they clung to their ancestral eating habits and their hometown delicacies in the midst of an alien land, I like to imagine the Roman legionnaires of 2,000 years ago slogging through the damp forests of Germany, where such civilized little niceties as a sack of flour very rarely reached them via their already thinly stretched supply lines. And bearing in mind my own experience of military home cooking, I can imagine some Roman soldier turning loose a little of his precious flour to keep alive his memories of mother's homemade pasta in the midst of this culinary wasteland.

Admittedly, my hypothesis takes us back a little further than the authorities consulted by Dr. Lerch, who proposed that spätzle might as well have originated in some medieval monastery kitchen. At any rate, suffice it to say that anyone who is interested in perpetuating one of Germany's proudest culinary traditions, in what is its purest and most ancient form, has only to follow this recipe.

Spätzle are served on all sorts of occasions and in a variety of different forms and "presentations," the more prominent of which are listed below; they go best with a roast or other robust meat dish that has ample amounts of rich-tasting gravy —with game, braised beef or *Bifflamot,* or sauerbraten.

·   ·   ·   ·   ·   ·   ·   ·   ·

Stir together the flour, eggs, and salt in a bowl with ½ cup of cold water, then beat this mixture until bubbles start to appear and you have a smooth batter that no longer adheres to the spoon. Add just as much water—a little bit at a time— as is necessary to achieve this consistency. This is rule number one of spätzle-making. Rule number two is that you should be prepared to write off your first couple of attempts as pure research; mastering the delicate task of grating or slicing off the requisite amount of spätzle dough (called *schaben,* or "shaving," in Swabia) really does take a certain amount of practice.

3 cups flour
4 eggs
1–2 teaspoons salt
1 quart cold water

That being said, the next step is to bring salted water to a boil in a large pot. To cut the dough, you will need a wooden cutting board—ideally, a "spätzle board" *(Spätzlebrett),* which is shaped like a little cutting board with a broad handgrip and front edge that tapers to a point like a knife blade. Moisten the board with a little of the boiling water, take a very little bit of dough, and press it out flat with a broad knife (although, of course, there is a special implement called a *Spätzleschaber* that's available for this purpose), then, while repeatedly dip- ping the knife blade in water, cut off fine strips of dough and push them off the edge of the board and into the pot of boiling water with the knife.

When the spätzle bob back up to the surface, remove them with a skimming spoon (or, if you prefer, with a customized spätzle-skimming spoon), briefly (and gently) swish them around in a pan of cold water to remove the floury film from the surface, then leave them in hot water to keep warm. I might add that though this second phase of the operation may only seem frustratingly difficult the first couple of times, it will always have to be performed while bathing in the steam that comes billowing out of the pot—a situation that I still find a little too clammy and uncomfortable for my tastes (and too close to the one described by the classic phrase "slaving over a hot stove").

It's easy to see why even the Swabians have devised so many of these mechanical aids to assist them in spätzle-making, though on the other hand, the modern, pre-prepared products can hardly hope to compare with the genuine hand-crafted article—a delicacy that's worth paying a special price for (even worth sweating for a little).

MAKES 4 SERVINGS

Spätzle in Clear Broth   Spätzle in der Brühe

1 recipe of spätzle (see above)
2 cups clear beef stock
1 tablespoon finely chopped fresh parsley or chives

Make the spätzle as described above; heat in the broth and serve garnished with parsley or chives.

MAKES 4 SERVINGS

Spätzle in Vinegar Sauce   Saure Spätzle

1 recipe for spätzle (page 319)
2 tablespoons butter or lard
2 tablespoons flour
Beef stock
Vinegar
¼ cup sour cream
2 bay leaves
Salt and freshly ground black pepper

Make the spätzle according to the basic recipe above; it's perfectly all right if you let them get cold. Melt the butter or fat in a skillet, add the flour, and cook until golden. Start pouring in beef stock until you have a thick, viscous sauce; season with vinegar, sour cream, bay leaves, salt, and pepper. Simmer for about 15 minutes; add the spätzle and heat it in the sauce. Remove the bay leaves, if possible, and serve—preferably with fricadelles (*Frikadellen,* ground beef patties), in my opinion.

VARIATIONS: You can also add 2 small minced onions to the sauce. Sauté these in butter before you add the flour; serve with 1 kirby (small cucumber, about 4″ long) that has been peeled, cut in half, seeded, and thinly sliced, then mixed in with the sauce along with the spätzle.

Alternatively, you can halve or quarter the 2 onions (large ones this time), then fry the half (or quarter) onion rings in 2 or 3 tablespoons butter until golden brown. Pour both the onions and browned butter over the spätzle and serve with lettuce salad. This dish is called *Abgeschmälzte Spätzle.*

To make *Brägelte Spätzle,* first prepare the spätzle separately; they can be left over from the day before if you like. Melt 4 tablespoons (clarified) butter in the pan and fry the spätzle, turning constantly, until they are crispy around the edges. Beat together 2 eggs and 3 tablespoons sour cream, sprinkle with salt and pepper, and pour this mixture over the spätzle in the pan. Sauté until the egg mixture solidifies, like an omelette, and serve with green salad.

MAKES 4 SERVINGS

Liver Spätzle   Leberspätzle

Other spätzle recipes in this book are *Allgäuer Käsespätzle* (Cheese Dumplings), *Spätzle und Linsen* (Spätzle with Lentils), and *Gaisburger Marsch* (Swabian Beef Stew with Spätzle).

Leberspätzle are especially popular with a green salad as a late afternoon "meat tea" *(Vesper)* or as a substantial snack, or they can be lightly sautéed in butter and served with fried eggs as a meal in their own right. The deluxe version of this dish, *Rehleberspätzle,* is made exclusively with venison liver.

3½ cups flour
1 pound liver, ground
3–4 eggs
*Salt and freshly
ground black pepper*
*3–4 tablespoons very finely
chopped fresh parsley*

•   •   •   •   •   •   •   •   •

Combine the flour, ground liver, eggs, salt and pepper, and beat this mixture until it has the consistency of spätzle batter; then it's best to let it sit for an hour or so.

Cook the spätzle as described in the basic recipe on page 319. Garnish with the parsley.

MAKES 4 SERVINGS

SOUTHWESTERN   GERMANY

Homemade Egg Noodles   Hausgemachte Nudeln

3 eggs
6 tablespoons water
A few drops of
  vinegar
2⅓–2⅔ cups flour

Granted that factory-made, store-bought noodles are not too bad, the best of all are the ones that are made at home. I've never met a German *Hausfrau* who wasn't convinced that *her* homemade noodles weren't better than anyone else's, though perhaps that has something to do with the fact that anyone who still goes to the trouble of making homemade noodles must care very deeply about such matters in the first place.

Nowadays, even the process of making noodles in your own kitchen has been semi-mechanized, with all sorts of little machines to help us out. The following recipe dates from the pre-industrial era of noodle-making and is borrowed from a cookbook published in 1912 by Hermine Kiehnle, director of a cooking school organized by the Swabian Women's Association—a volume, I might add, that still has its legions of loyal adherents up to the present day.

.   .   .   .

"For every egg, add half an eggshell full of water [2 tablespoons]; beat together well in a bowl. So the noodles will dry faster, add a few drops of vinegar, then mix in the flour [2⅓ cups per 3 eggs] and knead the dough on the board [*Nudelbrett*] until it starts to show little air pockets when you cut through it with a knife. Then divide the dough into 4 or 6 separate pieces, form each of them into a ball, then roll each out flat until the dough is so transparent that you can read a line of print through it. While you are rolling out one piece, make sure to keep the others underneath an upturned bowl so they will not dry out. Put the rolled-out sheets of dough on a clean cloth, and when they are almost dry, cut them down the middle, lay one half on top of the other, roll them up, and cut out strips of noodles between ⅓" and ½" wide. Spread out the noodle spirals and allow them to dry once more. You can cook the noodles in boiling salted water for about 10 minutes, drain them through a sieve [colander], and then put them on a plate after the water has drained out."

NOTE: Nowadays, you'll probably knead the dough and roll it out with the help of your kitchen machines.

MAKES 4–6 SERVINGS

S O U T H E R N   G E R M A N Y

Batter-Fried Sage Leaves   Salbey zu Backen

This old-fashioned savory, known in Swabia as *Mäus* (mice) or *G'schwänzte Küchle* (little cakes with tails), has been restored to favor by the electric frying pan and the renewed popularity of little treats that can be cooked right at the table.

In this case, the bitter herb taste of the sage leaves blends perfectly with the delicate crispy batter. This recipe is taken almost verbatim from a cookbook originally published in 1709; the language has been slightly modernized, but only 2 ingredients have been added (sugar and salt).

• • • • • • • • •

Scant cup flour
3 tablespoons cold water
1 egg, beaten
A few tablespoons dry white wine (or hard cider)
1 egg white
1 tablespoon melted butter that has been allowed to cool
Pinch of salt
Small pinch of sugar
Plenty of nice fresh sage leaves
Oil or shortening for deep-frying

Take the flour and mix with the cold water into a thick batter that must be smooth. Then mix in the beaten egg and stir well; pour in a little sour wine, yet not too much. Beat the egg white into soft peaks and fold it into the batter. Finally, add the butter as well as a very little salt and sugar and stir the batter once more. Wash and dry off the sage leaves, dredge them in the batter, and fry them on both sides in hot lard (see Note) until crispy.

NOTE: I would also suggest that you fold in the egg white last of all and let the batter sit for about 30 minutes beforehand. Also, vegetable oil or shortening is recommended for deep-frying rather than lard.

MAKES 8 SERVINGS

Forbach, Black Forest

SCHWARZWALD

Popovers   Quellende Küchle

3 teaspoons yeast
2 tablespoons lukewarm
  water
  Pinch of sugar
3½ cups flour
  Large pinch of salt
2 tablespoons butter,
  softened
1 cup milk
1 egg
  Oil or fat for deep-
  frying (or lard, for
  those who care more
  about folkloric
  authenticity than
  cholesterol)

This translation is approximate, since popovers are normally baked rather than deep-fried, but the basic principle is the same (*quellen* = "to bulge," "to swell up"). *Quellende Küchle*, customarily served with fresh ham and sauerkraut or other robust meat dishes, are something of a rarity in Germany today, surviving only in a few secluded valleys in the Black Forest region. Nevertheless, they make an excellent surprise side dish, especially if your family and friends are the sort of jaded worldlings so often depicted in television advertisements, who are "tired of just meat and potatoes."

•   •   •   •   •   •   •   •   •

Sprinkle yeast over the lukewarm water and sugar. Set in a warm place for 15 minutes so the yeast will start to rise. Sift the flour into a mixing bowl; add salt and separate little dabs of soft butter. Add the yeast mixture to the flour along with the milk and mix well. Knead the egg into the batter, cover the bowl, and allow the dough to rise for 1 hour. Then roll out the dough into a thick sheet and cut it into 2-inch squares or diamond shapes. Allow the dough to rise a little more for 20 minutes, then deep-fry in hot fat until golden brown.

The *Küchle* should have "puffed up" considerably, since a good-size bubble of steam forms inside them while they're cooking. Pile up the *Küchle* on the platter and serve hot, preferably with pork.

MAKES 4–6 SERVINGS

B A D E N

Hügelsheim Pancakes Hügelsheimer Pfannkuchen

Hügelsheim is a village between Baden-Baden and the Rhine. It is noted for its asparagus and the so-called pancakes that are actually more like dough spirals. The recipe for the *Pfannkuchen* is a proprietary secret of an inn called The Swan in Hügelsheim. I had been trying to get somebody there to give me the recipe for many years, and after my attempts at espionage failed, I returned to my own kitchen to make a few experiments. This, then, is the recipe for a kind of spiral pastry that looks and tastes exactly like *Hügelsheimer Pfannkuchen,* and I know of nothing that goes better with fresh asparagus. (Note that you will need a pastry bag to make the spirals.)

2 *cups water*
Generous pinch of salt
7 *tablespoons butter*
1¾ *cups flour*
4–6 *eggs*
Cooking oil

•   •   •   •   •   •   •   •   •

Combine the water, salt, and butter in a pot and bring to a boil. Add the flour and keep stirring until a large mass forms around the spoon and a white residue becomes visible at the bottom of the pot. Remove from the heat, allow to cool off somewhat, and beat in the eggs, one after the other; keep adding the eggs until the dough starts to get shiny and tears off when you lift it with a spoon.

Pour about ¾" of cooking oil into the bottom of a skillet, heat up, and, using a pastry bag with a round nozzle, squeeze out a spiral of dough (tight enough, for example, that the individual strands will be able to fuse together while expanding during the cooking process) onto the hot oil. When the dough is golden brown on the underside, turn it over with a ladle or skimming spoon. When the *Pfannkuchen* are done, drain them on paper towels and serve with asparagus. (It's best not to make the *Pfannkuchen* too big, or you may have trouble turning them over.)

MAKES 4–6 SERVINGS

Vegetables, Potatoes, and Stews

. . . .

Since the last of these three categories usually includes a sampling of the other two, it seemed reasonable to put them all in the same section of the book. It also seemed reasonable to exclude basic or extremely well-known recipes that might be found in almost any other cookbook published in any country. I have tried to concentrate, here as elsewhere, on little-known regional specialties or on recipes that were once popular and are now largely forgotten, also on traditional cooking techniques that have yet to win wider fame outside their native regions.

Salsify, Oyster Plant   Schwarzwurzeln

This is another European peasant or poor man's staple that has just started to turn up—along with mâche *(Feldsalat)*, sorrel, endive, radicchio, porcini, chanterelles, and various other European forest mushrooms—as a high-priced gourmet novelty in the produce bins of urban America. On the other hand, the consumer demand for *Schwarzwurzeln* in Germany (and hence the acreage under cultivation) has steadily been decreas-

ing since 1977. Perhaps the reason for this is that so much of
the black coloring of the roots is involuntarily transferred to
one's hands while peeling it (and subsequently very difficult
to remove).

One way of avoiding this, of course, is to wear rubber
gloves; the other is to boil the salsify (as described in the
following recipe) before attempting to peel it, a procedure that
is quite effective but does not seem to have been very well
publicized. Using canned or frozen salsify will eliminate this
problem. Canned salsify is widely available in North America;
the fresh *Schwarzwurzeln* (that becomes white after peeling)
may be rather difficult to come by in this form.

Salsify—greatly prized in the old days as "winter asparagus" and a bit reminiscent of turnips in flavor—is said to be
rich in iron and insulin. It figures prominently in a number of
interesting regional recipes, and, as an endangered species (at
least from a culinary standpoint), seems deserving of some
encouragement.

CENTRAL GERMANY

Black Salsify with Meatballs
Schwarzwurzeln mit Fleischklösschen

Salsify prepared this way is an excellent vegetable dish even without the meatballs. Best served with potatoes boiled in salted water.

• • • • • • • •

Soak the roll in water to soften, then press out the excess moisture. Mix the ground veal with the roll, sprinkle with salt and a pinch of grated nutmeg, and mix in the 2 eggs—if the resulting mixture is too runny, you can add some bread crumbs to thicken it. Form the mixture into little meatballs and dredge these in 2 tablespoons of the flour.

Thoroughly scrub the salsify under running water, then soak in 2 tablespoons vinegar for 15 minutes before peeling off the black husk. Cut the salsify into 2″ pieces and transfer these immediately (the peeled salsify "tarnishes" very quickly when exposed to the air) to a saucepan with the water, to which 2 tablespoons vinegar and 2 tablespoons flour, as well as a generous pinch of salt, have been added. Simmer for about 50 minutes. Cook the meatballs for the last 10 minutes or so in the salsify broth. Remove the meatballs and keep warm; save some of the broth as well. Drain the salsify in a colander.

Melt the butter in a skillet, sprinkle in the remaining 2 tablespoons flour, and cook the roux very briefly; before the flour starts to change color, pour in some of the salsify broth to make a sauce; thicken the sauce with the egg yolks, but do not boil. Add 1 cup cream to make a richer sauce and season with a little lemon juice. Mix in the salsify and the meatballs with the sauce and serve.

MAKES 4 SERVINGS

1 small dinner roll, crust removed
½ pound ground veal
Salt
Grated nutmeg
2 eggs
6 tablespoons flour
2 pounds salsify (Schwarzwurzeln)
4 tablespoons vinegar
1 quart water
2 tablespoons butter
2 egg yolks
1 cup cream
1 tablespoon lemon juice

BADEN

Winter Squash Savory   Pikantes Kürbisgemüse

1 pumpkin (2¼ pounds)
  Salt
  Juice of 2 lemons
2 medium onions, finely
  chopped
1 quart milk
2–3 tablespoons cornmeal
  or cornstarch
  Sugar
  Grated horseradish

In Germany, winter squash (including the ones that are called pumpkins in North America) are mainly used for making children's jack-o'-lanterns, or *Martinslaternen;* there is also a well-known sweet-and-sour squash recipe that is still customarily served with boiled beef. The older cookbooks provide a more extensive repertoire for this admirable vegetable; this one is taken from a handwritten recipe collection from the Upper Rhine region.

· · · · · · · · · ·

  "Scoop out round balls of flesh from a yellow marrow [squash or pumpkin]. Marinate for 2 or 3 hours in salt, lemon juice, and finely chopped onions. Cook carefully in milk until glassy [i.e., translucent] but not too soft. Bind the milk with cornmeal or cornstarch and season with salt and sugar. Finally add a few spoonfuls of grated horseradish."

NOTE: More specifically, I'd suggest using about 2¼ pounds of winter squash, or pumpkin if you like—the soft flesh only, without the rind or the seeds. For the marinade, use the juice of 1 or 2 lemons along with 2 or 3 small onions, finely chopped. I've found that this "savory" goes very well indeed with roast veal and roast chicken, and I can imagine that it would be quite good with pork chops as well. A worthy addition to anyone's kitchen recipe file.

MAKES 4 SERVINGS

BAAR (BADEN-WÜRTTEMBERG)

Sour French Beans   Sure Wälschbauna

Wälsch (Welsh) is a convenient Germanic term that means "foreign." In this case the dialect term refers to their rather gnarled and scrawny relatives known as scarlet runner beans —which seem to do very well in the rather gnarled and unfruitful countryside of the Baar; green beans can be used as well. Serve with home-fried potatoes.

2 pounds scarlet runner beans or green beans or pole beans
Salt
1 heaping tablespoon lard or butter
1 tablespoon flour
2 bay leaves
Generous splash of vinegar
Freshly ground black pepper

• • • • • • • • •

Wash and snap the beans, then cut them into thin strips and cook them in a small amount of salted water. Drain the water from the beans. Reserve this cooking liquid. Heat the lard in a thick-bottomed non-reactive skillet or saucepan, add the flour, and cook the roux till browned while stirring constantly; then pour in enough of the reserved cooking liquid to make a thick brown sauce. Add the bay leaves, vinegar, and a few grindings of pepper, and simmer this for about 15 minutes. Discard the bay leaves, add the beans, and mix well; allow all the ingredients to heat up together for a few more minutes, test for seasoning, and serve.

MAKES 4–6 SERVINGS

Neu-Brandenburg, not far from Berlin (after a drawing by Borussia)

Saint Vitus Beans   Veitsbohnen

Grüne Bohnen (green beans) have been very shabbily treated in German kitchens—overcooked and then embalmed in savory and flour paste. A more effective traditional way of dealing with green beans may be found in Carl Friedrich von Rumohr's *Spirit of the Art of Cooking* (1822).

.   .   .   .

"There are different ways of cooking fine-cut German-style [i.e., thin and diagonally cut] green beans. You might cook them in beef stock until they are quite done, then add some butter, flour, and chopped parsley, or you might cook them in butter and season them with a little estragon [tarragon], basil, and other strong-tasting herbs of that kind. Finally, you can make 'sweet' green beans with sweet cream, some butter, and flour."

NOTE: With the first method, the butter and flour should be heated together in the usual way to make a roux. The "strong-tasting herb" that von Rumohr had in mind for the second method was probably savory, which—as suggested by its German name, *Bohnenkraut* (bean herb)—has traditionally been associated with green beans. This herb undoubtedly has its uses, the most important of them being, in my opinion, to restore some flavor to canned green beans, which are otherwise rather tasteless. In connection with the third method, it may be worth noting that von Rumohr was from northern Germany, where similar "sweet" recipes for strong-flavored foods served with cream are still very much in vogue.

BRANDENBURG

Braised Cucumbers   Schmorgurke

Cut the cucumbers in half lengthwise, remove seeds, and cut the cucumber halves into short segments. Combine these with 2 tablespoons vinegar, 1 tablespoon sugar, salt, and pepper, and marinate for 2 hours, turning occasionally.

In a large pot season the beef stock with allspice, 1 or 2 tablespoons sugar, and 2 tablespoons vinegar, then cook the cucumber pieces in the stock until they're just beginning to get tender.

Meanwhile, cook the diced bacon until the fat has been rendered, remove from pan, and sauté the onion in the remaining fat until it is translucent. Sprinkle the flour into the pan, cook until the roux is browned, and stir in some of the liquid the cucumbers have been cooking in. Stir well, add the cucumber pieces, and cook for another 15 minutes or so. Garnish with the bacon bits and serve.

MAKES 4 SERVINGS

*2 pounds cucumbers,
   peeled*
4 tablespoons vinegar
2–3 tablespoons sugar
   Pinch of salt
   *Freshly ground white
   pepper*
2 cups beef stock
*2 allspice berries,
   crushed, or a pinch of
   allspice*
3 strips bacon, diced
*2 tablespoons minced or
   grated onion*
1–2 tablespoons flour

RHINELAND

Stewed Chard Stalks   Stielmus

Swiss chard is a kind of beet whose leafy green tops are sold in large bunches on vegetable stands in Hesse and the Rhineland. In other parts of Germany, *Rübstiele* are used; they are specially cultivated turnip stalks. Try these stalks with boiled potatoes and bratwurst.

• • • • • • • • • •

Cut the chard stalks into 2″ sections. Wash the stalks and cook in salted water until tender.

In another saucepan, cook the butter and flour to make a light roux. Pour in the milk and cook together to make a white sauce; pour in enough of the liquid in which the chard stalks have been cooking to make the sauce smooth and creamy. Drain the stalks in a colander and add them to the sauce; season with salt, pepper, and nutmeg. Simmer gently for another 10 minutes and serve. A splash of vinegar or lemon juice should enhance the flavor of this interesting vegetable dish.

MAKES 4–6 SERVINGS

*2 pounds Swiss chard,
   stalks only*
2 tablespoons butter
2 tablespoons flour
1 cup milk
   *Salt and freshly ground
   black pepper*
   *A very little bit of grated
   nutmeg*
   *Splash of vinegar or
   lemon juice (optional)*

N O R T H   B A D E N

Asparagus with Dumplings
Spargelgemüse mit Klössen

*2 pounds white asparagus
(canned may be used,
omitting the cooking)*
2 eggs
*2 tablespoons butter,
melted*
Salt
Grated nutmeg
*5 tablespoons crumbled
zwieback*
*5 tablespoons fresh bread
crumbs*
2 tablespoons butter
2 tablespoons flour
½ cup cream
Small pinch of sugar
3 tablespoons lemon juice
2 egg yolks

White asparagus is the principal farm product of north Baden, part of the former domain of the Elector Palatinate; it is cultivated particularly in the area south of Heidelberg. This is an adaptation of a handwritten recipe I once came across there, probably dating from the last decades of the previous century; it appears to have no counterpart in present-day regional cuisine.

•   •   •   •   •   •   •   •   •

Peel the stalks of the asparagus, cut into not-too-small pieces, and cook until quite tender, 15 to 20 minutes. Drain in a colander and save all the cooking liquid. Beat the 2 eggs with the cool melted butter. Add the salt and grated nutmeg and stir in equal amounts of crumbled zwieback and bread crumbs (at the same time) until you have a pliable dumpling dough. Use 2 teaspoons to scoop out and shape the dough into little dumplings and cook in the reserved asparagus broth for no more than 10 minutes. Keep warm.

Heat the butter and flour together to make a light roux; stir in the cream and some of the asparagus broth to make a white sauce. Season with sugar, salt, and lemon juice. Remove from the heat and add 2 egg yolks to thicken the sauce. Reheat the asparagus pieces in the sauce, but do not allow them to become overcooked, and do not allow the sauce to boil. Add the dumplings and serve together in a single serving dish. Green asparagus tastes very interesting when prepared that way (but shorten cooking time).

MAKES 4 SERVINGS

Assorted Vegetables with Dumplings and Crayfish   Leipziger Allerlei

This dish was said to have been first concocted for a university professors' banquet in Leipzig some time during the last century. The Wilhelminian (Victorian) era of prewar culinary splendor in Berlin was also the golden age of *Leipziger Allerlei,* and its decadent period began when the commercial canning companies decided to appropriate that term for their bargain vegetable assortments.

I have already successfully gone on record with a public appeal to our protocol chiefs in Bonn to start serving really outstanding "native" dishes like this one (not the canned variety, obviously) at their official state functions, receptions for distinguished foreign visitors, and so on. This is one of the earliest published versions of the recipe. Don't be afraid of the work involved: it's a special dish for very special occasions every cook can be proud of.

·   ·   ·   ·   ·   ·   ·   ·   ·

"This dish tastes best in spring and summer, when all the ingredients will be truly fresh in accordance with taste and price; the desired quantity of asparagus, fresh [baby] peas, small carrots, kohlrabi, cauliflower, and morels should each be prepared for cooking in the customary way. Once again, each vegetable should be cooked in water for as long as the taste and wisdom of the cook suggests and then tastefully arranged on a serving plate—provided solely that the cauliflower should go on top. The assorted vegetables should be served with crayfish [one may reckon, incidentally, on one crayfish per person], which should be boiled, the shell cracked open, and the snouts filled up with bread dumpling dough. These last [the dumpling dough] should be fried [separately] in butter. The crayfish meat, the filled crayfish snouts, and the dumplings should all be considered an indispensable accompaniment to this dish. The [tail] shells of the crayfish should be pulverized and mixed with butter and later dissolved in a

½ pound of each of the following: asparagus, fresh baby peas, small carrots, kohlrabi, and cauliflower

¾ cup dried morel mushrooms

20 or more crayfish

butter sauce, enriched by 2 to 3 egg yolks and seasoned with salt and nutmeg. This sauce is poured over the vegetables. This dish goes quite well with veal cutlet, tenderloin steak, roast pullet or squab, etc."

NOTE: To make *Leipziger Allerlei* for 4 people, I suggest you start out with about ½ pound of each vegetable, plus about ¾ cup dried morels that have been well soaked in water. If certain fresh vegetables are not available, I'd suggest leaving them out rather than using canned or frozen ones; likewise, canned Chinese straw mushrooms do not make a very good substitute for morels.

See page 98 for a little more information on crayfish and their snouts. Crayfish or lobster meat, precooked, may be substituted without all the trouble involved in stuffing the snouts.

This recipe also gives a fair idea of how much work was involved in the classic *bürgerlich* recipes of the last century.

MAKES 4–6 SERVINGS

City Hall, Leipzig, Saxony
(engraving by C. W. Arldt,
after a drawing by G. Täubert)

BADEN

Cooked Escarole   Endiviengemüse

This recipe comes from the cookbook of "Mamsell" König, Karlsruhe, 1844:

•   •   •   •   •   •   •   •   •

"The escarole (or Bibb lettuce) should be cleaned and washed, then cooked in boiling water until it is tender but not too soft. Then drain in a colander and cool by pouring cold water over it; squeeze out the moisture and chop very well. Then melt a little pat of butter and cook a handful of onion, a little parsley, and a cooking spoon of flour, then add the escarole and simmer for about a quarter hour, then stir in some good beef broth, add a little salt and nutmeg, and simmer for another half hour."

NOTE: Escarole and other salad greens go well with veal, brains, sweetbreads, and chicken fricassee.

MAKES 4 SERVINGS (1 SMALL HEAD OF ESCAROLE PER PERSON)

BADEN

Fricasseed Boston Lettuce   Kopfsalat Frikassiert

Here is a recipe from the Upper Rhine region that dates back to the beginning of the nineteenth century.

4 firm heads of Boston
    lettuce
1–2 tablespoons butter
    Salt and freshly
    ground white pepper
1–2 cups beef stock
2 egg yolks, or 1
    teaspoon butter and 1
    teaspoon flour,
    kneaded together

•   •   •   •   •   •   •   •   •

Remove and discard the hard green outer leaves and tie up the heads of lettuce with cooking twine to keep the leaves together. Drop them into boiling water and simmer gently until the leaves begin to soften, which should take only a few minutes. Remove them from the water with a slotted spoon and place in (or rinse with) cold water.

In a fairly large heavy-bottomed saucepan or skillet melt the butter. Carefully press the moisture out of the lettuce, pat dry if necessary, and place the heads of lettuce next to one another in the pan, lightly sprinkle with salt and pepper, and cover. When the lettuce becomes yellow on one side, turn it over and sprinkle once more with salt and pepper. Then pour in the beef stock and simmer for at least 5 more minutes.

Remove the lettuce from the pan, place in a heated serving dish, and untie the thread. Thicken the sauce in the pan with egg yolks (after removing it from the heat) or add little flecks of flour and butter paste and stir with a whisk over high heat until the sauce attains the desired thickness. Pour the sauce over the heads of lettuce and serve.

MAKES 4 SERVINGS

SAXONY

Cooked Greens   Negenschöne

1¾ pounds mixed greens
   (see Headnote)
3 tablespoons butter
1 medium onion, finely
   chopped
Salt and freshly
   ground black pepper
Small pinch of sugar
4–5 tablespoons crême
   fraîche (for which
   heavy cream may be
   substituted)

In former days, wild growing herbs were often the very first of the season. According to Carl Friedrich von Rumohr: "In several regions of Germany, all sorts of wild herbs and greens are gathered during Easter Week, such as orache, nettles, dandelions, watercress, the young sprigs of wild thyme, and so forth. These are chopped up fine and cooked into an exceptionally good-tasting vegetable dish, like spinach greens, which in the Saxon dialect is called *Negenschöne*."

I have not been able to locate an authentic recipe for this dish in any of my old cookbooks, but the following represents what might be thought of as a reasonably accurate reconstruction. The selection of greens may include garden orache, nettles, dandelions (only the whitish or pale yellow leaves and the stalks), sprigs of wild thyme, watercress, garden cress, chervil, and parsley; if you come up short on some of these ingredients, a couple of spinach or lettuce leaves (which also help to tone down the tart or bitter taste of the herbs) may be substituted. Although we now have a luxuriant selection of spring salad greens grown in greenhouses or imported from more southerly climates, one should not forget the healthy and exceptionally good-tasting traditional dishes made with wild growing herbs. Serve with new potatoes and pork chops, or just with hard-boiled eggs.

·   ·   ·   ·   ·   ·   ·   ·   ·

Sort through the greens, remove woody stems, wash thoroughly (do not dry off), and coarsely chop. Melt 2 tablespoons butter and lightly sauté the wet greens. Heat 1 tablespoon butter and cook the onion until quite transparent. Mix this together with the greens and season with salt, pepper, and sugar. Bind lightly with crème frâiche (or heavy cream if you like).

MAKES 4–6 SERVINGS

Frauenstein, Saxony

NORTH   BADEN

Cooked Sorrel   Sauerampfergemüse

1¾ pounds sorrel
1 tablespoon butter
2 teaspoons flour
1 cup rich beef stock
Salt
Grated nutmeg
3–4 tablespoons sour cream

Sauerampfer (sorrel) is another exceptionally good-tasting vegetable that grows wild in Germany and has been part of the traditional peasant cookery of Europe for many centuries. It has recently been rediscovered by the practitioners of *nouvelle cuisine*. Sorrel soup was especially popular in East Prussia (see "Soups" chapter), and it is invariably to be found in several versions of the famous "green sauce" of Frankfurt.

•   •   •   •   •   •   •   •

Carefully pick through the sorrel, remove the stems, wash, and blanch briefly (by placing it in a generous amount of boiling salted water and allowing it to come to a second boil), then remove from heat and let stand for 5 minutes. Drain, press dry, and finely chop the sorrel.

Cook the butter and flour together to make a golden roux, pour in the beef stock, and stir to make a lightly bound sauce. Mix in the chopped sorrel, season carefully with salt and a few grindings of nutmeg, and cook for an additional 15 minutes on low heat. Blend in the sour cream just before serving.

MAKES 4–6 SERVINGS

Sorrel with Raisins   Sauerampfer mit Rosinen

1¾ pounds sorrel
Salt and freshly
ground black pepper
Grated nutmeg
Raisins
2 tablespoons butter

Sorrel contains a relatively high concentration of a corrosive substance, oxalic acid (*oxalis* = "sorrel" in Latin), most of which can be leeched out of the sorrel leaves by blanching the leaves beforehand in boiling water. Nevertheless, as our rural forebears were perfectly well aware, all dishes containing it should be avoided by those suffering from rheumatism, arthritis, and various kidney ailments. Sorrel grows in damp, low-lying meadows and can be gathered from spring to early fall. It is also sometimes grown in home vegetable gardens and commercial market gardens in Europe and North America. (The American wild sorrel, known as "sourweed" in many areas, is not as tasty as the cultivated variety.)

·　　·　　·　　·　　·　　·　　·　　·　　·

Carefully pick through the sorrel, remove the stems, wash, and blanch briefly in boiling salted water. Remove from the heat and let stand for 5 minutes, drain the sorrel, and press dry. Put the sorrel through the meat grinder (or food mill or processor), then cook in a small amount of water for about 10 minutes. Season with salt, pepper, and a few grindings of nutmeg.

In the meantime, wash the raisins and cook them in a small amount of water until they are soft and tender. Drain the raisins and mix with the cooked sorrel. Melt the butter, pour it over the sorrel and raisins, and serve.

MAKES 4–6 SERVINGS

Castle Hohenstaufen and the Rechberg, Swabia

Mushrooms Forestière   Steinpilze Försterinart

1½ pounds forest
    mushrooms
    (Steinpilze) (yellow
    boletes and/or
    whatever variety you
    prefer), washed
4 slices fatty bacon, cut
    into thin strips
1 tablespoon butter
2 shallots, or 1 small
    onion, finely chopped
½ cup cream
2–3 tablespoons chopped
    fresh parsley
    Salt and freshly
    ground white pepper
1 small garlic clove
    (optional)

Steinpilze are wild forest mushrooms, "yellow boletes" to the mycophile, and this is, at least as far as the name of the recipe is concerned, "the way the forester's wife makes them." This is a traditional Bavarian dish that has become popular all over Germany in the last few decades. In Bavaria, this particularly tasty variety of mushrooms was formerly known as *Herren-pilze,* "squire mushrooms," because anyone who came across them in the forest was (theoretically) obliged to turn them over to the owner of the land.

Serve with veal or lamb, with dumplings, or on toast as an appetizer before the main course.

•   •   •   •   •   •   •   •   •   •

Cut the mushrooms into medium slices (not too thin). Sauté the bacon strips and the shallots or onion in the butter until the bacon has turned translucent, then add the mushrooms and cook over moderate heat, turning frequently. As soon as the cooking liquid has evaporated, stir in the cream, then sprinkle with the parsley and season with salt, pepper, and, if you wish, a small crushed garlic clove. Mix all these ingredients together well.

MAKES 4–6 SERVINGS

Mushroom Cutlets   Pilzkoteletts

This dish is a particular favorite during the summer months. Serve with a green salad.

•   •   •   •   •   •   •   •   •   •

Slice the mushrooms and sauté for about 5 minutes in 2 tablespoons butter. In another skillet, sauté the diced onions in the remaining 1 tablespoon butter until they are quite translucent.

Cut the rolls into slices, soak in water or milk, and press out as much of the moisture as possible. Once the mushrooms have cooled, put them and the rolls through the meat grinder, then combine with the onion, browned butter from the mushroom pan, eggs, parsley, salt, and pepper. Knead all these ingredients together and taste for seasoning. Add bread crumbs if too moist. Shape this mixture into flat little patties (cutlets), dredge in bread crumbs, and fry them in the clarified butter.

MAKES 4–6 SERVINGS

1½ *pounds forest mushrooms (Steinpilze) (yellow boletes and/or whatever variety you prefer), washed*
3 *tablespoons butter*
1 *medium onion, diced*
4" *piece French bread (inner parts must not be too soft), crust removed*
½ *cup water or milk*
3 *eggs*
1 *tablespoon chopped fresh parsley*
Salt and freshly ground black pepper
3 *tablespoons bread crumbs*
3 *tablespoons clarified butter for frying*

CENTRAL GERMANY

Red Cabbage with Bacon and Apple
Rotkraut mit Speckäpfeln

1 2-pound head of red
cabbage, washed and
quartered
2–3 tablespoons cooking
fat (originally lard or
Gänseschmalz,
rendered goose fat)
½ cup red wine or water
¼ teaspoon ground cloves
Salt and freshly
ground black pepper
2 teaspoons sugar, or 3
teaspoons red currant
jelly
3 tablespoons vinegar
6 strips medium-lean
bacon, diced
1–2 medium onions, finely
chopped
¾ cup cooked ham, finely
diced
4 large apples (Rome
variety), washed and
cored but leave the
bottom intact to hold
the filling

A peasant dish from Saxony and Thuringia, this is a great favorite of families with many children. However, it's much too delicious to be enjoyed only during periods of financial crisis. Serve with potatoes that have been boiled in salted water or mashed potatoes.

•   •   •   •   •   •   •   •   •

Shred the cabbage; drain and press dry. In a large non-reactive heavy-bottomed pot, cook the cabbage in the hot fat for a few minutes. Add the red wine or water, cloves, salt and pepper, sugar or red currant jelly, and the vinegar; mix well and simmer for a good hour over low heat.

Preheat the oven to 350°F. In another pan cook the bacon until the fat is rendered. Remove it from the pan and sauté the onion(s) in the same pan until golden (but not brown). Mix together the bacon, onions and diced ham and use this mixture to stuff the apples.

Place the stuffed apples on top of the cooked cabbage in an ovenproof baking dish and bake for about 25 minutes. You may have to add a little more liquid to keep the cabbage from drying out. The apples should be nice and tender, like ordinary baked apples.

MAKES 4 SERVINGS

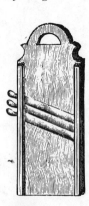

FRANKFURT AM MAIN

Home-Style Red Cabbage
Rotkraut Bessere Deutsche Art

This is my mother's recipe.

•   •   •   •   •   •   •   •   •   •

Remove bruised or damaged outer leaves and cut the cabbage into quarters. Cut out the stem, then shred the leaves or cut them into matchstick strips. Peel and halve 2 of the onions and cut into paper-thin slices. Heat the lard (or other fat) in a large heavy-bottomed pot to sauté the onions, then add the cabbage, and stir until everything is thoroughly coated with the fat. Leave the remaining 2 onions whole; add them to the pot to flavor the gravy but remove before serving. Stir together the vinegar and red wine with just 2 tablespoons beef stock (for the time being) and pour this over the cabbage.

Season with salt and pepper, ground cloves, and bay leaf (which also should be removed before serving). Mix in the apple. Simmer for at least 1 hour over low heat, stirring twice; add a few more tablespoons beef stock if necessary. Season with red currant jelly and the other spices just mentioned. Cook for another 30 minutes (uncovered if it looks like there might be too much liquid). Serve hot.

MAKES 4–6 SERVINGS

2 pounds red cabbage
4 small onions
2–4 tablespoons rendered goose fat, Gänseschmalz (or other cooking fat)
1 tablespoon vinegar
¼ cup red wine
2 tablespoons beef stock (and possibly a few more later)
Salt and freshly ground black pepper
"As much ground clove as will fit on the point of a knife"
1 bay leaf
1 large Granny Smith apple, peeled, cored, and coarsely grated
3–5 tablespoons red currant jelly

SOUTHWESTERN   GERMANY

Glazed Chestnuts   Glasierte Maronen

1 pound chestnuts
2 cups beef stock or milk
1 medium-size slice
  celery root, peeled, or
  1–2 celery stalks
2–3 tablespoons butter
1–2 tablespoons sugar

These homemade glazed chestnuts are especially popular with game or fowl, also with Brussels sprouts, red cabbage, or sauerkraut.

•   •   •   •   •   •   •   •   •

Wash the chestnuts, make a cut or puncture a hole in the shell of each chestnut, bring water to a rolling boil, and boil the chestnuts for 15 minutes. Drain, allow them to cool somewhat, and you should find it fairly easy to remove the shells and skins. Cook the chestnuts in beef stock or milk with the celery for 30 minutes; the chestnuts should still be firm and not at all crumbly. Drain through a colander.

After the chestnuts have been thoroughly drained, heat the butter in a large skillet and start to cook as many of the chestnuts as will fit comfortably in the pan at one time in the melted butter. Sprinkle with sugar and keep turning so the chestnuts will be caramelized. Place them in the center of the serving dish, surrounded by meat or vegetables. (Brussels sprouts are customarily mixed in with the chestnuts before serving.)

MAKES 4 SERVINGS

Home-Fried Potatoes   Bratkartoffeln

This once enormously popular homemade specialty is gradually losing out to the infamous deep-fried, deep-frozen *pommes frites* (French fries), which, for all their other faults, are a bit easier to prepare than *Bratkartoffeln* (variously known as *Röstkartoffeln, geröste* or *gebrätelte Kartoffeln,* or *Scheibenkartoffeln* in different parts of Germany). Things have reached such a pitch that a restaurant's reputation among truly serious eaters may stand or fall on whether or not it still serves *Bratkartoffeln* (or whether it has finally started serving them again), and of course how good they are. Here, in lieu of an actual recipe, are a few basic principles of *Bratkartoffeln:*

• Never use potatoes that have been peeled and boiled in salted water. If the potatoes have been boiled in their jackets, what the Germans call *Pelkartoffeln,* then they should have a chance to cool completely; in fact, it's best to make them the day before. Don't use soft boiling potatoes.

• Whether you slice them or dice them, they taste very much the same.

• Apart from salt and pepper, other possible spices include marjoram and caraway seeds; other additives might include diced ham, wurst, or bacon, leftover roast or any other cooked meat.

• The *Bratkartoffeln* can be fried in leftover drippings from a roast (a particularly robust and flavorful medium), butter (in which case the potatoes should be cut up in very small pieces), or *Wurstfett* (the fat skimmed off when sausages are cooked; very good-tasting, but not so easy to come by these days, even in Germany).

• Finely minced onions help to give the fried potatoes a richer taste.

• If *Bratkartoffeln* are to be made from scratch (i.e., from raw potatoes), then they should be sliced very thin to start with— as with the traditional Westphalian version, known as *Scheibenkartoffeln*—and not mashed up or manhandled too badly once they're in the pan.

Potato Croquettes   Kartoffelkroketten

This is another staple item that is much more likely to be encountered in its prefabricated and deep-frozen forms than homemade. Serve with fish and/or a green salad. The breading, not mentioned in the original *bürgerlich* recipes, reflects the influence of French-style gastronomy; in the old days,

2 pounds potatoes,
  peeled
1 cup mik
1 egg
1 tablespoon butter,
  softened
1 teaspoon salt
2–3 tablespoons flour
  Grated nutmeg
  Clarified butter

these croquettes were normally fried in butter in a skillet and only rarely deep-fried in oil.

•   •   •   •   •   •   •   •   •   •   •

Boil the potatoes and mash them while still hot; for this phase of the operation, *Grossmutter* would have used the same kind of potato press used to make potato dumplings. Allow this to cool somewhat, then add the milk, egg, butter, salt, and as much flour as this mixture will readily absorb; knead all these ingredients together and season with grated nutmeg.

Shape the mixture into small flat oval cakes about ¾" thick. Dredge in flour, let stand for a little while, then fry in clarified butter until crispy on both sides.

MAKES 4–6 SERVINGS

Fried Potatoes with Marjoram   Marjorankartoffeln

2 pounds potatoes,
  peeled and sliced or
  diced
2–3 tablespoons lard
8 strips medium-lean
  bacon, cut into
  matchsticks
  Crushed marjoram
  Salt and freshly
  ground black pepper
½ cup water

Sometimes known on their native heath as *Majoran Grumbiehre*, the second element in this compound (*Grundbirnen*, "ground pears") is the local word for "potatoes." This savory potato dish is customarily served with a roast or with home-made wurst.

•   •   •   •   •   •   •   •   •   •   •

First of all, although this is a recipe for fried potatoes, the potatoes themselves should be of a type that will remain fairly firm if they've been boiled. Heat the lard in a large skillet or in a heavy-bottomed saucepan. Add the bacon to the lard, along with the potatoes. Fry the bacon and potatoes for a good 5 minutes, turning frequently.

Sprinkle a generous amount of crushed marjoram, as well as salt and pepper, over the contents of the skillet. Add the water, stir once more, then cover and cook over medium-low heat for just about 30 minutes, stirring every 10 or 15 minutes.

MAKES 4–6 SERVINGS

Worms, city of the Nibelungen in the Rhine valley (engraving by Johann Poppel, after a drawing by L. Lange)

Potato Pancakes   Kartoffelpfannkuchen

Some foreign epicures are convinced that German traditional cuisine has never gotten beyond the peasant—some would say primitive—stage of development, often citing these starchy, crispy little morsels of potato dough as evidence for this accusation. However, the fact remains that even the most sophisticated Germans can never quite rid themselves of an obstinate craving for potato pancakes, and whenever two or three Germans are gathered together, no matter where in the world they might be, some sort of *Kartoffelpuffer* feeding frenzy is bound to ensue at some point.

Potato pancakes are thought of primarily as a Rhineland specialty, perhaps because they are sold by vendors from stalls on the sidewalk there, though they are probably eaten and enjoyed just as much in any other region of Germany.

There are a great many local variants on the basic concept, each with its regional or colloquial nickname, depending on whether the potato is locally regarded as a "ground pear" *(Grumbiehr-Pannekuche,* enhanced with semolina and chives, in the Palatinate) or an "earth apple" *(Erappelspankauken,* pan-size potato pancakes with bacon, from the Ruhr district) or merely a "tater" (*Tuffelpankok* from northern Germany), or whether the fact that the potatoes should be grated is emphasized (as in Bavarian *Reiberdatschi* and Rhenish *Rievekooche* or *Rievkoche,* also *Reibeplätzchen* in the region around Münster), or finally whether the pancakes themselves are classified as "fritters" (*Krebbelcher* in Koblenz), "muffins" (*Kartoffelplätzchen* in Westphalia), waffles (*Kartoffelwaffeln* in the Ruhr, which are actually cooked in the waffle iron), Swabian "pan-scratchers" *(Kartoffelkratzete),* or genuine "pancakes" (*Kartoffelflinsen* in East Prussia).

In all regions, potato pancakes tend to be eaten hot out of the skillet and without the benefit of knife and fork, though applesauce (sometimes apple compote) is always welcome as a side dish (and makes plate and fork a must). In the Rhineland, *Rievekooche* may be served on a slice of black bread, with or without butter, occasionally with *Knollekruk* (dark syrup) on top. Westphalian *Kartoffelplätzchen,* which are made with yeast, go very well with marmalade, and *Reibeplätzchen* in the Münsterland are eaten with a kind of sweet roll called *Stuten.* East Prussian *Kartoffelflinsen* are sprinkled with sugar and cinnamon or spread with bilberry (in Thuringia, blueberry) jam. The Bavarians eat them occasionally with sauerkraut, but mostly they eat their *Reiberdatschi* with applesauce. Elsewhere, they're simply eaten as is, with coffee. Modern gourmet restaurants all over Europe serve them as an accompaniment with roasts.

Basic Potato Pancake Recipe
Grundrezept für Kartoffelpfannkuchen

Combine the potatoes and onions. Add the salt, eggs, and flour, then stir into a batter. Heat a generous amount of the fat in a skillet and, using a small ladle, pour out little islands of batter onto the bottom of the skillet—making sure the edges do not overlap—and fry on both sides until crispy around the edges.

There is some difference of opinion as to whether potato pancakes should be thick and slightly squishy inside or thin and crispy all the way through. Perhaps it's best to poll your guests on their personal preferences beforehand. Serve hot and straight out of the skillet.

MAKES 4 SERVINGS (20 PANCAKES)

2¼ pounds potatoes, peeled and grated
2 small onions, grated
1–2 teaspoons salt
3 eggs
2–3 tablespoons flour
Lard or shortening for frying

KOBLENZ

Pan-Size Potato-and-Onion Pancake with Bacon   Döbbekoche

On either side of the Rhine from Worms down to Koblenz and beyond, the land stretches out to a distant rim of mountains on the horizon; this is the domain of *Döbbekoche* (*Topfkuchen,* "pot-cakes"), which, as the name perhaps implies, are very large pancakes, bearing roughly the same relationship to other potato pancakes as do the giant flour dumplings of the North Sea coast to ordinary *Klösse.*

•   •   •   •   •   •   •   •   •

Preheat the oven to 400°F.

Drain off any water that might have accumulated after grating the potatoes and onions. Mix these and season generously with salt, pepper, and grated nutmeg, then stir in the eggs.

4¼ pounds potatoes, peeled and grated
2 very large onions, grated
Salt and freshly ground black pepper
Grated nutmeg
2 eggs
½–¾ pound medium-lean bacon (it has to be smoked bacon to give the right flavor), diced
Oil for frying

Cook the bacon briefly and add to the potato mixture, along with the rendered fat.

Grease the sides and bottom of a cast-iron casserole with an ample amount of cooking oil so that there is a thin layer of oil along the bottom. Pour the mixture into it; poke a few holes in the surface with one finger and dribble in a little oil, then brush the surface of the mixture with oil as well. Place the skillet in the oven and bake for about 2 hours.

VARIATIONS: In the hills of the Westerwald, *Döbbekuchen* have slices of bacon baked into them on both top and bottom; they go very well with plum sauce or plum jelly.

In the Rhineland, *Döbbekooche* are eaten with apple or fruit compote, and further east, in Hesse for instance, *Dippedotz* have little bits of apple and dried salami (or bits of leftover roast or homemade wurst) baked into them and are customarily served with applesauce and café au lait (or rather, *mit Milchkaffee*).

Aschkloss is a Thuringian specialty, formerly cooked on the embers of the family hearth (as the name suggests) and made with partly raw and partly cooked potato and served with a hearty wurst.

The popularity of homemade *Topfkuchen* seems to be on the upswing, and a ceramics firm in the Westerwald (Kannebäckerland) has just put a specially designed *Topfkuchen* baking dish on the market.

MAKES 6 SERVINGS

WESTPHALIA

Pan-Size Potato Pancakes   Lappenpickert

There are a great many varieties of *Pickert,* a Westphalian specialty that is not exactly a potato pancake (the caption above notwithstanding) and yet not entirely a pastry either; the region around the Teutoburg Forest is its original habitat, and this particular recipe comes from the town of Bielefeld. Another popular variant, *Dicker Pickert,* is made with yeast as well as flour and is served sprinkled with sugar and cinnamon, like a cruller. To cook a genuine full-sized *Lappenpickert,* you will need a special cast-iron skillet with a handle on either side; many large professional omelette pans are so equipped, but failing that, you can cook *Lappenpickert* in an ordinary skillet in several smaller and more manageable installments. *Lappenpickert* is customarily served either with marmalade or with herring or some other salt fish; both are recommended, though possibly not to be sampled simultaneously.

2 pounds potatoes, peeled, washed, and grated
3 tablespoons sour cream
3 eggs
2–3 tablespoons flour
Salt
Lard or bacon to grease the pan

· · · · · · · · · ·

Drain off the water, then gently press down on the grated potato to extract additional liquid. Mix the sour cream and the eggs, add the flour little by little into the potato dough, and sprinkle with salt.

Grease a small or medium-size cast-iron skillet. Form the dough into a flat cake about ¾″ thick and cook on both sides until crispy and golden yellow. The heat should not be set too high, so the *Pickert* will have had a chance to cook on the inside by the time the outside is done. As with all other varieties of *Pickert,* the experts maintain that it tastes better if you let it cool and then warm it later.

MAKES 4–6 SERVINGS

Labskaus   Lobscouse

1¾ *pounds corned beef*
1 *medium onion*
2 *bay leaves*
2 *cloves*
3 *pounds potatoes,*
  peeled and sliced
4 *large onions, finely*
  chopped
1–2 *tablespoons lard*
  Freshly ground white
  pepper
  Salt

ACCOMPANIMENTS:
6 *dill pickles, halved*
  lengthwise
6 *matjes or Bismarck fillets*
  or rollmops (see Note)
  Pickled beets, sliced
6 *eggs, fried*

One of the most controversial German specialties, *Labskaus* originated on the high sea. It is a dish from the time of the majestic square-rigged sailing vessels, though the origin of the word *labskaus* itself is obscure. The basic idea is that since potatoes could not be kept very long aboard ship, a sailor's stew would have to be made with ship's biscuit and salt beef plus whatever else of interest was available.

Though this may not have been the sort of food that sailors, or anyone, would have chosen to eat voluntarily while on shore, *Labskaus* eventually became a sentimental symbol of the rigors and small rewards of the sailor's life, and any on-shore reunion of old shipmates, merchant marine and navy, would have been unthinkable without it. After *Labskaus* came ashore, there was no reason not to make it with more conventional and high quality ingredients.

The recipe that follows is based on my own seafaring experience as well as the recollections of a number of ancient mariners, veterans of the days of iron men and wooden (sailing) ships.

.   .   .   .

Cook the corned beef along with the whole onion, bay leaves, and cloves in a generous amount of water for about 1 hour. Cook the potatoes in unsalted water. Sauté the chopped onions in lard until translucent. Pour some of the cooking liquid from the corned beef into the onions, then allow to cook for another 15 minutes, until the onions are quite soft. Slice the corned beef and put it through the meat grinder (coarse grind) or food mill, then combine with the potatoes and onions (along with their cooking liquid); mash and blend together into a sort of hash.

Season with a generous amount of pepper and perhaps a little salt (the quantity of the latter depending on the saltiness of the corned beef). Finally, add some more of the cooking liquid. The lobscouse will have acquired a distinct reddish color from the corned beef. Serve each portion in the center of the plate, surrounded by a pickled herring fillet, dill pickles, halved lengthwise, pickled beets, and topped with a fried egg (sunny side up).

NOTE: Sticklers for authenticity should choose ordinary pickled herring over Bismarck or rollmops (rolled pickled herring stuffed with pickle and onion); others will probably prefer the latter two. Similarly, a fried egg was a delicacy that would undoubtedly have been saved for the captain's table in the old days but was (and is) greatly appreciated by other ranks when available.

MAKES 6 SERVINGS

Cuxhaven, North Sea fishing port

HUNSRÜCK

Kartoffelwurst

This "potato wurst" was an ersatz specialty—a "protein extender," as we might say nowadays—devised by the hearty (and hungry) mountaineers of the Idar-Oberstein region; this particular recipe is another example of the immense culinary legacy bequeathed to us by my dear friend August Görg, the Barbecue King of Birkenfeld county. Serve with sauerkraut; no bread or potatoes are necessary, since both are already well represented in the sausage stuffing mixture.

·   ·   ·   ·   ·   ·   ·   ·   ·

2¾ pounds fatty pork
   (originally, fresh pork
   belly)
½ pound lean beef
4¼ pounds potatoes,
   peeled and sliced
 2 kaiser rolls
   Salt and freshly
   ground black pepper
⅛ teaspoon ground cloves
⅛ teaspoon grated nutmeg
½ teaspoon dried savory
   Clean ring-shaped (O-
   shape) sausage casings
   (Kranzdarm) or
   different molds as for
   terrines

Cook the pork and beef in just enough water to cover. Cut the potatoes into smaller pieces. Soak the rolls in some of the cooking broth from the meat, then put all these ingredients together through the meat grinder (or food mill), which you may want to rinse out with a little more of the broth from the pot. Add the spices to the *Kartoffelwurst* stuffing mixture and knead vigorously; add a little more broth if the mixture seems too thick or dry. Wash out the ring-shaped sausage casings thoroughly, fill (not too tightly) with the stuffing mixture, and tie off the casings. Alternately the mixture can be placed in 2 or more terrine molds.

Allow 1 "sausage ring" per person (which is to say either double portions all round or enough leftovers to make another substantial meal for 4 people). Allow these to steep for about 1 hour in lightly salted scalding, but not boiling, water (about 185°F.); at least 2 hours for molds.

MAKES 8 SERVINGS

R H E N I S H   H E S S E

Hessian-Style Potato Casserole
Backesgrumbeere

The *Backes*-part (pronounced more like "boggis") means "baker's" rather than "baked," since this unique specialty of the little wine-growing village of Framersheim near Alzey was originally cooked in the village baker's oven. This updated version of the recipe, in which salt beef has been replaced with bacon or salt pork in accordance with current practice, comes to us from the Klenk family winery (courtesy of the lady of the house). Serve *Backesgrumbeere* with pickled beets, a green salad, and a thick slice or two of *Bauernbrot*.

•   •   •   •   •   •   •   •   •   •

Preheat the oven to 400°F.

If necessary trim the rind from the bacon strips and spread these out to cover the bottom of a fairly heavy 4- or 5-quart enameled pot (or ovenproof casserole). Make long, but not too deep, cuts in the rind of the pork belly about every ¾" or so; rub thoroughly with salt and pepper. Layer the onions and potatoes on top of the bacon; sprinkle lightly with salt, and somewhat more vigorously with pepper. Stick the bay leaves and the cloves down between the potatoes; press the pork down into the layer of potatoes and onions as well, so that the rind is about level with the tops of the potatoes.

First pour in the wine, then the cream; the meat and vegetables should just be covered. Sprinkle with a little cinnamon and place a few little dabs of butter on top. Place in the oven and bake for about 2 hours, or until both the potatoes and the pork are quite done. After the first 30 minutes, if you reduce the heat to 300° and extend the cooking time a little, you can expect to be well rewarded for your patience.

NOTE: Readers who have reservations about using (or difficulty in obtaining) so much fatty pork may prefer to substitute a leaner cut, such as pork shoulder or lightly smoked butt *(Kammbraten)*.

MAKES 6–8 SERVINGS

¾ *pound lean bacon (must be smoked to give the right flavor— smoked ham hocks could be sliced and substituted); use thickly sliced bacon if available*
2 *pounds fresh pork belly, as lean as possible, or pork shoulder (see Note) Salt and freshly ground black pepper*
2 *large onions, quartered then thinly sliced*
4¼ *pounds potatoes, peeled and quartered*
3–4 *bay leaves*
3 *cloves*
2 *cups dry white wine*
½ *cup cream Ground cinnamon A few little dabs of butter*

Mainz near Wiesbaden, Rhine valley (engraving by J. Barker, after a drawing by W. Tombleson)

BAVARIA

Three Meat Stew with Vegetables   Pichelsteiner

1 tablespoon lard
1¼ pounds pork and beef
    as well as lamb or
    mutton (mutton gives
    an excellent flavor),
    cut into ¾" cubes
2–3 medium onions, diced
    Salt and freshly
    ground black pepper
    Crushed marjoram
3 medium potatoes,
    peeled and finely diced
1 small celery root,
    peeled and diced, or 4
    celery stalks,
    diagonally sliced
½ pound carrots, peeled
    and diagonally sliced
1 large leek, white part
    only, washed and
    sliced
2 cups beef stock
    Chopped fresh parsley

Also known as *Büchelsteiner,* this is one of the most popular of all German stews—also, unfortunately, a dish that has largely been displaced in recent years by such "gourmet" novelties as Hungarian goulash or ratatouille. But I dare to maintain that *Pichelsteiner* tastes better than these two. It is also sometimes known as *Bismarck-Ragout,* since Prince von Bismarck is said to have developed a taste for it while he was taking the cure at Bad Kissingen, in Bavaria. The origin of *Pichelsteiner,* however, is in the Bavarian forests in the vicinity of Regen (not to be confused with Regensburg), which is where the official Pichelsteiner Festival has been celebrated since 1874. A slice of hearty *Bauernbrot* and a glass (preferably a stein) of beer are the obligatory accompaniments to this dish.

Heat the lard in a heavy-bottomed pot (or an ovenproof Pyrex casserole or the like). Lightly sear and mix together the meat cubes and the onions; season with salt, an ample amount of pepper, and a very little bit of marjoram. Remove two-thirds of the meat and onions from the pot and set aside.

Mix the potatoes and vegetables together; spread a third of these over the bottom layer of meat cubes in the pot or casserole. Sprinkle with salt and a little pepper. Alternate 2 more layers of meat with 2 more layers of vegetables. Each layer should be separately seasoned with salt and pepper; the top layer *must* consist of vegetables and potatoes. Pour in the beef stock. Cover tightly and cook over medium-low heat for just about 2 hours. Cooking in a 350°F. oven is also possible. You should not stir the stew, but you can tilt the pot back and forth to circulate the liquid and prevent the bottom layer from burning. Serve sprinkled with chopped parsley.

VARIATIONS: Savoy cabbage is frequently added to the roster of vegetables, and it tastes delicious. Sliced kohlrabi would be fine as well.

For a truly gourmet *Pichelsteiner*, 6 to 8 slices of bone marrow should be briefly sautéed with the onions at the beginning, then added later to one of the in-between layers of meat. Doubling of ingredients is advisable. *Pichelsteiner* tastes excellent reheated.

MAKES 4 SERVINGS

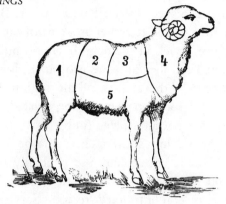

1. *Keule* (leg of lamb)
2. *Nierenstück* (loin)
3. *Koteletts* (rib or rack)
2 & 3. *Rücken, Sattel* (saddle), *Hammelrücken* (if cut lengthwise)
4. *Hals* (neck plus shoulder, British "sorag end")
5. *Blatt und Brust* (breast and shank)

B E R L I N   A N D   C E N T R A L   G E R M A N Y

Lamb Stew with Green Beans
Hammelfleisch mit Grünen Bohnen

Place the lamb and onions in a generous amount of water, bring to a boil, and allow to cook vigorously for about 30 minutes, skimming off the impurities from the surface from time to time.

Add the potatoes to the pot in which the lamb is cooking. Put the savory into a tea egg or a little cheesecloth bag and add this to the lamb as well. Add the green beans after another 10 minutes. Add salt and pepper to taste, and continue cooking 20 minutes more until the lamb is tender and the potatoes have started to cook down a little bit to provide a binding ingredient for the sauce—the stew should still have enough liquid that you may want to eat it with a spoon. Stir the stew once more and remove the savory; garnish with parsley. Total cooking time: 60 minutes.

MAKES 4–6 SERVINGS

1½ pounds stewing lamb (if mutton is used the flavor becomes more intensive and the cooking time is longer), cut into 1" cubes
2 large onions, halved, cut into thin rounds
1¾ pounds potatoes, peeled and cut into cubes
½ teaspoon savory
2 pounds green beans, cleaned, washed, and snapped
Salt and freshly ground black pepper
2 tablespoons chopped fresh parsley

MÜNSTERLAND

Sweet-and-Sour Veal Stew   Töttchen

1½–1¾ *pounds boneless stewing veal (preferably assorted cuts— breast, neck, shoulder, etc.)*
1 *carrot, peeled and diced*
1 *stalk celery, diced*
1 *leek, washed and sliced*
2 *sprigs parsley*
2 *bay leaves*
1 *clove*
   Pinch of crushed thyme
10 *peppercorns*
   Pinch of salt
2 *tablespoons butter*
2 *large onions, finely chopped*
2 *tablespoons flour*
1 *cup white wine*
   A dash or two of vinegar
   Pinch of sugar
1 *tablespoon mustard*

Devised as an accompaniment to the after-church pint on Sunday, this dish goes especially well with an Alt-Bier, and the two are frequently served together as a sort of Sunday brunch or early-afternoon snack in the neighborhood pubs of Münster, as well as in a number of more prominent local establishments specializing in the cuisine of the region. In the days when veal was far too expensive to be wasted on the free-lunch buffet of the corner *Kneipe* (pub), this dish was made with the "lights and lungs" as well as the head of the calf. Nowadays, it's more convenient and probably no more expensive to make *Töttchen* with a selection of choicer cuts, as called for in this contemporary recipe. Serve with small "cocktail slices" of rye bread or *Bauernbrot,* or possibly with parslied potatoes.

· · · · · · · · · ·

Wash the veal thoroughly; combine the vegetables with the veal and simmer along with the seasonings in a generous amount of water until the veal is quite tender, which should take about 1½ hours. Remove the veal from the broth, trim all gristle, sinew, and excess fat, and cut into little cubes. Pour the broth through a strainer; you may want to boil it down a little more to make it more concentrated.

Melt the butter in a large non-reactive skillet; sauté the onions until translucent. Sprinkle the flour over the onions and brown it lightly. Add the white wine and as much of the broth as is necessary to make a smooth, creamy sauce for the stew; cook for another 15 minutes or so. Season with a dash or two of vinegar, sugar, and mustard stirred with a couple of tablespoons of broth. The sauce should have a nice piquant flavor, be a little vinegary, and have the sweet-and-sour taste clearly discernible but not dominant. Add the veal pieces to the sauce and continue cooking until they are heated through.

MAKES 4 SERVINGS

SCHLESWIG-HOLSTEIN

Plockfinken

This favorite stew's ingredients are usually suggested by a quick inventory of the larder and the spirit of last-minute improvisation rather than by any particular recipe. I learned the recipe for this especially tasty version from some friends from Kiel, where this dish is called *Kort Recht,* "short dish," because it doesn't take all that long to make. For the record, other versions of *Plockfinken* often contain green beans or white beans, possibly both.

· · · · · · · · ·

Trim all the skin, tough membranes, and gristle from the meat and cut it into bite-size pieces. Place the meat and vegetables in enough water to cover, bring to a boil, and season with salt and pepper, sugar, and vinegar. Cover the pot, simmer for 30 minutes, then add the apples to the stewpot. When the stew appears to be just about ready (total cooking time: 75 minutes), cook the flour in the lard (in a separate skillet or saucepan) but do not color, add a little of the broth from the stewpot, and stir; pour this sauce back into the stewpot to bind the gravy a little. Test for seasoning; you may want the sweet-and-sour effect to be a little more pronounced. Sprinkle with parsley and serve.

MAKES 4–6 SERVINGS

1½ *pounds pork and beef (one-third should be corned beef)*
3 *large onions, coarsely diced*
1 *pound carrots, peeled and diced*
  Salt and freshly ground black pepper
  Small pinch of sugar
  Dash of vinegar
4 *apples, peeled, cored, and chopped*
1 *tablespoon flour*
1 *tablespoon lard*
  Chopped fresh parsley

Borscht, East Prussian-Style   Beetenbartsch

2 pounds stewing beef or
    soup meat
1 large soupbone
1 onion, into which 4
    cloves and 2 bay
    leaves have been
    inserted
10 peppercorns
    Salt
1 carrot, peeled and
    chopped
1 stalk celery, chopped
1 leek, washed and
    chopped
2 pounds fresh red beets
    (canned and pickled
    may be used as well)
    Vinegar
    Freshly ground pepper
2 tablespoons sugar
    Crushed marjoram
1–2 tablespoons potato
    flour or cornstarch
½ cup sour cream plus
    sour cream to garnish
4–6 boiled potatoes

This can be prepared as a soup or as a casserole.

•   •   •   •   •   •   •   •   •

Thoroughly wash the stew meat and the soup bone. Place these with the clove-studded onion in a pot with the peppercorns, salt, and vegetables, excluding beets. Add just enough water to cover, and cook for about 1½ hours, or until the meat is tender.

In the meantime, scrub the beets thoroughly with a brush and cook in water until tender; then peel and puree in a food mill or processor. Stir in a couple of tablespoons of vinegar and 1 tablespoon sugar. Pour the soup stock through a fine strainer, reserve the stew meat. Combine the stock and the pureed beets, and season with salt, pepper, vinegar, sugar, and marjoram.

Mix the potato flour in the sour cream, blend into the borscht with a whisk, and bring to a boil. Cut the stew meat into strips and heat once more in the borscht. Serve with potatoes that have been cooked in salted water and, of course, additional sour cream; it's best to allow your guests to work out the correct proportions for themselves.

MAKES 4–6 SERVINGS

Celery Root and Potatoes with Bacon Gravy
Selleriekartoffeln

Place the potatoes and celery root in just enough salted water to cover and cook until both are tender. Fry the bacon and onions in a skillet until the onions are golden yellow. Season with salt to taste. Serve the celery root and potatoes in soup plates, spooning out some of the bacon-and-onion sauce for each portion.

MAKES 4–6 SERVINGS

2 pounds potatoes, peeled and diced
1¾ pounds celery root, peeled and diced
¾–1 pound medium-lean bacon (smoked), cut into little strips or squares
4–5 small onions, finely diced
Salt

L O W E R   S A X O N Y

Rutabaga Stew with Pork
Wruken mit Schweinefleisch

Rutabagas may not be very prestigious vegetables in English-speaking countries. In Germany, where these "stick turnips" (*Steckrüben*) never figured in the city dweller's diet before the desperate wartime shortages of 1917–18, they came to be remembered by many as a last-ditch alternative to starvation during the "Rutabaga Winter" of the First World War. In northeastern Germany, *Wruken* have a somewhat longer history as a staple article of diet for both man and beast, and a number of very tasty rutabaga recipes have evolved over the course of several generations.

3 tablespoons lard
2–3 onions, finely diced
2 pounds rutabagas, peeled, washed, and diced or sliced
1¼ pounds potatoes, peeled, washed, and diced or sliced
1¼ pounds fatty pork (preferably a piece of fairly lean pork belly), cut into bite-size pieces
2 cups water
Salt
Small pinch of sugar

• • • • • • • • •

Heat 2 tablespoons of the lard in a large heavy-bottomed pot and sauté the onions until they turn pale yellow. Add the rutabagas, potatoes, and pork, stir, pour in the water, and season with salt and a small pinch of sugar. Cover and cook over low heat, stirring occasionally, for about 1 hour. Sprinkle the remaining tablespoon of lard over the stew and test once again for seasoning.

MAKES 4 SERVINGS

WESTPHALIA

Westphalian Vegetable Stew   Blindhuhn

1¼ pounds ham or lean
   bacon (or "belly
   bacon" if you prefer;
   both have to be
   smoked varieties),
   sliced into matchstick
   strips
½ pound each of green
   beans and white
   beans (the latter
   should be soaked in
   water overnight)
½ pound carrots
¾–1 pound potatoes
2 apples and 2 pears
   and perhaps a little
   lemon juice "to
   impart a tart and
   tangy flavor" if the
   fruit is too sweet
   Salt and freshly
   ground black pepper
2 tablespoons flour
   stirred into 2
   tablespoons water or
   vinegar

This vegetable stew has been around long enough to acquire a number of interesting nicknames—*Blindhuhn,* which means "blind chicken," *Nachlese* (gleaning, grain picked up after the harvest), *Gänsefutter* (goose feed), and *Husch und Susch* (Hoosh and Soosh). The idea behind the first three of these seems to be that of an assortment of different ingredients, chosen as if at random (the fourth one seems to be open to a variety of different constructions). There are even more possible recipes to choose from, though it seems only natural that the one proposed by Henriette Davidis-Holle, the grande dame of German cookbook writers and a native of Westphalia, should take precedence over all the rest. This is from her nineteenth-century *Practical Cookbook:*

•   •   •   •   •   •   •   •   •

"To a small piece of ham [Smithfield type] or belly bacon [smoked belly] that has already been boiled add green beans, which need not be of the very freshest, thoroughly washed and then thinly sliced on the cutting board, shelled white beans, and half as many carrots as green beans, cut into little cubes, all to be rinsed in water and cooked all the way through, then added to the ham as each is done in turn. If you have some pears, add them as well, peeled and quartered, and when the vegetables are almost done, some potatoes with as much salt as needed along with some apples, peeled and cut up in pieces, that have been cooked till they are soft. Next, the piece of ham should be removed [but returned to the stew before serving] and some pepper added and some flour that has been stirred into a little water and the vegetables all stirred round together. *Blindhuhn* should be cooked until it is quite thick and creamy and succulent and the apples have imparted a tart and tangy flavor to the stew. If you use no apples, then the flour should be stirred into the vinegar. Cooking time, 2 to 2½ hours."

NOTE: The syntax of this recipe has been slightly revised—

though not enough, you might think, to make it thoroughly comprehensible. However, please don't be too quick to throw your flintlock into the cornfield, as the Germans say—or in other words, to throw in the dishtowel. As with many great literary classics, this recipe may require a second or third reading before it begins to make much sense.

MAKES 4 SERVINGS

NORTHERN   GERMANY

Pears, Green Beans, and Bacon
Birnen, Bohnen, und Speck

Here is an ingenious combination that many may find bizarre at first acquaintance. Most of those who have actually sampled it, however, are obliged to admit that this northern German specialty is not at all bad, and there are even some from the other side of the Main Line (myself among them) who find it quite delicious. Serve with potatoes that have been cooked in salted water. (The potatoes are often added to the stew at an

Hamburg harbor

4 *large thick slices of*
medium-lean bacon
(total weight 1¼
pounds; use thickly
sliced bacon or slab
bacon if available;
smoked bacon gives the
authentic flavor)
1½ *pounds fresh green*
beans, washed and
snapped
Salt and freshly
ground black pepper
Pinch of dried savory
8 *small, hard stewing*
pears (with stems still
attached), washed
1–2 *teaspoons cornstarch*
dissolved in several
tablespoons cold water

earlier stage, but I've found that they taste better if cooked and served separately.)

.   .   .   .

It's best if this dish can be made in a pot or casserole that can eventually be brought to the table as a serving dish. Start by covering the bottom of the pot with a layer of bacon slices, topped by the green beans. Pour in just enough water to cover the green beans; season with salt, pepper, and a little savory. Cook, covered, for about 10 minutes. Remove the hard little nubs (flower stems) at the base of the pears but leave the main stems (on top) in place. Put the pears on top of the green beans in the pot, cover the pot once more, and cook over low heat until the pears are soft but still fairly firm.

A good deal of the cooking liquid may have evaporated by now; pour off the remainder into a saucepan and bind lightly with the cornstarch in water. Pour this sauce over the contents of the pot; for a more attractive presentation, remove the bacon slices from the bottom of the pot and arrange them between the pears.

MAKES 4 SERVINGS

BAVARIA

Baked Sauerkraut Rolls   Krautkrapfen

This is a rare conjunction (one that I've encountered only once in my Bavarian travels) of two great Bavarian passions—pastry and sauerkraut. My Bavarian friends tell me that this dish is rarely served these days, though apart from the homemade pastry dough it isn't all that much trouble to make.

.   .   .   .

Combine the flour, eggs, water, and pinch of salt, stir and then knead into a pliable noodle dough; you may want to add a little more flour or water, depending on the consistency. On a clean, flat surface that has been dusted with flour, roll out the dough into thin sheets and divide into smaller rectangles. Let stand for a little while so the dough will start to dry out.

Fry the bacon in the lard until translucent. Separate the strands of drained sauerkraut, combine with the grated apple, mix together, and fry in the same pan, turning frequently, until the sauerkraut is golden yellow. Allow to cool somewhat, then place a flat layer of cooked sauerkraut filling mixture on each of the rectangular sheets of dough, roll up into little bundles about 2″ in diameter, and cut each of these bundles into wide sections just about 1¼″ to 2″ long.

Preheat the oven to 350°F. Heat the lard in a large flat-bottomed saucepan or skillet (or an ovenproof ceramic casserole will do as well). Arrange the sauerkraut rolls with the cut side up and close to one another; they should just about cover the bottom of the pan. Pour in the beef stock to a depth of about ½″, place the pan or skillet in the oven, and bake until the rolls have acquired a light crust, which should take about 20 minutes or so. Add a little more stock to the pan if necessary and sprinkle some stock over the tops of the rolls as well. Diehard traditionalists who refuse to count calories will want to pour some melted butter (or lard) over the sauerkraut rolls before serving.

MAKES 4 SERVINGS

DOUGH:
 2½ cups flour
 2–3 eggs
 3–5 tablespoons cold water
  Pinch of salt

FILLING:
 5 strips medium-lean
  bacon, diced
 2 tablespoons lard
 2 cups sauerkraut, drained
  of any liquid
 1 small apple, peeled and
  grated

 4 tablespoons lard
  Beef stock

Kale Grünkohl

This hardy winter vegetable has deep roots in the culinary traditions of several German regions, primarily in the north, where it is known, among other things, as the "Oldenburg palm tree" *(Oldenburger Palme),* though it also has its admirers in slightly more southerly climates. In the Oberbergischen Land (North Rhine-Westphalia, near Cologne), it was customarily served, with bratwurst, on the second night of Christmas. In the town of Herford, in Westphalia, the *Kohlfest* has been celebrated on the first Thursday in Advent since 1590. This is also a school holiday, and I've heard the children of Herford skipping through the streets at an alarmingly early hour chanting *"Heut ham wir frei, das danken wir dem Grünkohl!"* ("We've got today off and the *Grünkohl* to thank for it!")

In Bremen, the *Grünkohl* is still known as *Braunkohl* (brown kale), though the original brown-leafed variety, said to have been very tasty in its day, has long since been supplanted by the green, which produces a much higher yield. As in Bremen, the fine old Hanseatic tradition of the *Schaffermahlzeit,* or *Eiswette* (a bet on whether the river will have a solid ice cover that can hold a tailor and his iron) has been carried on in Bremen on an annual, if no longer on a daily, basis with a great municipal banquet where *Braunkohl* is still a featured specialty.

Kale tastes best after the first frost, when its rather strong flavor is somewhat offset by a greater concentration of sugar in the leaves. In northern Germany, from November on, this fact has furnished the pretext for the slightly raffish all-male gatherings called *"Kohlpartien"* (kale parties), ostensibly to sample the first and finest leaves of the season—which, after a long and concerted struggle, have been successfully infiltrated by women in recent years. *Een beeten good un een beeten veel!* (literally "a little good and a little much," translating into "as good as possible and as much as possible") is an old saying that should always be remembered when putting together the ingredients. Kale is one of those vegetables that certainly tastes none the worse for being warmed up and served a second time.

MOSEL VALLEY

Sauerkraut Tossed in White Wine Sauce
Weincräwes

This is a traditional favorite in the wine country, where a lot of hard work has to be done outdoors in the vineyards in cold weather. Often this dish is featured in restaurants that cater to the tourist trade—as *Weincräwes,* presumably, rather than its alternate local name of *Stampes,* which just means "mashed." I came across the recipe in Traben-Trabach.

·   ·   ·   ·   ·   ·   ·   ·   ·   ·

Separate the strands of sauerkraut. Heat the lard in a non-reactive heavy-bottomed pot or large skillet with a tight-fitting lid, and sauté the finely chopped onion until it turns pale yellow. Add the sauerkraut, bay leaves, juniper berries, and wine; heat gently. Place the pickled spareribs on top of this mixture, cover, and cook about 50 minutes, until tender.

Boil the potatoes in salted water. Pour off the water, mash the potatoes, and mix with the milk.

Fry the bacon until the fat has been rendered. Add the onion rings and fry them in the same pan until well browned.

Remove the pickled spareribs as soon as they're cooked all the way through. Mix together the sauerkraut and mashed potatoes. Garnish this with the spareribs, bacon, and fried onion rings (plus, if you wish, the remaining contents of the pan in which they were cooked).

MAKES 4–6 SERVINGS

2 pounds sauerkraut
2 tablespoons lard
3 medium onions, 1 finely chopped, 2 halved and sliced into rings
2 bay leaves
A few juniper berries
1 cup dry white wine (Riesling is preferred)
4 pickled spareribs (thick slices of smoked ham are an excellent substitute)
2 potatoes, peeled and quartered
Hot milk
10 slices medium-lean bacon, cut into matchstick strips

BREMEN, FRIESLAND,
SCHLESWIG-HOLSTEIN

Kale with Homemade Sausage
Braunkohl mit Pinkel

PINKEL (MAKES 6 SAUSAGES):
- *¼ pound fresh (or blanched smoked) bacon, coarsely chopped*
- *¼ pound leaf fat, coarsely chopped (fresh pork back fat)*
- *2–3 medium onions, sliced*
- *1 cup (oaten) groats*
- *Salt and freshly ground black pepper*
- *1 pinch ground allspice*
- *Clean sausage casings*

- *3½ pounds kale (or about 2½ pounds if the ribs have not already been removed)*
- *2–3 tablespoons rendered pork fat*
- *2 medium onions, finely chopped*
- *1 cup beef stock*
- *Salt and freshly ground black pepper*
- *1 level teaspoon sugar*
- *¾ pound salt pork, corned beef, or medium-lean bacon*
- *1 link Pinkel or other sausage (like sweet Italian sausage)*
- *¾ pound dried smoked sausage (mettwurst) or kielbasa*
- *4 teaspoons rolled oat flakes*

Garnish each plate with a ring of crispy fried potatoes, preferably very small ones. To make them even crispier, it's best to boil them in their jackets, peel and fry them, and sprinkle with a few drops of dark syrup to obtain a nice crust.

·   ·   ·   ·   ·   ·   ·   ·   ·

To make *Pinkel,* also known as *Grützwurst,* combine and stir together the bacon, fat, and onions over heat until the onion slices are quite translucent. Allow to cool somewhat, then put all the ingredients through the meat grinder. Knead together with the groats and all the rendered fat until you have a pliable sausage stuffing. Season with salt, pepper, and allspice powder. Stuff into sausage casings or wrap tightly in cheesecloth. The cheesecloth, of course, unlike the sausage casings, will have to be removed before you can eat *Pinkel.*

Next, separate the leaves from the ribs and wash the kale. Kale that has never been frozen (in the ground, i.e.) should be parboiled briefly and then shaken dry. The leaves may be chopped or ground; I recommend the former.

Heat the fat in a large heavy-bottomed pot. Sauté the onions for a couple of minutes, then add the kale and allow it to cook down somewhat while stirring constantly. Pour in a small amount of stock (if necessary, you can add more later), add salt, pepper, and sugar, and simmer gently for at least 30 minutes.

Place the pork, corned beef, or bacon on top of the kale and cook for another 15 minutes, covered, then add the Pinkel or other sausage and the hard-smoked sausage and braise covered for a good 25 minutes over low heat. Stir in the rolled oat flakes and leave on the heat for 5 more minutes, until the oat flakes have had time to bind the cooking liquid into a sauce for the kale. Wait until the dish is brought to the table before you slice the bacon and the wurst.

VARIATIONS: Various local traditions allow considerable latitude in the choice of accompaniment for the kale. Salt pork or corned beef can readily be substituted for the fresh bacon—so can fresh pork belly and hog jowls (briefly seared or pickled in brine, a Holstein specialty), though perhaps not quite so readily available. Feel free to use bratwurst (as is the custom in Lower Saxony) or a boiled sausage of the kielbasa type in lieu of *Pinkel.* (Further south, the Westphalians refer to this dish as *Mettwurst and Grünkohl,* characteristically giving top billing to the smoked sausage.)

Along the northern German coast, a canister of sugar is normally set beside the tureen full of *Braunkohl mit Pinkel,* but this practice is not necessarily recommended. On the other hand, be careful not to put too much salt on the kale, since it can easily absorb a little too much of the salty tang off the salt pork, corned beef, or bacon.

MAKES 6 SERVINGS

Braised Cabbage Rolls Krautwickel

1 *head of white cabbage*
1 *large dry-baked or stale kaiser roll, soaked in milk or water*
1¼ *pounds ground beef, pork, and/or veal (preferably a mixture of beef and pork)*
1 *large dry-baked or stale kaiser roll, soaked in milk or water*
1 *egg*
  Freshly ground black pepper
  Grated nutmeg
  Salt
1 *large onion, diced*
¼ *pound fatty bacon, diced*
4 *slices of medium-lean bacon*
1–2 *tablespoons lard*
1 *tablespoon flour*
½–1 *cup beef stock*
  Boiled potatoes

Separate the leaves from the cabbage stalk and blanch them for a few minutes in boiling salted water. Remove the leaves from the water, drain, and pare the thick projecting center ribs with a knife.

Press the roll dry and mix together with the ground meat, egg, pepper, grated nutmeg, and some salt. Cook the onion and fatty bacon until both are translucent, combine this with the stuffing mixture, and knead well. Fry the medium-lean bacon in the same pan until crispy, then set aside. Reserve the rendered bacon fat.

Spread out the cabbage leaves you intend to use for the rolls and place a healthy spoonful of the stuffing mixture on each one; roll the leaves up and secure them with cooking twine.

In a large skillet or stewpot, heat the lard and the rendered bacon fat; sear the cabbage rolls on all sides, then sprinkle the flour into the pot and allow to cook until well browned. Turn the cabbage rolls once. Pour in enough stock to braise the cabbage rolls, stir, and cook, covered, for at least 1 hour. The rolls should be a lovely dark-brown color on (at least) one side. Serve with potatoes cooked in salted water and the reheated bacon slices.

MAKES 4 SERVINGS

THURINGIA

Red Cabbage Rolls   Rotkohlrouladen

Add the vinegar, 1 whole onion, clove, 1 bay leaf, salt, and sugar to 2 quarts of water in a non-reactive saucepan and bring to a boil. Separate as many undamaged whole leaves as possible from the cabbage head; remove the stem from each. Blanch the cabbage leaves in the boiling liquid until they are just beginning to get tender, then remove and drain.

Press the roll dry and combine with the ground meat. Sauté the 2 diced onions in 1 tablespoon lard until translucent; add the entire contents of this pan to the stuffing mixture. Mix in the eggs and season with salt and pepper.

Spread out the cabbage leaves, place a proportionate amount of the stuffing mixture in the center of each one, roll up the leaves, and fasten with poultry skewers or cooking twine.

Heat the 2 tablespoons lard in a non-reactive skillet or stewpot. Sear the cabbage rolls. Add the carrot, coarsely chopped onion, and the other bay leaf. Pour in the red wine and beef stock, a little at a time, cover, and braise over low heat for about 45 minutes, or until the rolls are done, turning at least once. Remove the rolls from the pan and keep warm; strain the sauce and bind with the dissolved cornstarch. Bring to a boil and cook for 5 minutes. Test for seasoning and serve the sauce separately.

MAKES 4 SERVINGS

1 generous splash of vinegar
4 medium onions, 1 whole, 2 diced, 1 coarsely chopped
1 whole clove
2 bay leaves
½ teaspoon salt
1–2 tablespoons sugar
1 young head of red cabbage
1 large stale or dry-baked kaiser roll, soaked in milk or water
1 pound ground meat (half beef, half pork)
3 tablespoons lard or butter
2 eggs
Salt and freshly ground black pepper
1 carrot, peeled and diced
½ cup red wine
½ cup beef stock
1–2 teaspoons cornstarch dissolved in 2 tablespoons cold water

BERLIN

Dried Peas with Potatoes and Pickled Pork
Löffelerbsen mit Pökelfleisch

½ *pound dried peas,*
preferably yellow ones
1 *pound brine-cured*
bacon, not too fatty,
cut into bite-size
pieces
1 *leek, white part only,*
finely chopped
1 *medium onion, finely*
chopped
1 *tablespoon lard or*
butter
½ *of a medium-size*
celery root, peeled and
chopped, or 3 stalks
celery, chopped
1 *parsley stem, chopped*
1–2 *bay leaves*
3 *medium potatoes,*
peeled and diced
Crushed marjoram
Salt and freshly
ground black pepper

According to a cookbook published in 1882, "The pulses, or legumes—peas, beans, and lentils—are fully the equal of meat in their nutritional content, and cooked up with a bit of bacon, they are as satisfying and nourishing as a serving of roast meat with vegetables." The fact that legumes are also very rich in carbohydrates is not mentioned, though these days that un- doubtedly is a plus. In Hamburg, the "bit of bacon" in this particular dish would have consisted of pickled pork trim- mings—a pickled pig's ear plus half of the snout was a popular combination—for which brine-cured bacon, not too fatty, makes a highly acceptable substitute.

•   •   •   •   •   •   •   •   •

Soak the peas in water overnight. Transfer to a soup or stewpot, and add enough water to the soaking liquid to make about a quart in all. Add the bacon to the pot and bring to a boil. Sauté the leek and onion in the lard until translucent, then add this to the pot along with the celery, parsley stems, and bay leaves. Cook all the ingredients in the pot together for about 1 hour, or until the salt pork is tender and the peas are soft, but not too soft. Add the potatoes to the pot after about 35 minutes. Season with marjoram and (very carefully) with salt and pepper. Serve in soup plates and eat with a spoon (since *Löffelerbsen,* after all, means "spoon peas").

MAKES 4 SERVINGS

WESTPHALIA

Broad Beans with Bacon   Dicke Bohnen mit Speck

The broad-bean season furnishes the occasion for a lovely summer festival in the Münsterland, the high point of which is, of course, a tremendous bean feast, as commended in an old regional song:

In the season that's the finest	*Ja, de schönste Tied von'n Sommer*
Of all the summertide—	*Is de Grautebaunentied—*
In the broad-bean season	*In de Grautebaunentied,*
Belly, be thou twice thy size!	*Buk, dann wär no mal so wied!*

•   •   •   •   •   •   •   •   •

Shell the beans and simmer gently, along with the bacon and a pinch of salt, in the water for about 1 hour. Drain the beans and reserve the cooking liquid.

Remove the bacon. Heat the butter or lard in a saucepan, add the flour, cook together to make a light roux, then pour in enough of the cooking liquid to make a smooth creamy sauce for the beans. Season with pepper and savory. Simmer gently for about 15 minutes, stirring occasionally. Return the beans and the bacon slices to the sauce and continue cooking until everything is heated through.

MAKES 4–6 SERVINGS

3½ *pounds unshelled broad beans (if the beans inside are small, you may need up to twice as many)*
1 *pound medium-lean bacon*
    Pinch of salt
1 *quart water*
2 *tablespoons butter or (originally) lard*
2 *tablespoons flour*
    Freshly ground white pepper
    Pinch of crushed savory

SILESIA

Silesian Heaven Schlesisches Himmelreich

8 cups mixed dried fruit
  (preferably unpeeled
  and home-dried)
2 tablespoons sultana
  raisins
4–6 dried figs
1¾ pounds smoked pork
  (see Headnote)
1 large onion studded
  with 1 bay leaf and 4
  cloves
8 peppercorns
  A little salt
  Peel of 1 lemon
4–6 tablespoons sugar
2 tablespoons cornstarch
  dissolved in ¼ cup
  cold water
1 jigger of brandy
  Lemon juice

The popularity of the Silesian national dish has survived numerous wars, famines, invasions, and even the forcible "repatriation" of most of the region's German-speaking inhabitants after the eastern part of Silesia had to be ceded to Poland in 1945. On first acquaintance, non-Silesians might be tempted to describe the taste of this dish as "unearthly" rather than "heavenly," but with practice, they may begin to feel an unaccountable longing for *Schlesien hold in Wiesen* (Silesia's lush and lovely meads, or, rather freely, "my little gray [green] home in the east"). The main ingredient in this dish is smoked pork—originally either unsliced lean bacon or smoked pork loin *(Kasseler Rippespeer),* for which a smoked pork butt may readily be substituted.

•   •   •   •   •   •   •   •   •

Wash the dried fruit, raisins, and figs, and soak in cold water overnight. Place the pork, onion, peppercorns, and salt in a pot with a very little water and simmer gently for about 1 hour.

Add the lemon peel to the dried fruit and cook (in the soaking liquid) until soft. Add some of the broth that the pork is simmering in, in order to combine the smoky taste with the sweet-sour flavor of the stewed fruit; season with sugar, if necessary, and bind lightly with cornstarch that has been dissolved in cold water. Bring to a boil. Add the jigger of brandy and lemon juice to taste, and the sauce is all ready.

NOTE: As the regional poet tells us:

The secret—lemme tell yuh
  somethin'—
Of our Silesian heaven's
in the little dumplin's!

*Die Hauptsach—doas soa ich
  Eich—
vun insem schläs'cha
  Himmelreich,
das sein do bluss de Klieβla!*

Unfortunately this instructive verse fails to mention exactly what kind of dumplings the author had in mind, and as we know, there are several possibilities. *Semmelknödel* (Bread Dumplings) are often mentioned in this connection, likewise Silesian potato dumplings. After making some inquiries among my Silesian friends who are best informed on matters touching their national cuisine, I can report that *Hefeklösse* (Yeast Dumplings) steamed inside a napkin (as described in the recipe found in the dumpling chapter) are the dumplings of choice.

As the local pastor most likely would not be able to give information about the "Silesian heaven," I might mention that the smoked pork should be cut into serving slices and placed on a platter with the stewed fruit and the dumplings. The sweet-sour sauce is for the pork and the dumplings—that way, the secret of Silesian Heaven would be revealed even unto the scoffers and unbelievers in a minimum of three bites.

Home-dried apples and pears with the peels left on make the fruit component of this dish taste twice as good, by the way.

MAKES 4–6 SERVINGS

Breslau, Silesia, now Poland (engraving by Johannes Rybicka, after a drawing by Wilhelm Kandler)

Lentil Stew with Bratwurst
Linsengemüse mit Bratwurst

1 *pound lentils*
2 *medium onions, 1 chopped, 1 grated*
2 *tablespoons lard*
1 *carrot, peeled and finely diced*
   Salt and freshly ground black pepper
1 *tablespoon flour*
1 *cup dry white wine*
   A few tablespoons vinegar
2 *tablespoons grated horseradish*
1 *large gherkin, sliced*
2 *eggs, hard-boiled and chopped*
4 *large bratwursts*
   Clarified butter or shortening

This recipe is taken from an old handwritten cookbook and, though I can't say for sure, probably originated in Hesse or the Rhineland.

•   •   •   •   •   •   •   •

Soak the lentils overnight in water. Sauté the chopped onion in 1 tablespoon lard. Transfer the lentils to a pot of fresh water, add the carrot and the sautéed onion, season generously with salt and pepper, and cook for about 1 hour.

Heat the tablespoon of lard and cook with the flour to make a brown roux; pour in the white wine and some of the cooking liquid from the lentils and stir. Add to the pot to provide a lightly bound sauce for the lentils.

Add the grated onion, vinegar, horseradish, gherkin slices, and hard-boiled eggs to the stew; keep warm. Fry the bratwursts on both sides in clarified butter and add the bratwursts and the remaining fat to the stew; you may want to fry a couple of onion rings along with them, and if the bratwursts are on the small side—feel free to use twice as many.

MAKES 4 SERVINGS

SWABIA

Spätzle with Lentils Spätzle und Linsen

The Swabians claim that if you eat lentils on Good Friday, you will be sure to come into some money during the rest of the year. Like the Scots, the Swabians are famous for their keen understanding of the mysteries of finance. The original meat component of this dish is *Rauchfleisch,* pork or beef that has been both salted and smoked, for which smoked ham or ham hock can readily be substituted.

. . . .

Pick over the lentils, soak in water overnight, then transfer to a pot of fresh water and cook, along with the ham or ham hock and the carrot, for about 45 minutes, or until tender.

In the meantime, in a non-reactive saucepan heat the lard and cook with the flour until golden brown; pour in some of the cooking broth from the lentils and stir into a smooth sauce. Season the sauce generously with salt and pepper; pour in half the vinegar and simmer for at least 10 minutes. Add the lentils, test for seasoning, and allow to cook for a few more minutes. Shortly before serving, cut the meat into serving slices and add more vinegar—which helps to make the lentils more digestible as well as adding savor to the stew. Serve with the spätzle on the side.

VARIATION: Frequently Vienna sausages (knockwurst) or other boiled sausages (*Siedwurst,* or *Saitenwürste* in Schwäbisch) are substituted for the smoked meat. These are cooked separately, and a piece of Canadian bacon (originally, lean smoked pork belly), chopped and fried with a finely chopped onion until both are translucent, is added to the pot with the lentils.

MAKES 4 SERVINGS

¾ *pound lentils*
1 *pound ham or ham hock (or knockwurst— see Variation)*
1 *carrot, peeled and diced*
2 *tablespoons lard*
1 *tablespoon flour*
Salt and freshly ground black pepper
2–4 *tablespoons vinegar spätzle (page 320)*

SWABIA

Beef Stew with Spätzle   Gaisburger Marsch

1 pound lean stewing beef
 (see Headnote)
 Several soup bones
1 carrot, peeled and diced
1 stalk celery, diced
1 leek, washed and diced
3 sprigs of parsley
1 bay leaf
¾ pound potatoes, peeled
 Salt and freshly ground
 black pepper
 Pinch of grated nutmeg
½ recipe for spätzle (page
 319)
1 large onion, diced
1 tablespoon butter

Around the turn of the century, Gaisburg (now part of Stuttgart) was still a country village; the story is that there was an inn that served a delicious beef stew, and the troops from one particular barracks in Stuttgart willingly undertook the long march out to Gaisburg to fill up on the specialty of the house, which thus came to be known as *Gaisburger Marsch* (Route to Gaisburg). Readers anxious for any reason to re-create the original *Schwäbischer* taste of this dish will use as little meat as they think they can get away with (maybe less than ½ pound), though it tastes quite a bit better if you use almost three times as much.

•   •   •   •   •   •   •   •   •

Wash the beef and the soup bones thoroughly. Place both in cold salted water with all the vegetables, parsley, and bay leaf, bring to a boil, and cook until the beef is tender. Strain the broth and reserve; remove the beef and set aside. Discard the vegetables.

Cut the potatoes into medium-size oblong pieces and cook in the reserved broth until tender. Dice the beef and add to the broth. Season with salt, pepper, and nutmeg. Cook the spätzle separately and add to the stew; blend all the ingredients together. In a skillet brown the onion in the butter; pour the entire contents of the skillet over the stew. *Gaisburger Marsch* is a complete meal in itself, requiring no accompaniment, though you will have to eat it with a spoon.

MAKES 4 SERVINGS

SOUTHERN AND
SOUTHWESTERN GERMANY

Ham with Noodles   Schinkennudeln

This is one of the most popular German casseroles, especially south of the Main Line.

·   ·   ·   ·   ·   ·   ·   ·   ·

Preheat the oven to 350°F.

Cook the noodles in salted water and drain; they can also be left over from the day before. Fill a soufflé pan with alternate layers of ham and noodles; salt lightly and put some of the sour cream and some grated cheese over each layer. The top layer should consist of noodles. Dot with little bits of butter and sprinkle with bread crumbs.

Bake in the oven for about 30 minutes.

VARIATIONS: This version of the recipe comes from Swabia; feel free to increase the proportions of the costlier ingredients (ham, butter, sour cream) as your fancy dictates.

In another version of this casserole, the ingredients are all mixed together in a bowl, along with 3 eggs, the soufflé pan is well greased with butter (always recommended), and the contents of the bowl transferred to the pan, then proceed as described above.

MAKES 4 SERVINGS

*¾ pound fresh egg
    noodles (see page 322)*
*½ pound ham, diced
    Salt*
1 cup sour cream
*3 tablespoons grated
    Swiss cheese
    (Emmentaler)*
1–2 tablespoons butter
*2 tablespoons bread
    crumbs*

Pickles, Relishes, and Preserves

. . . .

Homemade preserves—*Eingemachtes,* since what would be "put up" in English is "done in" in German—have started to come back into favor in recent years. In spite of the fact that canned and frozen foods from virtually every place on earth are now available in abundance, more and more German homemakers have started putting up their own marmalades, pickles, and relishes in the approved "*grossmutter*-ly" fashion. Though it is true that what might be called the "cuisine of nostalgia" is very much in vogue at the moment, this seems to be at least partly a matter of genuine personal preference—people seem to have developed, or rediscovered, a taste for "real food."

Sweet-and-sour relishes and preserves have benefited especially from this revival, even though the more utilitarian aspects of home canning and preserving have mainly been taken over by the deep freeze. The drying of fruit and other produce, for example, was once an important homemaking activity in Germany; old houses in the Schwarzwald were equipped with special drying lofts, few of which are still in active service today. In the region around Kissingen-am-Main, the preparation of oven-dried peeled and pitted plums ("prunelles," as the gourmet specialty items are called) was a lucrative cottage industry for many years.

Damson Cheese Zwetschgenmus

The English name of this highly concentrated version of damson plum preserves is not to be taken too literally; no dairy products are involved, and all that's needed are the damsons themselves, a fair amount of perseverance, and a strong right arm. In Germany, "damson cheese" is sometimes referred to as *Pflaumenmus,* or *Latwerge,* terms that are more commonly (and correctly) used for a straightforward puree, like applesauce, made with ordinary plums rather than damsons.

5 pounds plums
1 cup water

. . . .

Pit the damsons and mince them (or put them through the meat grinder or puree in the blender or food processor), retaining as much of the juice as possible. Add a little water to the minced damsons and the juice and slowly bring to a boil; reduce the fruit pulp over low heat for several hours, but do not stir or the damson pulp is quite likely to scorch on the bottom.

When the pulp has thickened somewhat, it will have to be stirred—continuously—for several hours, until it is literally thick enough that a spoon will stand up in it. It may sputter and bubble during this stage. (In former days, it was usual for several families to convene in the village washhouse for a cooperative *Zwetschgenmus*-cooking session, with story-telling and other impromptu entertainments to give encouragement to the stirrers.)

When the damson cheese has sufficiently thickened, transfer it to stoneware crocks and bake in the oven until a dry crust has formed on top. The damson cheese will keep better if a piece of parchment paper that has been soaked in rum is placed on top of this crust before the crock is sealed with plastic wrap (formerly a piece of linen or parchment was used). A good imported product is available on the American market under the name of "Pflaumenmus" (pronounced Flaumenmoose).

Ginger Pear Preserves   Ingwerbirnen

4¼ pounds sugar
2 cups water
6 slices of fresh ginger
4¼ pounds small, firm
  pears, peeled, cored,
  and quartered

No pear preserve from a supermarket shelf can match the wonderful flavor of this recipe. It makes an excellent relish for a variety of meat dishes.

· · · · · · · ·

Boil down the sugar and water until it is thick enough that a drop of it placed on a saucer will retain its shape and not trickle off like water (between thread and soft ball stage) . Add the ginger to the sugar water. Blanch the pears, a few of them at a time, for several minutes in boiling water, then place in the sugar water with ginger to cook for just about 1 hour; they should be soft but not mushy or pulpy. Store the pears in clean mason jars, allow to cool, and seal tight with wax paper or cellophane.

MAKES 12 CUPS

Assorted Fruits and Berries Preserved in Rye Whiskey   Chinois

The *Rumtopf* (mixed fruit preserved in rum) is a popular party dish in Germany today and has even lent its name to a variety of "natural" yogurt in the United States. The turn-of-the-century ancestor of the *Rumtopf,* the *Chinois,* has a more exotic origin than most of the other dishes in this book: it is said to have been introduced into Germany by returning members of the marine artillery battery stationed from 1898 through 1914 in the German protectorate in Tsingtau-Kiaochow in northern China. This recipe dates from c. 1902 and certainly seems worthy of revival in this current Year-of-the-*Rumtopf.*

·   ·   ·   ·   ·   ·   ·   ·

"Take a large empty jar from ginger preserves [or a large stoneware crock of any kind] with a thick, tight-fitting stopper. Fill halfway up with the best aged rye [or clear corn] whiskey [or even vodka] and pack with unbruised, unblemished, and washed ripe berries and fruits of the season, including as many of the following as possible: strawberries, raspberries, blackberries, green walnuts 'spiked' with whole cloves, currants, apricots, greengages, tangerines, and grapes. Add sugar to taste, a cinnamon stick, and a very little bit of vanilla, then let sit for several weeks in a not-too-cold place. The fruit should be served in shallow bowls of Chinese porcelain and eaten with chopsticks; the fortified juice should be drunk from eggshell teacups."

NOTE: The different kinds of fruit may best be added when they are in season, i.e., at different times. After each fruit addition pour in whiskey to cover as well as more sugar. Nowadays Weinbrand (German cognac) is most often used.

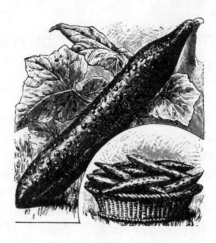

SPREEWALD (BERLIN)

Lübbenau Dill Pickles   Lübbenauer Salzgurken

*Small pickling cucumbers
(preferably the slender
rather than the plump
ones)
Sour cherry leaves
Fresh dill
Grape leaves
Fresh horseradish
Fresh tarragon
1 heaping tablespoon salt
for every quart cold
water*

Dill pickles are still a specialty of the town of Lübbenau on the outskirts of Berlin, as celebrated by the Berliner folk rhyme (or early advertising jingle), *"Was klärt den Kopp bei Mann und Frau?* [What clears a man or woman's head?] *Saure Gurken aus Lübbenau!* [Dill pickles from Lübbenau!]" Part of the Spreewald pickle country is still accessible to day-trippers from West Berlin, but as a rule in Germany nowadays, nice juicy "delicatessen-style" dill pickles are not all that easy to come by, since the powers-that-be in the pickle industry have decided to concentrate on gherkins and other vinegar-cured varieties rather than brine-cured dills because the first mentioned have a much longer shelf life. On the other hand, *Grossmutter*'s dill pickle recipe is readily available to make up for this deficiency. Dill pickles were put up in a stout little wooden keg *(Gurkenfass),* the household version of the old country-store pickle barrel. For our purposes, a large, wide-mouthed stoneware crock will do just as well—better in some ways, since it is easier to keep clean and watertight.

. . . .

Start by scrubbing the cucumbers thoroughly with cold water and draining onto paper towels. Rinse the cherry leaves thoroughly with hot water (since there are a great many more pesticides about than there were in *Grossmutter*'s day), and cover the bottom of the crock with them. Pack the cucumbers fairly tightly, inserting a generous amount of dill into the spaces between them and add the other ingredients (grape leaves, horseradish, fresh tarragon) in amounts according to your taste.

The salt should be completely dissolved in cold water; pour the salted water over the cucumbers until they are entirely submerged. Place a small saucer over them (weighted down with a stone or other heavy object if necessary) to keep them from bobbing up to the surface later on, since they are not meant to be exposed to the air. Cover the crock loosely with a cloth; the seal should not be airtight, since the acidophilus bacteria that build up on the surface of the pickling brine need oxygen to survive; this is to be encouraged, since bacterial action makes the pickles taste better, digest easier, and keep longer. (On the other hand, if a thick white scum builds up on the surface of the brine, it should be thoroughly skimmed off; you may have to replace the brine as well.)

In 10 to 14 days, the miracle of brine pickling should be complete: if all goes well, the pickles will be glossy on the outside and delicious all the way through. They should be kept at room temperature for the first few days, which also promotes the pickling process and makes them keep a bit better. In any case, you should be sure to eat them in a month or two, which rarely presents a problem in the average household.

Pickled Walnuts   Eingelegte Grüne Nüsse

2 pounds unripe walnuts
2 pounds sugar
4–5 cinnamon sticks
20 whole cloves
   Juice and yellow peel
   of 2 fresh lemons

This is an excellent homemade relish, especially good with boiled beef, roasts, or game dishes of any kind and recommended to anyone with a moderate amount of patience and access to an orchard with a couple of walnut trees.

The walnuts should be picked while still green at the end of June or thereabouts—when the nuts are fully developed but the shells are still soft. Bore a number of holes in the shells with a stainless steel or silver darning needle; it's best to wear gloves while doing this to keep the black "soot" from the inside of the shells off your fingers. The walnuts have to soak in cold water for 2 weeks; the water should be changed every day, and the nuts will eventually turn black.

·   ·   ·   ·   ·   ·   ·   ·   ·   ·   ·

Place the nuts in a generous amount of salted water and blanch for just 5 minutes. Leave to soak overnight in cold water; the next morning, put enough water in another pot so that eventually the nuts can be covered completely, and add the remaining ingredients. Bring to a boil and cook until the sugar can be spun out in thin, thready filaments between your fingers.

Strain the spices from the sugar water and return the sugar water to the stove and bring to a boil. Drop the walnuts into the boiling sugar water, a few at a time. When the pot comes to a second boil, remove the walnuts with a slotted spoon and place in warmed mason jars or a ceramic crock—the jars will have to be warmed up, since you're going to be pouring boiling liquid into them shortly. Let the sugar water come to boil once more and immediately fill the jars; wait until the liquid has had a chance to cool before you seal them. In 2 weeks' time, pour the pickling liquid out of the jars again, boil it down some more, and pour it back over the nuts; they should be well covered. In 3 or 4 weeks' time, the pickled walnuts will be ready to eat.

MAKES 6 CUPS

Sweet-and-Sour Pumpkin Relish
Süss-Saure Kürbis

This relish goes very well with corned beef (or any other kind of boiled beef) or a large roast, and will keep for 6 to 8 months.

· · · · · · · · ·

Cut the pumpkin flesh into cubes or other small pieces. Dilute the vinegar with the water and pour this over the pumpkin pieces. Turn the pumpkin cubes a few times in the marinade, then pour the vinegar into a non-reactive saucepan, bring to a boil, and pour back over the pumpkin cubes. Let stand overnight.

Pour off the vinegar again, add the sugar and spices to it, and cook for about 15 minutes. Add the pumpkin cubes to this and cook until they turn quite translucent. Transfer the pumpkin cubes to storage jars or a large stoneware crock or two; boil down the vinegar water a little more, strain out the spices, and pour into the jars after the liquid has had a chance to cool. Seal with parchment paper (or plastic wrap). The pumpkin relish should be ready to eat in a couple of days.

MAKES 6–7 CUPS

2¼ *pounds pumpkin flesh (or other large winter squash), seeds removed*
2 *cups vinegar*
2 *cups water*
3 *cups sugar*
16 *whole cloves*
15 *peppercorns, crushed*
2 *3" pieces of cinnamon stick (about ⅓ ounce)*
1 *2" piece fresh gingerroot, sliced*

Ingelheim, ancient imperial
castle of Carolus Magnus in the
Rhine valley

Sweet-and-Sour Pickle Relish   Süss-Saure Gurken

1¾ cups sugar
1 cup vinegar
8–10 peppercorns
1 2" piece of cinnamon
  stick
1 tablespoon whole
  cloves
½ tablespoon minced
  fresh ginger (or
  preserved if the
  ginger is not too
  pronounced)
1½ large cucumbers,
  halved lengthwise,
  seeded, and thinly
  sliced

This homemade chutney will keep for as long as two years, so you may want to make a substantial amount of it—perhaps doubling the quantities suggested below. It is delicious with boiled beef and in Rhenish Hesse is customarily served with boiled meat. This recipe is courtesy of the Klenk family winery in Framersheim bei Alzey (of baked potato fame).

•   •   •   •   •   •   •   •   •

Combine the sugar, vinegar, and remaining spices (tied up in a little muslin bag if you'd like to save yourself trouble when removing them and then putting them back a little later) in a non-reactive saucepan, bring to a boil, and stir until the sugar is dissolved. Add the cucumber slices and cook for about 5 minutes; remove them with a slotted spoon and pack them in a glass storage jar or stoneware crock. Boil down the pickling liquid (with spices) until it is reduced by at least half, then allow it to cool, take out the spices, and pour the liquid over the cucumber slices. Let stand for 4 days, then pour the pickling liquid back into a saucepan, boil down some more, allow to cool, and pour it back into the jar.

Repeat this process for a third and final time 1 week later; by now the pickling liquid should have cooked down to a thick syrup. Put a little saucer (weighted jar lid, etc.) on top of the cucumbers to keep out the air, and seal the jar with wax paper or cellophane.

MAKES 3–4 CUPS

Green Tomato Chutney   Eingelegte Grüne Tomaten

Here is an excellent use for those little green tomatoes that are left on the vine at the end of the season. Serve as an appetizer with bread and butter or on any other occasion that "mixed pickles" (as the Germans say) would be appropriate.

• • • • • • • • •

Give the tomatoes a good scrubbing and puncture the skins in several places with a toothpick. Pack the tomatoes in glass storage jars, sprinkling salt between each layer of green tomatoes, and keep in a cool place for 2 or 3 days.

In a non-reactive saucepan heat the vinegar with the spices and sugar but do not bring to a boil. Scrub the horseradish and cut into little slivers; press these (or the hot peppers if you prefer) down between the tomatoes. When the pickling liquid has cooled sufficiently, pour it over the tomatoes and seal the jars. In 10 days, the green tomatoes will be ready to eat. They will keep for 4 months.

MAKES 8 CUPS

25 small, firm green
  tomatoes
2 tablespoons salt
1 quart vinegar
1 heaping tablespoon
  peppercorns
5 whole cloves
1 tablespoon mustard
  seed
1–2 tablespoons sugar
1 4" length of fresh
  horseradish root, or
  4–5 small hot peppers

Pickled Mushrooms   Pilze in Essig

2 pounds assorted fresh-
  picked mushrooms,
  carefully washed
2 cups vinegar
1–2 teaspoons salt
1 tablespoon sugar
  Pinch of freshly
  ground white pepper
12 peppercorns
12 allspice berries
1 tablespoon mustard
  seed
4 bay leaves
1 2" piece of cinnamon
  stick

This is a recipe from the days when mushrooming was a kind of weekend treasure hunt in which the entire family took part. Since mushrooms were generally available on an all or nothing basis, it was useful to have some way of saving them for future festive meals. These make an excellent savory to go with meat or fish.

.   .   .   .

If you have mushrooms of various kinds, sort them out, then coarsely chop or quarter them and blanch them separately in boiling water for 1 minute; after that it's all right to mix them up again.

In a non-reactive saucepan combine the vinegar and the remaining ingredients, bring to a boil, and cook for 10 minutes. Turn off the heat, add the mushrooms to the broth, and allow this to cool.

In the old days, the mushrooms were put up in jars sealed with paraffin, but nowadays a glass storage jar with a pressure seal will do as well, as long as it's thoroughly rinsed out with boiling water. If the pickling liquid is strong enough, the mushrooms should keep for several months if stored in a cool place.

NOTE: There are those who prefer to strain out the spices before adding the mushrooms to the pickling broth; on the other hand, the flavor is appreciably stronger if they go into the jars with the mushrooms, and I've never found their presence to be especially troublesome.

MAKES 4–5 CUPS

Homemade Herbal Vinegar Kräuteressig

Certainly there is no shortage of ready-made herbal vinegar these days; the advantage of *Grossmutter*'s homemade over the multitude of imported store-bought varieties, of course, is that you can adjust the spices to suit your own personal cravings. With a hand-crafted label a bottle will make a fine gift.

•   •   •   •   •   •   •   •   •

Add salt to the vinegar as desired. Dry the herbs thoroughly, and coarsely chop them, then spread them out and let them dry out for a little while.

Mix everything together in a large bottle (one that will hold a bit more than a gallon) and shake vigorously; cover the mouth of the bottle with cheesecloth and let stand for 2 or 3 weeks in a bright, sunny spot. Strain out the spices (perhaps leaving a decorative sprig of tarragon or peppermint) and transfer the vinegar to smaller bottles with corks or pressure-sealed storage jars. The vinegar will keep for 1 year.

MAKES 1 GALLON

Salt
1 gallon pure vinegar
2 sprigs of tarragon, washed
A few sprigs of fresh peppermint, washed
Other herbs and/or garlic may be used as well
6 shallots, thinly sliced
Peel of ½ lemon (without inner white layer)

B A D E N

Sweet-and-Sour Cherries   Kirschen in Essig

3 cups vinegar
3 pounds sugar
7 pounds firm sweet or sour
   cherries

This makes a splendid accompaniment for any game dish.

•   •   •   •   •   •   •   •   •

In a non-reactive saucepan combine the vinegar and sugar and bring to a boil. Wash the cherries; leave about half of the stem on each one. Pack the cherries in stoneware crocks, and when the liquid has cooled to lukewarm, pour it over the cherries. Every day for the next 4 days, the liquid has to be poured out of the crocks, boiled down a little more, allowed to cool, and poured back into the crocks.

The last time you do this, bring the liquid to a rolling boil, drop the cherries into it (which is where the short stems prove useful), and allow to cook for several minutes; then fill the crocks again. When the cherries and syrup have cooled a little, seal the crocks again with wax paper or cellophane. The cherries will be ready to use after 3 weeks, and will keep for 6 to 8 months.

MAKES 10 CUPS

Desserts

. . . .

Desserts, *Nachspeisen,* is what we would call them nowadays, but in former times, as far as the vast majority of the German population was concerned, "dessert" was a special treat that could be expected to arrive promptly at the end of the week, not the end of the meal. Saturday's dinner, in other words, generally consisted of a thick, hearty soup followed by a special sweet or even a cake—like the "plum cake" (*Zwetschen-kuchen,* really Damson Plum Tart, see next chapter) that is still, together with a soup, a Saturday favorite in German households today. The basic categories of traditional German *Nachspeisen* that are presented in this section include, in approximate order of appearance, puddings, and custards; fruit desserts; baked desserts of several different kinds; sweet dumplings; crêpes, pancakes, and waffles; and an elaborate ice-cream parfait.

A great many of the recipes in this book, particularly in this section, are derived from handwritten recipe collections rather than printed cookbooks. In *Grossmutter*'s day, every self-respecting cook had a stout little buckram-bound book of blank pages, the edges of which were often impressively gilded, with a thumb index and elaborate frontispieces for the various sections.

This book might never have existed were it not for the diligence and enterprise of a great many *Grossmutters* and *Ur* (great)-*Grossmutters;* this seems like an excellent opportunity to offer them all my *herzlichen Dank*—sincerest thanks.

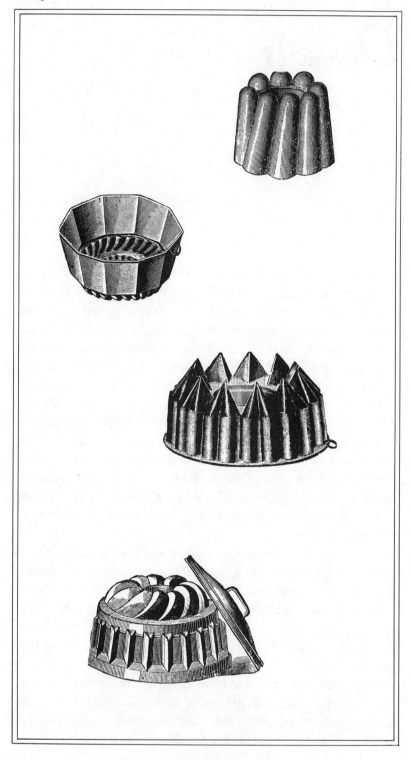

Grandmother's Chocolate Mousse
Grossmutter's Schokoladenspeise

This recipe for an old-time dessert that closely resembles a chocolate mousse was written down by my friend Hans Buch's grandmother, just as she had gotten it from *her* grandmother, and preserved in the Buch family's voluminous recipe archive. This was one of the most popular Saturday night treats in good *bürgerlichen* households before the packaged dessert-mix era.

9 ounces chocolate (bittersweet or milk chocolate, according to preference), cut into pieces
7 tablespoons butter
⅓ cup sugar
6 eggs, separated
1–2 ounces kirsch (cherry brandy may be substituted)
Whipped cream and/or macaroons

. . . .

In a heavy saucepan combine the chocolate with the butter, and melt over a very low flame. Stir in the sugar until completely dissolved, remove from the heat, and allow to cool.

Beat the egg yolks with the kirsch or cherry brandy and mix in the chocolate and butter. Beat the egg whites into stiff peaks; take a quarter of the egg whites, add to the chocolate mixture, and fold in well to lighten the texture a bit. Carefully fold the remaining egg whites into this mixture.

Place in individual serving dishes and chill thoroughly in the refrigerator, 3 to 6 hours. Before serving, garnish each portion with a dab of whipped cream and/or a macaroon.

MAKES 4 SERVINGS

POMERANIA

Ambrosia   Götterspeise

5 cups canned or frozen
   whole cranberries
1¼ cups sugar (more or
   less, according to
   tartness of berries)
1 teaspoon ground
   cinnamon
   Juice of 1 lemon
10 slices of black bread or
   pumpernickel
   (American
   pumpernickel must be
   thoroughly toasted)
3–4 tablespoons grated
   chocolate, plus extra
   for garnish
2 cups whipping cream
1 small packet of
   vanilla sugar, or
   3 tablespoons sugar
   and 1 teaspoon vanilla
   extract

Briefly poach the berries in a heavy non-reactive saucepan with 1 cup of the sugar, the ground cinnamon, and lemon juice; stir and allow to cool. Pour off any excess juice. Crumble or grate the black bread into fine crumbs and mix with the grated chocolate. Combine the cream with the remaining ¼ cup sugar and the vanilla sugar and whip the cream into stiff peaks.

To fill a large glass bowl (or several individual serving bowls), alternate layers of bread crumbs, berries, and whipped cream beginning with the crumbs. There should be room for 2 layers of each, if possible, and the top layer should definitely be whipped cream. Garnish with grated chocolate, or save some of the berries and arrange these in a decorative design. Serve chilled.

MAKES 4–6 SERVINGS

Bavarian Cream Bayrische Creme

The original Bavarian cream *(crème Bavaroise)* was a specialty of Procope's famous café in Paris, an establishment that was assiduously patronized by the princes of Bavaria at the beginning of the eighteenth century. In short, the connection with Bavaria is rather tenuous, though this delicious dessert, which today only vaguely resembles its Parisian ancestor, eventually became popular in Germany as well as France and has since gone on to achieve genuine international celebrity.

• • • • • • • • •

Combine the sugar and egg yolks and beat until light in color. Place the split vanilla bean in a pot with the milk and bring almost to a boil, then remove the bean and whisk the milk into the yolks. Return the mixture to the pan. Heat it, stirring constantly until it thickens. Do not allow the custard to boil.

Stir the softened gelatin into the hot custard mixture. Allow the mixture to cool completely. Combine the heavy cream and vanilla sugar and beat into stiff peaks, then fold into the custard mixture. Transfer the Bavarian cream to a fluted mold or a large glass bowl (or individual serving bowls) and chill 4–6 hours in the refrigerator.

MAKES 8 SERVINGS

1 cup sugar
6 egg yolks
1 vanilla bean, split
1¼ cups milk
2 envelopes (or 5 teaspoons) powdered unflavored gelatin, soaked in 3 tablespoons water for 15 minutes
1 cup heavy cream
1 teaspoon vanilla sugar (or 1 teaspoon regular sugar and a few drops vanilla extract)

Apricot Soufflé   Soufflé mit Aprikosen

10–12 fresh apricots
1½–2 cups water
¾ cup confectioners'
 sugar
6 egg whites

Here is a recipe that originally appeared in *The Pocket Cookbook,* published in Berlin in 1891.

* * * * * * * *

   "Remove the pits from 10 or 12 apricots, then stew them in boiling water until they are thick and syrupy. Press through a hair [fine] sieve and mix with [¾ cup] confectioners' sugar; beat the whites of 6 eggs until they are perfectly stiff and mix together with the apricots. Put this mixture into a [buttered and sugared] soufflé pan, sprinkle some sugar over the top, and bake slowly. Before bringing the soufflé to the table, sprinkle with sugar once again."

NOTE: After the soufflé batter is in the pan, it helps to moisten the blade of a knife and run it along the inner edge of the pan so the soufflé will rise evenly.

   I've sometimes permitted myself the indulgence of lining the bottom of the pan with a thick layer of sponge cake crumbs (or coarsely crumbled macaroons), generously sprinkled with apricot schnapps (perhaps apricot brandy would do as well). This is an innovation that the author of *The Pocket Cookbook* might not have thought entirely suitable, but I know that my great-grandfather, who was also around in those days, would have approved (so much so that I trust he would have thrown out his old *Pocket Cookbook* and run right out to get a copy of this one).

MAKES 4–6 SERVINGS

POMERANIA

Apple Cream Apfelcreme

This is a recipe from a country-house kitchen, where they specialized in concocting elegant banquet dishes out of the homeliest ingredients.

. . . .

Wrap the apples in aluminum foil or place in a covered earthenware (or Pyrex) casserole and bake in the oven until done. Peel the apples and press through a fine strainer or a food mill. Mix with the egg yolk and sugar and beat until light in color and texture.

Heat the white wine in a non-reactive saucepan until it is almost starting to boil and add the softened gelatin, mixing until it is thoroughly dissolved. Mix this together with the apple custard and allow to cool. Shortly before this mixture starts to set, add the salt and vanilla extract to the whipping cream, whip into stiff peaks, and fold it into the apple custard mixture, using one third of the whipped cream to lighten the mixture before adding the rest.

Place the macaroons, ladyfingers, and candied fruit on the bottom of a flat baking dish. Carefully fill the remainder of the baking dish with the apple custard mixture, then chill in the refrigerator for 4–6 hours.

When the custard mixture has set, tip it onto the serving dish like an aspic—so that the cookies and crystallized fruit end up on top, in other words. Here it helps to partially immerse the baking dish in hot water for a few seconds (or cover the outside of the pan with a cloth soaked in hot water) until the *Apfelcreme* starts to loosen its grip on the sides of the dish.

MAKES 6–8 SERVINGS

6 large Rome baking
  apples
1 egg yolk
2 tablespoons sugar
½ cup white wine
1 tablespoon powdered
  unflavored gelatin,
  softened in 3
  tablespoons cold water
  for about 10 minutes
  Small pinch of salt
1 teaspoon vanilla extract
1 cup whipping cream
6 tablespoons crumbled
  macaroons
6 tablespoons crumbled
  ladyfingers
½ cup candied fruit

Red Groats   Rote Grütze

Here is a dish that is as popular in Denmark as it is in North Germany. It is not clear exactly where it originated, nor is it especially important since what we have learned to call lifestyles (and particularly people's eating habits) are much more durable than political boundaries. In the course of many decades, red groats have also spread out from their original stronghold in Schleswig-Holstein to the North Sea and the Baltic coast, as far as East Prussia in the latter case, and in the 1970s, they were unexpectedly acclaimed as a treasure of home-grown haute cuisine and started turning up on "gastronomic" menus all over Germany.

Cereal groats were one of the mainstays of the peasant diet in northern Europe and were customarily served on an enormous wooden trencher that was strategically placed in the middle of the table so that family and hired hands could dig in with their long wooden spoons. The groats were heated in water, stock, milk, or in this case, berry or fruit juice. Red groats *(Rodegrütt)* is probably the only one of many different versions of this dish that are still popular in Germany—which may be explained by the fact that the groats themselves have long since been phased out, and cornstarch, sago, or tapioca starch is now used as a thickening agent in their stead.

SCHLESWIG·HOLSTEIN

Raspberry-Currant Coulis   Rodegrütt

Based on the earliest printed recipe that I know, this dates from the very beginning of the nineteenth century. The dish is so delicious that it is celebrated in a famous nursery rhyme:

> *Rodegrütt, Rodegrütt!*
> Look at Hansel eating it,
> Staring round him like a dumb thing,
> *Rodegrütt* is really something!
> *Rodegrütt, Rodegrütt!*
> *Kiek mol, wat lütt Hein hütt itt,*
> *Alles rundum het he vergeeten,*
> *Rodegrütt, dat is en Eten!*

· · · · · · · · · · ·

2½ cups red currants, stems removed (see Variations for substitutions), washed
1¼ cups raspberries, washed
3 cups water
1–1½ cups sugar (depending on the tartness and acidity of the berries)
½ vanilla bean
5–6 tablespoons cornstarch, dissolved in ¾ cup cold water

Cook the berries for 15 minutes in the water—until they are quite soft. Press through a fine strainer; add to the fruit juice the sugar and the vanilla scraped out of a slit bean, bring to a boil in a non-reactive pot, and reduce while stirring vigorously. Add the dissolved cornstarch to the sweetened fruit juice. Bring to a boil once more, then transfer the *Rodegrütt* to a glass baking dish that has been rinsed with cold water. Chill in the refrigerator and serve.

NOTE: Nowadays, it's more customary to serve *Rodegrütt* in individual bowls rather than in a giant family-size trencher. Serve with cream, cold milk, or cold Vanilla Sauce (*Vanillesauce,* see "Sauces" chapter), which only should be poured over the "groats" before you're ready to eat.

Make sure that the "groats" are not too thick. The correct consistency is somewhere between that of a pudding and a puree (like thick pea soup). When you first taste *Rodegrütt* made according to these specifications, it may easily seem too sweet or the berry flavor may seem a little overwhelming. However, bear in mind that after the "groats" have cooled off a bit and milk or cream has been poured over them, the taste will be considerably milder.

VARIATIONS: Some or all of the strained berry pulp may be replaced with an equivalent amount of fruit juice, and quick-frozen berries or preserves will do just about as well as fresh ones. Cherries, morellos (sour cherries), and black currants are often used instead of or in addition to red currants and raspberries. Many cooks like to hold back some portion of the berries until after the straining so they don't cook down like the others and you can still taste them when eating the dish.

As noted earlier, tapioca is often used as a binding agent, and there are those who maintain that this is the only "authentic" method of making *Rodegrütt*. In Saxony and East Prussia, red groats have been made with farina (semolina) for a number of years now, and since the words for farina (*Griess,* "grits") and groats *(Grützen)* are closely related, sometimes even used interchangeably, it is no less possible that this is in fact the "original" version. All questions of authenticity aside, a deluxe fortified *Rodegrütt* can be made by stewing the berries in red wine or with some higher-proof alcoholic beverage.

MAKES 4–6 SERVINGS

Fruit-and-Berry Coulis, Sylt-Style
Sylter Rote Grütze

Sylt is a small island off the North Sea coast, a popular seaside resort that is sometimes referred to as the "German Riviera." This is the sumptuous local version of *Rodegrütt* with which the islanders have regaled vacationers from every region of Germany.

. . . .

Place 1½ cups red currants, 1 cup raspberries, and ½ cup black currants or cherries in enough cold water to cover, bring to a boil in a non-reactive saucepan, and cook for about 15 minutes. Pour through a fine strainer; do not press the berry pulp through the mesh. This way the liquid will remain clear.

Remove the stems from the remaining handful of currants. Take two-thirds of the strained berry juice, add the remaining red currants, black cherries, plums, raspberries, and the black-berries, and cook for a short while—just until the currants have cooked long enough so they can be eaten. Add the wine, brandy, and rum, plus sugar to taste.

Stir the vanilla pudding mix into the fruit coulis and bring to a boil, then cook according to the directions on the package. Serve the "groats" in chilled bowls with cream that has also been chilled.

MAKES 4–6 SERVINGS

2½ cups red currants, plus
    1 handful
2 cups raspberries
½ cup black currants or
    1 cup black cherries
10 black cherries, pitted
3 plums (or greengages),
    pitted and coarsely
    chopped
½ cup blackberries
½ cup red wine
1–2 tablespoons brandy
1–2 teaspoons rum
    Sugar to taste

½ small package
vanilla pudding mix
Chilled cream

EAST PRUSSIA AND
CENTRAL GERMANY

Stewed Rhubarb   Rhabarbergrütze

1¾ pounds rhubarb
1¼ cups sugar
  Juice and peel of
  ½ lemon
1 cinnamon stick
2 cups water
1 cup white wine
¾ cup pearl tapioca

Serve with cold milk, cream, or Vanilla Sauce.

• • • • • • • • •

Scrub (but do not peel) the rhubarb and cut into 1-inch sections. Place in a non-reactive saucepan with the sugar and the lemon juice and peel. Add the cinnamon stick, pour in the water and wine, sprinkle with the tapioca, and stir well. Simmer all these ingredients together over low heat for about 20 minutes. Test for sweetness. Remove the lemon peel and the cinnamon stick and allow to cool.

VARIATIONS: In central Germany, they prefer to use farina (*Griess*) as a thickener, about ¾ cup farina and ½ cup water for every 1½ pints stewed rhubarb.

Optional ingredients—"refinements," as the Germans say—might include a little melted butter, chopped walnuts, slivered almonds, or cherry slices, either singly or in combination.

MAKES 6 SERVINGS

SOUTHERN   AND
SOUTHWESTERN   GERMANY

Sweet Dumplings   Dampfnudeln

Also called "raised dumplings" because they are made with
yeast, *Dampfnudeln* are thought to have originated in Bavaria,
though they have been just as much at home in other regions
of Germany for several centuries now. Henriette Davidis-
Holle's *Practical Cookbook* gives three different recipes, presumably from her native Westphalia, that were current in the
1840s; certainly my own boyhood in Frankfurt would have
been unimaginably different without them, and we had
Dampfnudeln at my aunt's house in the Rhineland as well.

Dampfnudeln make an excellent light meal with soup—and
as such were greatly in evidence at Saturday lunch—and are
still often served as a dessert. Due to competition from packaged "convenience" foods, they are perhaps no longer as om-
nipresent a feature of Bavarian life as suggested by this old
children's rhyme:

3½ cups flour
2½ teaspoons yeast
1¼ cups milk
¼ cup plus 2 tablespoons
  sugar
2 eggs
  Grated lemon peel
  Salt
7 tablespoons butter, 5
  tablespoons melted and
  cooled

We had *Dampfnudeln* yesterday,	*Dampfnudel hamma gestern* *g'habt,*
Dampfnudeln again today We have *Dampfnudeln* every day, We like it fine that way!	*Dampfnudel hamma heut* *Dampfnudel hamma alle Dag* *Weil's uns halt gefreut!*

•   •   •   •   •   •   •   •

Pour the flour into a large mixing bowl and press a well in
the top. Sprinkle the yeast over 4 tablespoons warm milk.
Pour this mixture into the crater in the flour, add 1 tablespoon
sugar, cover with a little flour, and let stand for 15 minutes.
Then mix the dough with ½ cup milk, the eggs, ¼ cup sugar,
grated lemon peel, and small pinch of salt. Pour in the cooled
melted butter and knead into a dough. Cover and let rise,
about 1 hour, knead briefly, and then let stand once again so
the dough again has a chance to rise.

Combine the 2 tablespoons butter, ½ cup milk, 1 tablespoon sugar, and small pinch of salt in a large pot with a tight-
fitting cover, stir well, bring to a boil and turn off the heat.
Roll the dough into little balls and place these closely together
inside the pot. Cover the pot tightly but there must be ample
space for the dumplings to rise—it's best to place several
thicknesses of paper towel or a dish cloth between the edges
of the pot and lid to make sure that none of the steam escapes
(and that none of the condensation that collects on the underside of the lid will drop back down onto the dumplings).

Steam the dumplings over medium heat for about 20 minutes; they'll let you know when they're ready, since the bottom crust produces a faint crackling sound when it's attained
the proper degree of crispness. Then (and only then) remove
the cover and remove the dumplings with a spatula. Serve
immediately.

VARIATIONS: Try with fruit compote or the fruit sauce of your
choice, Vanilla Sauce, or *Weinschaumsauce* (Wine Custard
Sauce, see "Sauces" chapter). At home, we always had
Dampfnudeln with *Weinschaumsauce,* which is still my favorite.

In Bavarian farmhouse kitchens, the tops of the dumplings
are slit open and a skilletful of crispy lean bacon (plus drippings, of course) is poured over as a garnish; these hearty
Bavarian-style *Dampfnudel* (without the final *n*) are served
with stewed plums.

Rohrnudeln are "oven noodles," as opposed to *Dampfnudeln*
("steam noodles," though they're both really dumplings). In
the old days, *Rohrnudeln* were usually provided with a dab of
plum puree (*Pflaumenmus,* roughly the same consistency as
applesauce) as a filling, then baked in an uncovered pot inside
the oven, which gave the dumplings a nice crispy crust all
over instead of just on the bottom, with other ingredients and
procedures as described. Alternatively, *Rohrnudeln* might be
cooked in a buttered baking dish, in which case the sweetened
milk was added after the dumplings had already been in the
oven for about 20 minutes.

MAKES 4–6 SERVINGS

BADEN-WÜRTTEMBERG

Fluffy Swabian Muffins Pfitzauf

Every well-stocked hardware store in southwestern Germany sells a special-size *Pfitzauf* baking dish that looks almost like a deep earthenware muffin pan. This traditional pastry can also be made in small Pyrex bowls (less than 1 cup content) or in muffin tins lined with paper cupcake molds.

• • • • • • • • •

Preheat the oven to 400°F. Grease the baking dish thoroughly with butter or line the muffin tins with paper molds.

Stir the flour into the milk, beat in the eggs, and stir the salt, sugar, and melted butter into the cake batter one by one. Pour the batter into the baking dish or muffin tins, but only until it comes about halfway up to the top. Bake for about 30 minutes, until golden brown. Turn the baking dish upside down, remove the *Pfitzauf,* sprinkle with the confectioners' sugar, and serve.

NOTE: *Pfitzauf* is sometimes made without sugar and served with a green salad.

MAKES 6 MUFFINS

2¾ *cups flour*
2 *cups milk*
4 *eggs*
Small pinch of salt
1 *tablespoon sugar*
9 *tablespoons butter,*
melted and cooled
Confectioners' sugar

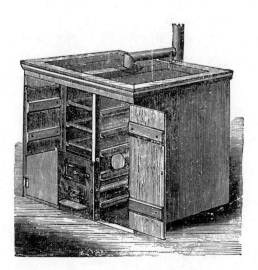

SWABIA

Apple Fritters   Apfelküchlein

3 tablespoons sugar
2 ounces kirsch
3–4 large Granny Smith
   apples, peeled, cored,
   and sliced
   Scant cup flour
   Small pinch of salt
   Peel of ½ lemon,
   grated
⅓ cup sweet white wine
1 egg yolk
1 teaspoon oil
3 egg whites
   Oil or clarified butter
   for deep-frying
   Confectioners' sugar
   Ground cinnamon

The Trojan War was said to have been started by an apple, but this deep-fried apple pastry can only claim to have *almost* wrecked one of the most important European peace treaties, when representatives of all the major powers had assembled at the Congress of Vienna in 1815 to reorganize a war-ravaged Europe along sound monarchical principles. The story is that the delegate from the Kingdom of Saxony grew suspicious as he watched the Austrian delegate, Prince Metternich, in close conclave with the French, Prussian, and Russian ambassadors. Metternich was doing the talking, and the others were listening with evident fascination, nodding their heads at intervals to signal their agreement. Suspecting that some sort of unholy alliance was in the making, the Saxon delegate drew closer and managed to overhear the tail end of Metternich's monologue—the recipe for apple fritters, the way they were made in his old home in the Rhineland. Unfortunately, I was unable to locate a Rhenish recipe for *Apfelküchlein* from the Metternich era, so I hope that this traditional Swabian recipe will do.

. . . .

Combine 2 tablespoons sugar and the kirsch; soak the apples in this for 30 minutes.

Combine the flour, 1 tablespoon sugar, salt, and grated lemon peel, wine, egg yolk, and oil, and stir together until you have a smooth batter with no apparent lumps. Let stand for about 30 minutes. Beat the egg whites into stiff peaks, and fold them into the batter just before you're about ready to make the fritters.

Dredge the apple slices in the batter, deep-fry them in hot fat, and drain on several thicknesses of paper towel. Sprinkle with confectioners' sugar and cinnamon and serve while still warm.

NOTE: If the batter seems too thick, add a few tablespoons of sweet white wine.

MAKES 4–6 SERVINGS

SCHWARZWALD

Soufflé with Cherry Liqueur
Auflauf mit Kirschwasser

This is a recipe from the mid-nineteenth century.

• • • • • • • • •

"Cut a French roll [or use slices of toasted bread] into slices of the desired thickness and fry them in hot lard or shortening. When they have cooled off a little, dip them in kirschwasser, set them on a platter, and sprinkle generously with sugar. Then take ¼ pound crushed almonds and fry with 2 table-spoons sugar until the almonds turn golden yellow; put them in a bowl and stir to cool them off a little. Beat 8 eggs into a froth [beat yolks until light, then fold in beaten whites last] and, together with the minced peel and juice of lemon, stir with the almonds. Then place some of the bread slices in a deep pan [preferably a Pyrex soufflé dish] that has been well greased with butter, place half a finger's breadth [¼–½″ layer] of the almond mixture on top of them, then more of the bread slices, and so forth, until the ingredients are all used up. Then put the baking pan [bowl] into the oven [350°F.] and bake [1 hour] until the soufflé has risen nicely."

MAKES 6–8 SERVINGS

1 loaf French bread
  Butter or lard for frying
1 cup kirschwasser
  Sugar to sprinkle on
  bread
¼ pound ground almonds
2 tablespoons sugar
8 eggs, separated
  Grated peel and juice of
  1 lemon

SWABIA, ALLGÄU

Cider Cakes   Mostküchle

1⅓ cups flour
2 eggs
1 cup milk
5 tablespoons sugar
   Small pinch of salt
4 breakfast rolls
   (Semmel) or kaiser
   rolls, cut into
   4 or 5 slices each
   Oil for deep-frying
2 cups alcoholic cider
   (which comes very
   close to German Most)
1 cinnamon stick

Combine the flour, eggs, milk, 1 tablespoon sugar, and salt and stir well; let the batter sit for 30 minutes.

Dip the roll slices in the pancake batter and deep-fry in hot oil until golden brown on both sides. Drain on paper towels, then place in a large bowl or a shallow baking dish (as long as there's enough room for them to lie flat). Heat the cider or German *Most* with the remaining sugar (4 tablespoons) and cinnamon stick in a non-reactive saucepan but do not allow it to come to a boil. Pour the cider over the little cakes and wait until they have absorbed as much of the liquid as they can. Serve warm.

MAKES ABOUT 20 CAKES

BADEN

Freiburg Waffles   Freiburger Waffeln

7 tablespoons butter
1¾ cups flour
8 eggs
1 cup sour cream
1 tablespoon sugar
½ teaspoon salt
   Grated peel of ½
   lemon
   Bacon fat
   Confectioners' sugar

This is an old family recipe from the university town of Freiburg in Breisgau.

•   •   •   •   •   •   •   •   •

Whip the butter until it turns white and creamy. Stir in the flour, eggs, and sour cream—no more than a tablespoonful of each at a time, however—then stir vigorously. Next, add the sugar, salt, and the grated lemon peel to the batter. If the batter is too thick, thin it out with a little more sour cream.

Do not let it stand; grease the waffle iron with bacon fat and cook the waffles until golden brown. Sprinkle with confectioners' sugar and serve.

MAKES 6–8 SERVINGS

Prince Pückler's Parfait   Fürst-Pückler-Eis

Prince Hermann von Pückler-Muskau (1785–1871) was famous in his own right as a writer, traveler, and landscape architect, and went on to achieve posthumous immortality after the owner of an ice-cream parlor in Lausitz (Herr Schulz) named this attractive *bombe glacée*—a multicolored Neapolitan ice-cream parfait—in his honor.

Nowadays, every layered block of ice cream that is colored yellow, brown, and red (pink) is called *Fürst-Pückler-Eis*. The original recipe is time-consuming but worth every minute of it. It became especially popular in Berlin during the decade or

Freiburg in Breisgau (Baden)

so after the prince's death; this recipe seems to have been written down about 1880.

.   .   .   .

"For this you will need to make vanilla ice cream. When the ice cream is ready and comes out of the churn, it should be divided into three parts—the first of which remains as is ['yellow'], the second is tinted pink by food coloring and mixing in some maraschino liqueur, and the third should have some grated chocolate mixed in with it. The basic ice cream should have been made with 1 pint cream and 4 eggs. After having come out of the churn and softened a bit, fold in 1 pint whipped cream mixed with ¼ cup crumbled, unsweetened macaroons. Then put the three separate layers of ice cream, one after the other, in a mold and pack in crushed ice and salt. Dip the mold in cold water before you turn it over to remove the completed dessert."

NOTE: The cleaned churn may be used as a mold for the three layers. Nowadays, we might be tempted to upgrade the pink section of the ice cream tricolor by substituting strawberry ice cream or raspberry sherbet for pink-tinted vanilla. We should not be tempted to fiddle around with the rest of the recipe, however, since the macaroons and the whipped cream are essential to the light and airy texture of the parfait.

MAKES 4–6 SERVINGS (1 QUART)

EAST PRUSSIA

Pirogi, East Prussian-Style   Schaltenoses

Schaltenoses means "cold noses" in East Prussian colloquial dialect, which is probably the best the East Prussians could do with the original name of this dish that came from one of the Baltic languages.

.   .   .   .

Soak the raisins in rum for 2 hours.

Combine the flour, 4 eggs, a little salt, and 1 tablespoon sugar and knead into a smooth noodle dough.

Rub the cottage cheese through a fine sieve and combine with the butter and 2 egg yolks, and stir together until creamy. Season with the grated lemon peel, 3 tablespoons sugar, saffron, and the raisins along with their soaking liquid.

Roll out the dough in a very thin sheet. Cut out circles about 4″ in diameter and place a dab of cottage cheese filling in the center of each one. Paint the edges of the dough circles with beaten egg white so the edges will adhere when you press them together to make half-moon shape *Schaltenoses.*

Cook in lightly salted water for 10 to 15 minutes and drain. When you've brought the *Schaltenoses* to the table, pour a little browned butter over them and sprinkle with sugar and cinnamon.

MAKES 4 SERVINGS

¾ cup raisins, washed
½ cup rum
2¾ cups flour
6 eggs, 2 separated
Small pinch of salt
4 tablespoons sugar
2¼ cups cottage cheese
3 tablespoons butter, softened
Grated peel of 1 lemon
Pinch of saffron, stirred into a little lemon juice
Browned butter
Confectioners' sugar
Ground cinnamon

BERGISCHES LAND

Bergisch Smorgasbord Bergische Kaffeetafel

"Coffee table" is not a piece of suburban furniture but rather a kind of miniature smorgasbord that appears in response to a request for *Kaffee mit Essen* (coffee with something to eat) in the Bergisches Land, a mountainous district in the West German state of North Rhine-Westphalia. This local dish has helped to preserve the bountiful eating habits from my great-grandfather's day and has become something of a tourist attraction in its own right.

In addition to a pot of excellent coffee (in Westphalia the coffeepot still has a long spout and is known in the local parlance as a *Dröppelminna,* or "Dripping Minnie"), a typical *Kaffeetafel* might include raisin cookies, currant buns, pretzels

1 cup plus 2 tablespoons butter, melted and cooled
4 eggs
6 tablespoons sugar
½ teaspoon salt
2 tablespoons honey
3½ cups flour
1 teaspoon vanilla extract
1 teaspoon baking powder
Confectioners' sugar

(Burger Bretzel), zwieback with icing, a small mountain of butter, rice pudding, sweet apple syrup, farmer cheese *(Klatschkäse),* and warm, crispy waffles. This old-time recipe for Bergische waffles should be a foretaste to the *Kaffeltafel* feast.

•   •   •   •   •   •   •   •   •

Combine the first 6 ingredients on the list (adding them in the order indicated) and stir with enough warm water to produce a fairly thick waffle batter. Add the vanilla extract and the baking powder at the same time.

Grease the waffle iron, cook the waffles until crispy on both sides, sprinkle with confectioners' sugar, and serve while still warm.

MAKES 12 WAFFLES

Pastries and Baked Goods

. . . .

Pastries were customarily reserved for Sundays and holidays, and over the centuries, a great many traditional recipes have come to be associated with Christmas Eve and *Fastnacht* (Mardi Gras and the week before the beginning of Lent). These recipes were generally prepared both by homemakers and professional bakers—and very often in the same oven, since during the days when most families cooked their meals over an open hearth fire (well into the twentieth century), relatively few homes had their own baking ovens. Pastries were either deep-fried in lard (*Schmalzgebäck*, which we'll be getting back to in a moment) or baked communally when the village or neighborhood baker's oven was fired up on bread-baking day.

Traditional pastries that have recently come into the domain of the professional baker have not been included in this collection; as examples of this category, I might mention the *Dambedei*, something like a gingerbread man in general appearance but made out of sweetened yeast dough, and the beloved "Easter Lamb" made from biscuit dough, which is very popular in the Catholic regions of Germany. The recipes in this section are arranged in more or less descending order of size: starting with cakes and other more substantial baked goods (*Grossgebäck*) that are baked in a mold or baking dish, ranging through tortes, tarts, and other pastries that are baked on a cookie sheet (*Blechgebäck*), to miniature fruit and cream tarts, cookies, and other "fancy pastries" *(Kleingebäck),* then winding up with traditional pastries for Christmas and New Year's and *Schmalzgebäck* for the pre-Lenten season.

Even now in southern Germany, a special day during Mardi Gras week—so-called *Schmuziger Donnerstag*—is expressly set aside for the preparation of *Schmalzgebäck.* For the benefit of those with some knowledge of German, it may be worth pointing out that *schmuzig* (pronounced "schmoo-tzick," with a very long *oo*) is derived from *schmalzig* (hence, "Schmalzy Thursday") and has nothing whatsoever to do with *schmutzig,* which means filthy, dirty, obscene. Of the enormous number of cookies *(Plätzchen)* and other *Kleingebäck* that are not connected with any religious holiday, I was only able to include a very small sampling, for which I beg the reader's kind indulgence.

NOTE: All the yeast used in these recipes is granular yeast.

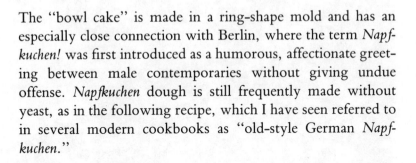

NORTHERN AND
CENTRAL GERMANY

Napfkuchen

1 cup plus 2 tablespoons
　butter
7 eggs, separated
1 cup sugar
　Pinch of ground
　cardamom
⅔ cup chopped almonds
1 tablespoon rum
1½ cups flour, sifted
　Confectioners' sugar

The "bowl cake" is made in a ring-shape mold and has an especially close connection with Berlin, where the term *Napfkuchen!* was first introduced as a humorous, affectionate greeting between male contemporaries without giving undue offense. *Napfkuchen* dough is still frequently made without yeast, as in the following recipe, which I have seen referred to in several modern cookbooks as "old-style German *Napfkuchen.*"

Preheat the oven to 350°F. Generously butter a 9″ bundt pan.

Whip the butter until it is frothy. Beat the egg yolks into the butter one at a time, alternating with a little sugar after each addition. Add the cardamom, followed by the chopped almonds and rum. Stir the flour into this to produce a smooth batter. Beat the egg whites into stiff peaks; take one-third of them and stir them into the batter to make it a little lighter, then fold in the rest.

Fill the ring mold with the batter—it should be about two-thirds full—and bake for 1 hour. Tip out of the mold, sprinkle with confectioners' sugar, and serve.

NOTE: Nowadays, a teaspoon of baking powder is sometimes added to the dough as well.

Those in search of a textural richness and variety may feel free to add about ½ cup of chocolate chips or chopped semisweet chocolate.

MAKES 8–10 SERVINGS

EAST PRUSSIA

East Prussian-Style Suitor Cake Anhalterkuchen

The language of flowers is known to many cultures, but the language of pastries was particularly well understood in East Prussia. The *Anhalter* cake is named for a suitor, a young man who comes courting, and not (as would be the case in Germany today) a hitchhiker, or perhaps a resident of Anhalt, an historic region of Saxony. When a suitor met with the approval of a young woman and her parents, he would be offered coffee and cake—*Anhalterkuchen*. Otherwise, he would just get the coffee, a tactful hint that he should spare himself the trouble and embarrassment of making a proposal that was almost certain to be rejected.

· · · · · · · · ·

Preheat the oven to 350°F. Grease a deep rectangular baking dish generously with butter and sprinkle with bread crumbs (or zwieback crumbs).

Whip the softened butter until frothy and add the egg yolks one by one, alternating with additions of sugar in between. Mix in the flour and the baking powder, followed by the rum and the grated lemon peel, and stir into a batter. Add a little salt to the egg whites and beat into stiff peaks, then fold into the batter in three turns.

Transfer the batter to the baking dish and bake in the oven for just about 45 minutes. Allow to cool a little and sprinkle with the confectioners' sugar.

MAKES 8 SERVINGS

3 tablespoons bread crumbs or zwieback crumbs
1 cup plus 2 tablespoons butter, softened
6 large eggs, or 8 small ones, separated
1¼ cups sugar
1¾ cups flour, sifted
1½ teaspoons baking powder
2 tablespoons rum
Grated peel of 1 fresh lemon
Small pinch of salt
A few tablespoons confectioners' sugar

THURINGIA

Thuringian-Style Coffee Loaf   Schietchen

14 cups (4 pounds)
    flour
1 quart plus 1 cup
    lukewarm milk
2 tablespoons plus
    1 teaspoon yeast
1 cup plus 2
    tablespoons
    butter, softened,
    plus extra for
    topping
1½ cups sugar
    Small pinch of
    salt
1¼–1½ cups currants,
    washed and dried
¾ cup almonds,
    slivered

This is something like the well-known Christmas stollen, only not quite as sweet and substantial. I now suspect that the reason my grandmother in Ilmenau had such an enormous cook-stove in her kitchen was to make enormous batches of *Schietchen*, which she baked every month; they were served for breakfast and with afternoon coffee. Since the *Schietchen* was meant to be dunked, my childish requests to spread mine with butter were strictly ignored. Clearly as a result of these thwarted boyhood cravings, I now prefer to eat them not only with butter but with jelly as well—which to the old folks at home in the Thüringer Wald would have seemed like a sinful extravagance.

•   •   •   •   •   •   •   •   •   •   •

Sift the flour into a large mixing bowl and let stand until it reaches room temperature. Press a crater into the top of the mound of flour, into the crater pour 1 cup of the lukewarm milk, sprinkle the yeast on the milk, cover with flour, and let stand once again while the yeast foams (20 minutes). Add the soft butter and the sugar to the flour, as well as a little salt, and knead into a fairly firm dough while gradually adding the rest of the milk. Now give it time to rise, 1 to 2 hours.

When the dough has risen, knead the currants into the dough, and let stand for just a short while (20 minutes) this time.

Preheat the oven to 350°F. Divide the dough into 3 separate loaves (stollen) and let stand for 20 minutes more, then brush with water. Spread the slivered almonds over the loaves and bake for 50 to 60 minutes until golden brown. When the *Schietchen* are still warm from the oven, spread them with butter (contrary to my grandmother's practice), which makes them keep longer as well as taste a bit better. (In the old days, when slivered almonds were still an expensive luxury, the *Schietchen* was often sprinkled with fine confectioners' sugar at this stage, as a substitute for the almonds.)

MAKES NUMEROUS SERVINGS (BREAKFAST SUPPLY FOR A FAMILY OF 4 FOR 1 WEEK)

BERLIN,   STETTIN

Tree Cake   Baumkuchen

The *Baumkuchen* is undoubtedly one of the most notable achievements of the German baker's art—a cake baked on a horizontal rotary spit, so called because the cake is shaped more or less like the knobby trunk of a tree. The pastry chefs of the port city of Stettin (now Szczecin) were especially famous for their *Baumkuchen*. During the Wilhelmine era, the

1½ cups plus
   1 tablespoon
   butter, softened
3 cups sugar
14 eggs, 4 separated
1¾ cups flour
¾ cup cornstarch
   Grated peel of
   ½ lemon
1 heaping tablespoon
   crushed almonds
   Generous pinch of
   cardamom
1 teaspoon vanilla
   extract
   Small pinch of salt
   Lemon or chocolate
   icing

deluxe *Berliner Baumkuchen* of Hofkonditor★ Jaedicke was celebrated all over Europe.

Professional bakers use a special self-contained apparatus (a descendant of the one shown in the picture on page 423) with rollers turning in front of or directly above a gas or electric grill. A good approximation of the traditional method of baking *Baumkuchen* can be achieved by the home chef with a standard upright barbecue, a (horizontal and preferably self-turning) rotary spit, and a bit of homemade rather than store-bought special equipment—a wooden roller (preferably hardwood) about 2″ or 3″ in diameter, bored out and sawed in half lengthwise to fit around the spit. The roller should be wrapped in several layers of greased parchment paper that can be held tight with fine wire; it's useful, but not essential, if the roller tapers slightly at one end, which will make it easier to slide out of the center of the completed *Baumkuchen*.

Here is the recipe using the modern way of baking.

• • • • • • • • •

Combine the butter and sugar and beat until the butter is quite frothy. Add the eggs one by one—10 whole eggs plus 4 egg yolks. Stir in the flour and keep stirring until you have a smooth mixture. Beat the 4 egg whites into stiff peaks and fold into the batter. Add the cornstarch and the remaining seasonings, and work into a smooth, slightly fluid batter. If the batter is still too stiff, beat 2 whole eggs until frothy and stir in. Formerly, the batter would have had to be dripped over the horizontal roller, coating it by rotation and baking it in front of the flame layer after layer. German homemakers have developed a method to bake *Baumkuchen* as a torte, which is much more convenient and lets us enjoy the same wonderful taste.

Pour a thin layer of batter, about the thickness of a crêpe, in a greased springform mold and brown under the broiler. Continue like this with layers of batter and brown each one

---

★ A *Konditor* is a pastry chef or a confectioner (or just the proprietor of a café, a *Konditorei,* where these delicacies are served); the prefix *Hof-* means something like "by appointment to the royal court," or in this case, the imperial court of Berlin.

before adding the next. The finished cake (more like a torte) has to be covered with lemon or chocolate icing.★ It keeps fresh for at least 2 weeks.

MAKES 12 SERVINGS

★ Icing: Blend together 4 tablespoons butter, 1–2 teaspoons heavy cream, and 2 cups confectioners' sugar. When creamy, mix in 3 tablespoons lemon juice. Spread on *Baumkuchen*.

NORTHERN AND
CENTRAL GERMANY

Butter-Top Cake   Butterkuchen

DOUGH:
3½ cups flour
  1 cup lukewarm milk
    Scant ½ cup sugar
2½ teaspoons yeast
  5 tablespoons butter,
    softened
  1 egg
    Pinch of salt

TOPPING:
11 tablespoons butter (for
    the butter top)
⅔ cup sugar
1–2 teaspoons ground
    cinnamon

This is a venerable but nonetheless very tasty example of the *Blechkuchen,* which is made on a baking tin rather than in a mold or baking dish.

•   •   •   •   •   •   •   •   •

Using the quantities listed here, prepare the dough according to the "Basic Yeast Dough Recipe" (see page 431). Let rise 1 to 2 hours.

Preheat the oven to 400°F. Grease a large baking sheet. Roll out the dough and place it on the baking sheet and puncture the surface of the dough with the tines of a fork in several different places. Whip the butter until frothy and spread on top of the dough, then sprinkle with sugar and cinnamon. Bake for about 30 minutes, or until golden brown.

VARIATIONS: Some of the old cookbooks suggest that rosewater and slivered almonds may be added to the dough, according to preference.

Instead of puncturing the dough, one can make several indentations with the thumb that result in little pools filled with butter.

MAKES 8–10 SERVINGS

Old-Fashioned Cheesecake
Käsekuchen auf dem Blech/Bätscher

Those who have acquired a taste for the insipid cardboard-flavored confection that passes under the name of cheesecake these days should read no further; others, however, may be interested in trying out *Grossmutter*'s recipe. The cheese topping is only about a quarter as thick as the store-bought variety, but it's guaranteed to taste at least four times as good. *Bätscher* is the name by which this cheesecake is known in the Hessian-Rhön district—elsewhere, more prosaically, it's just "cheesecake [baked] on the metal sheet."

.   .   .   .

Using the quantities listed here, prepare the dough according to the "Basic Yeast Dough Recipe" (see page 431).

Preheat the oven to 425°F. Grease a large baking sheet.

Make the topping. Combine the cottage cheese with the currants and the other ingredients; stir into a thick paste. When the dough has risen, roll it out, place it on a large greased baking sheet (or 2 small ones), and pinch a little border all around the edges to contain the topping. Puncture the sheet(s) of dough all over with the tines of a fork and cover with the topping mixture. Bake for about 30 minutes, until light golden.

MAKES 12 SERVINGS

DOUGH:
- 3½ cups flour
- 1 cup lukewarm milk
- Scant 1 cup sugar
- 2½ teaspoons yeast
- Pinch of salt
- 7 tablespoons butter

TOPPING:
- 2½ cups cottage cheese, rubbed through a fine sieve to smooth out the curds
- 1¼ cups currants, washed
- ½ cup cream
- 3 eggs
- ¾ cup plus 2 tablespoons sugar
- 1 teaspoon vanilla extract
- Grated peel of 1 lemon

CENTRAL   AND
EASTERN   GERMANY

Sour Cream Cake   Rahmkuchen/Schmantkuchen

DOUGH:
  3½ cups flour
  ¾ cup lukewarm milk
  ¾ cup sugar
  2½ teaspoons yeast
    Small pinch of salt

PASTE:
  1 cup milk
  2 tablespoons farina
    (semolina)
    Pinch of salt
  1 tablespoon sugar
  2 tablespoons raisins
  3 tablespoons sultana
    raisins

TOPPING:
  1 cup crème fraîche
  2 eggs
  2 tablespoons sugar
    An ample amount of
    confectioners' sugar

It seems like Parisian and Pomeranian cuisine would have very little in common. Perhaps the only thing they do have in common is *Schmant,* the thick, rich, and not-too-sour sour cream that is very similar in taste and texture to the French *crème fraîche,* which is also produced by German dairies and marketed (as in the United States) under the French name.

•   •   •   •   •   •   •   •   •   •

Using the quantities listed here, prepare the dough according to the "Basic Yeast Dough Recipe" (see page 431).

In the meantime, make the paste: heat the milk, add the farina, a little salt and sugar, and stir into a thick paste. Wash the raisins and sultanas and dry them off.

Preheat the oven to 400°F. Grease a large baking sheet.

Roll out the dough onto a large baking sheet (or 2 smaller ones), pinch a little border around the edges of the dough, and prick the dough all over with the tines of a fork. Spread the farina paste, which should have cooled by now, over the sheet of dough.

Combine the topping ingredients except confectioners' sugar; stir well. Place the raisins on top of the farina paste, pressing gently, then cover with the topping mixture. Bake

Zittau, Saxony (engraving by
Johann Poppel, after a drawing
by L. Rohbock)

for a good 30 minutes, until light golden, then sprinkle with a generous amount of powdered sugar while still warm from the oven, and serve.

VARIATION: Many of the older cookbooks advise adding a little mace to the topping, which results in an especially piquant and flavorful cheesecake.

MAKES 8–10 SERVINGS

Coffee Cake with Streusel Topping
Streuselkuchen

Back home in Frankfurt, we called this a *Krümmelkuchen,* which corresponds exactly to the English "crumb cake." To bake this sort of cake in a little round torte pan is considered an abomination by all right-thinking persons; the baking sheet should be rectangular, and it can't possibly be too big.

• • • • • • • • • •

Using the quantities listed here, prepare the dough according to the "Basic Yeast Dough Recipe" (see page 431).

To make the streusel topping, start by combining the flour, sugar, crushed almonds, and cinnamon. The melted butter should no longer be hot but still fluid; sprinkle the butter over the other ingredients, coat your hands with flour, and rub the streusel mixture back and forth between your palms until you have little clumps *(Streusel)* or nuggets of streusel topping.

Preheat the oven to 325°F. Grease a large baking sheet. When the dough has risen, roll it out, place it on the baking sheet, cover with the streusel, and bake in the oven for 35 to 45 minutes. Sprinkle with confectioners' sugar while still warm.

DOUGH:
3½ cups flour
1 cup lukewarm milk
Scant ½ cup sugar
2½ teaspoons yeast
¼ cup butter
2 eggs

STREUSEL TOPPING:
1¼ cups flour
⅓ cup sugar
1 tablespoon crushed almonds
½ teaspoon ground cinnamon
5 tablespoons butter, melted
Confectioners' sugar

NOTE: *Streuselkuchen* tastes best when very fresh, perhaps even a little warm from the oven. The next day, the *Streuselkuchen* can still be rehabilitated by dunking it in café au lait—a process that is known as *ditschen* to the common folk, *stippen* to Berliners, and *tunken* to more respectable people (assuming that they even acknowledge the existence of such a practice).

MAKES 10–12 SERVINGS

Basic Yeast Dough Recipe

All ingredients must be at the same room temperature (except for the lukewarm milk). Eggs coming directly out of the refrigerator may ruin the dough.

•   •   •   •   •   •   •   •   •   •

Sift flour into a large bowl and make a crater in the center. Into the crater pour one half of the milk; add in the sugar and sprinkle the yeast over the top. Sprinkle some of the flour over the yeast. After the yeast begins to foam (15 to 20 minutes) add the butter, eggs, and salt and slowly work in the remaining milk to make an elastic dough.

Knead the dough for 15 minutes by hand. It should not stick to the table or bowl anymore. (Kneading time with the dough hooks of an electrical kitchen helper is only 2 to 4 minutes.) Cover dough with a clean kitchen towel and let rest for 1 to 2 hours. During this time it should rise and double in bulk. Shape as desired and/or put in a form. Let rise another 15 minutes and bake in a preheated oven at about 350°F. for 35 to 45 minutes.

MAKES 4–6 SERVINGS

3½ cups flour
⅔ cup lukewarm milk
Scant ½ cup sugar
2½ teaspoons yeast
6 tablespoons soft butter
2 eggs
1 pinch salt

Bee-Sting Cake   Bienenstichkuchen

DOUGH:
  2⅓ cups flour
  ⅔ cup lukewarm milk
  ¼ cup sugar
  2 teaspoons yeast
  5 tablespoons butter
  1 egg
    Small pinch of salt

ALMOND TOPPING:
  7 tablespoons butter
    Scant ½ cup sugar
  1 cup almonds, slivered
    "As much ground
    cinnamon as will fit on
    the point of a knife"
  3 tablespoons milk

FILLING:
  3 egg yolks
  ½ cup sugar
  ½ teaspoon vanilla extract
  1 tablespoon cornstarch
  1 cup milk
  6 tablespoons butter

This delicious cake, so called because of the slivered-almond topping, dates from around the turn of the century and is still very popular in Germany.

.   .   .   .

Using the quantities listed here, prepare the dough according to the "Basic Yeast Dough Recipe" (see page 431).

To make the almond topping, start by melting the butter in a skillet over moderate heat; add the sugar, stir well, then add the slivered almonds, cinnamon, and milk. Stirring constantly, keep over the heat until this mixture becomes soft and spreadable—but the butter and sugar should not be allowed to brown.

Preheat the oven to 350°F. Grease a 10″ springform pan. Place the dough in the pan and press flat. Allow the almond topping mixture to cool off, then spread evenly over the dough. Bake for about 45 minutes, or until golden brown.

To make the custard filling, beat the yolks with the sugar and vanilla extract in a heavy saucepan until the yolks are frothy and the sugar has entirely dissolved. Add the cornstarch and milk, and, while stirring constantly, heat until just about to boil. Remove from the heat and allow to cool, stirring vigorously for brief intervals. Whisk the butter until frothy and whisk into the custard filling mixture when it has had a chance to cool.

When the torte has cooled, cut it in half horizontally so you can spread the custard filling onto the bottom layer. Cover again with the upper almond crusted layer. If you'd like to double this recipe, the *Bienenstichkuchen* can be baked on a large baking sheet instead and then cut into rectangular pieces.

MAKES ONE 10-INCH CAKE

Poppyseed Tarts Mohnkuchen

Here is a delicious central German specialty that, for some reason, has never caught on with West German families.

.   .   .   .

Using the quantities listed here, prepare the dough according to the "Basic Yeast Dough Recipe" (see page 431).

The poppyseeds should be washed several hours in advance. Steep them in boiling water, then pour them into a very fine strainer and allow to drain thoroughly. Put the poppyseeds through the meat grinder or food mill twice (you could also use a blender or crush with a mortar and pestle until they are very finely ground). To the crushed poppyseeds add the egg and sugar. Combine the milk, butter, and farina, and cook into a thick, porridgelike paste. Mix this into the poppyseed mixture, add the candied lemon peel, almonds, and raisins, and stir into the farina mixture.

Preheat the oven to 350°F.

Once the dough has risen, roll it out on a baking sheet, let stand for a short while longer, spread the topping mixture over the sheet of dough, and bake for about 40 minutes.

NOTE: The canned poppyseed filling that can be bought in most supermarkets saves the trouble of grinding.

MAKES 8 SERVINGS

DOUGH:
  3½ *cups flour*
  1⅓ *cups milk*
  ¼ *cup sugar*
  2½ *teaspoons yeast*
  2 *tablespoons butter*

TOPPING:
  2 *cups poppyseeds (see Note)*
  1 *egg*
  ¾ *cup sugar*
  1 *quart milk*
  2 *tablespoons butter*
  ½ *cup farina (semolina)*
  ¼ *cup candied lemon peel (Zitronat), diced*
  ¼ *cup almonds, coarsely chopped or slivered*
  ¼ *cup raisins, washed and dried*

Damson Tart Zwetschenkuchen

The premier German fruit tart, this is also known as *Zwetschgendatschi* in Bavaria and as *Pflaumenkuchen* in northern Germany, since the tart is always made with damsons rather than ordinary plums—preferably those picked late in the season, which tend to be firm rather than juicy. As with *Streusel-*

DOUGH:

3½ cups flour
¾ cup lukewarm
milk
⅔ cup sugar
2½ teaspoons yeast
9 tablespoons butter
2 eggs
Pinch of salt
1 level teaspoon
baking powder

3½–5½ pounds ripe
damson plums,
pitted, and halved
Confectioners'
sugar (optional)

kuchen, the large rectangular baking sheet—rather than the little round torte pan—is de rigueur.

The *Quetschekuche,* as we called them at home in Frankfurt, was the centerpiece of a colossal multifamily outing that took place in the early fall. We all trooped out to a country restaurant, sat around in the warm September sun, stuffed ourselves with fresh-baked plum tarts while the adults ordered coffee in large pots and the kids stood guard over the heaped-up platters of *Quetschekuche* to keep the bees and wasps away. This was called a "plumcake feed," which was certainly what it was. Ah, blessed memories of youthful overindulgence.

.   .   .   .

Using the quantities listed here, prepare the dough according to the "Basic Yeast Dough Recipe" (see page 431). The baking powder should be added in together with the butter, eggs, and salt.

Preheat the oven to 400°F. Grease a large baking sheet with butter, then lightly sprinkle with flour. Roll out the dough into a thin rectangular piece; place on the sheet and crimp a border around the edge with your thumb and forefinger. Cover with a dish towel and let stand for another 10 minutes.

The damson halves should be opened up like a book and slit in half once more without separating the quarters. The flat damsons should be placed in tight upright rows on top of the dough sheet (otherwise the topping will probably be too thin). Bake for about 35 minutes, by which time the little raised strips of dough around the edges should have baked golden brown. *Zwetschenkuchen* are at their best when still a little warm from the oven, but don't sprinkle them with sugar too soon, since this is likely to "draw up" too much juice from the plums.

NOTE: *Zwetschenkuchen* should always be made with yeast dough.

I have suggested adding a teaspoon of baking powder to give the crust a little extra zest.

If you find yourself compelled to try making *Zwetschenkuchen* too early in the season, when the damsons are still too full of juice, try sprinkling the dough with zwieback flour or oat flakes to soak up some of the excess.

Zwetschenkuchen will survive quite well in the deep freeze.

VARIATIONS: Streusel or slivered almonds are sometimes added to the damson topping, which in my view is quite gratuitous, if not actually offensive. The same goes for whipped cream, even though that's the way it's often served in some of our finest *Konditoreien* these days.

Potato soup plus *Zwetschenkuchen* was a popular combination for a Saturday night.

MAKES 8 SERVINGS

HESSE,   BADEN,   SWABIA

Cherry Cobbler   Kirschenmichel

Called *Kerscheplotzer* in Baden and the Palatinate, in the old days, cherry cobbler was a particular favorite with potato or chervil soup on Saturday for lunch. Nowadays, it is frequently served in restaurants with a dollop of whipped cream on top, but this seems to me a dubious and certainly unnecessary refinement.

Preheat the oven to 350°F. Take a round springform or a 1½-quart soufflé pan, grease generously with butter, and sprinkle with bread crumbs.

Stir the butter and sugar until frothy; blend in the egg yolks, one by one, until you have a smooth batter. Add the kirsch.

Soak the roll slices in milk, and then stir these into the batter. Wash and drain the cherries thoroughly, then mix them into the dough. Add a little salt to the egg whites, beat into stiff peaks, and fold into the dough.

1 tablespoon bread crumbs
9 tablespoons butter
⅔ cup sugar (or more if the cherries are sour)
6 eggs, separated
4 tablespoons kirsch (cherry liqueur)
6 stale dinner rolls, sliced, or 6 thick slices of white bread, dried in the oven
½ cup milk
1½ pounds cherries (sweet or sour, fresh or out of a jar), pitted, washed, and drained
Small pinch of salt

Spread the dough in the pan and bake for about 1 hour, or until golden brown. The *Kirschenmichel* tastes best when still warm from the oven, but takes to the freezer very well and still tastes quite good when reheated.

MAKES 8 SERVINGS

FRANCONIA

Apple Tart   Apfelkuchen

FILLING:

4½ *pounds Granny Smith apples, peeled, cored, and quartered*
1¼ *cups sultana raisins*
4–5 *tablespoons rum*
1–2 *tablespoons lemon juice*
3–4 *tablespoons sugar*

DOUGH:

2 *cups flour*
Pinch of salt
⅔ *cup sugar*
8 *tablespoons butter*
1 *egg*
1–2 *teaspoons baking powder*

1 *egg beaten with 1 tablespoon condensed milk*
Whipped cream (optional)

Here is a recipe that has been preserved for many generations by the Wissmath family in Nuremberg.

•   •   •   •   •   •   •   •

To make the filling, in a mixing bowl combine all the ingredients and let stand for several hours, tossing or mixing a little from time to time.

To make the dough, sift together flour, baking powder, salt, and sugar in a bowl. Add the butter and egg to the bowl. Mixing lightly with your fingertips, combine all the ingredients to make the dough. Do not overwork the dough. Chill the dough for 30 minutes.

Preheat the oven to 350°F. Take about two-thirds of the dough and make a bottom crust with raised edges in a greased springform pan. Overlap the apple halves so that the cut edges are standing perpendicular or slantwise with respect to the bottom crust; they should be in concentric circles. Add the raisins in among them, and pour any liquid remaining in the mixing bowl over the apple halves.

Use the remaining dough to make a top crust, place the top crust over the fruit filling, and crimp the crusts together firmly all around the edges. Brush the top crust with the egg-milk glaze and bake until golden brown, about 50 to 60 minutes. Whipped cream is optional.

MAKES 6–8 SERVINGS

Frugal Honey Cake   Einfacher Honigkuchen

A familiar pastry that was once popular in every region of Germany, this particular version is based on a handwritten recipe in the possession of the Seidel family of Baden-Baden.

•   •   •   •   •   •   •   •   •

Preheat the oven to 350°F. Combine all the ingredients and blend into a thick, viscous dough. Bake in a rectangular baking pan with 2-inch raised sides for about 1 hour. Test with a toothpick to see if the inside is properly cooked.

MAKES 10 SERVINGS

3½ cups flour
 1 tablespoon baking powder
   Grated peel and juice of 1 lemon
⅓ cup brown sugar
¾ cup corn or cane syrup (originally, sugar beet syrup)
¼ cup oil
½ cup coffee (rather strongly brewed)
   "As much powdered ginger as will fit on the point of a knife"
 1 heaping teaspoon crushed aniseed
 2 tablespoons finely chopped candied lemon peel (Zitronat)

HESSE

Almond Pralines Frankfurt-Style
Frankfurter Brenten

Strictly a municipal rather than a regional specialty since the raw materials were too expensive for the ordinary citizen or the countryfolk in the outlying villages, this was a delicacy reserved primarily for the city's patrician class, one of whose errant offspring, Johann Wolfgang von Goethe, wrote some very nice letters to his mother begging her to send some to him in distant Weimar.

Another great poet with a taste for *Frankfurter Brenten* was the Swabian clergyman Eduard Mörike, the author of the recipe that follows. Since there are very few pastry recipes

written in verse by major poets, it would be unthinkable to
pass this one up.

> Start out with almonds, I'd suggest to you—
> Four pounds is best, but three will do,
> Apportioning them as you are best advised.[1]
> Mix up with some rosewater
> And crush them in the mortar
> Until they're completely pulverized!
> For every pound of almonds add precisely
> Twelve ounces sugar, blend in nicely,
> Then pour this mixture through a fine hair sieve.
> That being done, I'd suggest you next give
> An eye to your array of kitchenware.
> A stoneware crock that's surely lurking there
> Can be entrusted to the flames—
> A *Kachel,*[2] to call it by its rightful name.
> Fill up with praline mixture from the bowl,
> And set it over ev'nly glowing coals,
> And stir and stir without surcease,
> This while the mixture thickens, for an hour at least,
> Till not a particle—when you thrust in your thumb—
> Adheres thereto (not yet depends therefrom).
> Then take the praline dough and roughly throw it
> (Or rather, place it gently) in a bowl—the poet[3]
> Cares only that the rhymes come out all right—
> Then press down flat and let stand overnight.
> And in the morning you had best begin
> By kneading thoroughly and rolling out thin,
> As thin as a knife blade, and as you roll each piece,
> The right amount of flour is certainly the least.
> And now, t'impose a little further on your patience,
> Press down the patterns to provide the decorations[4]
> Then off to the baker's, and bid the honest fellow
> Not bake them overlong, but just till golden yellow.[5]

  • • • • • • • • •

NOTES: [1] That is, the relative proportion of sweet and bitter
almonds is left to the discretion of the cook; bitter almonds
can be replaced by extract.

[2] In southwestern Germany, the word *Kachel* is still used for an ovenproof crockpot or terrine.

[3] The original text has been slightly altered here (for the sake of the rhyme, to be sure). In the original version, Mörike instructs the reader to put the praline mixture *(Gebrodel)* in a "mold" *(Model)* rather than a mixing bowl *(Schlüssel),* then immediately retracts this advice, explaining that "to the poet the rhyme comes ahead of everything else."

[4] This refers to the favorite German practice of using an intricately carved wooden mold or pattern—the *Model* referred to above—to imprint a decorative design on pastry dough. In those days, the *Brenten* was not baked individually but in great yard-long sheets that were cut into pieces after it came out of the oven.

[5] The *Brenten* would have been baked on large wax-coated metal sheets; for our purposes, greased aluminum foil or a lightly oiled baking pan will do quite well. As suggested, the praline mixture should be allowed to dry out overnight, then baked in a 275°F. oven for about 20 minutes until golden yellow—but, as the Reverend Mörike reminds us, it should not be allowed to brown.

RHINELAND

Aachen Honey Bars   Aachener Printen

1 cup plus 1 tablespoon
  honey
2 tablespoons butter
  Scant ½ cup sugar
1 teaspoon ground
  cinnamon
  Pinch of ground cloves
  Grated peel of ½
  lemon
3 tablespoons candied
  lemon peel (Zitronat),
  minced
3 tablespoons candied
  orange peel, minced
1 cup ground hazelnuts
2 teaspoons potash or
  baking soda
2 tablespoons rum
2¼ cups flour
1 teaspoon cornstarch
5 tablespoons water

Napoleon is indirectly credited with the invention of this well-known confection from the ancient city of Aachen. The emperor imposed the so-called Continental Blockade, a straightforward assault on the economic power of his enemy, the British, little thinking that in doing so he was also depriving the confectioners of Aachen of their normal supplies of sugar from the West Indies. And so, they were obliged to make their *Printen* out of honey and sweet fruit syrup, an experiment that turned out very well, though when the blockade was lifted, they put some of the sugar back in just to be on the safe side.

.   .   .   .

Heat the honey, butter, and sugar in a saucepan, and keep stirring until it comes to a boil. Remove from the heat. Allow to cool, mix in the spices, peels, and hazelnuts, and stir well. Dissolve the potash or baking soda in the rum and add these as well. Stir about two-thirds of the flour into this mixture and knead in the remaining third. The honeycake dough, which no longer sticks to the sides of the bowl, should have a chance to sit for an hour or two.

Preheat the oven to 400°F. Grease a baking sheet with butter. Roll out the dough into a flat sheet a little less than ¼" thick, cut into bars about 3" long and 1¼" across, and place on the baking sheet.

Stir the cornstarch into the water, bring to a boil, and brush the *Printen* with a thin layer of this cornstarch paste just before they go into the oven. Bake for about 10 minutes. *Printen* are very good with tea at any time of the year.

MAKES 32–36 HONEY BARS

WEST   PRUSSIA

Gingerbread Men   Thorner Kathrinchen

The most popular kind of Christmas gingerbread in eastern Germany was associated with the city of Thorn (present-day Toruń), which was founded by the Teutonic Knights, was a member of the Hanseatic League, and was the seat of a famous medieval university. In later years, Thorn/Toruń belonged both to Poland and Russia for several centuries apiece; it reverted to Poland after the First World War, though the famous *Thorner Kathrinchen* (Little Kates) are still very much part of the popular culture of the city . . . and of Germany.

.   .   .   .

Melt together the butter, sugar, and honey over low heat, then allow to cool. Add the gingerbread spices, salt, grated lemon peel, sugar, and the egg yolk; stir until lightened. Stir the baking soda into the rosewater and add to the egg yolk mixture. Combine this mixture with the flour and knead into a dough. Let stand overnight.

Preheat the oven to 400°F. Generously butter a baking sheet. Roll out the dough on the sheet about ¼″ thick, and cut the dough into long rectangles or stamp out little gingerbread men with a cookie cutter (the original *Kathrinchen* are shaped like the pastries called *langues du chat,* or "cat's tongues"—or ladyfingers with broadened ends). Whatever design you decide on, bake for 15 to 20 minutes. And, if you choose, frost with chocolate or vanilla icing when cookies are lukewarm.

MAKES 10 SERVINGS

2 tablespoons butter
Scant ½ cup sugar
1 cup plus 1 tablespoon honey
1 tablespoon gingerbread spices (ground cardamom, anise, cloves, cinnamon, ginger—mixed together according to taste)
Small pinch of salt
Grated peel of 1 fresh lemon
2 tablespoons sugar
1 egg yolk
2½ teaspoons baking soda
2 tablespoons rosewater
2¼ cups flour
Vanilla or chocolate icing (optional)

FRANKFURT AM MAIN

Marzipan Balls   Bethmännchen

7 ounces raw marzipan
  paste
1⅓ cups confectioners'
  sugar
  A few tablespoons
  rosewater
72 whole almonds, halved
1 teaspoon sugar
1 egg

These are probably the choicest of all traditional German Christmas cookies, so much so that they are now enjoyed all year round in their native city of Frankfurt. When you check into the Hotel Frankfurter Hof, you will find some *Bethmännchen* greeting you in your room. The name has been explained in different ways, the minority opinion holding that

Falls at Triberg, Black Forest

Bethmännchen were originally *Bet–Männchen* (little praying men), the majority that they were invented by a cook in the household of a prominent banker called Bethmann, c. 1840. The story is that there were originally four sons in the family (hence, four almond halves decorating the marzipan balls), but the number was reduced to three when one of them died in childhood, and three it has remained ever since.

Combine the raw marzipan, confectioners' sugar, and rosewater and knead into a smooth paste, then roll into little balls about ¾″ in diameter. Crimp into the shape of an old-fashioned three-sided top, slightly pointed at one end, and press 3 almond halves into the sides so that the pointed ends of the almonds are also at the top. Let stand overnight in a well-heated room.

Place the balls on greased aluminum foil and warm up for 2 or 3 minutes in a 450°F. oven, with the broiler turned on as well. Stir the sugar with the egg until the sugar is completely dissolved, remove the *Bethmännchen* from the oven, brush thinly with this egg glaze, put back into the oven, and bake until golden yellow (crispy brown around the edges).

MAKES ABOUT 3½–4 DOZEN BALLS

EAST PRUSSIA

Königsberger Marzipan

The Baltic seaports of Lübeck and Königsberg each gave their name to a variety of marzipan, the Königsberger being a bit less sweet (and browner around the edges) than the Lübecker. Marzipan cookies were baked for Christmas in almost every East Prussian household—not just as a symbol of family gaiety and piety but, inevitably, as a sort of showpiece of one's abilities as a *Hausfrau* and a woman of accomplishment.

1 pound almonds, including a few bitter almonds, shelled and peeled
2¾ cups confectioners' sugar
2–3 tablespoons rosewater
2–3 egg whites, unbeaten

Blanch the almonds and drain well, then grind them up *very* fine—this is clearly the key to success when you're making marzipan. Combine with the rosewater and sugar and knead together very well (see Notes). Roll into a cylinder and let stand overnight in a cool place.

Roll out a sheet about ¼-inch thick and cut out various decorative shapes with cookie cutters or just the point of a knife blade. Bake in the oven (under the broiler if you like) until the marzipan starts to turn brown around the edges, take out of the oven and glaze with egg white.

NOTES: If you prefer to use ready-made marzipan, which is much more finely ground than the homemade variety could ever hope to be, knead together with a relatively small amount of sugar—about ¼ cup confectioners' sugar and 1 tablespoon rosewater for every 3½ ounces marzipan—and then proceed as above.

Even though the crisp sculptural contours of traditional marzipan ("our most beautiful still-lifes," as the poet Agnes Miegel has called it) are awfully difficult to achieve in the home kitchen, shaping and decorating the marzipan is clearly not to be stinted on.

MAKES 2 POUNDS

NORTHERN GERMANY

Rum Balls   Rumkugeln

½ cup sultana raisins
5 tablespoons rum
1 cup grated chocolate
1¼ cups confectioners' sugar
5 tablespoons vegetable shortening
1⅓ cups chocolate morsels or sprinkles

Serve these rum balls in small bowls with coffee or tea.

•   •   •   •   •   •   •   •   •

Wash the raisins in warm water, drain, and dry off thoroughly with paper towels. Mince very finely, stir together with the rum, and let stand for 1 hour.

Mix together the chocolate and sugar. Melt the vegetable

shortening over low heat, allow to cool somewhat, then stir together with the grated chocolate and sugar. As soon as this mixture has cooled a bit and is starting to solidify, knead together with the rum-soaked raisins and let stand for a little while before rolling out little balls about 1¼″ to 1½″ in diameter. Turn these in the chocolate sprinkles, press lightly to fix the sprinkles in place, and allow to chill in the refrigerator.

MAKES 12–15 BALLS

Prune Fritters   Omas Schlosserbuben

The title of this Swabian family recipe proclaims these pastries to be "Grandma's Little Locksmith's Apprentices," perhaps so called because the latter tended to get oil-smeared and grimy, hence prune-colored, in the course of their professional activities.

.   .   .   .

Cook the prunes in a little water, but do not allow them to get too soft; drain and allow to cool. Stuff each prune with 1 of the almonds.

Combine the batter ingredients, dredge the prunes in it, and deep-fry in hot fat. Mix the sugar and grated chocolate, and turn the deep-fried *Schlosserbuben* in this mixture while they are still warm.

MAKES 12 FRITTERS

12 large prunes, pitted
12 almonds, shelled

BATTER:
 ¾ cup flour
 ½ cup white wine
 2 tablespoons sugar
  Pinch of salt
 1 egg, separated, white beaten to soft peaks

  Oil or fat for frying
 2 tablespoons sugar
4–5 heaping tablespoons grated chocolate

Meissen, Saxony, famous for
its china (engraving by Johann
Poppel, after a drawing by
L. Rohbock)

SAXONY

Old-Fashioned Stollen   Stollenrezept von Einst

The following is based on a handwritten recipe of *Grossmutter*
Schönfelder's that her grandson Fritz gave to me. This is one
of the great stollen recipes that were especially popular in
central Germany, the most famous of which is known as
Dresdner Christstollen (Dresden Christmas Stollen):

"First add the butter to the yeast sponge, then milk, flour,
and sugar. Flour, milk again. Blend together thoroughly—
but not before this. Then add the raisin mixture and the candied lemon peel [as well as the other ingredients]."

•   •   •   •   •   •   •   •   •   •

Handwritten recipes are often more like cryptic memoranda
for the use of a veteran than helpful guides for the inexperi-
enced; this one is no exception. My grandmother did not need
to remind herself, for example, that the yeast first has to be
crumbled and stirred into lukewarm milk with a few grains of
sugar to make the "yeast sponge." The lemon juice and peel,
vanilla extract, and rum are supposed to be added at the same
time as the candied lemon peel, though this is not mentioned
explicitly; the dough, of course, has to be kneaded for a considerable length of time—my grandmother used to put a little

bit of white cotton thread into the dough and kept on kneading until she turned it up at least two or three times—and then
given a chance to rise.

I remember—and this was during the 1920s—how the
homemakers in Frankfurt used to make up big batches of
stollen dough and take them around to Geisshäcker the baker
on a Wednesday. The big back room where the ovens were
(the *Backstube,* which does not mean "back room," by the
way, but "baking room") was crowded with women and
children from the neighborhood; the children (myself among
them) started to fidget after a while, but the mothers were
already nervous the moment that they set foot in Geisshäcker's baking room. There was no telling how any particular
batch was going to turn out until the moment of truth arrived:
the baker read out the names that had been written on little
slips of greased paper sticking out of the loaves. The perfect
batches of freshly baked stollen were proudly reclaimed by
their creators. Those that had not risen properly or had otherwise come to naught were received with embarrassed
blushes or shrieks of horror and dismay. I'll never forget one
of the neighbor ladies' anguished cry of "Ah, merciful heav-
ens! These ain't nothing but flapjacks!" *("Ei, du lieber Himmel,
des sin ja Pannekuche!").*

These dramatic events were also part of the preparations for
Christmas in those days. Traditionally, the last of the Christmas stollen was supposed to be saved until Easter, and if all
went well, it would still be fresh and moist when it was sliced.
When stollen is still warm from the oven, it should be brushed
all over with butter (at least once) and sprinkled with confectioners' sugar.

Modern Stollen Recipe

3¾ cups flour
1 cup confectioners'
   sugar
½ cup lukewarm milk
   (approximately)
3 teaspoons yeast
8 tablespoons softened
   sweet butter
1 tablespoon lard (or
   butter)
1 large egg
½ teaspoon salt
1 teaspoon vanilla
   extract
1 tablespoon rum
   Pinch of ground
   cinnamon
   Grated peel of
   ½ lemon
1 cup almonds, slivered
¼ cup candied lemon peel
   (Zitronat)
¼ cup candied orange
   peel (Orangeat)
1¼ cups raisins

FOR BASTING:
6 tablespoons milk, room
   temperature
8 tablespoons butter
¾ cup powdered sugar

The traditional Stollen recipe gives excellent results, but unfortunately it is rather complicated. For all newcomers to Stollen baking here is a modern recipe that is a lot easier to follow. It makes one loaf only.

•   •   •   •   •   •   •   •   •

Sift the flour into the bowl and make a crater in the center. Into this put ¼ cup confectioners' sugar and ¼ lukewarm cup milk. Sprinkle the yeast over the milk and dust the yeast with a little of the flour. Let the yeast develop for 15–20 minutes. Add the butter, lard, egg, salt, remaining sugar, vanilla extract, rum, cinnamon, grated lemon peel, slivered almonds, candied lemon and orange peels, and raisins to the bowl. Add only enough of the remaining milk to make the dough pliable. Knead very thoroughly. Cover the dough with a damp towel and let it rise overnight. Knead again for 1 minute. Shape the dough into one loaf and put it on a large buttered baking sheet. All raisins that may have popped up should be pushed back into the dough with a fingertip in order not to be scorched when baking. Baste the loaf with several tablespoons of milk and bake it in a preheated oven for about 50 minutes at 350°F. Stollen must turn golden brown. Test for doneness with a toothpick or a wooden match that should come out clean.

Baste the Stollen lavishly with butter when still hot and sprinkle with powdered sugar. Repeat this in order to give the loaf a nice white surface that at the same time keeps it fresh and moist for several weeks. Try to store it for at least a week before serving.

MAKES 1 LOAF (ABOUT 30 SLICES)

BADEN-WÜRTTEMBERG,
SOUTHERN GERMANY

Pear Bread   Hutzelbrot/Schnitzbrot

Also called *Bierewecke* (meaning "pear rolls," not "beer rolls") or just plain *Früchtebrot* (fruit bread), since other kinds of dried fruit are often involved as well. *Hutzeln* (pear pieces dried with the peel still on) show up in the grocery stores in Baden every fall, but those who are a bit fussy about quality control like to pick out their pears and supervise the drying phase themselves. This recipe is richer than most, almost like a fruitcake, and the quantities involved are quite substantial, since the family supply of *Hutzelbrot* was supposed to last from late fall until Groundhog Day (better known in Germany as *Lichtmess,* or Candlemas), February 2.

.   .   .   .

Remove the stems from the pears, wash the pears and other dried fruit, soak in enough water to cover for a couple of hours, then coarsely chop the dried fruit and cook in the soaking liquid for about 30 minutes. Keep the cover on the pot and let stand overnight.

The next day, start by sifting the flour into a large mixing bowl. Make a crater in the flour. Place 3 tablespoons lukewarm milk in it and sprinkle the yeast over the milk. Dust the yeast with flour and let stand for 15 minutes. Then add the sugar and salt plus the dried fruit and a cup of the cooking liquid (reserving the remainder), and knead into a dough. Work the raisins and nutmeats into the dough along with the candied orange and lemon peels, the spices, and the kirsch. Do not knead too vigorously, however, or the dough is likely to get overworked and pulpy.

Transfer the dough mass to a second mixing bowl, the inside of which has been coated with a thick layer of flour, and roll the dough back and forth until it no longer sticks to the sides; sprinkle with a little more flour from time to time if necessary. Cover the bowl with a damp towel and let the

3¼ pounds dried pears (including a certain amount of dried figs and pitted prunes if you like)
4 cups flour
2–3 tablespoons lukewarm milk
3¼ teaspoons yeast
1 cup plus 2 tablespoons sugar
Pinch of salt
1¼ cups sultana raisins, washed and dried
4 cups whole hazelnuts or walnuts, coarsely chopped
⅓ cup diced candied orange peel
⅓ cup diced candied lemon peel (Zitronat)
½ teaspoon ground cinnamon
½ teaspoon ground clove
1 tablespoon fennel or anise seed
3–4 tablespoons kirsch (cherry liqueur)
2 tablespoons sugar
1 tablespoon cornstarch

dough stand until cracks or "stretch marks" start to appear in the surface (40 to 120 minutes).

Preheat the oven to 400°F. Grease a baking sheet. Separate the dough mass into several small loaves, place these on the baking sheet, then let stand for one hour before baking.

Take about 2 cups of the reserved liquid in which the dried fruit was soaked and cooked, add the remaining 2 tablespoons sugar, and bring to a boil, then stir in the cornstarch. Brush the loaves of *Hutzelbrot* with this mixture while they are still warm.

NOTE: If you like, the loaves can also be garnished with almond halves, which will stick on very nicely if pressed into the warm glaze. Adding a little extra kirsch to the glaze gives the *Hutzelbrot* a nice Black Forest flavor.

Hutzelbrot is sometimes served for breakfast, or with tea or coffee. In any case, it tastes best when thinly sliced and spread with plenty of fresh butter.

CULTURAL NOTE: *"Stuttgarter Huzelmännlein"* ("The Little Pear Man of Stuttgart") is the very famous novel by Mörike about a shoemaker's apprentice who is rewarded with a *Hutzelbrot* that during the night always grows again to its original size— no matter how much you have eaten of it. The *Hutzelbrot* you'll bake will probably be eaten up in a very short time— but, sorry, it won't grow during the night.

MAKES 6–8 LOAVES

SILESIA

Liegnitzer Bombe

This is an old-style Silesian Christmas pastry that can easily stand comparison with the better-known *Dresdner Christstollen* (see above) as far as both deliciousness and longevity are concerned. It is made in the form of a blunt-ended cone about 3¼" to 4¾" in diameter and about 4" high—shaped like a howitzer shell, a bomb of the Bismarck era. *Bomben,* however, are not regarded with the same sort of interest in German households nowadays—especially at Christmastime—and this perhaps accounts for the waning popularity of even the *Liegnitzer* variety during the postwar years.

Liegnitz, by the way, is a city in Silesia, once the capital of a little principality, and this recipe comes to us courtesy of my good friend Heinz Schwarz. The Scharfenberg family originally came from Silesia too, and for many years I have been in the habit of sending out a good many *Liegnitzer Bomben* in early December by way of Christmas greetings to family and friends.

The list of ingredients is rather long, but there's nothing especially mystifying about the recipe itself—with the help of a food processor, it's really quite easy, though you'll note that the *Bombe* has to sit in a cool place for at least 2 weeks before it's ready to eat.

·   ·   ·   ·   ·   ·   ·   ·   ·   ·

Melt and blend together the honey and butter over a low flame and then allow to cool. Beat the eggs and sugar until light and foamy, then add the honey and butter mixture; sift in the flour and baking powder as well. Add the cocoa powder, spices, and salt (1 envelope of prepackaged gingerbread spices can be substituted for the spices) plus the grated lemon and orange peels. Stir the dough quite thoroughly, then blend the currants, almonds, and candied lemon peel into the dough.

Grease three 10-inch springform or other baking pans with 1 or 2 tablespoons butter; if you like, you can use several smaller rectangular baking pans, or—more in keeping with the roughly cylindrical shape of the original *Bombe*—coffee cans or other large metal cans that had their lids neatly removed. Only fill the pan(s) about halfway up, since the dough is going to rise quite a bit while baking. Preheat the oven, then bake at moderate heat (350°F.) for 30 to 60 minutes, depending on the size of the pan you decide to use. If in doubt, you can perform the famous toothpick test—inserting a toothpick (or wooden spit) into the interior to see if any moist particles adhere to it.

DOUGH:
1¾ cups honey
9 tablespoons butter, plus extra for greasing
4 eggs
1¼ cups sugar
3½ cups flour
2–3 teaspoons baking powder
⅓ cup cocoa powder
⅓ teaspoon ground cardamom
"As much ground clove as will fit on the point of a knife"
½ teaspoon ground cinnamon
Pinch of salt
Grated peel of ½ lemon
Grated peel of ½ orange
¾ cup currants, washed
1½ cups slivered almonds
¾ cup diced candied lemon peel (Zitronat)

FILLING:
1¼ cups apricot marmalade
2–3 tablespoons apricot schnapps (or liqueur)
9 ounces raw marzipan paste
1⅓ cups confectioners' sugar
¼ cup rosewater or rum

FROSTING:
¼ pound semisweet baker's chocolate
1 teaspoon cocoa powder
2¼ cups confectioners' sugar
2 tablespoons water
10 whole almonds

In the meantime make the filling. Blend together the apricot marmalade and the apricot schnapps (or apricot liqueur) over low heat and stir into a smooth mixture; push through a fine strainer if necessary. Combine the raw marzipan paste, sugar, and rosewater, and knead vigorously (see Note). Press into wide, flat wafers about ¼″ to ⅓″ thick.

When the baked *Bombe(n)* has had a chance to cool, make 2 horizontal cuts, separating it (them) into 3 layers, like a layer cake. Place the marzipan wafers on top of the bottom layer(s), spread the next layer(s) with a generous coating of apricot marmalade, and cover with the top layer(s).

Stir together the chocolate, cocoa powder, and sugar with 2 tablespoons water over low heat to make the frosting, and spread the frosting over all the *Bombe(n)* on all sides—including the bottom, to keep it from drying out. Decorate the frosting with almonds. Each *Bombe* should unquestionably be allowed to sit for at least 2 weeks before it is ready to eat, and, if wrapped carefully in aluminum foil, will keep very well in the cellar or other cool place for 1 or 2 months.

NOTE: Prepared, store-brought marzipan can be used instead.

VARIATIONS: Either the raisins and candied lemon peel (or both) can be left out of the dough, though you may also want to try increasing the amount of currants by half.

Sour-cherry marmalade (or preserves) and nougat can readily be substituted for the apricot marmalade and marzipan.

MAKES 3 BOMBES IN COFFEE CANS

BREMEN

Hanseatic Christmas Stollen   Klaben

Here is a Christmas pastry that is frequently more liberally endowed with raisins, currants, and almonds than the better-known *Dresdner Stollen*. It's important that all the ingredients be at room temperature before they're added to the dough, otherwise the dough may fail to rise properly.

•   •   •   •   •   •   •   •   •

    Using the quantities listed here, prepare the dough according to the "Basic Yeast Dough Recipe" (see page 431).

    Work remaining ingredients into the dough. Allow the dough to rise once more, about 40 minutes.

    Preheat the oven to 400°F. Generously grease a baking sheet with butter, place the dough on the sheet, and roll the dough up into a log *(Klaben)*. Let it stand a little while longer (20 minutes), then bake until golden brown, about 1 hour. Use a toothpick to test for doneness. Brush the *Klaben* with butter while it is still warm from the oven.

NOTE: The word *Klaben* is cognate with the words for "log" *(Kloben)* or "lump" *(Klotz)* because it's supposed to look like one (somewhat), not because it's supposed to lie like one in your stomach.

MAKES 2 LOAVES

6½ *cups flour*
½ *cup milk*
   Scant ¾ cup sugar
5 *teaspoons yeast*
1¾ *cups butter, plus extra*
   for topping
1 *teaspoon salt*

   Grated peel of 1 lemon
1¾ *cups raisins, washed*
   and dried
2¼ *cups currants, washed*
   and dried
1 *cup crushed almonds*
⅔ *cup diced candied*
   orange peel
⅓ *cup diced candied*
   lemon peel (Zitronat)

SILESIA

Poppyseed Loaf Mohnstriezel

DOUGH:
3½ cups flour
½ cup lukewarm water
⅔ cup sugar
2½ teaspoons yeast
1 egg
Small pinch of salt
Grated peel of 1 lemon

PASTE FILLING:
1 cup boiling milk
2 cups ground
poppyseeds (they can
be ground in a
blender)
2 tablespoons butter,
melted
1⅓ cups sugar
1–2 tablespoons zwieback
crumbs
½ cup almonds, coarsely
chopped
½ cup packed raisins or
currants, washed
1 egg
½ teaspoon ground
cinnamon

TOPPING:
Several tablespoons
butter, melted
Confectioners' sugar

This is the Silesian counterpart of Christmas stollen, though the Silesians seem to like it so much that they sometimes bake it at other times of the year as well.

•   •   •   •   •   •   •   •   •

Using the quantities listed here, prepare the dough according to the "Basic Yeast Dough Recipe" (see page 431). The lemon peel should be added in together with the egg and salt.

To prepare the filling, pour the boiling hot milk over the ground poppyseeds. Stir the butter and sugar into the poppyseed paste, and depending on the consistency of the latter, add zwieback crumbs to absorb any excess liquid. Stir the remaining ingredients into the poppyseed paste.

When the dough has risen, preheat the oven to 350°F. and sparingly butter a baking sheet. Roll the dough out into a rectangular sheet about as thick as your finger. Except for a thin strip all around the edges of the rectangle, cover the dough sheet with the poppyseed paste and roll up into a cylinder (stollen). Place on the baking sheet, making sure the seam side is facing downward, brush with a little melted butter, and bake for about 1 hour, or until golden brown. Brush the *Striezel* with an ample amount of melted butter while it is still warm from the oven, then dust generously with confectioners' sugar; sprinkle on a little more sugar after the *Striezel* has had a chance to cool a bit.

MAKES 1 LOAF

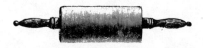

Falls of the Aderbach

Gingerbread House   Knusperhäuschen

Knuspern means "munch" or "nibble," and this most delight-
ful of all traditional Christmas confections is also known as a
Hexenhäusle, "witch's house" (as in the story of Hänsel and
Gretel), or simply a *Lebkuchenhäusle,* "gingerbread house." It
would be a great pity indeed if the classic prototype of "gingerbread" architecture were only available in store-bought
prefabricated form; this is a recipe that has already given satisfaction to four generations of Scharfenbergs, amateur building contractors and consumers alike.

.   .   .   .

Start out by mixing the dry ingredients. Heat the honey,
sugar, and butter, and stir together. Allow to cool. Preheat
the oven to 350°F. Grease a baking sheet with butter and dust
with flour. Pour the honey mixture over the flour mixture and

GINGERBREAD:

3⅔ *cups flour*
 5 *teaspoons baking*
   powder
   Pinch of salt
   Grated nutmeg
 1 *teaspoon ground*
   cinnamon
½ *teaspoon ground*
   cardamom
   "Twice as much
   ground clove as will fit
   on the point of a
   knife"
½ *cup honey*
1⅔ *cups sugar*
 8 *tablespoons butter*
   Grated peel of 1 or 2
   lemons
 1 *egg plus 1 egg yolk,*
   beaten

FROSTING AND "MORTAR":

3 *egg whites*
3 *cups confectioners' sugar*

DECORATIONS:

Red gelatin leaves or
cellophane
Chocolate candy
Chocolate cookies
Gumdrops
Candied fruit
Almonds
Marzipan fruit

knead together; add the grated lemon peel and the egg and yolk. Knead these into the dough as well. You can expect the dough to remain a little sticky to the touch. Roll out the gingerbread dough and bake on greased baking sheets for about 35 minutes. Allow the gingerbread to cool for a while after it comes out of the oven, and then the process of construction can begin.

It's best to cut out the sheets of gingerbread that are going to form the walls, roof, and foundation of the gingerbread house by tracing from a paper pattern or cardboard model, so the various pieces will fit together fairly snugly. Use a single large piece of gingerbread for the foundation; leftovers and remnants can be used for the chimney, fence posts, pine trees, and other landscaping accessories.

Make the "mortar" by beating the egg whites into the confectioners' sugar until you have a thick glaze. Then continue beating for 5 minutes with a wooden spoon. This develops its adhesive properties. Keep a very damp cloth over the top of the bowl of "mortar" to prevent it from hardening. Adjoining edges can be held together with this frosting, but the construction will be a great deal sturdier if reinforced with toothpicks; set toothpicks into the foundation piece, for example, so that they'll be protruding upward into the wall pieces for about ¾" to 1¼". The joints between the adjoining walls, gables, and roof pieces can be similarly reinforced if they seem a little shaky. Bear in mind a well-made gingerbread house should hold together for several years if kept out of harm's way.

Apart from being used to help secure the joints between the gingerbread pieces, the frosting can also be used to attach the edible decorations to the walls and roof of the gingerbread house or simply swirled around, in accordance with time-honored convention, to represent snow on the roof. Use a piping bag for icing with a fine, plain tip.

Attach red gelatin leaves behind the cut-out openings for the windows, which makes a very nice effect; little figures representing Hänsel and Gretel (whether made from gingerbread or some other, more pliable medium, or even store-bought) may be added to complete the scene. The decorations should include some or all of the following—chocolate candies and cookies, gumdrops and candied fruit, almonds, and marzipan, especially marzipan fruit—and if the *Knusperhäuschen* is to be truly worthy of its name, these decorations should be removed, munched, or nibbled by the small-fry clients on whose behalf the gingerbread house has been constructed, and then replaced the following year.

NOTE: If you have an extra-large kitchen and professional-size cookware, you can save yourself some trouble by tripling the quantities in the list of ingredients below. But those with more conventional-size kitchens will have to bake 3 batches in order to have enough raw materials for the *Knusperhäuschen*.

3 RECIPES MAKE 1 HOUSE

Crullers Ausgezogene Küchle

3½ cups flour
1 cup milk
½ cup sugar, plus extra
   for topping
3 teaspoons yeast
4 tablespoons clarified
   butter
2 eggs
Pinch of salt

Fat for deep-frying

These are a kind of holeless doughnut that have literally (but not exactly) been "pulled apart" *(ausgezogen);* they are also called *Pfosen* in Swabia and *Knieküchle,* "knee cookies," in Franconia—in honor of the anatomical region where the pulling apart can take place.

·   ·   ·   ·   ·   ·   ·   ·   ·

Using the quantities listed here, prepare the dough according to the "Basic Yeast Dough Recipe" (see page 431). However, you should only let the dough rise for 45 minutes.

Roll out the dough and separate into egg-shape pieces. Give the dough a little more time to rise again, 15 minutes. While continuously turning the dough egg around in your hands, press (rather than pull) the dough from the center outward so you end up with a thick doughnutlike circle of dough surrounding a thinly stretched membrane in the center. How about shaping them over your bent knee? Deep-fry the crullers on both sides until the outer ring is golden yellow; be careful the oil is not too hot or they will be too dark. The thinner crust in the center will be much lighter in color. Sprinkle with sugar while still warm.

MAKES 30 CRULLERS

Anise-Flavored Cookies Springerle

This recipe requires perhaps just a bit of baking artistry and, above all, a certain amount of care; traditionally, a decorative design is pressed into the dough with the help of a carved wooden pattern called a *Model,* a nice and moderately priced souvenir you can buy when traveling in Germany.

•   •   •   •   •   •   •   •   •

4 *eggs, separated*
2¼ *cups sugar*
3½ *cups flour*
½ *teaspoon baking*
  powder
½ *teaspoon dried grated*
  lemon peel
Butter for baking
sheets
½–1 *cup aniseed*

Beat the egg whites into stiff peaks, then combine with the egg yolks and sugar and stir vigorously. All the earlier recipes suggest that you keep stirring for at least 15 minutes, but with the help of an electric eggbeater, the time devoted to this task can be considerably reduced (7 minutes). Add the flour, baking powder and the dried grated lemon peel to the eggs and knead vigorously until the dough is soft and pliable.

Let stand for at least 1 hour in the refrigerator or other cool place, then roll out into a thin sheet. As mentioned, a carved wooden *Model* that has been dusted with flour is customarily used to imprint little figures or decorative patterns into the dough, and the cookies are cut out of the sheet of dough in accordance with these patterns. If no *Model* or reasonable facsimile is available, one or more metal cookie cutters can be used to much the same effect. (And if you don't use a *Model,* just sprinkle the flour directly on top of the cookies.)

Grease the baking sheet with butter and sprinkle with aniseed. Place the cookies on the baking sheet and allow to sit and dry out (at room temperature) overnight, or until the surface is quite dry and even hard. Those who have the patience to lift up each cookie, then brush a little water onto the underside to moisten it, will be rewarded with especially good results. Be careful, however, not to let so much as a drop of water get onto the tops of the cookies!

Preheat the oven to 300°F. Leave the oven door open a little ("a little" being a bit more than "a crack" in this case) during the first 20 minutes of the baking time; then close the door and raise the temperature to 350° and bake for another 20 minutes. The topsides of the *Springerle* should be almost white, and the flour can be dusted off with a brush but should be definitely allowed to remain in place until now. Also, since the hardened crust on top prevents the dough from rising any further in that direction, the cookies should also have acquired a sort of little platform or pedestal down below, called a *Füsschen* (little foot).

MAKES ABOUT 60 COOKIES

"Lay the napkin out flat and fold the four corners in toward the center, thus producing Fig. I. Then once again fold the corners marked 1 toward the midpoint, marked 2, which produces Fig. II. Turn the napkin over to the other side and fold the four corners in toward the center in the same manner, thus producing Fig. III. Turn the napkin over again and repeat this procedure of folding down the four corners, so that you end up with Fig. IV. Turn over the napkin once again, grasping by the folds marked 3 and 4, and pull these up and out (as has already been done with one corner in Fig. V) to produce the arrangement marked B above. If you turn B over, then you will have A."

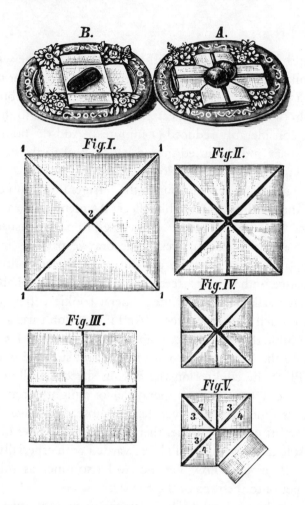

Shrovetide Pancakes   Krebbel/Berliner Pfannkuchen

Popular all over Germany and known by a variety of different names (including *Krapfen* and *Ballen* in addition to the above), these little pancakes were originally served on New Year's Eve and as part of the pre-Lenten festivities known as *Fastnacht* (Mardi Gras). In Mainz, for example, there is a famous parade on Rose Monday, the Monday before Lent, after which it's customary for the lord mayor to invite the local dignitaries and distinguished guests to a festive *Krebbel-Kaffee*.

The Berliners claim that these *Pfannkuchen* of theirs—which have a spherical shape not unlike that of a cannonball—were invented sometime around the middle of the eighteenth century by one of Frederick the Great's veterans who had found work as a baker after being wounded while serving in the Prussian artillery corps. Pancakes of a very similar kind were probably enjoyed by the ancient Romans, though the fruit filling in this recipe appears to be a fairly recent innovation. The American doughnuts, before having a hole in the middle, were called "fastnachts" by the Pennsylvania Dutch and were identical to this recipe of the German original.

3 cups flour
½ cup lukewarm milk
⅓ cup sugar
2 teaspoons yeast
4½ tablespoons butter,
　softened
2 eggs
　Pinch of salt
　Grated peel of 1 lemon

1 cup marmalade for
　filling the pancakes
　Fat for deep-frying
　Confectioners' sugar

・　・　・　・　・　・　・　・　・

Using the quantities listed here, prepare the dough according to the "Basic Yeast Dough Recipe" (on page 431). Add the lemon peel in with the butter, eggs, and salt.

Knead the dough thoroughly once more, then roll out in a sheet about ½″ thick. Cut out round pancakes about 3¼″ in diameter and place a little dab of marmalade in the center of half the pancakes. Brush the edges with water, set one of the other pancakes down on top of each, and press the edges together. Put a damp cloth over them and allow the dough to rise again for 30 minutes.

Heat the fat to about 350°F. and fry the *Krebbel,* turning just once, until golden brown on both sides; it's best to cook only 2 or 3 at a time so the temperature of the cooking fat will remain fairly high. Remove from the pan, drain onto paper towels, and sprinkle with confectioners' sugar.

NOTE: The tops of *Berliner Pfannkuchen* are also sometimes brushed with a glaze of sugar water. The original *Krebbel* were made without the marmalade filling, which meant that the dough was rolled out a little thicker.

MAKES 12–15 PIECES

Silesian-Style Gingerbread Men
Pfefferkuchenmänner

1½ cups honey
 Scant cup sugar
2 tablespoons butter
5½ cups flour
1 tablespoon baking
 powder
1¾ cups whole almonds
½ cup candied lemon peel
 (Zitronat), *minced*
½ teaspoon ground
 cinnamon
1 teaspoon ground
 cardamom
 *"As much ground
 clove and black pepper
 as will fit on the point
 of a knife"*
1 egg
1 cup confectioners'
 sugar
1 teaspoon lemon juice
1 tablespoon hot water

Gotthold Ephraim Lessing was Germany's first great play-wright and a leading figure during the eighteenth-century Enlightenment; at an earlier phase in his career (c. 1765), he was employed as a secretary to the military governor of Breslau, the capital of Silesia, and lodged with a gingerbread-baker in the Schweidnitzerstrasse. Lessing, later revered as Germany's great apostle of tolerance, liberalism, and moderation, was at that time given to late-night carousing and other bohemian behavior. His landlord hoped to induce him to mend his ways by executing a gingerbread caricature of Lessing while drunk.

The friend of Lessing's, theater manager Karl von Holtei, who recorded this anecdote, unfortunately neglected to provide further details, either as to the ingredients of the dough or the final presentation—whether the gingerbread was laced with schnapps or brandy, whether the gingerbread men were represented as weaving unsteadily, lying facedown in the gutter, or clinging to a lamppost, rather than in the traditional stiff-legged, full-frontal pose. The following is a typical Silesian *Pfefferkuchen* recipe, possibly dating from the same period.

· · · · · · · · ·

Combine the honey, sugar, and butter, and heat while stirring constantly until you have a smooth, well-blended mixture. Allow to cool.

Put 4 cups of the flour and the baking powder in a mixing bowl. Split a dozen of the nicest almonds and set aside; mince the rest. Add the minced almonds and candied lemon peel to the flour along with the spices; mix well. Add the egg and stir in vigorously, then work in the cooled honey mixture. Gradually add more flour to the dough using only enough to produce a dough that no longer adheres to the sides of the mixing bowl.

Preheat the oven to 350°F. Grease a baking sheet with butter. Roll out the dough about ¾″ thick on a surface that has been sprinkled with flour; cut out the gingerbread men (whether or not in the form of an intoxicated Lessing) with the help of a cardboard stencil or cookie cutter. Place the cookies on the baking sheet and bake for about 15 minutes. In the meantime, mix the confectioners' sugar with lemon juice and hot water; brush the gingerbread men with this sugar glaze when they emerge from the oven and attach the almond halves using the glaze as an adhesive. *Pfefferkuchen* that are stamped out with ordinary cookie cutters and not necessarily made in the image of G.E. Lessing are also very tasty.

MAKES 8–16 COOKIES (DEPENDING ON SIZE)

Court pastry chef at work in the former dungeons of the Kaiser's castle, Berlin.

Mock Ginger   Falscher Ingwer

1 pound ripe pumpkin
  flesh
1 pound sugar
2 tablespoons water
3–4 teaspoons ground
  ginger
1–2 tablespoons oil
  Chocolate frosting

This is a very old and formerly very popular Christmas confection in small towns and rural areas where real ginger was still very expensive and pumpkins abundantly available.

· · · · · · · · ·

Put the pumpkin flesh through a meat grinder, food mill, or processor, combine with the sugar and water, and cook for several hours over low heat until you have a very thick syrup, like marmalade. Remove from the heat and sprinkle with ginger; take the largest porcelain platter you can find, brush it with oil, and spread out the pumpkin "marmalade" on the platter in a layer about ½″ to ¾″ thick. Let stand overnight.

Cut into cubes or strips, coat with a thick layer of chocolate frosting, return to the oiled porcelain platter, and chill before serving.

MAKES 4–6 SERVINGS

SOUTHWESTERN   GERMANY

Scherben

A good example of traditional pre-Lenten *Schmalzgebäck,* this is from an old family recipe. The name means "shards" or "broken pieces of crockery."

· · · · · · · · ·

Combine all the ingredients except the fat and confectioners' sugar, and work into a smooth dough; let stand for about 15 minutes. Roll out the dough on a board that has been sprinkled with flour and cut out oval or rectangular pieces of dough just about as big as the palm of your hand. Deep-fry on both sides in hot fat until golden brown, then sprinkle with confectioners' sugar while still warm.

MAKES 8 SERVINGS

3½ *cups flour*
11 *tablespoons butter*
3 *tablespoons sour cream*
2 *tablespoons sugar*
2–3 *tablespoons rosewater*
Pinch of salt
2 *eggs*
3 *egg yolks*
Fat, lard, oil, or shortening for deep-frying
A few tablespoons confectioners' sugar

Marzipan Potatoes   Marzipankartoffeln

Here is a recipe that probably originated during some previous time of troubles, since it began to turn up in various parts of Germany immediately after the shortages brought about by the First World War had begun to make themselves felt.

•   •   •   •   •   •   •   •   •

Combine all the ingredients except the cocoa powder and mix well; knead vigorously and then let stand for 2 hours. Roll this mixture into little balls and shape like potatoes, dredge in cocoa powder, arrange the "marzipan" balls so they are almost touching one another, and let dry for several days. You may want to make a small cut in the tops with a knife to improve their appearance.

MAKES 15 BALLS

½ *cup farina*
¾ *cup sugar (superfine crystals)*
1 *teaspoon vanilla extract*
2–3 *tablespoons milk*
Dash or two of rosewater
A few drops of almond extract
Cocoa powder

FRANCONIA

Nüremberg-Style Christmas Cookies
Nürnberger Eierzucker

5 *eggs*
  Small pinch of salt
2⅔ *cups sugar*
  1 *teaspoon vanilla*
    extract
3½ *cups flour*
2–3 *teaspoons arrack or*
    dark (spiced) rum
    Food coloring
    (optional)

Once one of the great attractions of the famous Christ Child Market *(Christkindelmarkt)* in Nüremberg, these deliciously aromatic Christmas cookies are probably easier to bake yourself than to find in any store these days—even if you happen to live in Nüremberg. In either case, it's best to make them at least 3 or 4 weeks before Christmas in order to give the legendary aroma (to say nothing of one's expectations) a chance to build up to a peak.

•   •   •   •   •   •   •   •   •   •

Combine the eggs, salt, sugar, and vanilla extract, and beat until foamy—which is more easily accomplished with an electric eggbeater. Sift the flour and add gradually to this mixture, along with the arrack or rum. Knead thoroughly until you have a smooth dough, and let stand for at least 2 hours.

On a board sprinkled with flour, roll out the dough to a thickness of about ⅛″. Traditionally, a little figure or a decorative design is incised into the dough with a *Model,* or carved wooden pattern (see *Springerle,* page 458), and the cookies are cut into squares or whatever seems appropriate to the figures on the *Model.* Let the cutout pieces of cookie dough sit in a warm place to dry out for about 2 days.

Generously grease a baking sheet with butter. Place the cookies on the sheet and bake at 275°F. but only until they are a very light color, about 40 minutes. The next day the figures and designs on the cookies can be painted with food coloring. Store in a metal cookie tin for at least 3 or 4 weeks.

MAKES 50 COOKIES

FRANCONIA

Nüremberg-Style Gingerbread
Nürnberger Lebkuchen

Gingerbread, one of the most famous of all German regional specialties, has been serious business in Nüremberg for at least 600 years now, thanks to the happy conjunction of Franconian honey and the spice trade carried on by the *Pfeffersäcke,* or "peppersacks," as the city's prosperous medieval merchant adventurers were called. Commercial gingerbread was baked by the members of an exclusive guild, known as *Lebküchler,* rather than by homemakers or ordinary bakers, though no guild secrets are being betrayed by the publication of the present recipe, which has been handed down for many generations in a family of avid but nonprofessional gingerbread-makers. *Lebkuchen* is most closely associated with Nüremberg—specialists in the field will recognize this recipe as being quite similar to a popular variety of gingerbread known as *Elisenlebkuchen*—but the *Pfefferkuchen* of eastern Germany (see *Pfefferkuchenmänner*) and *Honigkuchen* of northern Germany are not really all that different.

•　　•　　•　　•　　•　　•　　•　　•　　•

"Take the vegetable chopper, mince up 1 pound almonds very fine, and roast them on the baking sheet. Stir up 1 pound fine sugar with 7 egg yolks for ¼ hour, then fold in the stiffened egg whites and work for an additional ¼ hour. Add ¼ pound candied orange peel, ¼ pound candied lemon peel, [2 tablespoons] cinnamon, just slightly more clove, 1 teaspoon cardamom, 1 [grated] lemon peel, ½ teaspoon white pepper, a little mace, and 1 pound flour. Mix well and let stand overnight. The next day, take 1 teaspoon baking soda and work into the dough until it becomes slippery and pliable. Take a knife blade [or the back of a metal spoon] dipped in water and spread the dough onto rectangular wafers (thin as the ecclesiastical variety), leaving a little raised border around the edge. Decorate with almond halves or candied lemon peel, sprinkle

1 *pound almonds*
1 *pound superfine sugar*
7 *eggs, separated*
¼ *pound candied orange peel*
¼ *pound candied lemon peel*
2 *tablespoons ground cinnamon*
2½ *tablespoons ground clove*
1 *teaspoon ground cardamom*
　Grated peel of 1 lemon
½ *teaspoon freshly ground white pepper*
　Pinch of mace
1 *pound flour*
1 *teaspoon baking soda*
　Almond halves or candied lemon peel for decoration
　Sugar

with sugar, and bake at moderate heat [or 350°F. for about 20 minutes]."

MAKES 25 COOKIES

E A S T   P R U S S I A

Walnut Cookies   Walnussschnitten

2¼ *cups confectioners'*
  sugar
 4 *cups whole walnuts*
  (⅓ to be crushed, ⅔
  ground)
 2 *eggs, beaten*
 2 *tablespoons water*
 2 *tablespoons lemon*
  juice

The expense involved in making real marzipan for a brood of five or ten children can be fairly daunting. This is a recipe devised by thrifty mothers in the region around Osterode (Osteróda) that substitutes homegrown walnuts and seems very much like a delicacy in its own right, with nothing "ersatz" about it.

•   •   •   •   •   •   •   •   •   •

Sift half the sugar (1 cup plus 2 tablespoons) and blend with the walnuts, add the beaten eggs, and knead into a smooth doughy mixture. Roll out about ½″ thick, and cut out stars, diamonds, etc., with cookie cutters. Place on a waxed baking sheet (or a metal baking sheet covered with wax paper).

Combine the remaining sugar, the water, and lemon juice into a thin, watery glaze; stir together over low heat, adding a few tablespoons of water or lemon juice if the mixture seems too thick. Brush the tops of the walnut cookies with the glaze and allow the cookies to dry out in a warm (150°F.) oven.

MAKES 20 COOKIES

Drinks

. . . .

To begin, I'll dispose of two possible misconceptions—beer is not necessarily the most popular drink in Germany and all German beer is not brewed in Bavaria. It is true that the Germans drink more beer than anyone else, and certainly they've been drinking it a lot longer than they've been drinking coffee. In fact, the evidence suggests that the durable German institution of the ladies' *Kaffeekränzchen* ("coffee party," a little more formal and less spontaneous than the celebrated *Kaffeeklatsch*) was originally convened wherever freshly home-brewed beer was made available for tasting.

As in America, German wine consumption has increased in recent years, and Germans now drink more sparkling wine than anyone else in the world. Mineral water and various fruit drinks come into their own during the summer months. However, this is usually not the sort of thing we mean when we talk about "drinks"; there are a couple of hot drinks made with tea or coffee included in this section, plus two "medicinal" beverages (both of them alcoholic). But more to the point, there are a great many alcoholic mixed drinks, punches, grogs, May bowls, and other concoctions—some of them involving beer as well as wine and distilled spirits—that are associated with particular regions. A few, such as *Knickebein* and Turks' Blood, are included here that were once in the mainstream of German conviviality but have now been largely forgotten.

NOTE: Alcohols, like vinegars, should never be heated in aluminum; always use a stainless steel or other non-reactive saucepan when heating them.

S C H L E S W I G - H O L S T E I N

Anglian Mug   Angler Muck

The residents of the strip of Baltic coast between the Flensburger Förde and the Schlei inlet, just below the Danish border, are still known as *Angeln,* and in Low German, a *Muck* (or *Mugge*) is what the Angles' distant cousins, the English, would call a mug.

1 cup rum (or vodka)
1 cup water
Juice of 2 to 3 lemons
2–4 tablespoons sugar

• • • • • • • • • •

Combine the rum and water, then heat until just about to boil. Season with lemon juice and sugar. Serve hot.

NOTE: The recipe for cold *Angler Muck* is even simpler—combine 1 pint of rum with an equal amount of (carbonated) lemonade; stir once.

MAKES 4 SERVINGS

NORTHERN GERMANY

Grog

1–3 sugar cubes
½–⅔ cup boiling hot
water
⅓–½ cup rum

"Old Grog" was the nickname of an eighteenth-century British admiral who commanded the West Indies fleet. He was so called because he wore a coat made out of a shiny fabric called "grogham." He became convinced that in tropical waters his crews would be much healthier if their (extremely generous) rum ration was cut with a little water. And so, the nickname "grog" was transferred from the admiral himself to the rum-and-water drink that he had introduced into general currency among seafaring folk. ("Popularized" is hardly the right word, since a fleetwide mutiny was only narrowly averted when this new policy was implemented.) Even today, on shipboard and on the offshore islets *(Hallige)* of Schleswig-Holstein, the rule about grog is that "rum most, sugar can, water need not."

    •   •   •   •   •   •   •   •

Put the sugar cubes in the glass, add the hot water, and stir until the sugar is dissolved; pour in the rum and stir once more.

VARIATION: Beat an egg yolk with some sugar in the glass (or *Muck*), add the rum and stir, then add a bit less hot water than you would otherwise (to counteract the diluting effect of the egg yolk); this is called *Eiergrog,* or "egg grog." In former times, this drink was sometimes made with Middle Eastern arrack instead of the West Indian rum, which is perfectly possible.

MAKES 1 SERVING

LOWER SAXONY

Egg Beer Braunschweiger Mumme/Eierbier

Mumme is a strong dark beer with a pronounced flavor of hops, like stout, that is brewed in Brunswick (the name is also applied to a kind of unfermented malt extract, which is something else altogether). This "egg in your beer" concoction can also be made with ordinary beer—both versions are given below—and is described in one early recipe as "an agreeable as well as nourishing beverage, particularly so when drunk on an empty stomach."

EIERBIER:
- ¼ *pound rock candy (made with white sugar, not brown)*
- 1½ *pints beer*
- 1 *cinnamon stick*
- 2 *whole eggs*
- 2 *egg yolks*

MUMME:
- 2 *teaspoons crushed rock candy*
- 1 *pint* Mumme *or stout*
- 2–3 *egg yolks*

· · · · · · · · ·

For *Eierbier,* crush the rock candy in a mortar, then sprinkle into the beer, add the cinnamon stick, and heat while stirring until the candy is dissolved. Beat the whole eggs and egg yolks into a froth, then continue stirring as you pour them into the beer. Keep stirring over the heat until the *Eierbier* is very hot, but do not boil. Remove the cinnamon stick and serve.

For *Braunschweiger Mumme,* sprinkle rock candy into the *Mumme* and heat up very slowly until the sugar is all dissolved. Remove from the heat; beat the egg yolks and then briskly beat them into the hot *Mumme* with an eggbeater.

MAKES 2 SERVINGS

Brandied Raisins   Sintbohntjesopp

2 cups large raisins or
  sultanas, washed
3 cups vodka or
  German
  Kornbranntwein
  (rye brandy)
¼–½ cup rock candy,
  crushed

Devotees of rum-raisin ice cream will immediately understand the rationale behind this "holy bean soup,"which is traditionally set out for the friends and well-wishers who come to congratulate an East Frisian family on the birth of a child. It is served in a special tin bowl, and the guests are all provided with tin spoons to scoop out the "bean soup." An expectant Frisian father who's mindful of his community responsibilities usually makes the *Sintbohntjesopp* at least 2 months in advance.

•   •   •   •   •   •   •   •   •

Dry off the raisins thoroughly to prevent even the smallest drop of water from contaminating the brandy. Put the raisins in a crock or jug. Add the vodka or brandy, and as much rock candy as you like. Put the stopper in the crock (or jug, bottle, etc.), and let stand for a couple of weeks. Serve in cups or in a glass, with cappuccino spoons.

MAKES 25 SERVINGS

Knickebein

⅓ part Maraschino (cherry
  brandy)
1 fresh egg yolk
⅓ part Crème de Vanille
  (creamy vanilla liqueur)

It's difficult to guess from the name alone (which means "knock-knee") that this is the German version of the French pousse-café, a colorfully multilayered novelty drink that reached its peak of popularity during the Deco era.

•   •   •   •   •   •   •   •   •

If a cylindrical liqueur glass of small diameter is unavailable, a small parfait glass can be substituted. Fill the glass with the ingredients listed below, in the order mentioned; be careful to do so in such a way that the 3 layers remain separate in the glass. (Other liqueurs and/or brandies can be used, but make sure that the one with the highest density is below.)

MAKES 1 SERVING

Turks' Blood   Türkenblut

Turks' Blood became popular during the second half of the nineteenth century.

⅓ part Burgundy (or other full-bodied red wine)
⅔ part sparkling white wine (Sekt) or champagne

·   ·   ·   ·   ·   ·   ·   ·   ·

In a large (Bordeaux) glass, first pour in the Burgundy and then the sparkling wine.

MAKES 1 SERVING

BERLIN

Berliner Weisse with Syrup   Weisse mit Schuss

"White" beer, made with wheat malt rather than barley malt, was first brewed in Hamburg during the sixteenth century but has since come to be identified primarily with Berlin; there's something in the water there, according to beer connoisseurs, that particularly enhances the delicate wheat-malt bouquet. A *Weisse* with a shot (i.e., of raspberry or pale-green woodruff syrup) is a wonderfully refreshing summer treat—a drink that conjures up memories for nostalgic Berliners of long summer afternoons in the shady suburban beer gardens of the Grunewald or on the elegant café terraces of the Kurfürstendamm, the Champs-Élysées of Berlin before World War II.

½ shot of raspberry or woodruff (Waldmeister) syrup
1 bottle Berliner Weisse beer (several brands are available in North America), well chilled

·   ·   ·   ·   ·   ·   ·   ·   ·

Pour the ½ shot of syrup into a glass, then fill with *Weisse*. You can expect the *Weisse mit Schuss* to have a substantial head on it, so that impatient drinkers should be provided with straws (not too thin, because of the syrup); those who like to defer their pleasures will simply wait till the foam has partially subsided.

MAKES 1 SERVING

EAST   FRIESLAND

Homemade Cherry Brandy   Karsenbranntwein

1–1½ pounds ripe, juicy
    sour cherries
1 quart rye or clear
    corn brandy
    (vodka is a good
    substitute)
1¾–2¼ cups rock candy,
    crushed or
    coarsely pounded

The concocting of mixed drinks—which would involve diluting their precious crystal-clear rye brandy that they call *Korn*, with other liquids, possibly even water—is not the sort of thing the Frisians would do willingly. But a little extra flavor and variety may be legitimately provided by "putting up" cherries or other seasonal fruit in a jug of brandy.

•   •   •   •   •   •   •

Pit the sour cherries, trying to conserve as much of the juice as possible while doing so. Pack the cherries into a large, widemouthed jug or carafe and pour in the liquor. Seal or stop up the jug and let sit for 3 to 4 weeks in a not-too-cool place; moderate exposure to sunlight is permissible.

Pour a very small amount of boiling water over the rock candy and let stand until the sugar is totally dissolved and the liquid has had a chance to cool. Pour off the brandy from the jug, then gently squeeze out the liquid from the cherries before discarding them. Sweeten the "cherry brandy" to taste with the sugar water, put the stopper back in the jug, and allow to mature for a few more days.

VARIATION: Red currants (especially the very dark ones) may be substituted for the sour cherries.

MAKES ABOUT 1½ QUARTS

Ratafia

Ratafia was a commercial liqueur made from brandy and various fruit extracts that was popular until around the end of the nineteenth century. This recipe for a somewhat simplified homemade *Ratafia* was composed about 150 years ago. Quantities have been reduced by half (i.e., the original recipe calls for 8 bottles of brandy).

· · · · · · · · · ·

"To make *Ratafia,* take 4 bottles of good brandy, 1 quart raspberry juice, ½ pint cherry juice, and 1 kilo [4¾ cups] sugar. Pour the fruit juice into a large bottle or a bowl, add the sugar, and stir until thoroughly dissolved. Then pour in the brandy, and when the brandy has separated out of the mixture and turned a nice clear color again, mix together once more, pour off into bottles, seal with a cork, and store carefully [until it is homogeneous]."

MAKES ABOUT 4 BOTTLES

Norderney, North Sea island

East Prussian Punches, Schnapps, and Other Specialties

When I was a very young man and traveling in East Prussia, I remember being puzzled by the fact that schnapps was served in rather large glasses and beer in rather small ones. When I asked about this, I was told, "Aye, young feller, we don't care to take so much moisture into our stomachs" *("Ja, Jungchen, wir wolln nich so viel Flissigkeit in 'n Bauch kriejen")*. Whatever the reason, Germany's "lost" provinces in the east were more inventive in devising new (and stronger) drinks than any other region—even without the inclusion of such noted commercial liqueurs as Danziger Goldwasser.

Nikolaschka

1 ounce Cognac (brandy)
1 fresh lemon slice (cut crosswise, without seeds, with peel)
1 teaspoon sugar

Here, the tartness of the lemon helps to counteract the alcoholic kick of the brandy, which enables one to savor and appreciate the various flavors involved without being immediately overwhelmed by the brandy. A drink (or at any rate, a technique) discovered by the inhabitants of the Masurian Lakes district, formerly in easternmost Prussia, has gone on to achieve a certain international renown.

.   .   .   .

The traditional big-bellied balloon glass will not be of much use in this case; a cylindrical liqueur glass of small diameter (or the like) is far more practical. Pour in the brandy (Cognac), place the lemon slice over the mouth of the glass, and spoon the sugar on top of the lemon slice. Next, convey the lemon slice and sugar to your mouth (by whatever means you choose), bite into the lemon, and take a sip of brandy, letting the liquid mingle voluptuously with the lemon and sugar in your mouth. Afterwards, you are presented with another choice—whether to swallow the lemon slice or to remove it discreetly and leave it sitting on the little plate that should be provided for that purpose. Alternatively, you may prefer to fold the lemon slice in half, then bite off the little semicircle of lemon and sugar and daintily remove the rind with your fingers.

REFINEMENT: Sometimes a couple of grains of coarsely chopped coffee beans are sprinkled on top of the sugar, which adds a very pleasant flavor.

MAKES 1 SERVING

Pillkaller

Recommended primarily to those who are already steeped in hearty, elemental East Prussian folkways. Pillkallen is the name of a little town on the outskirts of Gumbinnen (Gusev) in the Masurian Lakes district. The liverwurst absorbs the kick of the brandy, the brandy cuts the fattiness of the wurst, and the mustard makes one all the more eager to have another little taste of each.

⅔ ounce clear corn brandy or vodka
1 thick slice liverwurst, rind removed
Generous dollop of mustard

· · · · · · · · ·

Here you will need a liqueur (or schnapps) glass of the smallest possible diameter. Pour in the brandy, place the liverwurst slice on top of the schnapps glass, and put a dollop of mustard on it. The trick is to get the liverwurst slice from the top of the glass into your mouth. Beginners may feel more secure if they keep their fingers and a paper napkin at the ready; adepts will be able to dispense with these beginner's aids.

Bite gently into the liverwurst slice, let the brandy flow over it and on down, then finish off the liverwurst slice, and prepare to start in on the next; repeat this procedure as many times as required.

MAKES 1 SERVING

Bärenfang/Meschkinnes

½ cup water
1 cinnamon stick
1 vanilla bean, split
1½ cups honey (should
   flow smoothly)
1 pint "pure" grain
   alcohol (190 proof or
   over)

The first of these, which means "beartrap," is the more familiar name for this drink in West Germany today; the second is
the original East Prussian name. Nowadays, you can buy a
bottle of ready-mixed *Bärenfang* in West Germany, but in East
Prussia in the old days, every household made up its own
private stock . . . and you can too.

·   ·   ·   ·   ·   ·   ·   ·   ·

Bring the water to a rapid boil with the cinnamon stick and
split vanilla bean, then strain out the spices. Pour in the honey
and continue to stir over low heat until the honey is thoroughly dissolved. Allow this to cool somewhat before pouring in the grain alcohol. Stir well, pour into a bottle, insert
the stopper, and allow to "age" for about 2 weeks before
serving.

NOTE: Clearly, the more flavorful the honey, the better the
"Beartrap" will be.

A deluxe version can be produced by substituting dry white
wine for the water. The quantities given should be enough for
1 bottle.

For a milder version of *Bärenfang,* the pure alcohol (190
proof) may be substituted with vodka.

MAKES 1½ PINTS

POMERANIA

Pomeranian Punch   Vorpommerscher Umtrunk

At around the turn of the century, the social life of the eastern
garrison towns revolved around the officers' "casinos," or
mess halls, where the punch bowl and a peculiarly stylized, if
not very sophisticated, form of soldierly banter circulated
endlessly around the table. This recipe is taken from a little
booklet compiled by the conscripts of the gunnery school at

Jüterbog and entitled "Punches and Jorums [another kind of punch] for the Use of the German Army on Maneuvers and in the Field." The recipe does call for one ingredient that may be a little difficult to lay hands on today—"the dried peel of a fresh, green Seville orange." Seville oranges (formerly *Pomranzen* in German) are too bitter to be eaten fresh or squeezed for juice, and so are mainly encountered nowadays in the form of bitter orange marmalade, crème de Curaçao, and candied orange peel. The last sentence of the recipe is probably a good example of the bluff soldierly wit of the period.

. . . .

"Place the dried peel of a fresh, green Seville orange in a glass of red wine and let stand for about half an hour. To 2 bottles of good, light claret and 1 bottle of dry sparkling white, add as much of the Seville orange extract as is necessary for the taste to assert itself gently but distinctly. This punch is not only good for the liver but also for the heart and the kidneys, and is thus to be recommended in favor of the more conventional dosage of cod liver oil."

VARIATIONS: If you forget about the Seville oranges altogether, then you have a very popular punch recipe of yesteryear, called "cardinal"; if you substitute a still white for the sparkling wine, you have a "bishop."

NOTE: As a substitute for peel of Seville oranges steep the pieces of peel from "bitter orange marmalade" in some Curaçao liqueur and add to the red wine.

MAKES 2¼ QUARTS

May Wine   Maibowle/Waldmeisterbowle

The May Bowl, flavored with an herb known as *Waldmeister* or *Maikraut* in German and "sweet woodruff" in English, is the best known of a large selection of *Bowlen,* wine punches flavored with herbs, fruits, berries, and occasionally with flowers. The *Bowle* was (and is) the German summer drink

*1 bunch of fresh
woodruff
(Waldmeister)*
*2–3 bottles not-too-dry
white wine
Orange slices
(optional)*

par excellence, though it was most popular outside the wine-growing regions of Germany—in northern, central, and eastern Germany—where people liked their wine with a little flavoring (possibly since the ordinary table wine that was available in those days was highly acidic at the best of times).

This is the genuine recipe for what is sold under the name of "May wine" everywhere in the United States. A *Bowle* is often prepared in the wine country as well, and indeed all over the world, to celebrate the arrival of spring. May wine made with fresh woodruff actually tastes best in April, before the plant has come into bloom; the woodruff should not have any open blossoms on it and should be picked the day before you intend to make your May bowl, since the wine imbibes the woodruff flavor better if the leaves are a little dried out. Woodruff grows wild in wooded areas, covering the ground. It is worth picking.

·   ·   ·   ·   ·   ·   ·   ·   ·

Tie the stems of woodruff into a bundle with cotton thread; put 1 pint of the wine into a glass bowl (or other receptacle) and hang the bundle so that the leaves (but not the stems) are soaking in the wine. After 10 or 15 minutes, remove the bundle of woodruff and discard. Pour in the rest of the wine and serve; you may want to float a couple of very thin orange slices (with peel) in the punch bowl, though this is not an essential ingredient.

NOTE: Some prefer to sweeten the punch to taste with sugar, but this is an operation that's very easily botched, so it may be more prudent to start out with a mildly sweet wine in the first place.

Also, if the wine absorbs too much of the woodruff flavor, drinking even a cup or two of the punch may cause headaches and dizziness, so it's clearly important not to let the woodruff leaves steep for too long. In most American recipes it is advised to soak the woodruff several hours in wine—but that results in a very bad headache.

A nonalcoholic May bowl can be made with apple juice or even milk.

MAKES 1½–2¼ QUARTS

Königsberg, city of the philosopher Immanuel Kant, East Prussia, now Russian territory

Basic Principles of Fruit Punch Preparation
Grundregeln zu Bowlenbereitung

What follows is a sort of all-purpose list of dos and don'ts compiled in 1889 by an old gentleman who had served for many years as "casino officer" in a Prussian guards regiment (the equivalent title might perhaps be "morale officer" in an English-speaking formation).

·   ·   ·   ·   ·   ·   ·   ·   ·

"1. Do not allow yourself to be misled by the advice of your good friends and trusty comrades, but make sure to mix up your punch all by yourself. For there will always be someone who thinks it too sour, another who thinks it too sweet, a third who is convinced that the flavorings have not steeped enough, and a fourth who is convinced that the infusion is too strong. If you heed all this advice, the punch will be labored over and coaxed with sugar—they may even attempt to revive it with the despicable addition of Cognac or Madeira or Bombster of a poor vintage—and even so, it will end up tasting like Silesian sourbush wine of the very worst vintage.[1]

"2. In general, you should select only clear, light wines that are without visible sediment and those that have not been affected by the cork; test each bottle to make sure that this is the case.

"3. If you must use sugar at all, it is better to dissolve a little piece of it in clear spring water and sweeten your punch with this sugar solution. It is very easy for the punch to turn cloudy if you add even the smallest amount of granulated sugar.

"4. Be sparing in the use of herbs and other flavorings. The punch starts out as wine and wine it should remain; the assembled fragrances should be mixed in as discreetly as a beautiful woman puts on her perfume. A punch made with strawberries and peaches in particular should be clear and limpid and thus should not have the appearance of dirty dishwater.

"5. After the correct admixture of flavors has been achieved by stirring gently and (if the ladies are expected to partake) the punch has been sweetened with sugar water, the punch should be chilled before serving. This is not to be accomplished simply by tossing ice cubes into the bowl; a small bowl can more suitably be chilled in an ice bucket and then covered with a cool cloth. A larger bowl[2] can best be chilled by placing it in a vessel of slightly larger diameter and packing the intervening space with cracked ice."

NOTES: [1] *Bomster Wein* in the original; *Bomst* is a wine-growing community in Silesia, the source of a wine that was famous for its acidity. In the same year that this recipe was written, 1889, the Danzig poet and satirist Johannes Trojan maintained that "even diamonds that are soaked in *Bomster Wein* turn instantly as soft as plums."

[2] This may still be a problem if you have a refrigerator with nonremovable shelves; a portable Styrofoam cooler that can be packed with cracked ice, as described above, may provide the solution. In Germany you can buy special *Bowle*—vessels with a built-in glass tube to hold ice cubes.

Cold Duck   Kalte Ente

All the authorities seem to agree that the name of this classic warm-weather drink results from a slight alteration of the words *kaltes ende* (cold end). Some say that this refers to General Von Pape, a crony of Kaiser Wilhelm I, who preferred to be served a mixture of still and sparkling wines after dessert instead of coffee, explaining, "I like for a hot meal to have a cold finish." This original recipe makes a drink that is superior in taste to every commercially produced Cold Duck.

1 bottle dry (but not too tart) white wine, chilled
1 bottle dry sparkling white wine or champagne, chilled
Peel of 1 fresh lemon

• • • • • • • • •

Pour the chilled white wine into a decanter (preferably a tall, cylindrical one rather than the type with a spherical base and a narrow neck like a bottle); the sparkling wine should continue to chill until it is ice cold. Cut the lemon peel into a spiral and allow it to steep in the decanter; in 10 or 15 minutes, taste to see if the wine has acquired enough lemon flavor to suit you. If not, allow the lemon peel to steep a little longer, otherwise fill up the decanter with the ice-cold sparkling wine. Serve in wineglasses or in a punch bowl. You may want to chill the decanter by placing it in a large bowl or an ice bucket and packing it with cracked ice.

NOTE: There are those who like to sweeten the cold duck by pouring in a little saturated sugar solution ("purified sugar," see number 3 on page 483). I continue to maintain that better results can be achieved (and considerable effort avoided) by selecting an ordinary white wine and a dry sparkling wine, the combination of which, even taking the tartness of the lemon peel into account, should be sweet enough for all practical purposes.

MAKES 6–8 SERVINGS

NORTHERN GERMANY

Pharisäer

During the nineteenth century, the inhabitants of the chilly islets of the North Sea were not always readily won over to the prohibitionist sentiments of their Lutheran pastors, especially since grog and other hearty beverages were thought to be essential in warding off some of the ill effects of the chilly climate—"Better a little *Seever* [binge] than a little fever" is

½ cup freshly brewed coffee
½–¾ ounce rum, warmed
1–3 tablespoons sugar
1–2 tablespoons whipped cream

still a popular saying in the region. On the other hand, the Schleswigers were a God-fearing folk who would never think of openly defying the edict of a man of God.

On Nordstrand, one of the North Frisian Islands, around the middle of the last century, the pastor, a stalwart temperance crusader, liked nothing better than to spend a convivial evening with his parishioners in the village pub where everybody was drinking only coffee. On one occasion, he paused in mid-harangue and absent-mindedly took a sip from his neighbor's coffee mug. "O, ye Pharisees!" is what he cried out when he discovered the deception, and coffee laced with rum and topped (or camouflaged) with a dollop of whipped cream is still called *Pharisäer* in northern Germany.

•   •   •   •   •   •   •   •

Fill the cup about halfway with coffee, then the rest of the way with warm rum and sugar; stir briefly. Top with whipped cream, but do not stir—the rum and coffee are intended to be sipped through the whipped cream so that all three can be tasted at once.

MAKES 1 SERVING

Hoppelpoppel

2 cups strong hot tea
½ cup crushed rock candy (made from white sugar)
2 cups cream
4 egg yolks
1 cup rum (or arrack)

When we read in nineteenth-century novels and memoirs of an invalid being given a "strengthening draft" of rum or brandy that's been kept in the house "for medicinal purposes," *Hoppelpoppel,* or something very like it, is probably what the writer had in mind.

•   •   •   •   •   •   •   •

Gradually sweeten the tea with rock candy and keep stirring for some time until it is all dissolved. Combine the cream, egg yolks, and rum in a bowl and whip vigorously with the eggbeater. Heat the *Hoppelpoppel* by placing the mixing bowl in a pot of boiling water while continuing to whisk. Whisk in the tea. When the *Hoppelpoppel* is so hot you can barely stand to drink it, it's all ready for the patient.

MAKES 1½ QUARTS

East Frisian Tea Ceremony Ostfriesentee

The farmhouses in East Friesland have massive reed-thatched gables rather than sliding paper walls, but the tea-drinking ritual that takes place inside is, to my mind, much more enjoyable than anything that goes on in a Japanese teahouse. The conventional equipment and ingredients that are required for the ceremony include a hearty (preferably East Frisian) tea blend, soft (unchlorinated) tap water or bottled spring water, porcelain teapot, a set of eggshell teacups, a *Teestowke* ("tea-stoker," or a tea-cosy to keep the pot warm), white rock candy in as large chunks as possible, a little bowl for the cream, and a special spoon for the cream with a flat bottom (or the equivalent—perhaps a Japanese-style ceramic soup spoon).

1 heaping teaspoon East Frisian blended tea leaves
1 large chunk of rock candy (crystallized white sugar), or several smaller chunks (see Note)
1 teaspoon fresh cream

•   •   •   •   •   •   •   •   •

   Warm the teapot by rinsing it out with hot water, then pour it out and put in the tea leaves. Pour boiling water over the tea leaves, put the lid on the teapot, and cover with the "stoker." Allow the tea leaves to steep for about 4 minutes.

   Place a *Kluntje* (large chunk) of rock candy or several smaller ones in the bottom of each of the teacups and pour the hot tea over them; you may hear a faint crackling sound as you do so. Take the cream spoon and gently place a little swirl —in Frisian, a *Wulkje* (little cloud)—of cream on the surface of the tea. Do not stir.

   In this way, you should become aware of three successive "tea-sensations," as the Germans would say: first the pure, slightly bitter taste of the tea itself; next the cream should announce its presence, softly and harmoniously, like the statement of the secondary theme in a symphonic adagio; and finally there's the understated sweetness of the rock candy. An ordinary teaspoon will also be provided in the Frisian tea ceremony, but only so you can put it in your empty cup to indicate that you don't care for any more tea.

NOTE: The rock candy *Kluntje* should be big enough to last you through at least two refills, preferably three. Note that only white sugar rock candy should be used for this purpose; the brown sugar candy has a distinct caramel taste that obscures the flavor of the tea. As you may recall from grade-school experimentation with supersaturated solutions, sugar will readily crystallize around a string that is dipped into such a solution, and in the old days, rock candy was sold in long strings at the grocer's for so much per meter, like ribbon. The German grocer ordinarily rejoices in the title of *Kolonialwarenhändler* (because he dealt mainly in imported "colonial wares" like sugar and tea), but in the rural areas of East Friesland in the years between the wars, he was better known as the *Kluntjekniper,* or "*Kluntje*-snipper."

MAKES 1 CUP

HESSE

Hot Hard Cider Heisser Apfelwein

An old-time Frankfurter (by which I mean a native of Frankfurt am Main) who suspects that he might have "taken a chill"
immediately prescribes for himself a therapeutic course of hot
apple wine, which seems to be most effective if the patient
munches on a *Haspel* (pig's knuckle) or a couple of spareribs
in the intervals between treatments. Swabian *Most* (hard cider)
or any other kind of dry white wine can be substituted in cases
of life-threatening emergency.

1 cup apple wine
  (hard cider or a
  wine with high
  acidity)
1¼" – 1¾" cinnamon stick
1 clove
1 slice fresh
  lemon with peel
1 – 3 tablespoons
  sugar

•   •   •   •   •   •   •   •   •

Combine the apple wine, cinnamon stick, clove, and lemon
slice, and heat slowly. Add sugar to taste, pour through a
strainer to remove the spices and lemon pits, and drink while
still very hot.

MAKES 1 SERVING

U.S.-Metric Cooking Conversions

U.S. Customary System

CAPACITY		WEIGHT	
⅛ TEASPOON	1 ML	1 FLUID OZ	30 ML
1 TEASPOON	5 ML		28 GRAMS
1 TABLESPOON	15 ML	1 POUND	454 GRAMS
⅛ CUP	50 ML		
1 CUP	240 ML		
2 CUPS (1 PINT)	470 ML		
4 CUPS (1 QUART)	.95 LITER		
4 QUARTS (1 GALLON)	3.8 LITERS		

Metric

CAPACITY		WEIGHT	
1 ML	⅛ TEASPOON	1 GRAM	.035 OZ
5 ML	1 TEASPOON	100 GRAMS	3.5 OZ
15 ML	1 TABLESPOON	500 GRAMS	1.10 POUNDS
34 ML	1 FLUID OZ	1 KILOGRAM	2.205 POUNDS
			35 OZ
100 ML	3.4 FLUID OZ		
240 ML	1 CUP		
1 LITER	34 FLUID OZ		
	4.2 CUPS		
	2.1 PINTS		
	1.06 QUARTS		
	0.26 GALLON		

*I*ndex

. . . .